SIMULATION
AND
GAMING
ACROSS
DISCIPLINES
AND
CULTURES

David Crookall
Kiyoshi Arai
editors

SIMULATION
AND
GAMING
ACROSS
DISCIPLINES
AND
CULTURES

ISAGA
at a Watershed

SAGE Publications
International Educational and Professional Publisher
Thousand Oaks   London   New Delhi

For information address:

SAGE Publications, Inc.
2455 Teller Road
Thousand Oaks, California 91320

SAGE Publications Ltd.
6 Bonhill Street
London EC2A 4PU
United Kingdom

SAGE Publications India Pvt. Ltd.
M-32 Market
Greater Kailash I
New Delhi 110 048 India

Printed in the United States of America

Library of Congress Cataloging-in-Publication Data

Main entry under title:

International Simulation and Gaming Association. International
    Conference (25th : 1994 : Ann Arbor, Michigan)
      Simulation and gaming across disciplines and cultures: ISAGA at
a watershed / edited by David Crookall, Kiyoshi Arai.
          p.   cm.
      Includes bibliographical references and index.
      ISBN 0-8039-7102-8 (cloth : alk. paper). — ISBN 0-8039-7103-6
(pbk. : alk. paper)
        1. Game theory—Congresses.   2. Simulation methods—Congresses.
3. Intercultural communication—Congresses.   I. Crookall, David.
II. Arai, K. (Kiyoshi, 1950-   III. Title.
HB144.I58   1994   95-12230
519.3—dc20

This book is printed on acid-free paper.

95   96   97   98   99   10   9   8   7   6   5   4   3   2   1

Sage Production Editor: Astrid Virding
Sage Copy Editor: Joyce Kuhn
Sage Typesetter: Janelle LeMaster

Contents

Part I: Applications

Part II: Policy Exercises

Part III: Research

Part IV: Professional Matters

This volume is dedicated
on behalf of
all ISAGA Members and Conference Participants
to

Richard D. Duke

Co-Founder
International Simulation and Gaming
Association (ISAGA)

President
ISAGA, 1994-1995

Program Chair
Silver Anniversary ISAGA Conference

Founder and Director
Certificate Program in Gaming and Simulation

Dedicated and Talented Simulation/Gamer
an example to all in the profession

25th Annual International Conference
Silver Anniversary

International Simulation and Gaming Association
(ISAGA) Ann Arbor, MI, USA

July 23-29, 1994

Program Committee

Sandy Bartlett
James Brown
Marie Duke
Andrea Frank
Mark LeBay
Lisa Leutheuser
Colleen McGee
Mojtaba Naavab
William C. Purves
Charlene Schmult
Marjorie Efva Winful

Richard D. Duke, Chair

David Crookall, Consultant

Preface: Interdisciplinarity and Interculturality

This volume presents highlights of the 25th anniversary conference of the International Simulation and Gaming Association (ISAGA) held in the United States in Ann Arbor, Michigan, in July 1994. Publishing these particular proceedings is important for two related reasons. First, of course, they mark the silver anniversary of a vibrant, respected, and well-established professional association and the only international association devoted to simulation/gaming —a methodology destined for a great future if the authors in this volume are correct. Second, they record a conference organized by the co-founder of ISAGA and host of the first conference 25 years ago—Richard D. Duke.

At the time of the founding of ISAGA, Duke was regarded by many as one of the leaders, if not *the* leader, in simulation/gaming; a quarter century later, he is still held in that regard. His contribution to the field is unequaled, save that by his close colleague and friend, Cathy Greenblat. They produced several books together, including one that remains the foundation text in the field— *Principles and Practices of Gaming-Simulation.* Duke's own book, *Gaming: The Future's Language,* published in 1974, was a seminal work at the time. Some people, such as Jac Geurts in this volume, think it was too far ahead of its time to have had the impact it deserved, but that is often the fate of the work of a true visionary. The book still inspires many, when, that is, they can find it.

The 25th ISAGA conference is also significant in that it coincides with another silver anniversary, that of the association's official journal, *Simulation & Gaming: An International Journal of Theory, Practice, and Research (S&G).* The link between the two was established by Cathy Greenblat (the journal's previous editor) and by Klass Bruin (who organized the 1979 conference in the Netherlands, and who was the *ISAGA Newsletter* editor). For those of you wishing to read about the past quarter century in simulation/gaming generally, a series of special 25th anniversary issues of *S&G* is devoted to that theme— Vols. 25 (2 and 4) and 26 (2 and 4) (i.e., June and December, 1994 and 1995).

Theme

Finding appropriate, encompassing themes for general books on simulation/gaming such as this one is difficult because the field is relevant to so many areas and in so many places. It is becoming almost trite to say that simulation/gaming is able to achieve certain things where other methodologies have failed, be it in business, aeronautics, language learning, policy development, sustainability, international studies, cross-cultural communication, urban planning—the list is a long one. Previous ISAGA volumes have had titles that included such themes as global interdependence, uncertainty, and transferable skills. They are often discipline-generic themes—themes that are relevant to a wide range of disciplines. The double theme of this 25th anniversary volume—interdisciplinarity and interculturality—reflects an underlying characteristic of the field and profession of simulation/gaming.

Broadly defined, interdisciplinarity has to do with matter that draws on or involves two or more traditionally-defined disciplines, such as geography and business. Interculturality has to do with relations among two or more cultural groups, such as the Scots, the Catalonians, and the Japanese. The two themes have more in common than might otherwise meet the eye, for many of the hallmarks of interdisciplinary activity turn out to be special cases of more generalized intercultural phenomena.

Interdisciplinarity

Interdisciplinarity is evident in several ways throughout the collection:

- *Subject matter within chapters.* Some chapters deal with areas that by their very nature involve or bring together several disciplines. Examples are sustainability (Mackie) and academic integrity (Halleck).
- *Subject matter across chapters.* Obviously, as soon as one looks at subject matter across all the chapters, we are presented with a broad range of disciplines, concerns, and competencies. Examples are climate (Klabbers et al.), international relations (Bradford), language education (Coleman), and business (Wellington & Faria).
- *Contributors individually.* Some contributors' main work is at the interface of several disciplines or areas: The matter of their everyday work demands knowledge within and across disciplines.
- *Contributors collectively.* The contributors as a whole represent a large range of disciplinary backgrounds, quite apart from their interest in simulation/gaming.

Simulation/gaming is one of the truly interdisciplinary professions. It deals directly with the world and bases its selections on criteria relevant to the purpose at hand, a pragmatic procedure not commonly found among academic disciplines. These have traditionally tended to divide up the world before looking at it—a predetermined, historically enforced procedure.

Both simulation/gaming and disciplines are artificial constructs. The purpose, in both cases, is to make the world more manageable. As Joe Wolfe points out, disciplines are gatherings of like-minded people basically pursuing the same quest. They gather to offer mutual support, they run their own journals and conferences, engage in intellectual debate, and share experience and increase knowledge.

However, in so doing, many disciplines slide toward an ingroup-outgroup mode of behavior. People gather to offer mutual support—against attack from the outside (other disciplines). Although disciplines do pursue their academic endeavors with an eye on truth and beauty, increasingly this is being diluted by socio-political motivations. Disciplines define boundaries with other disciplines and determine internal rule systems, partly as ways of excluding material declared as extraneous or irrelevant to the pursuit of their fundamental academic goals. Disciplines thus must make certain that insiders remain faithful members and keep undesirable outsiders out. They also need to maintain adherence of their membership to internal frameworks (duty to the flag). They need, vis-à-vis other groups, to bolster viability, strengthen their prestige, and vie for resources. Above all (or rather, underneath all), a discipline must make certain that its active members derive a positive self-image from such membership. A discipline's view of the world is therefore partial at best and often distorted.

Simulation/gaming, however, creates an artificial world for almost opposite reasons. Its aim is to portray an accurate and balanced image of the world by bringing in all relevant elements (including such dynamics as above) from whatever disciplines that might contribute. It is, therefore, not surprising that simulation/gamers often consider themselves interdisciplinarists—as working among, across, or outside disciplines. This is one reason why some people working thoroughly within disciplines consider the simulation/gamer to be an outsider, that is, with suspicion. It may also be why simulation/gamers sometimes ally themselves with those working in general system theory and system dynamics.

This also underlies the reluctance of some to call simulation/gaming a discipline. The very nature of simulation/gaming may disqualify it from taking on all the characteristics of a discipline—at least as traditionally defined by the scientific community. This then raises the question of whether simulation/gaming can be called a science. Or is it an art? A technology? A methodology? Or all four?

Whatever answers are eventually forthcoming in regard to such speculation and questioning, we can safely assume that simulation/gaming is an interdisciplinary endeavor. Contrasting simulation/gaming with discipline is, of course, an over-simplification and may infuriate some simulation/game skeptics (it will not be the first time!). At the very least, the above thoughts may spark some debate about the relationship between simulation/gaming and other constructs, be they disciplines or techniques or others.

Laudable efforts are under way in many parts of the world to bridge the boundaries of (traditional) disciplines. Simulation/gaming is one of the tools contributing substantially to such a shift in outlook and to the redefining of what constitutes legitimate areas of study, that is, of the definition of discipline itself. Perhaps if such definitions are reshaped sufficiently, then we may be able to regard simulation/gaming as a discipline. Until that happens, it is unlikely that simulation/gaming will take on or manifest major traits as a discipline. It is difficult to see how a fundamentally *inter*disciplinary endeavor can turn tail and call itself a discipline in its own right. Additionally, simulation/gamers are quick to remind us of the uniqueness of this field, and yet some of these same people seem to clamor for recognition as an ordinary discipline just like any other. Such issues need to be debated, not with the preconceived notion that it is an unquestioned given that simulation/gaming must become, or indeed be defined as, a discipline, but by first asking if it really needs and wants to be a discipline, to what end, with what result? Indeed, would not the efforts put into achieving disciplinary status be better put into getting on with our simulation/gaming work? If simulation/gaming really does merit institutionalization into a discipline, then that will happen, whether we will it or not.

For simulation/gaming not to be a discipline in no way diminishes our work. On the contrary, it avoids the dangerous pitfalls of disciplines as traditionally defined. If simulation/gaming is to remain vibrant, it must avoid being bound by the straitjacket often imposed by the heavy edifice of discipline. If simulation/gaming is to remain an innovative undertaking and to inspire young professionals, it must build its own identity, without trying to emulate other areas. The circumspection with which simulation/gamers regard the systems they model should also be channeled into generating a healthy skepticism in regard to what we want the field to do and where we want it to go.

To return to the theme of this volume, we might simply remember that simulation/gamers are interdisciplinarists by profession—the matter of their everyday work is interdisciplinary—and they make it their business to be interdisciplinary. Today's world requires both breadth and depth—depth without breadth is like an ostrich with its head in the sand. Simulation/gamers are particularly good at pulling heads out of the sand, but we do not do enough to prepare those heads for what they are likely to see. Too many of them dive for the ground again as soon as they have glimpsed the vastness around them. The concern for interdisciplinarity generally and the maturing of the field of simulation/gaming is discernible in the field itself. In the 1970s, many simulation/games tended to be discipline based; they focused on conveying a certain portion of the subject matter. This is reflected, for example, in Horn's opus magnum that catalogued most of the simulation/games that existed at the time. Since the late 1980s, simulation/games have tended to focus more on problem areas or on issues or on sets of skills—that is, on interdisciplinary phenomena. A Horn directory today would probably be organized in a very different way. (More musings on such matters can be found in *Communication and Simulation: From Two Fields to One Theme,* co-edited by David Crookall and Danny Saunders and published in 1989 by Multilingual Matters.)

From Disciplinary to Cultural

In many ways, one can regard academic disciplines as cultures. The way that some academics from different cultures speak of, indeed treat, one another, one would quickly conclude that strong ingroup-outgroup dynamics are at work— the very same ones that underpin the more unfortunate consequences of contact across cultures, namely, bigotry and even institutional racism. Well before ISAGA had been thought of, in 1959 C. P. Snow, in his *The Two Cultures and the Scientific Revolution,* characterized this phenomenon in terms of literary intellectuals being at one end, scientists at the other, and between them mutual incomprehension. Unfortunately, this also happens between closer disciplines than science and literature; a notorious example (in many countries) is the hostility meted out between literature and language teachers. If such is an inevitable result of becoming a discipline, then simulation/gamers must pause to reflect on whether this is the best route to take.

Within simulation/gaming itself, such antics are relatively rare. This is due in no small measure to the fact that simulation/gaming is interdisciplinary and as such has been spared the worst effects of disciplines. It may also have something to do with the very nature of simulation/gamers. Druckman (this volume) suggests that the typical character and personality of simulation/gamers may influence the results of quantitative research. If indeed this is the case, then a great deal more qualitative research needs to be undertaken. The relatively bickering-free nature of simulation/gaming is also one of the reasons why people from many disciplines and many cultures come to ISAGA conferences and find them enriching events.

Although interdisciplinarity is a special case of interculturality, notable differences exist. Some people have made the former a cause (and a worthy one it is), but it tends to take on negative connotations in some circles, partly due to the kind of vested interest and intergroup dynamics outlined above. A discipline is threatened when one talks about interdisciplinarity. Interculturality, however, probably enjoys a more positive academic attitude and greater public interest and scrutiny. It is also the target of far more professional and academic activity—cross-cultural research, diversity training, studies in racism, and the like. This may be due in part to one of the main differences between the two concepts—one deals with campus-based edifices (with shoot-outs confined to academic ivory towers), the other with human relations (with conflict on the ground, reports in the media, and showdowns in courts). Also, issues of cultural identity (an essentially intercultural phenomenon) touch a far greater number of people with greater impact than one could ever imagine disciplinary identity doing.

Thus, although simulation/gaming is fundamentally interdisciplinary in its substance, it is more intercultural by way of the people involved and the places it happens. True, simulation/gaming has not produced many exercises to help interdisciplinarity or to increase greater tolerance among scholars from different disciplines, but many simulation/games have been designed to increase intercultural understanding. Indeed, several classic simulation/games have been developed by interculturalists. Moreover, it would probably be legitimate, and it would certainly be very useful, for simulation/gaming to call itself a culture rather than a discipline. The profession seems to have more in common with a cultural group than it does with a discipline. It is an idea that might bear more fruit than chasing after the notion of discipline. It is certainly an idea to be explored and debated in the years to come. In recent years, questions have been raised as to the cultural dimensions of simulation/gaming; in other words, we must ask in what ways simulation/games and their debriefing should be adjusted for the cultural context in which they are conducted. Cultural adaptation of simulation/gaming is an open field to be examined closely in the years ahead. Such musings bring us fully to the intercultural in simulation/gaming.

Interculturality

The positive aspects of intercultural relations are evident in the ISAGA conferences and in the various proceedings that have been published over the years. There are few international organizations that enjoy such great variety in disciplines and cultures. The cultural mix in ISAGA is indeed rich. It is not uncommon for a conference of 160 people to have 40 different national cultures represented. The latter number would increase considerably if we defined "cultural group" in more restrictive terms.

ISAGA's younger sibling, the International Society for Intercultural Education, Training and Research (SIETAR International), thrives and focuses on cultural mix, and yet its membership composition is less culturally varied than ISAGA's. Of course, both organizations overlap in many ways. Some people go to both conferences, and SIETAR has its Simulation/Game Special Interest Group. Simulation/gamers are probably one of the most culturally adaptable groups around, and interculturalists constantly use simulation/gaming in their work.

The intercultural dimensions of the ISAGA 25th anniversary conference in particular and of simulation/gaming in general are evident from the contributions in this volume. The theme of interculturality (as with interdisciplinarity) is manifest in several ways:

- *The subject matter within chapters.* Some chapters deal with intercultural issues or with aspects of intercultural phenomena. Examples are intercultural understanding (Sutherland et al.), Arab-Israeli relations (Bradford), and foreign language (Rising & Cedar).
- *Subject matter across chapters.* Here again, looking at subject matter across all the chapters, we are presented with a range of work, each influenced by its own cultural context, and with a range of cultural concerns. Examples are Britain (Ellington), Holland (Geurts), and Russia and neighbors (Rybalskiy).
- *Contributors individually.* Some authors are themselves of mixed cultural background (especially the expatriates and the global nomads). Their biographical sketches indicate this.
- *Contributors collectively.* The contributors as a whole come from a large variety of cultural backgrounds, and that variety can be gleaned from a glance at the affiliations of authors. Some chapters bring together, in a more intimate intercultural collaboration, co-authors from several cultural backgrounds.

A couple of concluding observations on culture and simulation/gaming help to reinforce the importance of the intercultural in simulation/gaming. First, it is not coincidental that both games and cultures can be characterized by rules. One conceptualization of culture is that it constitutes an elaborate set of rules regulating human relations within the culture and defining intergroup relations with other cultures. The notion of rule is, of course, essential to the game element in simulation/gaming. Indeed, some would say that a coherent (and self-consistent) set of rules in itself almost constitutes a game. These two are nicely brought together in some intercultural simulation/games, for example, BARNGA. Similar parallels can be drawn in the notion of roles—in role-play and in social behavior.

This may partially explain a second observation: that a comparatively (vis-à-vis many other professions) large proportion of simulation/gamers have had direct and sustained intercultural experience. Several come to mind immediately as having lived in three or more countries: Ivo Wenzler (Croatia, United States, the Netherlands), Doug Coleman (China, Poland, United States), Cathy Greenblat (United States, France, Spain), Leo Schapira (Argentina, Switzerland, England), David Crookall (Nigeria, England, Germany, France, United States), and Hubert Law-Yone (Burma, England, Israel). Many more can count two countries. In some ways, as in SIETAR conferences, each delegate brings several cultures.

Watershed

Behind the notions of interdisciplinarity and interculturality is a hazy idea that at some point a crossing is made into unfamiliar territory. Simulation/

gamers (and others) cross over to other disciplines in search of what they need to design their simulation/games. People travel to and live in new cultures for a number of reasons. In both cases, the notion of watershed comes to mind— invisible but palpable and influential. In moving from one quarter century to another, the simulation/gaming profession is crossing an intellectual and cultural watershed. Further, the concept of cultural group arises again in the idea of generation. Thus, interculturality also underlies the idea of moving from one generation to the next, somewhat like crossing from one culture to another. This notion of watershed and its implication for moving on is developed further by Richard Duke in his remarks, reproduced in the next section of these proceedings. We seem, as Joe Wolfe has pointed out, to have arrived at a plateau, and we have not yet found or decided which routes to take for the next stages in our professional travels.

Organization of This Volume

If you have already scanned the contents pages of this book, you are probably asking why the chapters are not divided into specialties. The answer is given partly in the discussion above on the themes of this volume (mainly interdisciplinarity) and partly in the focus placed on simulation/gaming as a professional endeavor rather than merely as a set of subject-relevant techniques. Indeed, a simulation/game in forestry may be of great relevance to language teaching or to teamwork. It should hardly matter that a simulation/game is for business or for geography or for pronunciation. Indeed, dividing up chapters into subject-related categories goes counter to the (interdisciplinary) spirit of simulation/gaming; simulation/gaming professionals should delve into and learn from the entire spectrum of interests. How many simulation/gamers working in ecology, for example, actually read papers on simulation/gaming for cross-cultural communication? One of the challenges of simulation/gaming is that it encourages us to move outside our sometimes narrowly defined disciplinary bunkers.

Dividing this book's contents into subject areas would have been a mistake; it is like saying "this section is for business trainers, so forget the rest." Of course, simulation/gaming books and articles can and do specialize in certain areas, such as language teaching or international relations or policy formation. These are legitimate because they manifestly and avowedly specialize, but a book that contains pieces that cover as wide a spectrum as this one does has a different strength. It sparks off new ideas from creative interaction among a variety of domains—one of the advantages of bringing together several disciplines. The sections selected for this volume have, therefore, been chosen along professional lines, using categories that will be more meaningful for the true simulation/gamer, the person who is concerned with the field as a whole, with the breadth and richness of simulation/gaming, and with the depth of their own discipline (e.g., geography, communication, urban planning).

Categories such as "design" or "computers" are also inadequate for a general volume such as this. Design is a consideration that is directly addressed by many chapters and is not beneath the surface in most others. Such a category would therefore have contained most of the chapters in this volume. Computers are either used or not used, and such a category would thus have made a binary division of chapters. None of those in this volume have as their main focus the use of computer technology, although many mention such technology.

The book, then, is divided into four parts: applications, policy exercises, research, and professional matters. These categories come close to the ones used by Kiyoshi Arai in his conference presentation of a survey of the field. Admittedly, some of the chapters belong in more than one category. They must, nevertheless, be located somewhere, and overall balance was a consideration, along with appropriateness. The reader will no doubt recognize those chapters that go beyond the bounds of their home categories.

Part I: Applications

Using the methodology for a particular purpose—applying it to achieve a certain goal—is one of the main concerns of simulation/gamers. The intent here is to show the links between the methodology as manifest in a given simulation/game or type of simulation/game and a given set of objectives. For example, Cunningham shows us how he used simulation/gaming to teach bushfire management. However, many of the chapters in this category also express more professionally-oriented concerns. Cunningham, for example, also discusses adaptation—how to modify a simulation/game for new audiences and evolving situations.

Part II: Policy Exercises

Although it could be argued that policy exercises belong in the Applications category, they are not so much a type of application (the purpose for which a simulation/game is applied) as they are a type of procedure (the form of simulation/game being used). Within ISAGA, those involved in policy exercises formed International Policy Exercise Group (IPEG), which organized an extra day of sessions at the end of the ISAGA conference. It is thus fitting that they have their own category, even though much of what they do is of relevance to other simulation/gamers, just as IPEG people see themselves as a part of ISAGA.

Part III: Research

Unfortunately, the chapters in this category are few: two specific pieces of research (one on business performance and the other on discourse analysis in simulation/games), two literature reviews (one on effectiveness and the other more general), and a description of a research instrument, which reports results relating to ISAGA as an association. One might argue that research should be included in the Professional Matters category (discussed below), and it is indeed a vital professional concern. It is so much so in fact that it warrants its own category.

Part IV: Professional Matters

This is the key category (at least for a volume that marks the silver anniversary of ISAGA), containing contributions that embrace a broad range of topics:

- Simulation/gaming as a profession (Rybalskiy on simulation/gaming in the Confederation of Independent States, formerly USSR)
- Status of simulation/gaming as a profession (Geurts on simulation/gaming in Holland)
- How things have developed over the years (Armstrong on the 25 years of simulation/gaming; Toth on the history of policy exercises)
- Ethical matters (Powers on dilemmas with a particular methodology)
- Techniques used by simulation/gamers (Lederman and Kato on debriefing)
- Predicting where we might go from here (Ellington on the British scene; Geurts on the Dutch scene)

The thoughts expressed in these chapters contain many seeds for ideas and efforts to be developed and undertaken in the next generation of simulation/gaming.

Missing from here is a chapter on professional standards. However, Crookall's guide to the literature (Chapter 19) contains a section on professional standards, summarizing the work done to date. This should appease those at the conference who complained that nothing was being done in this area. Still, more work is needed, so all those interested in contributing (which means time and commitment) or taking an active part in the discussions are invited to contact one of the editors.

Acknowledgments

Conference acknowledgments are made by Richard Duke in the next section. We will confine our thanks here to some of the many people who have helped in one way or another with these proceedings. Of great help, especially in the rewriting and copy-editing of certain chapters, was Alexandra Bernstein. Sandy Fowler provided valuable feedback on this preface and other parts of the book. Daniel Druckman agreed at very short notice to re-write a chapter especially for this volume, and Jan Sutherland swiftly revised and augmented a paper. Also, special appreciation must go to Joe Wolfe for his stunning performance in producing a completely new paper within a few days.

Local thanks are due many people, only some of which can be mentioned here. At the Institut d'Etudes Politiques (Sciences Po) de Lille are Yves Luchaire (Directeur), Noëlle Gorin, Florence Kaczmarek, Sandrine Terrier, and Michel Vlaeminck. They and others at the IEP made it possible for David Crookall to attend the ISAGA '94 conference. After the conference, David moved to the Université de Technologie de Compiègne, where he also received solid support, in particular from Nicole Bonis, Philippe Cremery, Abdi Seyed Hosseini-Kazeroni, Joëlle Lallier, Claude Moreau, Jean-Paul Narcy, and Michel Vayssade. From further afield, Mieko Nakamura spent some time in Compiègne while this volume was being prepared and lent a major hand in the office.

At Sage Publications, many people lent many hands. Nancy Hale, Production Assistant, provided invaluable guidance for general aspects of production; Joyce Kuhn, Copy Editor, did a terrific (almost terrifying) job on the manuscript; Janelle LeMaster, Typesetter, turned all those pages into a visually attractive form; Astrid Virding, Production Editor, deftly kept us on our toes and extracted from us the missing pieces—all wonderful people to work with. C. Deborah Laughton, Acquisitions Editor, deserves a big hug of thanks for her support and guidance throughout the development of these proceedings.

Finally, Richard Duke deserves the final applause for his prompt support during the preparation of the volume—swiftly supplying us with discs, e-mail files, and the like. It is to Dick that this volume is dedicated, and we know that gamers around the world join us in thanking him for offering to pay for sausage and beer all those years ago (would have liked to have been there) and for making it possible for us to celebrate that historic event a quarter century later.

—David Crookall,
Fresnel and Compiègne, France

—Kiyoshi Arai,
Fukuoka, Japan

Opening Speech: Welcome and Challenge

RICHARD D. DUKE

My thoughts this morning will be presented in two distinct phases. First, welcome to ISAGA '94, our 25th annual meeting! On behalf of the University of Michigan, the College of Architecture and Urban Planning, and the Graduate Program in Gaming and Simulation, I would like to welcome all of you to Ann Arbor.

On behalf of the ISAGA '94 Program Committee, I would like to thank all of you for making your long journey. You have come from many countries—literally from the four corners of the earth. Even by jet, travel of this kind can be arduous. I hope that the activities of the coming week will be adequate reward for your effort.

Acknowledgments

A conference of this kind requires the active support of many people; I have been fortunate in receiving this assistance. It is not possible to mention everyone, but I would like to acknowledge those who have been exceptionally helpful.

First and foremost, I would like to acknowledge David Crookall. David seems never to sleep, never to tire, never to be in the same country for more than a week at a time. The inverse is also true: David seems ever available on e-mail, ever knowing of how best to contact each of the hundreds of respondents, ever willing and able to advise on the mind-numbing list of particulars that have to be resolved as planning for the conference progressed.

I would like to acknowledge the Program Committee (see page x) for their assistance over the past year; these weekly meetings have helped greatly in shaping the conference. As you can guess, working out the particulars of the program required patience and attention to detail. We are all indebted to Andrea Frank for her effort in this regard.

EDITORS' NOTE: Duke's speech has been edited for these proceedings.

Robert Beckley, Dean, College of Architecture and Urban Planning, has made the appropriate arrangements to provide the conference with the exclusive use of the Art and Architecture Building. We also appreciate the support received from Robert Marans, Chair of the Urban and Regional Planning Program, and the students of the Graduate Certificate Program in Gaming Simulation. Allen Samuels, Dean of the School of Art, has been kind enough to assist the Program Committee in a variety of ways. We are also indebted to Heather Dornoff for her assistance with the arrangements for the Slusser Gallery.

We have two graduate programs in gaming and simulation here at the University of Michigan. The first is a year-long graduate program. The second is a new 12-week professional program. The students from these programs have worked with me on this conference over the past two terms. These students developed three games for this occasion; they will be presented in the Slusser Gallery throughout the week. You should participate if you get the opportunity.

Students in the Graduate Certificate Program in Gaming and Simulation have been active in the development of the conference throughout the process. Besides their participation as active members of the ISAGA '94 Program Committee, several students took on additional responsibilities:

Sandy Bartlett	Computer and technical assistance
James Brown	Speaker—specific room arrangements
Anne Carmichael	Assistance to the young professionals
Debra Darmofal	Support of various kinds
Andrea Frank	Completion of the detailed conference program
Mark LeBay	Building signs and decorations
Lisa Leutheuser	Tour information; e-mail messages
Colleen McGee	Support of various kinds
Mojtaba Navvab	Technical assistance; organizing the canoe trips
William Purves	Responsibility for the Tuesday student barbecue
Marjorie Efva Winful	Contacting speakers

Students in the Certificate Program in Gaming and Simulation developed three games for use at ISAGA '94. Students participating in these games presented on Sunday afternoon are Jee Young Ahn, Benjamin Bolger, James Brown, Darin Bufkin, Anne Carmichael, Robert Cohen, Delilah Ellis, Andrea Frank, Bernie Hsiung, and Han Sung Koo.

The North American Simulation and Gaming Association (NASAGA) has been supportive of the efforts to develop this conference. Special thanks go to the NASAGA Cooperation Committee: Barbara Steinwachs (Chair), Pierre Corbeille, and Chuck Plummer.

It is also appropriate to extend thanks to Al Feldt, whose band, The Eclectics, provided entertainment for the reception on Sunday. I would like to point out that Al was one of the participants at the first meeting of ISAGA 25 years ago. I would also like to acknowledge the Conferences and Seminars staff, in particular Penny Tully and Cindy Sakstrup. We would like to thank Sage Publications for their assistance with the awards reception.

Many others have contributed a great deal to the preparation for this converence; regrettably, they cannot all be mentioned. However it is appropriate to single out a few who have made a special effort: Mojtaba Navvab and Sandy Bartlett have assisted with the arrangements for the special Audio-Visual equipment required for some of the presentations; and Charlene Schmult, who has been kind enough to work with foreign students to locate accommodations in private homes.

As I complete these acknowledgements, I want to single out the person who has, perhaps, carried the largest burden over the past year. As you can imagine, there has been an unending stream of mail to be sent or received, messages and phone calls, a fax machine demanding attention at all hours of the day and night. I have to confess I did not do it all. Much of this was attended to and kept in an orderly manner by my wife, Marie. We are all indebted to her.

Theme

The theme for this conference is "The Next Generation." As you saw in the registration packet, every professor on the mailing list was sent a buy-one-get-one-free coupon. We have made a substantial effort to bring young professionals to this meeting; the result has been gratifying. We have more than 40 students from many different countries participating.

I would like to welcome these visiting students. It is gratifying to see you here, and I welcome you to Ann Arbor. I challenge you to join in the discussions and activities of the conference and to consider how you might best contribute to the profession in the years ahead. I also challenge you to become involved with ISAGA so that it might best be organized to meet your future professional needs.

It is time for ISAGA to focus on new perspectives, new techniques, and new technologies. This is in no way a denial of the legacy provided by the earlier generation—rather, it is an opportunity to celebrate the vitality of this profession and to pass the mantle on to young professionals worldwide.

It is important that all participants make a special effort to be in contact with those of other generations and other cultures. This conference provides the opportunity both to increase the network of professionals and to permit some of the veterans in the field to mentor a new generation. I challenge each of you to make contact across the boundaries of age and space and to use this opportunity to encourage, enlighten, and, whenever possible, amuse your colleagues.

Challenge

The second phase of my remarks is to offer a challenge to you in attendance at ISAGA '94. There is a mythical character in children's stories named Rip Van Winkle. Mr. Winkle's claim to fame was that he fell asleep, only to awaken 25 years later. This morning, I feel like Rip Van Winkle: I have taken a short nap, only to awaken to discover that a quarter century has passed.

To establish a frame of reference, consider some memorable events from 25 years ago:

- The moon walk by Neil Armstrong
- Vietnam, Richard Nixon, and peaceniks
- The first transatlantic flight on the Concorde
- The movies *I Am Curious (Yellow)* and *Midnight Cowboy*
- Broadway shows *Hair, Hello Dolly,* and *Oh! Calcutta*
- Woodstock
- Celebration of first Earth Day
- A jumbo jet hijacked to Cuba
- And, of course, the first meeting of ISAGA held in Bad Godesburg, Germany!

A quarter century later, the world has changed in many ways. But today, here in Ann Arbor, we find ISAGA still going strong.

How did this first ISAGA meeting come about? In 1969, I was doing a simulation of the housing market for Dortmund, Germany. Hans Hansen, Roy Miller, and Al Feldt were members of this team. In preparing for this conference, I discovered the original 28 letters that I had sent out, as well as their responses. The letter simply said, "Come to Bad Godesburg and talk about gaming, and I will buy the sausage and beer." No conference activities had been planned because, at best, no more than 5 or 10 people were expected. A total of 84 people showed up, including gamers from many countries, their wives, and children.

Fortunately, the small army that arrived was enthusiastic. We rented an old windmill that had been converted to a conference center. The group organized a semblance of a conference, sessions were held, and, thanks to Henk Becker, a constitution and by-laws were established. The group was enthusiastic, a great deal of information was exchanged, and a lot of beer and sausage was consumed. It was a terrific experience—a lot of fun. Many of the friendships established at that meeting have endured to this day.

The impromptu ISAGA meeting in 1969 started a chain of events that led to this silver anniversary meeting. ISAGA has met each year in many different countries. Organizing that first conference was simplicity itself. Basically, all I did was buy a lot of beer and sausage! I can tell you that, a quarter century later, mounting an ISAGA conference is a bit more complicated. For example, the mailing list for this conference exceeded 3,000 people; more than 60 countries are represented on this list. Of course, there are a lot more countries than there used to be!

Reshaping ISAGA

Over the past quarter century, gaming has become a robust discipline. As evidence, let me suggest that you review the many presentations that are in the program. The gamers who have shown an interest in this meeting come from a very broad range of professional backgrounds, and they reflect a wide variety of substantive interests. Closer observation reveals at least three common threads of interest:

- First, the presentations address a continuum of related *methodologies.*
- Second, they address a series of related *disciplinary* concerns.
- Third, they reflect loosely defined *substantive* interests.

These three are the glue that holds ISAGA together; they are the underlying drawing power for a conference such as this. They may also prove to be our Achilles' heel.

Few gamers have the luxury of spending their time doing gaming solely for the love of it. Most of us are employed in work that addresses a specific substantive area; gaming/simulation techniques are incidental to the demands of our job. First and foremost, we are required to establish substantive knowledge and gain access to a network of colleagues with similar interests.

Increasingly, these professional obligations result in the demand for substantively focused international gatherings. These meetings inevitably compete in both time and money with the annual ISAGA conference. It would be unfortunate if newly formed substantive groups were to threaten ISAGA's existence.

Our mutual underlying interests in methodological and disciplinary concerns, as well as our shared philosophy of experiential learning, argue for ISAGA to become a strong, overarching, professional organization. Those of us who are true believers feel with a passion that the gaming approach is not just another technique. We believe that, when properly employed, this approach can achieve significant social objectives that urgently demand attention—human concerns that cannot be adequately addressed with other approaches.

If my concerns about fragmentation are legitimate, we must work actively to keep ISAGA viable during the next quarter century. Let me suggest three concerns that ISAGA must address:

- First, we need to reconsider our organizational objectives. As now stated, they are to facilitate communication among specialists, improve communication with educators and policymakers, promote the training of specialists, promote improved disciplinary methods, and encourage comparable groups on a national and regional basis.

- Second, it is time to give serious consideration to rethinking the structure of ISAGA. ISAGA should serve as an umbrella organization that actively encourages special interest groups. We should take the opportunity to create an organization that will accommodate a variety of subgroups. For example, at this conference, we have at least nine special interest groups represented.
- Third, to ensure the viability of ISAGA, we need to establish a more effective central office function with the capacity to maintain a mailing list that reaches a large potential constituency and the ability to post a regular newsletter. ISAGA should depend no longer on the heroic activities of a single, unfunded individual.

This conference has been organized to stimulate discussion on these issues. Toward that end, seven distinct substantive channels have been developed. These do not reflect a preordained agenda; they are the result of an attempt to accommodate the abstracts that were presented. Thursday morning has been set aside to permit discussion to focus on the issue of professional divisions. There are nine special interest groups represented; all groups not listed are encouraged to identify themselves and facilities will be made available. [The ISAGA News & Notes section in *Simulation & Gaming* reports on the work of these groups.]

In summary, then, my charge to you as delegates to ISAGA '94 is to consider the possibility of the need to restructure ISAGA. In these deliberations, give careful thought to the possibility of having ISAGA become more of an umbrella organization that accommodates professionals who share our interests, no matter what their substantive context. If this is a valid concept, we must lay the groundwork now for future conferences.

Introduction for Robert Armstrong*

We are fortunate today to be able to hear from a gamer of long standing, one of the participants at the original ISAGA meeting in Bad Godesberg. Bob Armstrong has contributed a great deal to the underlying thought structure of this discipline. He has had long experience in the field; he has thought deeply about what gaming is and where it fits in our societal milieu. Bob has spent a considerable part of his life thinking and writing about these concerns.

Unfortunately, Bob has been taken seriously ill and is not able to be with us today. He has been able to put his thoughts on tape; his paper will be available in its entirety in the proceedings. At Bob's request, we have provided a few slides to go along with his text. Forgive us if the graphics intrude on his thoughts, but the tape arrived by air post on Friday, and we have done our best to make the presentation more lively than simply the taped voice. Bob sends his greetings and his regrets.

---

*EDITORS' NOTE: The first plenary of the conference was to have been given by Robert Armstrong. This is Duke's introduction to that plenary, edited for these proceedings. Armstrong's chapter appears later in this volume.

ISAGA

The International Simulation and Gaming Association (ISAGA) was founded in 1970. The aim of the association is to promote the use and study of simulation/gaming throughout the world. Its annual conference is held in a different country each year—see chart. The official journal of ISAGA is *Simulation & Gaming: An International Journal of Theory, Practice, and Research*, published by Sage Periodicals Press. Information about ISAGA conferences and other activities is presented in the *ISAGA News & Notes* section of the journal.

Previous ISAGA Conferences

Conferences held over the past quarter century are shown below, along with the first two conferences of the next quarter century. Thanks go to Jan Klabbers for supplying the information. This listing provides a summary impression of the international and intercultural character of ISAGA.

No.	Year	City	Country	Chair/Organizer	Proceedings Published?
1	**1970**	**Bad Godesburg**	**Germany**	**Richard Duke**	
2	1971	Utrecht	The Netherlands	Hank Becker	
3	1972	Birmingham	England	John Taylor	
4	1973	Gaithersburg, MD	United States	Cathy Greenblat & Peter House	
5	1974	Berlin	West Germany	Declan Kennedy	
6	1975	Milano	Italy	Gianluigi Sartorio	
7	1976	Caracas	Venezuela	Estelio Breto-Flores	
8	1977	Birmingham	England	Margaret Hobson & Robert Armstrong	
9	1978	Lund	Sweden	Mats Lorstad	
10	1979	Friesland	The Netherlands	Klaas Bruin	Yes
11	1980	Genève	Switzerland	Maurice Graber	Yes
12	1981	Haifa	Israel	Hubert Law-Yone	Yes
13	1982	Sterling	Scotland	Drew Mackie	
14	1983	Sophia	Bulgaria	Ognyan Panov	Yes
15	1984	Elsinore	Denmark	Eric Petterson	
16	1985	Alma Ata	USSR	Vladimir Burkov	
17	1986	Toulon	France	David Crookall	Yes
18	1987	Venezia	Italy	Arnaldo Ceccini & Giorgio Panizzi	Yes
19	1988	Utrecht	The Netherlands	Jan Klabbers	Yes
20	1989	Weimar	East Germany	Hans Gernert	
21	1990	Durham, NH	United States	Dennis Meadows	
22	1991	Kyoto	Japan	Kiyoshi Arai & Hiroharo Seki	Yes
23	1992	Edinburgh	Scotland	Fred Percival	Yes
24	1993	Bucaresti	Romania	Eduard Rădăceanu	Yes
25	**1994**	**Ann Arbor, MI**	**United States**	**Richard Duke**	**Yes**
26	1995	Valencia	Spain	Francis Watts & Amparo Garcia Carbonell	Yes
27	1996	Riga	Latvia	Valdis Bisters	

PART I

Applications

1

EXECUTIVE DECISION

Exploring the Psychological Contract: An Exercise

HAMILTON BEAZLEY

JOHN LOBUTS, Jr.

Basic Data

Objectives: To help the participants become aware of the importance of the unwritten psychological contract that exists between an employer and employee and of the way in which that contract is changing, to encourage participants to examine their own interpretations of the psychological contract, to expose the conflicting values and obligations that underlie major corporate decisions, and to enable participants to experience one or more counterproductive psychological phenomena (adjustive reactions) that commonly occur among managers making stressful decisions in small groups.

Target audience: Any group for whom small-group decision making and employer/employee relations are important, such as students of psychology, sociology, communication, and business. Managers, executives, human resource professionals, and labor leaders would also benefit.

Playing time: 90 minutes (30 minutes for instructions and play and 60 minutes for debriefing following conclusion of the game)

Numbers of players: From 6 (1 group of 6) to 120 (20 groups of 6)

Materials required: The Hudson Valley Corporation Briefing Paper to be distributed to each participant. An EXECUTIVE DECISION Game Packet for the facilitator contains a complete set of instructions, comments, and transparencies that facilitate the play of the game.

Equipment/room setup required: Either one room that is large enough for multiple groups of 6 to work without being influenced by the words or actions of other groups or one large room for discussion by all the participants and smaller rooms for individual groups to use during the small-group decision-making phase.

The Situation

The simulation is based on the plight of Hudson Valley Corporation, the largest employer in Hudson Valley, which has been steadily losing money in recent years. Edward Hudson, Sr., the company's 76-year-old founder and majority stockholder, has to decide whether or not to accept a buyout offer from Amalgamated Industries or one from the employees of Hudson Valley Corporation or choose some other alternative to reverse the losses. With Edward Hudson, Jr., his 46-year-old son and the president of the company, Ed Sr. has developed a list of seven dramatically different options to save the company. Each option represents a different interpretation of the psychological contract between the Hudsons and their employees. As role-playing members of the Executive Vice-President's staff, participants are divided into groups of six and asked to reach unanimous agreement on recommending one option of the seven provided.

Procedure: Notes for Facilitators

Explain to the participants that they will be doing a group exercise involving the Hudson Valley Corporation. Ask each participant to play the role of a member of the staff of the Executive Vice-President. The Executive Vice-President has asked her staff members to make a unanimous recommendation from among a list of seven alternatives provided to them. Distribute copies of the Hudson Valley Briefing Paper (below) to all participants and instruct them to read it and then decide which of the seven alternatives they favor.

After participants have finished reading the Briefing Paper and have reached their own decisions, divide them into groups of five to seven, using any convenient method. Then ask the groups to discuss the Hudson Valley case and to reach a unanimous decision as to which alternative they recommend. The groups have 20 minutes in which to reach that decision. Only one recommendation can be made by each group, and it must be one of the seven alternatives provided in the Briefing Paper.

When time is called, ask each group for its decision and write that decision on the board under the group designation ("Group A," "B," "C," etc.). If no unanimous decision has been reached, the facilitator records the individual decisions by option number (1-7) and notes in parentheses next to the option the number of participants favoring that decision. The debriefing begins after the results have been recorded.

Remind the participants that a role-play simulation permits them to participate emotionally in the decision-making process. It allows them to delve into perspectives other than their own and to see decision making in terms of values and emotions rather than strictly as an intellectual or abstract exercise. Remind the players to be alert to—and aware of—the dynamics of the group as they attempt to reach a decision.

The Briefing Paper

Hudson Valley Corporation is the largest employer in Hudson Valley, an ethnically diverse town of 150,000. Founded in 1946 by Edward Hudson, Sr., the company grew during the postwar boom years into a large and highly profitable operation. Over the past ten years, however, its profitability has declined, despite efforts by its founder to reverse the trend. For the past three years, the company has been in the red, with losses rapidly mounting. Edward Hudson, Sr., Chairman of the Board, CEO, and owner of 52% of the stock, has refused to lay off any employees. His son, Edward, Jr., who is Vice-Chairman and controls 22% of the stock, is anxious to downsize or sell the company in order to preserve his substantial inheritance. Various employees of the company own 16% of the stock. Hudson Valley Charities, Inc., a Valley-wide charitable organization, owns the remaining 10% of the stock, its largest source of funds.

Amalgamated Industries, the Big City conglomerate, has made a final cash offer for Hudson Valley Corporation that will expire in three days. The employees responded to that offer with one of their own. The Hudsons have studied both offers and prepared a list of the options they consider viable. However, they disagree so vehemently regarding these alternatives that they have asked the Executive Vice-President to make a single recommendation from the list of seven they have provided. Whatever recommendation she makes will alienate one or the other of the Hudsons.

"Mr. Ed" Hudson is 76 and in poor health. "Little Ed" is 46 and in the prime of life. Mr. Ed is Chairman of the Hudson Valley Bank, Chairman Emeritus of the United Way, Honorary Chairman of the Hudson Valley Hospital, and a member of the Board of Stewards of his church.

The Executive Vice-President has been approached by Hudson Valley Corporation employees begging her not to recommend closing or selling the company to Amalgamated Industries. Townspeople by the hundreds, it seems, have reminded her of how crucial the company is to Hudson Valley. Closing the corporation would, in the public mind, start a decline from which Hudson Valley would never recover. It would be financially and psychologically devastating. Everyone in town is related to someone who works for "the company," and they are all afraid. Some have hinted that the recent immigration of new families into the region has created a workforce that is not as well known and well liked by the founding family. They believe that the Hudsons would be more willing to fire them for that reason, but there is no evidence to that effect.

In fact, the problem with Hudson Valley Corporation is that it has not responded well to the global marketplace, to rapid technological change and swift product innovations, or to the need for more flexible management styles. Its production costs remain too high to be competitive in a global environment, its product designs are not quite cutting edge, many of its manufacturing processes involve tedious repetitive labor, and product quality does not meet the improved world standard. Little Ed blames the Japanese and the failure of the U.S. government to force open Japanese markets and stop them from dumping their products in the United States. Mr. Ed keeps his own counsel, but it is clear that he is deeply disturbed by the business trends he is witnessing. In unguarded moments among old friends, he laments the passage of the good old days. Time is running out for Hudson Valley Corporation.

Which recommendation should the Executive Vice-President make to the Hudsons?

As a member of her staff, you must resolve this question with the other staff members because the Executive Vice-President wants a unanimous decision. Choose one of the following alternatives and be prepared to discuss the reasons for your choice. No alternatives other than those below can be considered, and choices cannot be combined or otherwise modified.

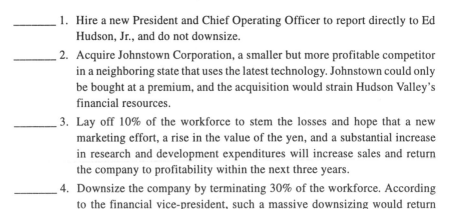

_____ 1. Hire a new President and Chief Operating Officer to report directly to Ed Hudson, Jr., and do not downsize.

_____ 2. Acquire Johnstown Corporation, a smaller but more profitable competitor in a neighboring state that uses the latest technology. Johnstown could only be bought at a premium, and the acquisition would strain Hudson Valley's financial resources.

_____ 3. Lay off 10% of the workforce to stem the losses and hope that a new marketing effort, a rise in the value of the yen, and a substantial increase in research and development expenditures will increase sales and return the company to profitability within the next three years.

_____ 4. Downsize the company by terminating 30% of the workforce. According to the financial vice-president, such a massive downsizing would return the company to breakeven within a year. If a sales increase could be achieved, the company would return to profitability within two years.

_____ 5. Accept a buyout offer from the employees with 40% down and a ten-year payout based on profitability. Total payment (if made) would amount to 25% less than Amalgamated's cash offer on a discounted cash-flow basis. If the employee proposal is not accepted within five days, the prime lender will permanently withdraw and the employees will never be able to purchase the company.

_____ 6. Sell the company to Amalgamated Industries for cash. Amalgamated may or may not close the plant, although Amalgamated's past predatory behavior indicates that it would do so if a brutal downsizing were not successful.

_____ 7. Break up the company, selling off its operating divisions and other assets, which, individually, are worth more than the integrated company and 10% to 25% more than Amalgamated has agreed to pay in its final offer. Some of the divisions would be permanently closed and the remaining sold to competitors in other states. The dismantling process would take at least two years.

Debriefing

There are two different aspects to the debriefing: One concerns the psychological contract and the other the adjustive reactions that occurred during the simulation. It has been our experience that participants become very emotionally involved in the simulation and are quite surprised that they cannot easily reach consensus as to the most appropriate recommendation to make. It has also been our experience that the participants grasp that the various alternatives represent different perspectives and that there seems to be no right answer. Furthermore, the various participants invariably manifest some of the adjustive reactions described below. During the ISAGA conference, we also used a confederate, as explained under Variations (below) to heighten the conflict. We found that the different responses chosen by the participants were highly dependent on their cultures.

The Psychological Contract

The first part of the debriefing deals with the psychological contract between employers and employees. Edgar Schein (1965) originally postulated the existence of such an unwritten contract based on mutual expectations and obligations. He saw the contract as being at the heart of employee motivation and performance.

Questions about the psychological contract include the following:

- Who are the parties to the psychological contract in the Hudson Valley case?
- What are their expectations?
- What are their responsibilities?
- Is there a right answer for the Executive Vice-President?
- On what does the answer depend? (Possible answers: your perspective, values, background, education, work experience, philosophy of life, religious views, etc.)
- How has the psychological contract changed in recent years?
- What are some examples of organizations with significantly changed psychological contracts (e.g., armed forces, IBM, Japanese automakers)?
- What kinds of contracts are represented by Edward, Sr. and Edward, Jr.?
- What are the implications for our society of the changing psychological contract?
- What happens when the psychological contract is broken by either side?

Adjustive Reactions

The simulation sets up a small group dynamic in which one or more of the following adjustive reactions usually comes into play. These reactions (formerly called psychological defenses) are important for managers because their use is counterproductive to the management process. The simulation helps participants experience these reactions in action both in themselves and in the other members of the group. Five of the reactions to be highlighted are as follows:

- *Psychological safety*—Going along with the majority decision even though you disagree with it
- *Psychological deafness*—Refusing to hear another side of the story; filtering out what is being said because you do not agree with it; being closed to arguments and data from others
- *Psychological amputation*—Being cut out of the discussion and ostracized from the group because of your unpopular views
- *Psychological deflection*—Blaming others for the problem rather than accepting responsibility for your part in it and thereby trying to solve it
- *Psychological deviance*—Strident refusal to agree with the group; relishing an adversarial role at odds with the group (a devil's advocate is a deviant role taken temporarily to achieve a specific and positive purpose)

Questions about adjustive reactions in the group dynamics include the following:

- Did you experience any of these adjustive reactions yourself? If so, which ones?
- Did anyone else in the group exhibit these reactions? If so, which ones?

- Have you experienced any of these reactions yourself at work? If so, which ones and under what circumstances?
- Has your boss or your colleagues at work exhibited any of these reactions? If so, which ones and under what circumstances?
- How can you reduce the likelihood that you will employ these reactions?

Interdisciplinarity, Interculturality, and ISAGA Watershed

Interdisciplinarity

The EXECUTIVE DECISION simulation calls upon many disciplines for its successful play: psychology, sociology, economics, finance, political science, and management. Diverse perspectives on the role of corporations in society and their own responsibilities to their employees and to the towns and states in which they are located emerge during the simulation, reflecting various schools of thought. Small group dynamics and adjustive reactions characterize part of the learning experience. The simulation provides a vehicle for using the knowledge of various disciplines within a single event—a testimony to the unique power of gaming/simulation to capture the complexity of the real world in a teaching environment.

Interculturality

The nature of the psychological contract between employer and employee is highly dependent on the specific culture in which an organization is located because it reflects the values and expectations of that culture. Notions of fairness, responsibility, and obligation are culturally derived. For example, the difference in employee and employer expectations regarding "permanent" employment by a firm in the United States and Japan is quite remarkable, at least traditionally. Even notions of what constitutes "hard work" or appropriate vacation time stem from cultural forces.

When workers from different cultural backgrounds work for the same company they will likely hold different versions of the psychological contract. Furthermore, their versions may not mesh with the corporate version based on the dominant culture. The psychological contract, then, plays a central role in the management of diversity, but it is culturally specific. Therefore, when the simulation is played by participants from a single culture, their decisions will reflect the diversity of values held by that culture. When the simulation is played with participants from different cultures, the impact of culture on the psychological contract and on management practices becomes abundantly clear.

ISAGA Watershed

The 25th anniversary of ISAGA that marks a watershed in simulation/gaming coincides with a watershed in the history of American business and the management philosophy that has guided it for almost a century. The EXECUTIVE DECISION simulation, in fact, explores that watershed. As the world economy makes its transition from an industrial to a technological to an informational base, management philosophy and the thought processes of managers themselves are changing to accommodate the new realities. Chief among these realities is ongoing turbulent change that requires a more participatory management style.

Participatory management means greater cooperation and collaboration among employees and between employees and employers. It means greater team effort. As the authoritative, rigid management style of previous decades gives way to collaborative management, managers will be called on to develop new psychological contracts and to make significant psychological adjustments. This simulation addresses the contract and some of the mechanisms involved in those adjustments in an experiential way.

Variations

In one variation of the game, a participant is chosen in advance to act as a confederate of the presenter in each of the groups. These "plants" are given the Hudson Valley Corporation case to read in advance. The confederate is instructed to express no opinion on the case until the group has begun to develop a consensus. At that time, the plant takes a position that is opposite to that of the group and continues to argue it until he or she either sways the group or brings it to a stalemate when time is called.

The functions of the plant are to make the play of the game more realistic by provoking the adjustive reactions of the other members of the group and to stimulate a more thorough discussion of conflicting perspectives on the responsibilities and obligations involved in the psychological contract.

Reference

Schein, E. H. (1965). *Organizational psychology* (Foundations of Modern Psychology Series). Englewood Cliffs, NJ: Prentice Hall.

2

Simulated U.S. Decision
Making in Arab-Israeli Crises

WILLIAM C. BRADFORD

Although many observers of the post-Cold War Middle East sense that the winds
of change are ushering in a new spirit of peace and cooperation, as evidenced
by the Jordan-Israel Treaty of Nonbelligerence and the Palestine National
Authority-Israel Declaration of Principles, there are still several important
impediments to a long-term solution of conflicts in the region. A multi-level
analysis of historical and contemporary conditions in the Middle East suggests
that future Arab-Israeli crises may erupt in the region as they have on an average
of once every eight years since 1948. For the United States, the sole surviving
superpower, decision making in times of these crises will continue to be both
rich with opportunities and fraught with dangers.

The history of U.S. foreign policy decision making in times of Arab-Israeli
crises is replete with successes, such as the defusing of the SCUD crisis in 1991
and the diplomatic termination of the October War of 1973, and failures, such as
the loss of more than 240 Marines in Lebanon in 1983 and the inability to prevent the Six Day War in 1967. Unfortunately, no real planning procedures have
guided the making of U.S. foreign policy, and Arab-Israeli crisis decisions have
tended to be made simply as reactions to rapidly changing conditions and on a
basis of incomplete and frequently incorrect information and assumptions.

Although the United States cannot expect to control completely the outcomes
of future Arab-Israeli crises, U.S. foreign policy decisions have historically
been instrumental in the production of certain political and military crisis
outcomes. Consequently, it is logical to suppose that future U.S. foreign policy
decisions in times of Arab-Israeli crises will determine to at least a large extent
which of the numerous potential alternative futures will indeed be realized.

AUTHOR'S NOTE: I thank Professors Harold Guetzkow and Tong Park for their extensive guidance, the participants in PROJECT PAX ISLAMICUS for their generous gift of time, and the Institute
for the Study of World Politics for the generous grant that made the project possible.

Although it is essentially reductionist to focus exclusively on the role of the U.S. president in determining the source(s) of U.S. crisis decisions, there is ample evidence, much beyond the scope of this chapter, to suggest that this is not theoretically unwise. Further, a number of primary causal factors that are the product of the psychological profile of the U.S. president can be identified as largely responsible for the substance of specific crisis decisions and, in turn, crisis outcomes (for a detailed description of a political-psychological model of U.S. presidential crisis decision making, see Bradford, 1994).

Until now, research has been rooted almost exclusively in post hoc analyses of historical crises. Further, the specific research area of Arab-Israeli crises is limited; only seven major crises exist for study. In fields such as this, traditional quantitative research is unproductive; hence, other methods are required. Simulation, particularly the variety known as political-military gaming, allows for the quasi-experimental generation of future crises and the testing of hypotheses concerning the relationships between presidential psychology, crisis decisions, and crisis outcomes. Further, policy selection can be designed on the basis of simulation research in a manner that reflects the objective and subjective values of the decision makers. Research efforts in this direction may ultimately lead to a global-level synthesis of regional models of the relationship between U.S. and other national crisis decisions and crisis outcomes.

PROJECT PAX ISLAMICUS

The Game

PROJECT PAX ISLAMICUS (PPI) is a scenario-driven, near-future-oriented, computer-assisted political-military simulation that I designed for the purpose of generating experimental data and testing a political-psychological model of U.S. foreign policy decision making in Arab-Israeli crises (for a detailed description of the model see Bradford, 1994). PPI incorporates much of Guetzkow's INTER-NATION SIMULATION (INS) (1968) and Gilboa's SIMULATION OF MIDDLE EAST CONFLICT (SMEC) (1980) as a structural and procedural foundation, with the future international context and crisis scenario having been developed specifically for the purposes of the present research. PPI consists of four 60-minute move periods and a 30-minute debriefing exercise; several weeks of participant preparation precede the game.

The specific scenario used in PPI is largely a replication of the October War of 1973 with several additions: An Islamic government is in power in Egypt, and the international context is altered to reflect the international system in the post-Cold War era of intensified regionalism, ethnic conflict, and nuclear proliferation.

Participants and Logistics

The participant pool was composed primarily of Northwestern undergraduate and graduate students with extensive prior political science, international relations, and national security coursework. Some of the roles, particularly those of the Arab and Israeli teams, were filled by consular officials and nationals of those states. Participants were assigned to teams and roles on the basis of personal biographical information and the results of a psychological test composed of relevant social psychological inventories that measured the aforementioned psychological causal factors. Participants committed to a minimum of ten hours of preparation for the simulation and performed specific preparatory exercises, which they received from the simulation director.

PPI was held at several locations on the campus of Northwestern University in Evanston, Illinois. Teams were assigned to separate rooms in a common hallway, and communications were facilitated by written messages and by telephone. All the runs of PPI were filmed on videotape for reconstruction and research.

Schedule

PPI began in September 1994 with the issuing of simulation kits to the participants. Participant preparation began at that time and continued into mid-October. The 12 runs of PPI started in mid-October and continued until completed in early 1995.

Debriefing

Participants completed an extensive, written, post-simulation questionnaire, individually and with their teams, prior to an oral interview with the simulation director. Questions concerned motivations for decisions, degree of success in implementing decisions, probable decisions that would have been made had the simulation continued, and a host of other items relevant to the research. Questions regarding the project, in particular the political-psychological model, the crisis scenario, and any decisions made by the simulation director in the course of PPI that affected crisis outcomes, were answered.

Future Research and Training

Limitations of the Current Project

Following my presentation of PPI at the ISAGA conference, several audience members noted that PPI does not attempt to model non-crisis decision making and does not focus much research attention on the role of the United Nations or other international organizations in the use of force to resolve crises. Both of these observations are accurate. Nonetheless, I stressed my rather modest expectation for PPI that it serve as a method for research in U.S. foreign policy decision making in Arab-Israeli crises. Routine foreign policy decisions are beyond the scope of the project, and the history of U.S. military involvement in Arab-Israeli crises suggests that relative inattention to the United Nations need not compromise the validity of the project.

Several members of the audience were familiar with Arab-Israeli crisis simulations, having examined the work of Edgar Taylor (1993) and his ICS at the University of Michigan. A final report of the results of the project has been readied for ISAGA '95 in Spain.

Global Model

At present, PPI is exclusively a means of testing theories of U.S. foreign policy decision making in times of Arab-Israeli crises. Nonetheless, the potential for the extension of the method and the model to other world regions and other foreign-policy decision units is evident; an important occasion for development in this direction was realized at ISAGA '94 at the University of Michigan in Ann Arbor. Professor Hiroharu Seki of Ritsumeikan University in Japan, Professors Tong-Whan Park and Harold Guetzkow (emeritus) of Northwestern University, Alexander Ryzhenkov of the University of Bremen in Germany, and Estelio Breto, former organizer of the ISAGA conference in Caracas, Venezuela, each expressed an interest in the globalization of the current study to address other world regions, particularly North Asia, Eastern Europe, and Latin America, other decision systems, such as parliamentary and formal bureaucratic structures, and alternative systems of values and ethics, such as Confucianism and indigenous perspectives, in international crisis research. As such, PPI must be viewed as an initial step in a rather lengthy and arduous journey.

Training

It is hoped that PPI will serve as a guide and training device for U.S. foreign-policy decision makers as they prepare to confront future international crises in the Middle East. The results of PPI may suggest means by which policy objectives can be realized in times of crises with minimal expenditures of lives and resources. Moreover, decision makers with personal psychologies that predispose them to decisions that lead to undesirable outcomes will have the opportunity to seek the modifying effects of additional advice and information.

Crisis Prevention

While it is quite premature to hope that PPI can serve as a means of crisis prevention, it is hoped that the extention of the project to incorporate additional world regions, decision systems, values and ethical systems, and emerging support technologies will enable progress to be made in that direction. If the sources of variation across crisis decisions and outcomes can be identified and if decision makers can be encouraged to select policies and make crisis decisions based on a desire to conserve life and resources, then the next step, preventing crises, may not be impossible. Progress in this direction will require extensive collaborative efforts, and some interest in this was evidenced at ISAGA '94.

Conclusion

The end of the Cold War, alas, does not spell the end of regional crises, and the Middle East remains a region of conflict. PROJECT PAX ISLAMICUS is a political-military game designed to penetrate the U.S. decision unit, test a political-psychological model of U.S. foreign-policy decision making in times of Arab-Israeli crises, and enable the probabilistic determination of potential outcomes of alternative U.S. decisions. The theoretical component of PPI maintains that combinations of psychological constructs in the person of the U.S. president are likely to produce particular decisions in times of Arab-Israeli crises that, in turn, will lead to particular associated crisis outcomes; simulation runs in PPI will test these hypotheses.

Although PPI is as yet limited geographically to the Middle East arena, theoretically to the United States decision unit, and culturally to the values and ethics of the West, it is hoped that, through the efforts of regional experts and simulators of other backgrounds, the project can be extended in the direction of global relevance. Moreover, opportunities exist whereby policies can be pre-tested, crisis outcomes can be tailored to conserve life and resources, and crisis prevention can be explored. In short, PPI is merely the beginning of an ambitious, wide-reaching, and, we hope, productive venture into cross-cultural crisis research and prevention that will extend well past the dawn of the next century.

References

Bradford, W. (1994). *U.S. foreign policy decision making in Arab-Israeli crises: The role of presidential personality constructs in the production of political and military crisis outcomes.* Evanston, IL: Northwestern University, Department of Political Science.

Gilboa, E. (1980). *SIMULATION OF CONFLICT AND CONFLICT RESOLUTION IN THE MID-DLE EAST.* Jerusalem: Hebrew University Press.

Guetzkow, H. (1968). *INTER-NATION SIMULATION.* Evanston, IL: Northwestern University Press.

Taylor, E. (1993). *ICS ARAB-ISRAELI CRISIS SIMULATION.* Ann Arbor: University of Michigan, Department of Education.

3

An Extended Simulation/
Game for ESL Composition

DOUGLAS W. COLEMAN

A detailed rationale for the use of simulation-based (and similar) materials in second/foreign language teaching is presented in Crookall and Oxford (1990), Jones (1982), and Di Pietro (1987) and hence is not repeated here. Rather, an outline is presented in terms of the three major elements of a language-learning simulation as defined by Jones (1982): simulated environment, structure, and reality of function.

Existentialist Hells Are
Not Limited to Plays by Sartre

Consider the following two situations for foreign language practice, one in which an environment is not simulated and the other in which it is. In the first situation, which is more accurately a kind of role-play, two students (A and B) participate. Learner A is told to imagine that she is waiting for a bus. Learner B is told that he must approach a stranger and ask for directions in the target language. Note that B has not been told where he must go. How often does a person ask for directions without first having a definite destination in mind? Note that no matter where B asks A how to get to, A really has no information about how to get there and therefore must make something up. When asked for directions, how often does a person simply make up a response out of thin air? Neither A nor B is making meaningful use of the target language; at the same time, to succeed in this activity, both must do something *in addition to* using

AUTHOR'S NOTE: I wish to express my thanks to Leslie A. Kosel, who has been primarily responsible for the classroom delivery of BRIDGES and who has made significant contributions to the revisions that have been made to it over the past year and a half. Her efforts have indirectly contributed to this chapter.

the target language (i.e., play act, creating a reality as they go). Such activities occasionally even degenerate into repartee that resembles nothing so much as an existential play, if, for example, A tries to beg off by saying "I'm sorry I can't help you, I'm waiting for a bus" to which B replies "What are you talking about? This isn't a bus stop!" and A counters with "Of course it is, there's the sign!" to which B replies "What sign?" and so on. This activity is clearly *not* a simulation because it lacks a simulated reality.

Now consider the other version of this situation in which a simulated environment is provided. A and B will be at the railway station in a small town in the country in which the target language is spoken. A is a resident of the country and familiar with the town; B is a visitor who knows nothing about it. The target language word(s) for "bus stop" are drawn on a piece of paper (or whatever would actually be found in that country, such as a silhouette of a bus). A is given a simplified bus route map of the town to study beforehand (she is not permitted to show the map to B). A is told that she is on the way to visit a friend and needs to take the No. 5 bus, which comes by only every half hour, to get to the friend's home. B is provided with no map. He needs to get to the bank (there is only one because it is a very small town) to change money because he needs to buy a rail ticket for a train that leaves in 3 hours, does not have enough cash in the local currency, and the clerk at the rail station will not accept his credit card. Thus, B does not know where the bank is or which bus to take to get there. A third participant, C, is added (perhaps a third student with a watch and a "bus schedule") who will speak over a public address system to announce the arrival and departure of each bus. In this version of the activity, participants do not make things up as they go along, the key factual elements are provided, and there is no opportunity for the repartee to sound like lines from Samuel Beckett's *Waiting for Godot*. There is a simulated environment.

The Way Out?

Thus, we avoid the necessity of abandoning all hope, so to speak: we escape an existentialist hell by providing for a coherent simulated environment. However, we want the right events to take place that will foster language learning. To ensure that these events occur, we need to create a structure for the activity. In the course of developing BUILDING BRIDGES and other simulation-based activities for college-level ESL composition (see Coleman & Kosel, 1994) I have become more and more convinced that it is through well-constructed documents provided to the learner—more than through any other aspect of simulation design—that the structure of the simulation is established.

This may seem like an overly obvious conclusion, but please bear with me. What some readers may not realize is that "structure" in a language-learning simulation may not be quite parallel to "structure" in a simulation designed to teach about most fields. When ISAGA members, for example, speak of the structure of a simulation, they typically use the term in more than one sense. First, there is the structure of the reality—how the simulated elements relate to each other. Then, there is the structure of the learner's task—the procedures that students use to get from "here" to "there" within the simulation. In most simulations, these are the primary senses of structure that apply. However, in a language-learning simulation, there is also the structure of the discourse in which students engage, and this is the primary sense that applies here. Thus, when I say that documents are critical to structuring a language-learning simulation, I mean that they are critical to structuring the discourse in which students will engage, and in turn, the kinds of discourse they will learn how to master.

What Jones (1982) calls the "reality of function" in the use of the language to be learned does not arise automatically just because there is a coherent world to be discussed. A structured discourse must emerge as well. This will not happen unless the simulation is designed so as to make it happen.

Building a Bridge

BUILDING BRIDGES is a 10-hour-long, simulation-based activity for college-level ESL composition. It was designed for English 105 at the University of Toledo, which is a course into which students are placed if they are judged unready for regular freshman composition on the basis of their abilities to organize and develop a basic essay and are non-native speakers of English. (A separate course exists for non-native-speaking students whose writing has problems dealing more with the language itself.) The course goals therefore focus on providing students with the rhetorical skills they will need to succeed in freshman composition. The course meets three times a week for ten weeks, with two "long" classes (100-minute sessions) and one "short" class (50-minute session) each week. BRIDGES thus covers a two-week span of classes.

Prior to the day on which BRIDGES begins, students are assigned readings consisting of a mock editorial and letters to the editor about an upcoming election in the city of Fenville. These materials provide some background to the simulation they will enter into but, more important, serve as models of the type of writing the students themselves will later have to do (comparison/contrast).

Day 1

All of Day 1 (a long class) consists of briefing for the task. Documents drive this briefing in which students analyze the readings they did earlier as homework. Students work in groups and in whole-class discussion. The primary document is a set of questions designed to lead the students through their analysis of the readings—to help them identify explicitly the structure of the discourses therein and to recognize the features of successful examples. (Not all of the models given to the students are equally successful.) The instructor ties up this class by leading students toward a consensus, helping them work out a single list of the features of a good piece of comparison/contrast writing.

Day 2

Day 2 (also a long class) begins with a review of the features of a successful comparison/contrast via a document generated from the students' own previous day's work. This document codifies the major aspects of the discourse structure that students will later use in their writing.

This is followed by a briefing for the students' roles within the simulation, using fairly conventional documents, the first of which is a role card. (Students take on the role of engineer in engineering firms that contract with the city of Fenville to build public works projects—in this case, bridges.) They are assigned to firms of three to five members each. A letter from the City Commission of Fenville awards a bridge project to each firm, explaining that it is in competition with the other firms for the contract for a future (and much larger) project. All students are also provided with a set of technical specifications that must be met. Each firm receives a packet of materials to be used in the construction of a paper-and-glue bridge.[1]

Students then have 45 minutes in which to construct their bridges. During this time, most of them will engage in a considerable amount of negotiation with fellow members of their respective firms about how to best complete the assigned bridge-building task. The audience who will judge the fruits of their labors has been defined by the letter, their relationship to this audience by their role cards, and the criteria on which their bridges will be evaluated by the letter and technical specifications taken together. The result is highly focused, very task-oriented discourse, much of it persuasive in nature. A great deal of the discourse is also (and not by sheer chance) implicitly or explicitly comparison/contrast—evaluating this possible design against that one, one possible action against another, and so on.

Day 3

On Day 3 (a short class), the instructor enters briefly into the role of Chief City Inspector. Using an Inspection Report Form for each firm's bridge, the inspector establishes major background "facts" that will serve as a basis for later comparison/contrast of the bridges. (Although couched in the context of the simulation, this also has the effect of an intermediate debriefing.) In the process, limits are implicitly set on the discourse in which students can engage when they do their later writing assignment.

Day 4

On Day 4 (a long class), drafting begins. A letter from the chief of each firm to its engineers tells them that each person is to write a report separately; the chief will select the best from his team's members to actually send to the city.

About 45 minutes or so before the end of this class, students are given a memo from their chief stating that, instead of selecting the best report, the best elements of all their reports will be merged and therefore they should help each other out by exchanging their drafts and making helpful comments. The chief provides a form (supposedly taken from a technical writing text the chief once studied) to help them with this task. In fact, the form directs the next stage of discourse in which they are to engage. Like the set of questions they used to help them analyze their model readings on Day 1, it is to be a meta-discourse—a discourse about the discourse of their writing task.

Day 5

At the end of Day 4, the instructor has collected both the students' drafts and their comments on their colleagues' drafts. Day 5 (a long class) then begins with an intermediate debriefing session that relates both to the students' performance in the task of drafting and to their performance in giving useful commentary to their fellow writers. This is done with the students and instructor free of their simulation roles; at this point, the students are students and the instructor an instructor—period. However, the discourse is still highly structured and strongly shaped by the drafts and the comment forms being discussed.

This session is followed by a reentry into the simulation roles, at least by the students. A new document (a memo from the chief of each firm) tells its members to revise their drafts. In doing so, this document reminds student writers of those elements that structure the discourse they are producing: the topic (the bridges), the audience (the City Commission explicitly but implicitly also the chief), the purpose (to convince the City Commission to award that future, more lucrative contract and to convince the chief that you are a valuable employee), and the background facts (found in the technical specifications, the inspection reports, and in the paper-and-glue bridges sitting in front of them).

Between Days 5 and 6

As an optional step, the instructor has sometimes added short meetings with students between Days 5 and 6 to debrief them individually on the progress they have made with their revised drafts.

Day 6

A final memo from the chief of each firm instructs each of its members to do some final polishing and editing of their writing. This takes the greater part of a short class. (The rest of this session is devoted to the introduction of the background materials for the next assignment.)

Concluding Remarks

In developing a new simulation for language learning, designers may focus only on generating the documents that establish the simulation reality per se. These documents define the simulated environment and provide structure to the elements of that environment or to a (non-linguistic) task to be accomplished within it. However, for a successful language-learning simulation, this is not enough. Documents must also be generated in such a way as to structure the discourses in which students will engage.

Note

1. I am indebted to Ken Jones, whose ROLLERCOASTER (Jones, 1987) provided the original inspiration for BRIDGES.

References

Coleman, D. W., & Kosel, L. A. (1994, March). *Building bridges: A simulation for college-level ESL composition.* Paper presented at the annual meeting of Teachers of English to Speakers of Other Languages (TESOL), Baltimore, MD.

Crookall, D., & Oxford, R. (Eds.). (1990). *Simulation, gaming, and language learning.* New York: Newbury House.

Di Pietro, R. J. (1987). *Strategic interaction: Learning languages through scenarios.* Cambridge, UK: Cambridge University Press.

Jones, K. (1982). *Simulations in language teaching.* Cambridge, UK: Cambridge University Press.

Jones, K. (1987, September). *ROLLERCOASTER.* Unpublished simulation demonstrated at the annual meeting of the International Simulation and Gaming Association, Venice, Italy.

4

Evolution of a Bushfire Simulation/Game

CHRIS J. CUNNINGHAM

BLACK CHRISTMAS and BLACK WEEKEND are versions of a simulation based on Australian bushfires. The scenario poses a serious emergency that is threatening an urban community. It is a simple pencil-and-paper simulation, is played out on a 1:25,000-scale topographic map of a real community, and it requires a period varying from three hours to a whole day, depending on the client group involved. Versions used so far are based on the Blue Mountains near Sydney, New South Wales, and the Adelaide Hills, a residential district immediately east of the South Australian capital city of Adelaide. Both of these areas have a long and reasonably well-documented history of urban bushfires, and the use of an actual rather than a fictitious community adds realism to the simulation.

Participants must manage a bushfire emergency in the community. In the prelude to play, they are given a description of the community and its fire history. They are provided with geographic information, such as topography, vegetation, and settlement patterns, and a list of available resources, including fire appliances, safe areas, and personnel in firefighting crews and logistic support organizations. As play gets under way they are given frequent bulletins of information on current weather, position of the fire front, and happenings in the community, all of which they must respond to.

The objectives and the form of the exercise have changed as it has been adapted to the specific needs of different groups of client players. It is the evolution of those changes that forms the main focus of this chapter.

AUTHOR'S NOTE: I gratefully acknowledge the support of Margaret Jones, of Adelaide, who provided invaluable assistance in collection of essential data and whose fire history of the Adelaide Hills was an essential component of the exercise. Russel Grear of the South Australian Country Fire Service and Inspector Derek Hunter of the South Australia Police helped fine-tune the scenario. Annette Mifsud and Merrick Chatfield of the Australian Emergency Management Institute encouraged development of the simulation. The willing participation of all players and their frank criticism are gratefully appreciated. My colleague, Elizabeth Teather, was closely involved in writing earlier versions. Funding for the project was provided by the University of New England and the Australian Emergency Management Institute.

Evolution of BLACK CHRISTMAS
and BLACK WEEKEND

This simulation was originally devised as a practical exercise for geography students in the unit *Natural Hazards* at the University of New England (Armidale, New South Wales). There were several objectives for this client group:

- Introduce students to key concepts in bushfire management and relate ideas of bushfire hazard and bushfire intensity to decision making in crisis situations.
- Help students become familiar with technical data on biomass, terrain, climate, weather, and fire behavior.
- Allow students to experience the uncertainty involved in decision making in crisis conditions.
- Make the learning process an enjoyable, active, and dynamic one and allow the student to learn by making mistakes.

In any such exercise, the complexities of the real world must be simplified so that key ideas can be brought out. Yet the situations described must be plausible and lifelike so that the student can role-play convincingly and can experience the emotional as well as the intellectual experiences of the crisis. For this reason, a real location, the Blue Mountains, was chosen. This area, between 60 and 100 kilometers west of Sydney (see Figure 4.1), is a rapidly developing tourist and suburban area with a long history of serious urban bushfires (Cunningham, 1984). The title of the simulation, BLACK CHRISTMAS, specifically draws attention to the time of year when bushfire disasters are most likely in the Blue Mountains.

In its original version, labeled Mark 1, the exercise was played by syndicates of three or four students, who were competing against similar teams. The players were asked to respond to a series of multiple-choice questions that tested both their understanding of technical matters and their judgment of the future development of the scenario. The simulation was based on the fires in late November 1968 that destroyed 130 houses in the area. The students thus replay, unknown to them, an actual emergency according to the precise conditions that occurred. They could subsequently compare their efforts with those of managers of the historical incident. The exercise generated enthusiasm among the students and helped them assimilate the technical information that was part of the syllabus for their course.

The simulation has also been successfully played by senior and intermediate high school students (Cunningham & Teather, 1990). The Mark 1 version also proved to be particularly effective for the training of external students of the university, who work by correspondence and may live up to 4,000 kilometers from the campus. A set of instructions allowed the students, as individuals, to play through the exercise, to make mistakes in management, and to learn from

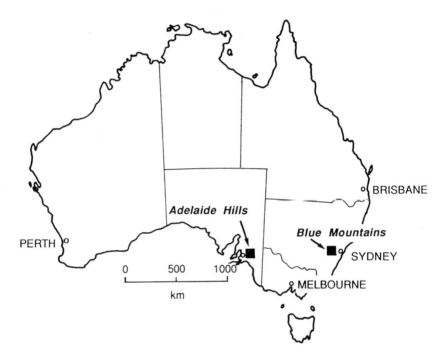

Figure 4.1   The setting for BLACK CHRISTMAS and BLACK WEEKEND.

them. Their written evaluations of the simulation were similar to those of on-campus students and confirmed the value of the exercise for teaching technically complex ideas.

One of these external students was an employee of the New South Wales Bushfire Council. Through his reports, the exercise attracted the attention of civil defense and disaster management authorities. It was played first at the Australian Police College (Manly, Sydney) and then several times as part of an intensive course, *Operational Disaster Management,* for senior emergency services personnel at the Australian Emergency Management Institute (Mount Macedon, Victoria).

The senior police officers, firemen, paramedics, and local government officials, who were the new clients, appreciated the inclusion of technical detail but were more interested in the way that information flowed in the crisis. This led to modification of the simulation for their purposes, including the use of larger syndicates of nine to 15 players, which were further divided into three subgroups with specialist roles. Those subgroups were then isolated in separate rooms from which they could only communicate by telephone (Cunningham &

Teather, 1992). This modification, the Mark 2 version, greatly improved the effectiveness of the exercise for these professional players, but there remained some deficiencies.

Chief among these was ambiguity between the roles of the three groups—boffins (technical experts), coordinators, and frontline workers—who made up the syndicates. Some players believed that the roles assigned to the groups did not easily correspond to those to which they were accustomed when working in emergencies.

A completely new scenario was written to clarify these roles. This is not a Mark 3 version, but a completely new model specifically designed for the training needs of the Australian Emergency Management Institute rather than for university and school students, for whom the earlier models are still appropriate and effective. The scenario was moved 1,500 kilometers westward to the Adelaide Hills in South Australia (see Figure 4.1) and was rewritten to conform to the totally different characteristics of a bushfire emergency in the new locality. It is based on the bushfire history of the Adelaide Hills written by Jones (1987). A new title, BLACK WEEKEND, was necessary. It reflects the high summer (January and February) fire season in the Adelaide Hills.

This version is based on the worst fire weather conditions recorded in the Adelaide Hills in January 1939, when temperatures reached 47 °C (117 °F), relative humidity fell to 4%, and wind speeds exceeded 70 kilometers per hour. A plausible scenario resulting from these conditions was developed in consultation with emergency managers in the Adelaide Hills area, using their experience of the Ash Wednesday fires in mid-February 1983. Those fires, in less severe weather conditions, cost 15 lives and more than 250 houses. Early in 1994, I carried out a reconnaissance survey of bushfire fuels and potentially difficult firefighting conditions. The settlement pattern and available community resources used in the game are those current in March 1994. Although simplified, the scenario is therefore faithful to the character of bushfire incidents in the Adelaide Hills.

Playing the Game

Participants are senior officers of emergency service organizations such as police, fire services, and ambulance and rescue services run by the federal and state governments. Participants may also come from overseas countries, especially New Zealand and Hong Kong. On the evening before the exercise, participants are given a formal lecture on technical aspects of bushfire weather and behavior that they will be expected to use in play. The emphasis in play is on information exchange between members of the syndicate. Usually there are about 30 players, enough for two syndicates.

Play starts with a familiarization session lasting about 40 minutes. Players are issued the following:

- A scenario describing the study area and the roles of players
- A kit of graphs, tables, and information on fire behavior, allowing players to make technically informed decisions
- The *Noarlunga North* (South Australia) 1:25,000-scale topographic map that covers the area of action and the 1:100,000-scale *Adelaide* and *Milang* sheets that give the regional background.

The exercise, which takes about six hours to play, leads the participants through the heatwave and bushfire crisis that purports to last for several days. Each syndicate is divided into three groups, each with its specific responsibilities: technical support (boffins), field intelligence (frontline workers), and control room activities (coordinators). Within the syndicate, players are not competing but cooperating to secure a maximum score for their syndicate. The groups operate from separate rooms and can only communicate by telephone, which represents the radio links used in emergency events. Frontline workers can only communicate with the boffins through the coordinators and vice versa. The coordinators, however, can communicate to each of the other groups (see Figure 4.2). Boffins and coordinators are allowed to exchange graphic information by "fax" (slipping the information under the door), but this facility is not available to the frontline workers. Transfer of information, such as fire fronts or locations of emergency situations, from the "field" to the coordinators requires careful verbal transmission of map grid references.

When players are familiar with the resource materials and the rules, they are issued with a bulletin of weather and emergency information every 15 minutes. Each bulletin is accompanied by a series of questions to which the players respond. The interval between bulletins can represent elapsed times of minutes, hours, or days. The action following each bulletin is therefore a snapshot rather than a continuous unfolding of events in real time. Players respond to the bulletins by exchanging information. Coordinators are the channel through which all information in the syndicate must pass. In addition, they must prepare rosters of firefighting crews and keep track of the movement of those crews in a diary. The exercise controllers may, by a chance process, determine the fate of crews and equipment sent to very hazardous locations, so it is possible to lose such resources throughout the action, incurring penalty points. Figure 4.3 indicates the complete unfolding of the scenario, which is only revealed progressively to players.

Each group is scored on its ability to understand the developing emergency, to plot the fire paths on the map from information received, and to forecast how the emergency will develop. They must then respond to questions, the answers to which can only be found by getting information from other groups in the

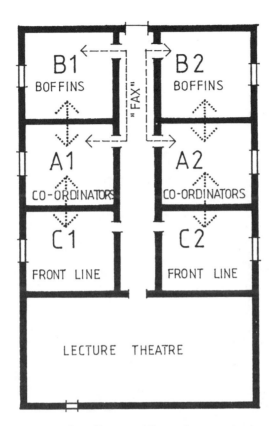

Figure 4.2   Organization of syndicates and lines of communication.

syndicate. Their responses are scored on the basis of their likely effectiveness in mitigating the disaster. The syndicate is required to defend up to 500 points. Each point lost by the syndicate represents a house or property destroyed, and each 10 points represents a life lost.

The players do not know in advance how the situation will develop. The game tests their skills in using information to forecast conditions, conserve resources, and make effective decisions. In fairness to the syndicates, it is made clear that a perfect score is unlikely. In the worst conflagration, fire conditions likely to be experienced in the Adelaide Hills, the loss of 100 houses and fewer than ten lives might well be considered the best result that the most perfect organization and management of the crisis could achieve. Although the competition between syndicates may well stimulate motivation to succeed, this is usually secondary to that generated by the simulation itself, that is, the wish to make the best possible decisions to save the towns and their inhabitants.

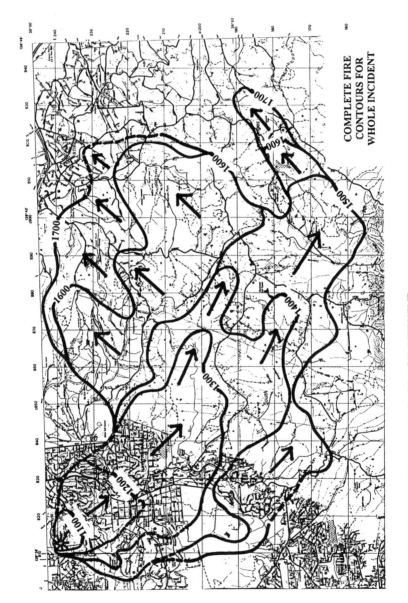

Figure 4.3 Outcome of the scenario for BLACK WEEKEND.

Outcomes

The desired outcome of the simulation is a better understanding of the critical role that clear communication and effective exchange of information play in management of any large-scale emergency. In the most recent playing, in April 1994, participants very quickly became confused by the rapid flow of information coming to them. The coordinators, in particular, became disoriented by this information flow and developed coping strategies that, in an emergency, could have potentially disastrous results. In one syndicate, they refused to provide their boffins with information on the fire front, maintaining a militaristic "don't need to know" stance. This information was vital for the boffins to forecast fire paths, which in turn would have been essential knowledge for both coordinators and frontline workers.

Within an hour of the commencement of the simulation it was obvious to the facilitators that power plays were emerging among the players. Instead of cooperating, groups within a single syndicate were seeing themselves as rivals. Information was seen as the key to power, and groups tended to hold rather than exchange it. Failure to exchange information led to poor performance of the syndicate as a whole.

These power games that emerged from the simulation are very common in real-life, large-scale emergencies. Management agencies, such as fire brigades or police, have their own culture, which works well in the routine situations they face in calls on their services. In major emergencies they are thrown together at short notice, and inter-service rivalry leads to reluctance to share information. In the January 1994 bushfires in New South Wales, there were many examples where police, bushfire fighters, and rescue services were at odds. Most commonly, police tried to evacuate able bodied and prepared residents from threatened streets and homes when the best advice of bushfire authorities was that such people are better off staying to defend their properties. It is therefore better that the consequences of such rivalry, and poor information management, should emerge from a simulation, rather than in a real emergency where they could cost lives and property.

Debriefing

A most valuable aspect of the simulation is the subsequent discussion. Having been through an active experience of crisis decision making, players are very receptive to the lessons that the exercise has to impart. At least 40 minutes is allowed for this evaluation. Syndicates meet first to review their operations and then all players join the game facilitators for a general debriefing. An atmosphere of exhaustion is usually characteristic of these final sessions, and players may need to be de-roled.

A great deal of humor, as well as motivation, is generated by posting progressive syndicate scores on a whiteboard. The scoring system is recognized by players as an indicator of the effectiveness of their decisions. An adverse score, for example, encourages players to question their own preconceptions of crisis management. It also prompts them to discuss and question the official assessment logic, a written commentary on each of the questions asked in the bulletins, which is given to players on conclusion of play.

In April 1994, participants recognized the breakdown of information flow but initially tried to blame the "unrealistic nature" of the scenario for their failure. They were uncomfortable at the way that weakness in their management skills had been exposed. The debriefing session was thus a fairly hostile one, with a lot of anger directed against the exercise controllers. Nevertheless, players continued to discuss the exercise in the subsequent days of their course. The necessity for better information management became a key issue of that discussion, and in their concluding course evaluation, BLACK WEEKEND was singled out for its contribution to their awareness of its importance. This was the major objective of the simulation.

BLACK WEEKEND at ISAGA

Because it takes an entire day to play through BLACK WEEKEND, it was not possible to demonstrate the game in practice to conference participants. The presentation was therefore planned to give them as close an appreciation of the game as could be obtained without playing through the scenario. Bound copies of all three major versions of the exercise were available for inspection during the presentation. In the 45-minute session, the audience was shown slides of the localities within which the scenario is set and of high-intensity Australian bushfires to give some idea of the emotional environment within which the game is played. The detailed physical setting for actual play, including room layouts and telephone links, was described graphically, along with many of the technical considerations involved in play.

The audience responded positively to the detail of the presentation. One participant commented that it was one of the few games presented in such detail. Valuable suggestions were discussed for the possible use of computers to allow playing groups to keep track of information while retaining the essential personal interaction character and information management objectives of the exercise.

Conclusion

BLACK CHRISTMAS and its successor BLACK WEEKEND are continually evolving to better meet the needs of client groups. In its initial form, the simulation was an enjoyable and effective way of teaching complex technical matters to undergraduate and high school students in a relatively short time period. In its latest version, it has reproduced the problems of lack of information management that beset large-scale emergencies. It is currently being revised to throw more light on these problems.

The search for more effective ways of running the simulation is continuous. There is no endpoint in its development. As with the real-life events it purports to imitate, it is necessary to adapt and change to meet new needs of the client groups who play it. One likely revision arising from discussion at ISAGA is the use of computers to allow participant groups to store, recall, and review information. The Australian Emergency Management Institute is well set up to incorporate such changes, which could also reflect the increasing use of electronic data in the emergency control center.

References

Cunningham, C. J. (1984). Recurring natural fire hazards: A case study of the Blue Mountains, New South Wales, Australia. *Applied Geography, 4,* 5-27.

Cunningham, C. J., & Teather, E. K. (1990). BLACK CHRISTMAS: A bushfire simulation game. *Simulation/Games for Learning, 20*(1), 7-17.

Cunningham, C. J., & Teather, E. K. (1992). Civil emergency training: A new context for BLACK CHRISTMAS. *Simulation/Games for Learning, 22*(3), 173-182.

Jones, M. A. (1987). Urban settlement and natural hazard: A case study of the Adelaide Hills, South Australia. In *Geography and society in a global context: Proceedings of 56th ANZAAS Conference and 14th New Zealand Geography Conference.* Palmerston, North New Zealand: Massey University, Department of Geography.

5

Modeling Equipment Breakdown
in the Electrical Supply Industry

JIM FREEMAN

The British electricity-supply industry reaches into the homes and workplaces of almost every citizen in the country. The industry is a major employer of skilled labor both directly and indirectly, and its performance is thus crucial to the long-term prospects of the workforce and, indeed, to the financial well-being of the nation. Figure 5.1 presents an overview of the current post-privatization industry structure (Bunn, Larsen, & Vlahos, 1993).

Like all the other 11 regional electricity companies in England and Wales, NORWEB is highly capital intensive. Because of its relatively large asset base, a significant proportion (39%) of NORWEB's annual capital expenditure is devoted entirely to asset replacement. The workload associated with this expenditure is considerable, not least because of the following:

- Many technically different types of equipment comprise the distribution network (summarized diagrammatically in Figure 5.2).
- The life expectancy of each equipment type is a matter of considerable uncertainty.
- Rapid change in technology means that replacement of any particular piece of equipment is rarely on a like-for-like basis.
- Electrical demands on the network are difficult to predict in the long run.

Yet this workload is unavoidable if the company is to continue to meet its obligations under the 1989 Electricity Act, which requires, in particular, that the supplies of electricity provided are regular and efficient and that the public is protected from dangers arising from the generation, transmission, or supply of electricity. In response to these and other (e.g., economic) constraints, NORWEB recently initiated a detailed appraisal of its long-term replacement practice.

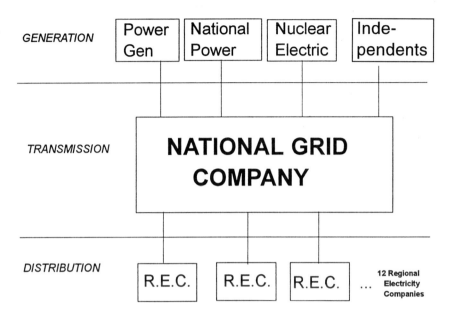

Figure 5.1   The electrical supply industry following privatization.

Asset Replacement Strategies

Historically, the company's strategy for replacing equipment has been to renew each item when it fails or after a period of 40 years, this being the duration over which most equipment is normally depreciated. The advantage with this approach is that outlays in future years can, allowing for inflation, be projected directly from those made many years previously.

In most other respects, regrettably, this policy is seriously flawed. Not only does it result in a very undesirable roller-coaster pattern of investment by the company, but it completely ignores the failure rate properties of the different types of equipment concerned—with unfortunate consequences in terms of either pointless wastage or unnecessary disruption.

In a search for more realistic policy options, various alternative procedures were investigated. Analytically, the aim was to find or develop a model that would accurately predict the outcome of different replacement strategies and so help identify an optimum, long-term cost solution. An important characteristic of the problem is that it is neither feasible nor economical, ordinarily, for the company to repair defective equipment.

Increasingly, modeling or simulation appeared to be the only workable options for dealing with the analysis. From experience, the critical balance for

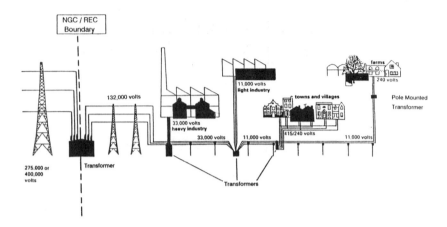

Figure 5.2   Electricity distribution from supplier to customer.

NORWEB has been found to be between planned preventive renewal and unplanned remedial replacement of parts, the costs of the latter significantly outweighing those of the former. Finding a balance between these two cost components is the conceptual basis of the computer model described here. As the company already had significant expertise in the use of (QUATTRO PRO) spreadsheet software, the motivation for adopting this particular approach was especially strong.

Pole-Mounted Transformers

For the feasibility project, model development was restricted to a single equipment type, that of 11kV/415V pole-mounted transformers (PMTs), one of six different kinds of transformer (Franklin & Stignant, 1989) currently in use at NORWEB. There were three reasons for selecting only PMTs for the exploratory analysis:

- The company has a large stock of transformers still operating after many years of service, so there are considerable data available.
- A national database (NAFIRS) provides comprehensive details for all transformers used in the industry (Electricity Council, 1992).
- Failure of PMTs cause little, if any, damage to adjacent buildings or equipment or, indeed, disruption to customers themselves. There are therefore no ancillary costs to consider in the modeling.

TARDIS

The model is presently known by the acronym TARDIS (Transformer Asset Replacement—Deciding the Ideal Strategy). TARDIS runs on the QUATTRO PRO (Version 4) spreadsheet system, its graphics and macro facility making it an attractive choice of software platform. TARDIS is a sizable application (353 kb) requiring a minimum 1 Mb of memory.

Input

Prior to the model being run, the following information must be provided for each equipment item covered by the model (see Appendix A for details):

- Total size and age profile of equipment population
- Failure rate with respect to age
- Rate of non-age-related failures
- Costs associated with planned (preventive) replacement, unplanned (remedial) replacement, and colateral damage in the event of failure
- Maximum age (years) of transformer permitted in the network
- Number of units to be replaced in a planned manner per year
- Number of years after which the model should pause (if parameters are to be reset partway through a run)

The basic sequence of events within the model are summarized in Appendix B.

Simulation Output

An example of the main output summary from TARDIS is shown in Figure 5.3. This gives a breakdown, by year, of transformer replacements and costs for a single run of the simulation. More detailed feedback is available on an individual year basis, namely, the numbers of emergency and planned replacements and related costs.

A graphics option is also available summarizing, for example, total and average costs per year of the test strategy. For relatively long experiments (where a period of 20 or more years is modeled for a particular replacement strategy), results from TARDIS have been found to be remarkably consistent. To allow for the relatively minor variations that can occur, output is currently averaged across a small number of independent TARDIS runs. Shortly, the model itself will take on this aspect of the analysis, although users will still be able to stipulate the number of replications to be made.

Experience to date suggests that the model is not overly sensitive to changes in the parameters used. Nevertheless, the need for quality estimates of parameters, particularly costs, should not be understated.

| Year | Replacements | | | Cost £k | Cost/yr of service | |
	Emergency	Planned	Total		£	Mean £
1	92	81	173	264	38.6	38.6
2	79	25	104	167	50.2	42.4
3	81	18	99	161	52.8	44.8
4	85	15	100	163	53.5	46.4
5	90	3	92	154	58.6	48.1
6	97	10	108	178	53.2	48.9
7	105	8	114	189	52.7	49.4
8	115	17	132	216	49.1	49.4
9	125	35	160	257	45.3	48.7
10	134	21	155	254	47.1	48.5
Grand Total	8,197	6,209	14,406	£m 22.1	Results Table	

Figure 5.3 Example of tabulated results from TARDIS.

When TARDIS was used to evaluate the type of fixed-term replacement strategy described earlier, the average replacement cost was found to be least when transformers were replaced, at the latest, after 47 years. The cost of this policy option was estimated to be over half a million pounds less than the corresponding 40-year replacement alternative.

If this saving could be verified by other methods, it is conceivable that development of a full-scale (or larger) TARDIS model could lead to major long-term cost improvements for the company. Translated industrywide, the benefits would be greatly magnified.

The Session

The small number of delegates who attended the ISAGA '94 session were obviously animated by the idea that spreadsheet modeling could have such cost-cutting potential. Following the presentation, there was a brief discussion of the political and commercial consequences of privatization in Great Britain. In response to various technical queries, the statistical theory underpinning the TARDIS model was quickly summarized.

APPENDIX A

Details of TARDIS Inputs

Total size and age profile of equipment population

Present details, built into the package on the number and age of PMTs used at NORWEB, were estimated from the company's plant file database.

Failure rate with respect to age

Failures in this category include those due to the loosening of electrical connections by vibration, contamination or deterioration of oil used to insulate transformer windings, and long-term metallurgical changes. In the program, age-related failures are modeled using the Gumbel, or extreme-value, distribution. Empirically, this was found to provide a much better fit to the appropriate hazard function than the usual Weibull option (Freeman & North, in press).

Non-age-related failures

Most non-age-related failures are due to lightning or willful damage; both are estimated in the model from NAFIRS data.

Costs of planned (preventive) and unplanned (remedial) replacement

Replacement costs are normally assessed in terms of labor-related and materials-related cost components. There is also the value to the company of energy not being used while replacement is taking place.

APPENDIX B

Stages in TARDIS Analysis

Stage	Description
1	Tabulate present transformer population by age.
2	Divide table into two parts: one for those in lightning-active areas and the other for the rest.
3	Simulate age-related failures and then non-age-related failures for each section of the data. All failures are treated as terminal and result in replacement with new transformers (having zero age).
4	Allow for planned replacements, assuming that the oldest surviving transformers are replaced first.
5	At the end of the iteration (corresponding with the completion of the yearly cycle), transformers in the current population are all aged a year.
6	The process is repeated starting at Stage 3 until the designated number of years (time horizon) covered by the simulation has elapsed.
7	At a predetermined point, the user can halt the simulation and check the results so far and, if necessary, adjust the simulation parameters set previously.

References

Bunn, D. W., Larsen, E. R., & Vlahos, K. (1993). Complementary modelling approaches for analysing several effects of privatisation on electricity investment. *Journal of the Operational Research Society, 44,* 957-971.

Electricity Council. (1992). *National fault and interruption reporting scheme: National system and equipment performance.* London: Author.

Franklin, D. P., & Stignant, S. A. (1989). *The J & P transformer book.* London: Butterworth's.

Freeman, J. M., & North, M. R. (in press). Analysing equipment failure rates. *International Journal of Quality & Reliability.*

6

Academic Integrity

Description of a Simulation/Game

GENE B. HALLECK

This chapter introduces a simulation created to orient international graduate students at U.S. universities to issues of academic integrity and dishonesty. Such issues need to be explored because international students are often unaware that academic standards and expectations in the United States may differ from those of the academic communities where they have previously studied (Moder & Halleck, 1994). The chapter also describes how participants at ISAGA '94 reacted to the simulation.

Participation in this simulation helps raise awareness of such issues as the kind of process due to a tenured professor accused of academic misconduct, the relationship between pharmaceutical companies creating new drugs and the large research institutions where the drugs are tested, and the role that agencies such as the National Cancer Institute should play in the experimental stages of such drugs. Participants in this simulation must decide whether universities are responsible for policing their researchers, what the role of outside agencies should be in overseeing the research they sponsor, and whether governmental agencies should be involved in establishing guidelines for the behavior of researchers on the faculty of public institutions.

This simulation can be used in orientation and training programs for international graduate students and in intensive English language institutes with advanced-level learners who are preparing to enter degree-granting programs. It can also be used with any group wishing to explore and debate the issues involved in the broader aspects of academic misconduct and integrity. Such groups would be university decision-making committees or industry boards and funding agencies.

The Simulation

INTEGRITY OR MISCONDUCT evolves in three phases. In the first phase, participants become familiar with the facts of the case by reading newspaper articles. Some of the articles give background information, others probe some of the issues that participants must consider during the simulation, and still others define academic misconduct and provide readers with explanations of the many acronyms they will encounter in the next two phases of the simulation, including HNU (Hamilton National University), NIH (National Institute of Health), NCI (National Cancer Institute), and NCUPI (National Coalition for Universities in the Public Interest).

An example of one of the news articles that simply details the facts of the case follows:

TOP RESEARCHER AT HNU
CHARGED WITH MISCONDUCT
by Carolyn Maxwell
Internet Press Corps

Washington. On Monday, July 11, 1994, a famous scientist and one of the most respected researchers at Hamilton National University was officially charged with scientific misconduct. Dr. A. N. Simmons, head of Hamilton's Cancer Research Unit and a recipient of a major grant from the NIH, was accused of fabricating data in a publication describing clinical trials of a new drug, XP 123.

Members of the administration at HNU have promised "a swift and thorough investigation of this matter," but unidentified sources question whether the university can provide the kind of impartial assessment necessary. Dr. Simmons was not available for comment.

Whereas the material in the Maxwell article introduces the facts of the case, other articles probe some of the issues that will be raised in the second and third phases of the simulation, as the following excerpts illustrate:

QUESTIONS FROM CAMPUS

Is Dr. A. N. Simmons guilty of scientific misconduct? Is Hamilton National University guilty of protecting "big money" scientists like Simmons?

These are the questions that you hear every day on college campuses all over the nation. But maybe they are the wrong questions. Perhaps Dr. Simmons is not guilty. Perhaps the finger of guilt should be pointed at the researcher involved in the clinical trials at Mercy Hospital. If so, then surely the University isn't guilty for protecting Dr. Simmons. Or should we hold Dr. Simmons accountable . . . ?

* * * * *

SENATOR QUESTIONS HNU'S
ABILITY TO JUDGE THE SIMMONS CASE:
LATEST WORD FROM WASHINGTON
by Hillary Chase
AP Education Desk

According to State Senator M. C. Bernstein, a democrat on the Senate Subcommittee on Medical Ethics, there have been several other misconduct cases at HNU in the past decade. . . . Senator Bernstein says that a review of HNU's record with regard to their handling of such cases of academic misconduct indicates that an independent body should be formed to deal with this latest case of fraud.

In an address to the League of Women Voters, Bernstein said, "We are all angry that a re-evaluation of the fraudulent data has not been presented to the American public. We hold Dr. Simmons, the NCI and the administration at HNU responsible for perpetrating this fraud, and we will not forget that the agencies involved are silent accomplices in this crime."

After reading the articles about the case, participants at ISAGA '94 took part in a mini-simulation (Phase 2) that served as a warm-up activity. Duke (1974) suggests that, as a game progresses, a player's "need for information increases." Although he warns that "players should be given no more information than is essential at any given moment," he points out that as participants become involved and motivated they can "assimilate surprisingly large quantities of information" (p. 142). Thus, in Phase 2 of the simulation participants had very brief roles. In this activity, they expressed opinions about the Simmons case by calling a radio talk show. At ISAGA '94, one participant was nominated by another group member to play the role of hostess of the show. There are also 16 roles for "callers" from different U.S. states. Because there were only 8 participants at ISAGA '94, two roles were assigned to each person. Because of the format of the radio show, everyone sat at their desks and talked to the backs of the people in front of them. Examples of roles used in this phase of the simulation follow:

Caller From Nebraska:

You believe that it is a national disgrace that researchers at top universities can get away with this type of fraud. We must send a message to the administrations of those large universities telling them that we won't tolerate scientific misconduct that is a result of collusion between the academy and big drug companies.

Caller From New York:

You think that the NCI is using Dr. Simmons as a scapegoat; the NCI is blaming Dr. Simmons in the hopes that no one will realize that the Institute was at fault for not supervising the clinical trials more closely.

Caller From Florida:

You had a family member who was taking XP 123 for 8 months without knowing that there were serious side effects! You feel that it is outrageous that the NCI knew there were problems with this drug, yet allowed patients to remain on it.

Caller From New Mexico:

You think that the media is making too big a deal about this case. Why should the public be following this case with such interest?

Caller From Michigan:

You don't believe how many callers have presumed that the scientist from HNU must be guilty! Ask the talk show audience what happened to the idea that a person is innocent until PROVEN guilty. Since nobody really has all the facts, ask everybody to just reserve judgment. That is the only fair thing to do.

During this phase of the simulation, there was little opportunity for discussion of the issues, although after expressing their assigned opinions, several callers tried to call the show back to engage the hostess in further discussion. Perhaps these attempts are evidence that the talk show segment was a success, in that it provided conflict (a useful ingredient for the type of discussion to follow) and created in the participants "a desire to communicate" (Crookall & Oxford, 1990, p. 13).

At the end of the radio show portion of the simulation the participants were familiar with the arguments for both sides and were ready to examine new roles. At this point everyone rearranged the chairs so that the third phase could be conducted with participants sitting around a circle facing each other.

Each participant received a new role card for the third phase of the simulation. Two roles represented the university (a colleague of the accused researcher and the academic integrity officer), three roles represented funding agencies (the NCI, the drug company, and the Office of Research Integrity of the NIH), and two roles represented interests outside the university (a U.S. senator and a representative of the NCUPI). Two examples of the roles are provided below:

FACULTY MEMBER AT HNU

You believe that

— when misconduct charges are brought against a colleague, everyone suffers: the scientist, the institution, her or his colleagues, and our confidence in the scientific community.
— to punish all faculty members (by denying anyone at an offending institution a research grant) would be wrong.
— most researchers are honest and their research reflects the highest standards; only 1 in 1,000 of your colleagues is actually guilty of fraud.
— Dr. Simmons didn't know that XP123 had such serious side effects because the researcher at Mercy Hospital, where the side effects were discovered, altered the data before sending Dr. Simmons the results.
— Dr. Simmons's only mistake was not to question the data received from the trials being run at Mercy Hospital.
— if anyone (besides the Mercy Hospital researcher) is guilty, it is the National Cancer Institute because the NCI was responsible for supervising the clinical trials.
— the NCI is using Dr. Simmons as a scapegoat; the NCI is blaming Dr. Simmons in the hopes that no one will realize that the Institute was at fault for not supervising the clinical trials more closely.

(continued)

UNITED STATES SENATOR (M. C. Bernstein)

You believe that:

— Hamilton National University protects all researchers who bring in large sums of money, regardless of their academic integrity.
— some researchers at major institutions like HNU are not scientists in search of the truth; rather they are in search of the big bucks.
— universities such as HNU that receive research grants from the NIH and charitable contributions from the drug companies whose drugs are being tested in the research trials have a poor record in terms of adhering to ethical standards of scientific integrity.
— officials at the NCI were not rigorous enough in overseeing the national trials being conducted under Dr. Simmons's direction.
— it took too long for the NCI to get involved in the investigation; their failure to act indicates that they can't be trusted to safeguard the public's interest.

Debriefing

Because of time constraints, the debriefing as a group at ISAGA '94 was very short. However, a handful of participants stayed afterward to share their observations. Several people noted that, after the conclusion of the radio show portion of the simulation, participants were quite eager to gather in a circle. Just stating opinions (with little opportunity for discussion) was somewhat frustrating for some of the participants of the talk show segment. Because most of the participants at ISAGA '94 session were native speakers of English, there was less of a need for this phase of the simulation, although even for people who have no difficulty expressing their opinions in English, it did serve the purpose of introducing the main issues in a fairly efficient manner. In any case, it was clear that for many of the participants, the chance for a real debate in the third phase provided some relief to the feelings of frustration engendered by the constraints of the radio talk show!

A question proposed by one of the participants during the initial phase of the simulation was whether it would actually be possible in the United States to have such a discussion of a researcher's academic integrity in public. She was assured that Americans do indeed discuss such matters publicly, even though such discussion would not be permitted in some countries where the rights of the accused would prevent public debate.

There was no reflection on the way the group at ISAGA '94 chose the hostess for the radio talk show or the moderator for the public discussion. Especially for a group of students who did not know each other well when the simulation began, this would be a topic for debriefing. There was also little time to discuss how the hostess's style might have affected the outcome of the talk show. Similarly, given more time, the group would need to reflect on how the moderator's style might have affected the outcome of the public discussion. Other issues that might be probed are the participants' satisfaction with the group's final decision and the way(s) in which they dealt with conflict during the discussion.

Although we ran out of time and could not finish the discussion, it was pointed out that if there had been more time it would have been the group's task to prepare a written document stating its recommendations. One of the participants suggested that this is a difficult assignment for any group and that it might be more effective if each of the participants were asked to prepare a statement outlining recommendations for future action. Adding a task requiring that each participant submit a written recommendation might strengthen the simulation. Jones (1983) suggests that writing tasks as follow-up assignments are appropriate additions to simulations for upper-intermediate and advanced students. Because the international graduate students for whom this simulation was created should have the necessary writing skills, the suggestion made at ISAGA '94 will probably be incorporated into future runs of the simulation.

The debriefing should also include a discussion focusing on issues related to academic integrity from a cross-cultural perspective. It would be worthwhile to compare and contrast the expectations of participants with any insights gained as a result of taking part in the simulation. Without such a discussion, the simulation is incomplete.

Conclusion

This simulation provides international graduate students with information about issues of academic integrity in a setting that enables participants "to develop a tolerance for ambiguity" (Crookall, Coleman, & Versluis, 1990, p. 154). At the same time it provides opportunities for participants to engage in the specific uses of oral language as outlined by Gredler (1994): conveying or abstracting information, using new vocabulary to plan or to develop information for dissemination, and using language to express and support opinions (p. 122). More specifically, participants are required to engage in a wide variety of language functions, especially in the final phase of the simulation. As they express their opinions and listen to their colleagues' ideas they are forced to "analyse, discuss, argue, report, state a case, question, negotiate, conciliate, mediate, explain, denounce, agree, tackle problems and make decisions in a cohesive manner" (Jones, 1982, p. 7). Thus, as the simulation unfolds, the participants not only become oriented to issues of academic dishonesty and scientific misconduct but also become involved in the authentic language of public debate.

References

Crookall, D., Coleman, D. W., & Versluis, E. B. (1990). Computerized language learning simulation: Form and content. In D. Crookall & R. Oxford (Eds.), *Simulation, gaming, and language learning*. Boston: Heinle & Heinle.

Crookall, D., & Oxford, R. (1990). Linking language learning and simulation/gaming. In D. Crookall & R. Oxford (Eds.), *Simulation, gaming, and language learning*. Boston: Heinle & Heinle.

Duke, R. (1974). *Gaming: The future's language*. New York: Sage/Halsted.

Gredler, M. (1994). *Designing and evaluating games and simulations*. Houston: Gulf; London: Kogan Page.

Jones, K. (1982). *Simulation in language teaching*. Cambridge, UK: Cambridge University Press.

Jones, L. (1983). *Eight simulations*. Cambridge, UK: Cambridge University Press.

Moder, C. L., & Halleck, G. B. (1994, March). *Solving the plagiary puzzle: Role-plays for international students*. Paper presented at the annual conference of Teachers of English to Speakers of Other Languages (TESOL), Baltimore, MD.

7

Gaming Sustainability

DREW MACKIE

At the 1992 ISAGA conference in Edinburgh, I demonstrated a similar game that explored a simple model of local economies and how these might be made more sustainable. This model has now been expanded to include the environmental and community aspects of sustainability in a "three capital" model.

I have now updated the Edinburgh game to encompass the new model. This chapter looks at the process of developing the model and its accompanying game. It also raises issues relating to the simulation of complex subjects and the reactions of public service clients. This is not a theoretical chapter but an expedition through the real-world jungles and deserts of public policy and the use of "thinking models" and games to chart unknown regions.

Policy problems become more complex by the year. The old certainties of the Western economies are becoming increasingly distrusted as a map for the future. The commercial and informational changes that are transforming Western society are mirrored by the collapse of many of the centralized economic systems and their replacement by a seemingly chaotic free-for-all. At the same time societies are revising their views on the value of the environment and of the role of the community in decision making.

Several years ago, if you had suggested to me that I might introduce an ISAGA topic in such apocalyptic tones I would have scoffed. Policy matters in Britain and elsewhere seemed well ordered and concerned with small changes— with adjustments to a generally accepted framework of ideas. Things have changed. Social, economic, and environmental policy is a minefield of conflicting views and serpentine complexities. The old right/left divisions of the traditional parties no longer seem relevant to these new realities.

Recently, we have been using games as a way of exploring policy options. Although a game will not demonstrate the specific outcomes of a policy, it will illustrate the cracks and loopholes. It will also indicate the stylistic aspects of policy. By this I mean the way in which the policy is implemented and the perceptions of other agencies affected by it. In this sort of area, gaming is very effective. Such information is invaluable for policymakers. The problem is that decision makers may not treat the results of gaming seriously or may consider that their own political skills may override any directions indicated by a game.

At this point we come to the whole problem of the credibility of gaming as a technique. My own experience together with a study of the literature indicate that gaming has a very good track record as a predictive technique. This is particularly true of the less numeric games, which depend on perception and intuition. Other techniques however, have a greater degree of credibility with both policymakers and politicians, even though the record of prediction is not so good.

This is not a new problem. There are examples of gaming giving way to other techniques, particularly computer analysis, for no other reason than fashion and the expectation that the newer technique might be better.

Some years ago I was involved in the design of a policy simulation for the Department of the Environment to gauge the effects of a new policy toward British inner cities. SPICE (Simulation of Policies for Inner City Expenditure) was a good predictor of the problems that the policy was later to encounter. However, questions were asked in the House of Commons about the use of games by the Department of the Environment. A rather half-hearted reply by the minister responsible was almost drowned out by jeers and catcalls from members of Parliament of which "why don't we give civil servants Monopoly sets for Christmas!" was among the most polite.

A number of commentators have suggested that the title "game" should be dropped and that a grander name should be adopted for this activity. The problem is that games are what they are, and terms like "strategic simulation" and "policy exercise" predispose people toward more numerical techniques, which, as I have already argued, are actually less effective in generating predictive results. All this means that gaming is difficult to sell in the competitive consultancy market (in the United Kingdom at least).

The SIMPLEX Approach

Some years ago at gaming conferences in Britain, I explored the idea of SIMPLEX—a game form in which complex outcomes could be produced by simple rules. Most of these were simple negotiation games in which the players often defined the situation to be simulated and created its roles.

Recently, the idea of complex outcomes generated by simple rules has been pursued in terms of chaos theory and lately in the studies of complexity undertaken by scientists and computer experts. The idea of simple rules generating very complex outcomes is fascinating and has largely been made possible by the availability of fast, powerful computers. Consequently, the detail of this approach is couched in complex mathematical formulae. The SIMPLEX approach holds out the possibility of modeling complexity with simple tools.

The problem with applying a SIMPLEX approach to policy is that policy-makers, overwhelmed by the complexity of the problems to be addressed, assume that any model used to tackle these should be equally complex. While this may be true of the outcomes of the model, it is not necessarily true of the model itself. In fact what is needed is a simple way of resolving the complexities that does not trivialize the issues.

The Three-Variable Model

A common problem in planning and other environmental disciplines is how to relate three different variables while giving a clear picture of how they behave over time. This has particularly concerned me in working with interdisciplinary teams, where there are few shared concepts, or in work with communities, where complex planning concepts are not understood. Let me give an example.

Streets

Some years ago, while working with a colleague in Norway we developed a simple way of analyzing the problems of urban streets. What we needed was a way of portraying the relationship of three types of street user—the resident, the visitor, and the traveler. Our doodles produced a simple matrix—3 × 3, the columns of which indicated the three groups and the rows a low, medium, or high count for each. Within this simple framework we were able to describe different streets and their problems. Because there are 64 different patterns achievable within the matrix, it gives a considerably fine grain of analysis and yet allows instant visual recognition of a simple pattern.

This was used as the basis for a simple game presented at the 1988 Norwegian Road Engineers conference in Trondheim. The game focused on deriving a pattern randomly and then suggesting how the pattern created problems and formulating solutions for these. Perhaps not the most exciting game, but it did demonstrate the use of the diagram as a "thinking machine."

The use of diagrams to think through concepts in this manner has a long pedigree. Charles Dodgson, the English mathematician more famous for his writings as Lewis Carroll, used a simple matrix framework with counters in *The Game of Logic* to explain the structure of philosophical syllogisms. Physicist Richard Feynman used simple diagrams to chart the behavior of subatomic particles. The three-variable model does the same thing but is applicable to any field in which a simple visual representation of three "stocks" is required.

Bathtubs, Hoovers, and Dustbins

Some years later, I was asked to present a paper to the annual conference of Rural Forum, a Scottish organization of rural interests. The only brief I was given for the paper was that it be visual and controversial. As part of my work with small communities I had developed a version of the three-variable model that looked at the economic performance of a small settlement. The three columns represented income to a community, circulation within that community, and outgoings from that community. Many common problems of growth, decline, and stability can be represented by this simple model. In particular, we had developed shorthand names for typical projects that a community might have to consider. *Bathtubs* were local projects that collected money as it passed through the local system and passed it on to other local bathtubs. *Hoovers* were projects that drew money from the local economy. *Dustbins* (trashcans) were hoovers that dumped pollution (environmental or social) into the local system at the same time as hoovering money from it. Perhaps this is a simplistic model to use for the complexities of a local economy, but it works very well with residents and local business, who can recognise their real problems portrayed in the diagrams.

I had presented this as a bit of lighthearted entertainment. I succeeded in splitting the conference right down the middle! Eminent Austrian economists were asking to use the model in their own work. A British economist sourly informed me that if I were in his first-year class in economics he would fail me. Another accused me of "Mickey Marx" economics. Veteran rural experts asked me how to create bathtubs. I was amazed. Several consultancy contracts followed from this conference, and we have used the model in regeneration work since then.

At the 1992 Edinburgh ISAGA conference, I demonstrated a game based on this application of the model. This asked players to develop a stable economy from a selection of project opportunities. Each project had several effects on the income, circulation, and outgoings sections of their boards, and the "winner" was the first player team to reach a balanced economy and hold it stable for two rounds.

The Three-Capital Model

Recently, I was part of a team of consultants asked by a number of public agencies to carry out a study of sustainability in Ettrick and Lauderdale, an area of rolling hills and moorland that lies in the southernmost part of Scotland. The study was concerned with establishing a local approach to sustainability. The results were to be used as a guide for national policy. The problems encountered in the course of the study highlight many of the problems that we face in policy issues generally and in "new" areas in particular. These are concerned with the portrayal of complexity and the development of effective tools to support policy makers dealing with complexity.

As part of the brief for the study we were asked to develop simple models for use with communities in explaining sustainability concepts. After several attempts we ended up with a version of the 3 × 3 matrix that looked at the interaction of the three capital stocks to which sustainability relates. The first of these is the environment. This comprises all the non-human-made aspects of flora and fauna, and it is categorized in terms of low, medium, or high quality. In environmental terms this is expressed as degrees of simplicity, diversity, and complexity. The middle column is concerned with human issues and registers the quality of life. The third column looks at the state of the local economy as it serves the local area.

Each column has inputs and outputs. The inputs are the resources that it requires to function. These can be externally and internally provided. They can also be classified as renewable or non-renewable. Outputs can also be directed externally or internally and can be positive (raising the quality of a stock or its external equivalent) or negative (lowering that quality). An initial analysis of an area gives the basic pattern of the diagram in terms of the way that the stocks perform. Applying a project to the diagram shows how the stocks change because of the action of that project.

We can now look at different types of sustainability. Simple sustainability is achieved when a project increases one of the stocks without decreasing any of the others. The implication is that such projects should be pursued. Complex sustainability is achieved when the increase in one stock is matched by decreases in others. An evaluation of the tradeoff has to be made.

SUSTAIN GAME

The SUSTAIN GAME is actually a cluster of games using the three-column model as a base (see Figure 7.1). The purpose of the games ranges from simple teaching to more complicated exercises in creating scenarios based on real situations and testing the results of projects on these.

Overview

This suite of games allows the use of the model in situations ranging from teaching to policy analysis and with a range of users from schoolchildren to policy analysts. The first game is concerned with data manipulation. It familiarizes people with some basic principles of sustainability and with the model as a way of thinking about these. It also indicates the likely results of types of project. The game is quite mechanical and does not allow much flexibility in the interpretation of play.

The second game, however, is rather freewheeling. It is useful for gatherings of experts in the field or of people who will have to cooperate to tackle sustainability problems. It can be used as the basis of a day's event.

The third game is a useful technique in the armory of planner or policy maker. It allows people to experiment with policy in safe environments and introduces the discipline of three-capital thinking in the resolution of real issues.

The Sustain Game

	Environment	Community	Economy	Jobs Total
				1600
				1550
				1500
				1450
				1400
				1350
Complex				1300
				1250
				1200
				1150
				1100
				1050
Diverse				1000
				950
				900
				850
				800
				750
Simple				700
				650
				600
				550
				500
				450
				400
				350
				300
				250
				200
				150
				100
				50
				0
				-50
				-100
				-150

SEQUENCE OF PLAY

1. Set out counters on the playing board according to the initial scenario. Play proceeds clockwise with each player carrying out the following actions in turn.

2. The current player picks and discards from the Enterprises stack. Announcing the class and title of the card (but not the values) to other players, and deciding whether to retain or discard, the player must then throw the die to determine whether to receive that card or not (a throw of 1-4 means that the player's decision is followed. A 5 or a 6 means that the decision is reversed). The Board markers are then moved according to the numbers in the boxed chart on the card. Numbers of jobs accruing from each enterprise are determined by t̶ ̶wing the die and multiplying the throw ̶ number given in the right hand of the unboxed chart. The jobs ̶ ̶then moved to indicate a ̶

3. Other players may bid for a card announced by the curren̶ ̶ ̶ ̶ by sec̶ ̶ ̶ player to spend so many resource markers. The highest ̶ ̶ ̶ carri̶ diately. Play resumes with the current player wh̶

4. A card may indicate that further action must b̶ ̶ ̶ ̶ ̶rigl̶ must select that number of cards from t̶ ̶ ̶b̶ number of cards from the discard pile ag̶ section 2 to determine if the card is selecte̶

5. At the end of every full round an external even̶

6. Play continues until any player manages to mainta̶ rounds of play.

7. Players must now describe their local areas according t̶

Figure 7.1   Three-column model used in SUSTAIN GAME.

Game 1

Following the precedent of the BATHTUB GAME, I have used the extended sustainability model as a basis for a game that can be used to explain the concepts and to study issues in hypothetical and real situations. The 3×3 matrix is used as the board. The initial pattern of the board is determined by dice throw. "Projects" are represented by cards that show effects on the three stocks, raising or lowering them. Players try to affect the level of their stocks by encouraging or resisting cards that are randomly selected. Some cards lead to other cards being selected, creating runs of development that might not produce the local results that players want. As in the BATHTUB GAME, a player who manages to hold the pattern steady for a predetermined number of rounds is deemed the winner.

The purpose of the game is to create informed discussion on aspects of sustainability by raising questions about planning policies. The game can be played in loose or tight versions. In the loose version, the players are involved in creating their own local scenarios and in setting up the cards (the structure within which play will take place). A series of roles can be generated for each area and the introduction of each enterprise can be handled naturally through the appropriate roles. In the tight version, the cards and the playing board are used to manipulate simple data with less role interaction and the decisions taken by teams with no role differentiation. Time available and the purpose of the session determine which version is used.

The debriefing session at the end focuses on using the game to draw scenarios of the likely future of your area. The complexities are generated by the players and the experience that they bring to the game. The game should allow the strategies that are available in real life. It is not as loose as many negotiation games, but the number of possible strategies generated by the simple framework is enormous.

Further twists have been introduced by allowing players to bid for desirable developments. Thus, the twin strands of planning, the power to discourage development and the power to encourage development, are simulated. The power to generate development is left to the mechanics of the game.

The game is disconnected. By this I mean that the actions that a player takes can influence results but will not totally determine them. Not only are decisions partially randomized but they are likely to lead to unexpected consequences, to runs of unwanted development that are difficult to control. In some cases, the game controller can intervene to upset a player's plans with unexpected events. This is often seen as unfair by the player. It is.

Game 2: Generating Scenarios

This is a team game that uses the model to define fictitious scenarios. Each team of up to seven people describes a geographic area. This can be urban or rural or any combination. The scale can vary from local to international. Under each column heading they are asked to compose a list of attributes—the definition of the stock. They are then asked to indicate whether this stock is low, medium, or high and to draw the base diagram accordingly. This base scenario is then passed to another group who try to devise policies to enhance and protect stocks.

In a third session, each team is asked to prepare a series of projects and to indicate the likely effects of these on parts of the environment, community, and economy. Teams then exchange project lists and apply them to the area scenario they now hold within the policy framework they have devised, debating whether the projects drive stocks up or down and what effect they may have on resources and outputs. Finally, each team presents its scenario, the changes brought about by the projects, and indicates what measures it might take to preserve or enhance the sustainability of the area described.

Game 3: A Real Situation

This exercise follows the sequence outlined in Game 2 but applies it to a real situation using real data. It is intended to be played as a way of analyzing an actual sustainability problem. It can be played as one session to explore policy options, or it can be used to test the effects of project proposals.

Conclusions

The games work well as thinking machines. They allow people to experiment with different courses of action and to plot linkages between different capital stocks. They make you think holistically rather than in a detailed way, and this is often a help in considering policy issues where the detail swamps the bigger picture. Importantly, they concentrate thinking about sustainability at the level of the individual project. The message is "you as an individual can make a difference."

The games are intended to be used to simulate actual situations or to build imaginary scenarios. They provide a structured language for assessing the way that projects will affect an area's capability for sustaining itself, and these provide a crucial test of how individual action can help or hinder the wider goals of sustainability.

8

Computer-Mediated Simulation/Gaming in Estonian High Schools

IVAR MÄNNAMAA

TERJE TUISK

Education systems tend to be ultra-conservative. Changes take place slowly, and in stable societies this may even be beneficial—acting as an immune system against risky experimentation. In societies where radical and rapid changes are taking place—as in the post-socialist countries today—both teachers and students are looking for new effective methods of learning, as new conditions demand a totally new quality of knowledge and entirely different belief systems. Under these conditions we decided to design a simulation/game that would bridge the gap between limited opportunities offered by the current educational system and the real needs of students. This chapter focuses on the main problems we faced while designing and running the computer-mediated simulation/game SIMUVERE, in which groups of university and high-school students of Estonia participated.

Setting Objectives

At the start of our adventure we discussed two different sets of simulation objectives. The first was at the university level. When the University of Tartu was connected to the Internet in 1992, one of our first discoveries was the international simulation Project IDEALS (Crookall & Landis, 1992; see Sutherland et al., chap. 13, this volume). Our students took part in this for two terms, learning something about team work and different strategies of problem solving. As a result we had a group of enthusiastic students who had some experience in simulations and who wanted to use their knowledge of problem solving together. This led to our decision not to speak about teaching and to focus on learning.

TABLE 8.1   Goals of the Simulation

Skills and Knowledge	Management
Computer literacy	Productive teamwork
Use of e-mail	Creative problem solving
How to write an application letter	Decision-making methods
Collective composition and process writing	

The second set of objectives was at the high-school level. About half of the high schools in Estonia have computers. All students in towns have access to computers even when there are none in their school, whereas in rural areas, computers are available to about half the students. However, computers are used very little for teaching subjects beyond computer science (informatics). A survey of Estonian school principals revealed that 95% of teaching is carried out in the old didactic style. Gaming/simulation was not known to be used in Estonia until 1993, with our participation in Project IDEALS. Also, e-mail is a very new thing in our schools. Our school-level objectives were based mostly on these conditions.

Our first task was to answer the question "What do we want our students to learn?" In one sense, we tried to kill two birds with one stone: We assumed that simulation was a tool that could be used both to develop concrete skills and to acquire new management practices (see Table 8.1).

A third objective soon became clear. This arose out of our ambitious plans to improve the practice and conditions of teaching in our high schools and to encourage teachers to use novel methods in their everyday work. We wanted to bring active learning into teaching practice. We also wanted to support the learning of social science; this is a new subject in our high school curriculum, for which not enough teachers are employed, nor any good textbooks published.

Planning and Preparation

The group that participated in Project IDEALS comprised only students. For SIMUVERE, we felt that the simulation would benefit from the participation of some experienced teachers. We asked a few colleagues to join us, and together we organized three brainstorming sessions and group discussions. During these sessions, nearly 200 ideas for future simulations were raised. We built up the framework of the simulation—a game that was based completely on e-mail connections.

By June 1993, five schools were connected to e-mail. Our idea was announced to them, and all responded with interest. When we started in September 1993, 11 schools were able to participate in the project.

SIMUVERE required an electronic environment. As our schools have only UUCP connections, electronic letters and "listserv" lists were the only options available. We created three lists—one for the actual simulation, another for the teachers' discussions, and the third for game facilitators. We ran SIMUVERE during two terms: October-December 1993 and February-April 1994.

The First Term

SIMUVERE is an electronic town in which high-school students play the roles of citizens. Every team represents one of the social groups of SIMUVERE, the groups being chosen by the students themselves. In fall 1993, we had scientists, university students, businessmen, pet keepers, ex-hippies, an indigenous tribe, and many more. Game leaders play the role of Town Council.

The first assignment is to give a description of the chosen group and its problems. Descriptions must be based on a previously distributed ten-point instruction list. Then the annual budget of the Town Council is announced. Proposals to develop the town (again based on our instructions) are requested from every social group. Very different kinds of projects—from environmental protection (sent by scientists) to beer brewing (sent by ex-hippies)—were submitted during the first term. Projects are evaluated by citizens—all groups must evaluate all projects. The decision on how to distribute the budget is made by the Town Council, but is based on the opinions of the citizens.

At the end of the first term, a festive party took place. There, the Town Council's decision was presented to every team in one document, and one representative from every group signed the document. At the party we all met in person for the first time, and every team had readied a short presentation to introduce itself. All participants completed a short questionnaire. To our surprise, 100% answered "yes" to the question "Do you want to participate in a similar simulation again?" Although it is usually difficult to get children aged 13-17 seriously committed to this type of long-term group project, the majority found the SIMUVERE project interesting. Our project was novel for them, which was one reason why they liked it.

The Second Term

On the basis of the positive feedback from the first run, we felt obliged to create the next game. We created new activities for SIMUVERE citizens that enabled them to practice creative problem solving and teamwork. The main objective was to organize the election of a Town Council in SIMUVERE. The citizens of our town, aged 13-17 years, had never had a chance to take part in real elections. We thought a simulated election in SIMUVERE would be a more effective teaching tool than textbooks or lectures.

We had many new citizens in our town the second term, so our first step was to take a census—to get the register of electors. Many new citizens and social groups appeared. We called it "the emerging of reality in SIMUVERE." During the first term, we had student groups from rural areas or from our university town, Tartu—mostly peaceful persons. During the second term, students from Tallinn—our capital and business center—joined us. So did Mafia members, sex profiteers, and arms smugglers, among others. This is indicative of the high visibility of these problems in the Estonian capital. Even when children get to create a new society as they envision it, they are not able to get rid of everyday problems and may even find these problems exciting. We waited for our citizens' reaction to the new and negative elements of society—they reacted by asking why the Town Council is not doing anything. They asked us to ban the Mafia and sex business. As we existed only electronically, there was nothing we could do.

In spite of these problems, we tried to lead a normal life in SIMUVERE and to organize elections. Meanwhile, the census was taken, and we created an election law according to our electronic reality as close as possible to the Estonian election law. The registration of parties and electoral campaigns was electronic. The register of electors obtained as a result of the census was sent to the local election committees—located at the schools—by e-mail. All pre-electoral activities were electronic, and the election itself was as real as possible. There was a precinct in every school with real polling places and booths, ballot boxes, and ballots. The simulation ended with a two-day festival in one of the participating schools. The newly-elected Town Council had its first meeting during this festival.

Debriefing

Because a special characteristic of our project was its electronic environment, the facilitators could influence participating groups only through e-mail messages. As a rule, we intervened only in cases of procedural violations. Unfortunately, it was difficult to discern and assess any actual learning in the classroom. All participating groups actively expressed their opinions of events and processes taking place within the simulation but were uninterested in discussing their experience in learning. We concluded that debriefing cannot be carried out through electronic mediation if facilitators have no prior experience. It requires direct contact and direct facilitation.

Although the debriefing in our own university group was better, we nonetheless found that having an experienced facilitator on hand would have helped a great deal. Most of the work was done by e-mail, with each team member working on his or her personal tasks. The most important issues were discussed once a week, when all team members met in a relaxed atmosphere and reported on their achievements and problems. Our problem was that, although we could always start the debriefing session, we were not so successful in directing it.

When we discussed our plans for the following term, we decided to focus on improved debriefing for computer-mediated simulation/gaming. We decided to take an incremental approach rather than to make sweeping changes. The first step was to improve debriefing related to team dynamics and problem-solving methods. To accomplish this, we knew we should stress three aspects. First, the shift to metalevel must be clear and sharp, for the electronic environment is susceptible to misunderstandings. Second, debriefing sessions must be conducted with a certain amount of structure. Finally, debriefing a computer-mediated simulation requires, on the part of the facilitators, a great deal of information about the learning of all participants.

The improvements were encouraging, and they allowed some methodological conclusions to be drawn. The main problem encountered was language. Moving to the debriefing phase required a shift from concrete to meta-level analysis and language. This requires a certain minimum of knowledge, which must be supplied at some prior point in the simulation process.

Procedural Issues

SIMUVERE is multi-functional and, as such, bears the many advantages and disadvantages of a complex simulation. The shortcomings usually appear only during the simulation or after it has ended. The main difficulties caused by the large scale of our simulation project were these:

- Lack of cooperation between groups
- Evaluation bias due to intellectual/emotional investment of evaluators
- Fuzziness and ambiguity of game rules

Usually, these problems were caused by poor design of playing procedures and ineffective intervention methods on the part of the facilitators. To overcome these problems we decided to evaluate the learning process in the specific light of simulation/gaming.

Reflections on the Simulation Experience

With some reservation, we see gaming in education as offering a somewhat flexible model that can be used and transformed in dealing with real life. Usually, a simulation requires the solution of some real problems and is, therefore, an excellent means to test and, if needed, modify and re-test the model.

Unfortunately, this kind of theoretical statement is of little value in directing and analyzing the actual process of learning. With every educational task we ask the learners to change their mind; we ask them to abandon their earlier beliefs and acquire new ones. Thus, the first task of a designer of a simulation game is to adopt at the start the viewpoint of the learners. The question then is what are the conditions under which change occurs? What motivates students to acquire new knowledge, obtain new skills, or change their cognitive or other style?

Learning Through Resistance

In analyzing the change taking place in students minds, we usually tend to compare the starting level and the state reached after a learning activity. Yet the most important process, the transition from one state to another, occurs somewhere in the interim. As long as we do not understand and follow these elusive processes, we are unable to direct learners to the development we desire. It is this interim point that may be the most valuable.

When we designed the scenario and procedures for our second simulation project we brought in the concept of learner resistance. Most human beings are conservative in changing their approaches to problems. It is only when they find they are not able to surmount an obstacle that they are ready to change attitudes or ways of thinking. Resistance to obstacles mobilizes new energy and can be characterized as a motivating power in the learning process. Thus, we must try to manage the rising resistance; we make use of its positive aspects.

An obstacle may be the task itself or may arise during the process of attaining the real educational goal. When we have managed to define the current level of students' skills and have defined the desirable new state we want them to reach, we come up against existing obstacles that we attempt to integrate into the system. As a result, the problems that students must solve should direct them to think in novel ways and to apply information and knowledge acquired during the simulation/game.

Students are like persons to whom we offer tickets to another continent. Why should they go? Other than out of curiosity (which is, of course, of great importance), the need will arise only when they face difficulties that are not solvable in their current state with their existing knowledge and skills. This widely known principle might be considered a good starting point in designing and running a simulation/game.

Rules Around Empty Space

Next, we looked at the forces that help the students over the obstacles, over some kind of threshold. How can a simulation game push them to a new level? Usually, it cannot, and actually it is not even necessary. To explain what I mean

I would like to use the question that Dmitri Kavtaradze, of Moscow State University, asked the audience during his presentation at the ISAGA '94 conference. He asked about the forces that make airplanes fly. As you can imagine, only very few of us were able to give even an approximately correct answer. To our astonishment, he explained that a plane is not pushed but sucked up; a kind of rare space, a relative vacuum, is created over the plane's wings causing it to rise. This example, in a different context, is an apt explanation for the effectiveness of simulations/games in various spheres. Of course, it may be possible to use simulation/gaming as a baker uses his shovel and try to shove students along, but another essential advantage that gives real value to simulation/gaming lies in its ability to create that empty space. One must take care, of course, that the empty space (which nature does not love, as we know) appears in the right place and at the right time. That is why we try to give a great deal of attention to the essence and the functioning of rules. Our only way of maintaining control over the learning process lies in the creation of rules.

The model that a student is expected to acquire during the simulation/game is nothing more than a set of rules. Early on, this model is supposed to be usable (then changeable, as needed) within so-called real life. Thus, we are justified in speaking about simulation/gaming as an educational tool that enables us to test and, if needed, to modify and integrate the model. The model must be flexible in the best sense of the word. This kind of model is a connecting chain between real life and a game; it offers the possibility of overcoming the strictness of typical game rules and, at the same time, avoids the indeterminacy, the possibility of chaotic development, that is always possible in real-life systems.

Different researchers describe some fundamental requirements for rules in real life. First, they can be broken—this is the condition of breach. Another agreeable requirement is that rules must be capable of change—this is the condition of alteration. All rules of real life achieve value and importance because they may be violated. In the case of games, this is somewhat contrary. Only the integrity of its rules gives it its real value. Every change in rules must be accepted by all players, and in that case it makes sense to talk about a new game. Otherwise, the phenomenon of double-play, in which another game is played within the first one, will occur. For most facilitators of simulations/games, this is not a comfortable situation. So, both real life and games need rules because of their prescriptive value. Rules specify "correct" or "appropriate" procedures, and the community (real or virtual) thereby evaluates the performance of those individuals who fall within its jurisdiction. It is argued that even very specific rules—for example linguistic ones—have an imperative force in that violators of such rules are penalized because they run the risk of being misunderstood. (Both in real life and in simulations/games the rules must be supported by sanctions. Invocation of sanction can be considered a fundamental requirement of a rule.) This property—the opportunity to contrive a unique set of rules and to direct their influence upon the participants of the game —is one of the significant advantages of simulations/games as teaching tools.

Conclusion

Simulation/gaming is a powerful tool for enabling rapid and relatively enduring changes in learners' minds and thoughts. It can be effective even in cases where learners are not so eager to acquire new skills and knowledge, when they are not interested in complementing their current abilities. The obstacles that learners meet on their way may engender different kinds of resistance due to the different levels of knowledge and ability of each student. A simulation/game must, therefore, offer different ways of overcoming the obstacles, and different intervention methods must be worked out to direct rising resistance. We tried to use this resistance as a moving force and the results were at least promising.

Even if the motivational level of students is already high, the main objectives of a simulation/game must form a balanced set. This is possible only through analyses of the current status of participants and a description of the desired outcome. All developmental tasks and virtual goals of the simulation/game must be in synchrony with educational objectives.

In our project, because we could not use direct intervention, we chose, instead, a velvet glove strategy. We worked out a set of rules supported by all participants and tried to create a kind of self-regulating model of virtual society. Although we did not design our simulation/game as a predictive method, the behavior and decisions of participating groups mirrored real developments in Estonian society. This encourages us to believe that our next attempts at simulation/gaming will be even more successful.

Reference

Crookall, D., & Landis, P. (1992). Global network simulation: An environment for global awareness. In D. Crookall & K. Arai (Eds.), *Global interdependence: Simulation and gaming perspectives* (pp. 106-111). Tokyo: Springer-Verlag.

9

Statistics Games for Large Classes

MIEKO NAKAMURA

I have experienced several types of simulation/gaming since 1991 and have applied games such as KNOTS (see Fluegelman, 1976), SPACE GAME (Law-Yone, 1993), and PLANES OR BUST (Legg, 1994) in my classes. These games are effective in creating a friendly atmosphere, providing an opportunity for understanding social mechanisms, giving clues to the study of management theories, or supplying materials for data analysis. There is, however, a serious drawback in the applicability of the above-mentioned games in that they are not designed to enhance students' motivation toward learning general statistics, which is the main subject for which I am responsible. They are also basically designed for a class of less than 20 participants.

I have been in charge of teaching general statistics since 1988. It is one of the subjects in which most students are found to be weak. Although I have been using games in this class, to minimize unsettling the status quo I have also continued to practice the traditional lecture-style approach. One other reason for maintaining a traditional approach alongside games is large class size. However, after accumulating experience in a small class, I decided to run experimental trials of simulations/games in a general statistics class of about 100 students. Appropriately designed, the application of these games to such large classes of general statistics can benefit both the teacher and the students in a number of ways. Such games can facilitate the traditional teaching methodology and can also become tools to help the teacher in times of need. In addition, they can make learning enjoyable and thus spark learner interest in the subject. The purpose of this chapter is twofold: to outline a series of games for teaching statistics in large classes and to report results from their application.

Lecture Topics and Games Used

Table 9.1 shows the contents of the lecture topics and corresponding games used. Because of the registration delay, the number of players who attended the

TABLE 9.1   Contents of Lecture Topics and Corresponding Games Used

Lecture Topic	Game Used	Number of Players
Measure of average	AVERAGES GAME	45
Probability	BIRTHDAY GAME	106
Population and sample	SAMPLING GAME	90
Hypothesis testing	EXEX	113

first game was less than for later classes. Participants, numbering about 100, were all students taking a credit course in general statistics.

Each game has its own specific objectives, although all games have an overall objective of enhancing the students' motivation to study general statistics. An outline of each of the four games and comments on the results of running each one are presented below.

AVERAGES GAME

Basic Data

Objective:	To clarify the difference among mean, median, and mode.
Playing time:	30 minutes.
Materials required:	Pen and paper for each player.

Play Procedure

1. Distribute paper to each player.
2. Ask the players to choose one number from 0 to 9 and to write it on the paper.
3. Ask the players to guess the mean, median, and mode of numbers chosen by all players in the classroom and to write them on the paper.
4. Count the number of players that chose 0. Do the same with the rest of the numbers to see how many chose 1, 2, and so on.
5. Calculate the scores of mean, median, and mode.
6. Ask the players how close their answers were to the real scores.
7. Praise the player(s) whose answers was (were) closest to the real scores.
8. Ask the players to write their opinions about this game.

Results

The number of players that chose 0, 1, and so on are shown in Table 9.2. The scores of mean, median, and mode calculated from Table 9.2 were 4.46, 5, and

TABLE 9.2   Number of Players to Each Number Chosen

Number chosen	0	1	2	3	4	5	6	7	8	9	
Number of players	1	4	7	6	4	6	4	10	2	1	45 total

7, respectively. Rounding off 4.46, we get 4 as the mean score. Only 1 student among 45 gave the correct answers to all three scores. In the debriefing, students expressed their frustration in wrongly predicting the scores. This frustration is a sign of their absorption in the game. Also, a large number of students misunderstood what the median was and answered 4.5—the midpoint between 0 and 9. However, when the actual calculation of the median was done with them, their misunderstanding surfaced and they realized their mistake. Thus, first-hand experience helped the students learn something that the traditional method of teaching failed to cover.

BIRTHDAY GAME

Basic Data

Objective:	To understand what probability is through experience.
Playing time:	60 minutes.
Materials needed:	Pen and paper for each player.

Play Procedure

1. Distribute paper to each player.
2. Ask the players to write down their birthday (month and day).
3. Ask the players to predict and write the frequency of having the same birthday within a group of 10, 20, 50, and 100 members, respectively.
4. Ask the players to form groups of about 10 members each.
5. Check whether or not the same birthday can be found within each group.
6. Combine two or three groups to form a larger group.
7. Repeat Step 5.
8. Combine again to form a group of about 50 members.
9. Repeat Step 5.
10. Combine again to form a group of about 100 members.
11. Count the number of people in the group who have the same birthday.
12. Ask the players to write their opinions about this game.

TABLE 9.3   Number of Group Members and Number of Occurrences of People With the Same Birthday Found Within the Group

Number of group members	10	10	9	11	11	9	12	10	11	13
Occurrences of people with the same birthday	0	0	0	0	0	0	0	0	0	0

Number of group members	20		31		21		34
Occurrences of people with the same birthday	0		1		1		1

Number of group members	51		55
Occurrences of people with the same birthday	1		3

Number of group members	106
Occurrences of people with the same birthday	10

TABLE 9.4   Number of Group Members and the Probability That at Least One Pair Has the Same Birthday

Number of Group Members	Probability of the Same Birthday
10	0.117
20	0.411
22	0.476
23	0.507
30	0.706
50	0.970
100	0.999

Results

The number of group members and the number of occurrences of people with the same birthday within the group are shown in Table 9.3.

If we calculate the probability of the frequency of coinciding birthdays within a group of ten members, the probability that all members have a different birthday is $(365/365) \times (364/365) \times \ldots \times (356/365) = 0.883$. Therefore, the probability that at least one pair has the same birthday within a group of ten members is $1 - 0.883 = 0.117$.

In the same way, the probability that at least one pair has the same birthday within a group of 20, 22, and 23 members can be calculated. As shown in Table 9.4, the probability exceeds 0.5 when the number of group members is more than 22. The results of Table 9.3 are consistent with those of Table 9.4. When the number of group members was ten or so, coinciding birthdays were not found in any group but were in a group of 21. When the number of group members was over 30, students found one or more occurrences of people with the same birthday.

The debriefing of students showed that they were surprised by the fact that birthdays coincide so frequently and that this is proved by theoretical calculation. In the written report, one student complained about having to reveal his birthday, which was a secret for him, and felt his privacy had been invaded. Such a situation can be avoided by asking students to choose something less personal, such as the birthday of a relative (e.g., father, sister) or the last two digits of their student identification number.

SAMPLING GAME

Basic Data

Objective:	To understand what sampling is and see how well a sample represents a population.
Playing time:	30 minutes.
Materials required:	Pen and paper for each player.

Play Procedure

1. Distribute paper to each player.
2. Ask the players to make a table on the paper like that of Table 9.5.
3. Ask the players to go around the class and collect data by entering them into the table.
4. Ask the players to write in data about themselves below the table.
5. Count the number of students majoring in management.
6. Count the number of students whose sample data that show 10% as the rate of students majoring in management. Do the same with those whose data show 20%, 30%, and so on.
7. Compare the results of Steps 5 and 6 and explain that most of the samples show a rate very close to that of the general population.
8. Repeat Steps 5 through 7 about females instead of management.
9. Do the same with support for government.
10. Ask the players to use their own data to calculate the mean for hours of sleep and the mean for commuting time to school.

Results

Because of time limits, Steps 8 and 9 were omitted. The number of students majoring in management was 23 of the 83 partipating. Therefore, the rate of students majoring in management was 0.277. The distribution of the rate of students majoring in management is shown in Table 9.6.

TABLE 9.5   Table for Collecting Data

	Name	Major	Sex	Support for Government	Hours of Sleep	Commuting Time to School
1						
2						
3						
4						
5						
6						
7						
8						
9						
10						

Rate of Students Majoring in Management	Rate of Females	Rate of Support	Mean of Hours	Mean of Commuting Time

TABLE 9.6   Distribution of the Percentage of Students Majoring in Management

Percentage	Number of Samples
0	5
10	7
20	22
30	25
40	12
50	11
60	1
70	0
80	0
90	0
100	0

Taking a complaint regarding BIRTHDAY GAME into consideration, I set aside a place for those who did not want to play games; seven students chose to observe. A few of them later reported that they were bewildered by the idea of being required to participate in games.

EXEX

Basic Data

Objective: To learn about hypothesis-testing theory through experience.

Playing time: 30 minutes.

Materials required: (a) Two sets of handouts on Type I error and Type II error and their relationship in hypothesis-testing theory (Handout A contains descriptive text; Handout B contains the same text and a set of questions related to the text), (b) four sets of instructions, each identified by a suit of playing cards (spades, hearts, clubs, and diamonds), and (c) copies of a post-treatment questionnaire that asks how well the players understood the descriptive text about Type I and Type II errors and their relationship, and how much they enjoyed the task (see Kemmerer & Thiagarajan, 1993).

Play Procedure

1. Divide the players into four groups according to the suit of playing cards they had been asked to take from a few decks of playing cards beforehand.

2. Distribute handouts to the players according to the suit of cards as follows: **Spade**—Handout **A**, with instructions to read it silently for 20 minutes; **Heart**—Handout **B**, with instructions to read it silently for 20 minutes; **Club**—Handout **A**, with instructions to read it silently for 10 minutes and to discuss the content for 10 minutes with a partner within the group; **Diamond**—Handout **B**, with instructions to read it silently for 10 minutes and to discuss the content for 10 minutes with a partner within the group.

3. Let the players start reading. Make sure that Clubs and Diamonds begin to discuss the content after 10 minutes.

4. After 20 minutes, indicate that the time is up.

5. Distribute copies of the post-treatment questionnaire to the players.

6. Count the number of players' responses on a 5-point scale (1 = *not understood at all*, 5 = *understood very well*) concerning the degree of understanding of Type I error, Type II error, and their relationship, respectively. Count the number of players' responses on a 5-point scale (1 = *not enjoyed at all*, 5 = *enjoyed very much*) concerning the degree of enjoyment. Calculate the mean scores and compare the degree of understanding and enjoyment among the four groups.

TABLE 9.7   Mean Scores for Each Group

Group	Size	Type I Error	Type II Error	Relationship	Degree of Enjoyment (5-point scale)
		Degree of Understanding			
Spade	28	3.107	3.071	2.607	2.357
Heart	28	**3.500**	**3.464**	2.857	2.464
Club	29	3.241	3.207	2.759	2.966
Diamond	28	3.393	3.429	**3.036**	**3.464**

Results

The research hypotheses were that players in the Spade group (neither questions or discussion) would score the lowest in both understanding and enjoyment, that those in the Heart group (questions but no discussion) and those in the Club group (no questions but discussion) should score better than the Spade group, and that those in the Diamond group (both questions and discussion) should score the highest. Table 9.7 shows the mean scores for degree of understanding of Type I error, of Type II error, and of the relationship between the two and for degree of enjoyment. Scores in the Spade group were always the lowest, but those in the Diamond group were not always the highest. Degrees of understanding of Type I and Type II errors were highest, not in the Diamond group, but in the Heart group. Degree of understanding of the relationship between Type I error and Type II error, and degree of enjoyment were highest in the Diamond group. These results can also be analyzed in the classroom, thus providing further discussion on statistics.

Discussion and Conclusion

As described above, the four games were designed to aid students in general statistics. In terms of attitude, the students seemed to enjoy these games thoroughly. This does not necessarily mean that the students were really motivated to learn general statistics. They might simply have been bored with the traditional lecture style of teaching. This year's class attendance was higher than the previous year's, perhaps due to the simulation/gaming method's success in drawing students to the class. Of course, we need more data to prove it. However, as a first step this is very encouraging.

During the ISAGA '94 conference, the audience at my presentation suggested that I accumulate more data and report on the relationship between simulation/ gaming methods and the rate of attendance. This was a very good suggestion, which I am planning to implement for a future ISAGA conference.

Let us now consider another aspect of helping learners understand general statistics. Each game was integrated with lectures. To accommodate a time constraint, as one unit of lecture comprises only 90 minutes, debriefing was done by writing. This saved time and contributed to data collection. The data collected from the written debriefing were then used to improve the quality of teaching in both the lecture and the simulation/gaming methods. This also guaranteed the continuity of the lectures, as the data from one class were put to use in the next.

Written debriefing also helped overcome the size constraint, as oral debriefing is difficult in a class of over 100 students. There is also merit in having a large class where debriefing is done on paper because it provides the teacher with a large sample of data. In this way, a large class becomes an asset instead of a constraint.

Last but not least is the players' readiness. The simulation/gaming methods are very helpful if they are properly incorporated into lectures. However, as some showed in their debriefing, students do not like being forced to do something new or to be involved too much in classwork. This is a point to keep in mind. One alternative is to ask them to observe and report what happens. After participating as observers, they may be more willing to participate fully in these games.

References

Fluegelman, A. (Ed.). (1976). *The new game book.* London: Headlands; New York: Doubleday.

Kemmerer, F., & Thiagarajan, S. (1993). EXEX: An experiential activity on experimental research. *Simulation & Gaming: An International Journal, 24,* 116-119.

Law-Yone, H. (1993). *SPACE GAME.* Technnion-Haifa: Israeli Institute of Technology, Faculty of Architecture and Planning.

Legg, L. (1994). PLANES OR BUST: An OPT scheduling game. In R. Armstrong, F. Percival, & F. Saunders (Eds.), *The simulation and gaming yearbook* (Vol. 2, pp. 209-219). London: Kogan Page.

10

The Psychologist and Games in the Intensive Foreign Language Game-Based Course

NINA N. NEMITCHEVA

The Management Training Center in St. Petersburg is a private institution established as a business training center in 1988. With a staff of 170 it trains industrial managers, university officials, municipal officials, trainers, and entrepreneurs. It also does consulting in new technologies for language teaching and simulation modeling of socio-economic systems. The Center creates different programs to teach foreign languages to adults, running two to eight programs each year, each lasting from 10 days to 1 month. With the use of immersion techniques, English and Russian are taught as second languages. Moreover, the program is successful in this work because it reaches beyond the customary reliance on only language skills.

The idea of knowing a foreign language means to know not only its grammar rules, functions, and lexical peculiarities, but also how all these things are used in the complicated process of communication. It means language as a tool of communication. That is why, using the principles of communicative foreign culture teaching, we teach students in groups and integrate language teaching with the improvement of communications skills. Critical tools for improving these skills are simulations and games. As each group's language needs differ, the set of games/simulations used for each group is tailored to its needs. The language programs use many different kinds of games: grammar, vocabulary, structure, total physical response, moving, communications, and so on. Games and role-plays enable learners to generate new experiences as they solve different communications problems. Simulations, for example, allow students to practice and improve their skills in presentations, discussions, and negotiations. These new experiences result in learning that is profound and well retained. Moreover, the simulation/game reality is special; it is full of energy, creativity, imagination, and fun. It motivates students to do their best and to interact without fear of failure.

Structure of Language Courses

The process of language learning at the Training Center is very intensive. Placed in groups of 8 to 10 according to language level, students work more than 10 hours a day. Each group is taught by a foreign language teacher and is facilitated by a psychologist. There are several advantages of such teamwork. First, the complementary efforts of the two experienced trainers streamline the process of learning and improving communicative and linguistic competence. Much attention is paid to the feedback from students, facilitators, and video-tapes. Language learners become aware of the process and results of their verbal and nonverbal behavior, taking into account cross-cultural differences.

Second, video training of communicative skills can be used as a pre-program for the intensive foreign language course. This helps create a caring atmosphere and an attitude of working as a team. The communications pre-program also makes it easier to minimize the possibility of harming the trainees in their new and uncertain environment. Finally, due to the cohesiveness of learners and trainers, the responsibility for the learning process is shared between both parties. These factors guarantee better training and more effective learning.

A third advantage of the team approach is that it allows the learning process to unfold in all its complexity and richness as it takes into account the laws of group dynamics and the potential of each group of learners.

Beginning the Group

The work of the psychologist in our intensive course can be divided into four stages. During the first stage, the objective is to organize the most efficient group for the intensive course. To accomplish this, the psychologist pays particular attention to selecting the students who will work together most effectively, assisting students in an analysis of their learning needs, and leading the discussion concerning major issues to be considered in the target program.

To obtain the most efficient class, we group students homogeneously by the extent of their knowledge of the target language. Then we pay attention to age, sex, marital, and social status. For example, it is not easy to work when a married couple or a boss and a secretary are in one group. At the same time, the language needed for the boss and for the secretary is quite different. We also take into account the motivation to learn the target language in the group and the major channel of perception: visual, audio, or kinesthetic. Then we discuss the students' needs. In which areas of the target language do the students want the most practice? What do they need to do in the target language?

In the final part of this stage, the facilitators and the group discuss major issues of the target program. We use an individual approach and flexibility, trying to take into account the needs of each participant and the group as a whole. The responsibility for the content of the program is shared between the facilitators and the students.

Video Training for Communication Skills

The objectives of the second stage are to further improve communicative skills and to prepare students for the target program. Early on, students and facilitators realized that half the difficulty in speaking the foreign language stemmed, not from a lack of knowledge of vocabulary and grammar, but from fear of using new language skills. It was found that videotaping and then reviewing the tapes is crucial to breaking down this fear of making mistakes. The program makes great use of videotaping as a training tool.

The main aims of Stage 2 are the following:

- Work out the norms of group functioning to make the learning process efficient (norms such as confidentiality, active participation, focus on the "here and now," and constructive feedback)
- Verify the expectations and deal with fears (if there are any) of the participants and facilitators
- Assist in coping with the barriers that may affect the learning process (e.g., overdependence on the teacher, linguistic prejudice, inhibition about communicating in a foreign language, a mismatch between a learner's expectations of how learning should take place and actual teaching)
- Help students to be aware of how necessary it is that they construct their own strategy for learning the foreign language in the most appropriate way for them
- Create an attitude of team cooperation, teaching how to give and receive useful feedback that is clear, owned, balanced, specific and based on the behavior, free of judgments, and consistent about verbal and non-verbal behavior
- Encourage development of general communicative skills (e.g., active listening, expressing feelings, coping with tension in conflict, and making contact) that provide effective interaction
- Encourage development of more specific communications skills according to the major issues of the target program chosen in the first stage, such as making presentations and negotiating
- Give students the opportunity to work on their own issues with a video camera and to get acquainted with methods and techniques such as role-plays and relaxation that will be actively used during the target program
- Activate imagination and skills of non-verbal behavior
- Lead the group through forming, storming, and norming to the performing stage of group dynamics and to achieve student readiness for the target program

The results of the second stage greatly influence the success of the target program.

The Target Program

The objective of this stage is to continue solving problems touched on in the second stage and to streamline the process of foreign language learning. The main aims for the psychologist are the following:

- Create readiness for acquiring the program elements through appropriate warm-up exercises
- Monitor and manage group dynamics, balancing at any given moment the gestalt of the group and the element of the program in use
- Adapt role-plays and exercises for each group of learners, and create new ones using the current spoken language
- Deal with physical, mental, and interpersonal tension in the group
- Run meditation and relaxation exercises during the program
- Consult and support group participants and the language teacher (if needed) to cope with difficulties
- Carry out behavior briefing for games and role-plays
- Deal with ethical and cross-cultural issues
- Organize and carry out different kinds of feedback (debriefing)
- Analyze daily videotape of some parts of group work with the language teacher to assess what modifications of the program are necessary for the next day

Sometimes, the psychologist participates in warm-up exercises, role-plays, and free talks to demonstrate models of verbal and non-verbal behavior.

Completion of the Group

The objective of the final stage is to organize feedback from the group on the process and the results of the intensive course. The psychologist works to elicit participants' feelings about the completed coursework, namely, acceptance of their successes and disappointments, their expectations for the next steps in using the new language, and their appreciation of what they have accomplished. The main aims are to select and carry out appropriate verbal and non-verbal procedures for group completion, organize the final discussion or debriefing, and help the group to plan concrete actions for continuing with foreign language studies.

Conclusion

The two-person language teacher-psychologist team is a new approach in teaching foreign languages. The program integrates the improvement of communications and language skills, using deep debriefing with oral, written, and video feedback on the language, behavior, results, and process. Games and simulations used in the program create an excellent environment for learning and helping participants maintain open attitudes toward new ideas.

The contribution of the psychologist to the intensive course is powerful. She or he reflects on the behavioral and psychotherapeutic issues and is a resource both for an enjoyable and rich learning process and for effective and profound teaching of foreign language in a group setting.

11

A Large-Scale Simulation
for Teaching Business Strategy

DIANE H. PARENTE

Large-scale simulation or live-scale simulation (LSS) was used as an approach
to the delivery of an undergraduate capstone course in business administration.
LSS integrates theory, simulation, and role-event gaming to provide the student
with a context for experiential learning. Student comments reveal the impact of
LSS:

> Don't fall behind in your work, but don't get too scared in the beginning; get as
> much out of this course as possible. It will help you when interviewing for jobs!
> Teamwork is the key. Start off together. This class is a cannon. I hate doing work,
> but this is so rewarding once you complete the class, it's worth it.

One objective of this course is to provide a near-realistic setting for students
to demonstrate theory and practice skills learned in prior courses. A secondary
objective is to help prepare students for the challenges ahead in their careers.
Traditional case-study instruction organizes the facts of a particular situation.
The environment is set and the students then analyze and discuss appropriate
actions by the case actors. Thus, students examine the case from the outside, or
the position of an observer. Case methodology is widely used to provide
business students with experience in analyzing many specific situations. Thus,
they may call on this experience in situations in the future that may be similar
to the cases studied.

A dynamic case environment is set in LSS with a computer simulation that
illustrates the theory of the subject. Role-event gaming incorporates role-play
and gaming to build an environment from which the students can learn experientially. Therefore, the students analyze situations from the inside, or the
position of a participant. A dynamic or changing environment is created as a
result of student decisions made throughout the computerized simulation.

This chapter discusses the components of LSS and the contribution to student learning. A framework for learning is included, and various methods of management education are placed within the framework. An example in the use of LSS for a business policy/strategic management course is discussed in detail, including process components, game components, and course deliverables. The final section describes the impact of ISAGA '94 on my future work in LSS and business management pedagogy.

Large-Scale Simulation

LSS is an approach that integrates theory, simulation, and role-event gaming to provide experiential learning. The theory is introduced to students via a standard text. The simulation is used to set the live-scale environment and to illustrate the theory. Role-event gaming places students as actors in specific management roles in the semester-long experience. Purkey (1992) states that "the student's motor is always running. The function of the educator is to place the signs, build the road, direct the traffic, and teach good driving—but not to drive the car" (p. 6). LSS suggests that the instructor allow the students to drive the car.

The environments created by management games have been called "experiential in the United States . . . , action learning in the United Kingdom . . . , or active teaching within the Eastern bloc" (Wolfe, 1993, p. 447). Active learning is a technique that engages the learner with the material being learned. In the classroom, the instructor teaches the students how to function and how to get the task done within the context of the discipline, the course, and the class. Active learning distributes the learning between the students and the teacher. Traditional models of teaching are lecture, case studies, and presentations. These do not involve active learning. Therefore, the comfort level of the instructor may not be particularly high in his or her early use of active learning. LSS, like experiential learning and role-playing independently (Hsu, 1989), shifts the emphasis from teaching to learning. Mintzberg (1973) implies that this aspect is especially appropriate for management education. He states that formal education cannot make managers. Rather, it is the acquisition of a variety of skills through role-play, experiential learning, or on-the-job training. LSS acts as a link to job training.

Hsu (1989) defines a general model of learning that has four phases: retaining information, organizing knowledge, experiencing, and firming. He further identifies tools and methods that are appropriate at each of the four phases. If we assume that the phases are also levels of learning, the primary level, retaining information, uses lectures and readings as the methods of instruction. The second level, organizing knowledge, uses discussions, debates, and cases. The third level, experiencing, involves gaming and simulation and may be accomplished through on-the-job training. The fourth level, firming, may be dubbed feedback.

At the level of a capstone course, it is appropriate that the third level is achieved. The transition from organizing knowledge to experiencing helps to bridge the student from academe to the "real world." LSS not only reaches the third level but, may also achieve the fourth phase in the feedback that occurs throughout the simulation. Results of student decisions form the basis for the next live case or the next simulation situation. Further, a final critical evaluation of the corporation contributes to the feedback level.

Use of LSS in a Business Policy/Strategic Management Course

A business policy or strategic management course is designed to be a capstone course that integrates all prior coursework in a business administration program. *Webster's* defines capstone as putting the final stone in place. It is the intent of this course to fit the pieces of an entire business administration program together to form a cohesive whole. Students can then apply their knowledge in the real business world.

A live-scale simulation approach focuses on the "how," or the process of strategic management. Theory is taught in the classroom and applied within the context of the simulation and role-event gaming. The objective of the use of LSS is to provide a realistic setting to facilitate experiential learning in the last semester of business administration education.

Students enter the course with a formal resumé in hand. Students are chosen to be corporate chief executive officers (CEOs) based on their resumé and possibly an interview with the instructor. On the second day of class, CEOs conduct job interviews for positions in their mock corporations. Students are subsequently hired to be vice presidents of finance, marketing, administration, manufacturing, or research and development.

Teams (now corporations) manage several strategic business units (SBUs). Each student has two roles within the company: business unit manager and CEO or vice president of a functional department in the corporation. The corporations then compete with each other in a game that simulates real-world business competition in ten industries in a global setting. Each week each corporation must make strategic decisions regarding its SBUs, guided by its corporate mission and goals. It also uses the results of its computer simulation competition to produce deliverables. Reports or concrete documents that serve a purpose in the operation of an organization are defined as deliverables. These are the components for the role-event gaming portion of the course.

In addition to each corporation's deliverables, a case study is prepared at the end of the semester that analyzes the company over the three-year simulation period. Students are expected to use the tools learned in the theory portion of the course to analyze their own corporations (e.g., SWOT analyses, McKinsey matrix). Oral class presentations allow all groups to understand the strategies and tactics used by the other corporations during the simulation.

Process Components

Professionalism is set as a standard early in the role-event gaming when students dress in formal business attire to interview for positions as vice presidents. Professionalism is continued throughout the course in standards set for deliverables. All corporation reports are graded for typing, spelling, and grammatical errors. The fifth error in a report of any length causes a loss of 10% in the final grade. Each subsequent error results in an additional 5% loss. Deliverables contain large amounts of creativity besides structure. As an example, annual reports often include colored photographs of the corporate officers and pictures of the company's products. Illustrative graphs and charts, letters from the CEO, and statements from the auditors may also be included. Students use deliverables for job interviews. Thus, each semester's deliverables are better than the previous one's.

Both the individual and the team build confidence and true feelings of pride and accomplishment by the end of the semester. The students learn the value and contributions of disciplines other than their own in the operation of the firm. Marketing students appreciate the contributions of finance and accounting personnel in the application of creative ideas. Accounting students learn to appreciate the creative ideas that may be solutions for unprofitable businesses or industries in decline.

The mock companies may be considered the ultimate team. Other class group projects are usually short in duration, encouraging students to overlook either personal or professional differences because the project will finish within a week or two. The LSS class requires that dysfunctional behavior on the team be resolved to allow the team to complete its work. This simulates the real business world in that employees must find a way to work together to accomplish goals. One of the learning objectives is for students to determine how to accomplish the large volume of work within a limited time period with the resources and talents they have on their teams. They must learn to use each person's talents and to mitigate any weaknesses.

Limited direction on deliverables is provided by the instructor because students will soon graduate and move into the real business world. Learner autonomy as an objective is usually achieved. If they do not know how to complete a particular deliverable from a prior course, they should know how to find out how to do it! There are few instruction manuals provided on the job. LSS is an exercise applying the theory and content from this course or prior courses to create the deliverables required for their corporation to exist.

Deliverables

The game is processed quarterly for a simulated period of three years. Results of the simulation are used in the preparation of the deliverables. Table 11.1 lists each deliverable, briefly states the business purpose, and notes a specific learning objective. Students receive different point awards for each deliverable depending on the level of responsibility for the item. For example, the Vice President for Finance and Accounting has primary responsibility for the annual report and receives the highest number of points. Marketing, manufacturing, and the CEO also contribute heavily but receive fewer points.

The major purpose of all deliverables is to highlight the relationship to the mission and goals of the organization. The deliverables follow a logical progression throughout the three-year history of the firm. The deliverables are documents that would be prepared in the normal operation of an organization. Participants are involved in the preparation of the deliverables and operation of the corporation. They become caught up in the simulated situation and learn emotionally as well as cognitively.

A mid-semester in-game debriefing is the presentation to the board of directors. The instructor uses this one-hour session with each team to identify and resolve problem areas. These may be related to group dynamics or understanding of the business operation. The in-game debriefing is a powerful tool in the learning process, according to students. The final case analysis represents structured debriefing at the end of the simulation. Students report in an end-of-course questionnaire that the most valuable deliverable is the case analysis. In-depth analysis allows them the opportunity to reflect on their actions throughout the course. Some observations are made about their pre- and post-board performance and understanding that further attest to the power of the in-course debriefing.

Game Components

The course described in this chapter uses Hill and Jones's (1992) *Strategic Management Theory* as the text and Priesmeyer's (1992) STRATEGY! for the simulation. Although written by different authors, the book parallels the simulation. Both are sound theoretically, with the simulation illustrating the theory of the book.

STRATEGY! is easy to run and allows for individual participation and tracking due to the multi-SBU format. Strategies are identified by the simulation, based on the budgeting done on individual SBUs. If students do not achieve the expected strategy, they probably provided inconsistent information in the budgeting process. It is likely that the game response will be "strategy not established." The importance of an inconsistent approach is manifested by poor financial performance by the SBU.

TABLE 11.1 Corporation Deliverables

Deliverable	Business Purpose	Learning Objective	Vice President Primary Points
Job description and performance goals	Enumerate tasks that are necessary for day-to-day operations by position	Understand the difference between job-specific and person-specific functions; obtain agreement on job requirements	Administration
Annual operations plan	Develop short-term interface between marketing and operation	Note importance of sales forecast in short- and long-term operation of the business units	Manufacturing
Annual report	Historical and public report that provides stockholders with information on the performance of the corporation	Working with diverse disciplines to produce a quality and professional document	Finance and Accounting
Presentation to board of directors	Update board on strategic direction or request approval for significant change in direction	Formal 1-hour business presentation outside class; total integration of multiple disciplines in significant presentation	Marketing
Strategic plan	Evaluate alternatives and make recommendations for future actions	Integrate various functions of the corporation in evaluation of strategic alternatives	Marketing
Compensation and bonus plan	Statement of specific bonus programs by position and compensation plans of the organization by function, both of which are consistent with the mission and goals of the organization	Create compensation and bonus plans that advance the goals of the organization	Administration
Organizational design	Graphic representation of the organization on both SBU and portfolio level	Design of reporting relationships, taking into account the mission and goals of the organization	Administration
New business development plan	Strategic document proposing entry into new business areas	Develop three ideas for new business (new facilities use, new product, and product extension); determine cash flow, ROA, and pro forma profit and loss and balance sheet	Research and Development
Environmental position paper	Evaluation of decisions made in the implementation of environmental policies and procedures	Environmental issues of business, including cost and benefit	Research and Development
Performance reviews	Feedback session between employees and managers	Understanding of positive and negative feedback and agreement on performance criteria based on goals established at the beginning of the course	CEO

The game has fairly weak financials, and price setting is a bit awkward. However, other aspects of the teaching environment provided by this simulation far outweigh the minor disadvantages. The game is multi-industry, which means that the business situations provided are at both an industry and a portfolio level. This is clearly an opportunity for the student to explore strategies, such as vertical integration, and related industries that are not possible in a single-industry game.

Debriefing

LSS for strategic management has been used by five different instructors to date. Some have used different texts, and others have used a single-industry game. Although each has now switched to the text and simulation discussed here, it is not the specific theory or simulation that makes this a unique class. It is the application of role-event gaming with the process and task components that makes LSS effective in this course. Students become so involved that their corporations become real. They are participants in the live case. Active learning occurs in each class period and continues for many hours outside the classroom. Students and teacher take active roles in the learning process and share it in a special way.

Each semester, students are invited to give advice to those who follow. Student comments are copied without editing and included in the syllabus for the next semester. It is through these comments, student evaluations, and other questionnaires that instructors realize the impact of LSS on students.

Conference Session

The ISAGA '94 workshop helped me to focus on several important facets of LSS. Participants at the workshop were impressed with the quality of the deliverables produced by undergraduates. Comments were made that the quality of work was "professional." Several participants reminded me during the workshop and in personal notes received later that this approach challenges students at a high level of performance. Practical work experience has guided the development of the course.

Participants at ISAGA '94 identified transferability as a key issue. The *Instructor's Guide* (Parente, 1994) now appears more important than originally thought. In fact, the format was one that specifically outlined each deliverable. However, it is clear now that the complete operation of the course should be included in detail. Potential instructors may then replicate the total impact of the course and the LSS approach.

Mintzberg (1973) describes learning by simulation as the primary form of experiential learning that involves practicing the skill in as realistic a situation as possible and then analyzing performance explicitly. Students must be immersed, practice the skill, and receive constructive feedback on their performance from someone who understands the skill. LSS is an approach that provides the environment described by Mintzberg.

LSS can be applied in many situations and across many disciplines both within and beyond management. Higher-level integrative courses at either an undergraduate or a graduate level may lend themselves to LSS more easily (Wheatley, Roberts, & Einbecker, 1990). In an MBA course using LSS, Wheatley et al. (1990) discuss a two-semester course that goes even further in scope than the course described here. It integrates role-playing events such as labor negotiation and incorporates business managers' participation. The University of West Florida was cited as an award winner for this program.

Preliminary analysis of the end-of-course questionnaire reveals a high level of perceived learning from the course. Students also report self-satisfaction and achievement upon completion. Future work will involve refinement of the description of LSS, identification of additional applications, and development of LSS evaluation techniques.

References

Hill, C. W. L., & Jones, G. R. (1992). *Strategic management* (2nd ed.). Boston: Houghton Mifflin.
Hsu, E. (1989). Role-event gaming simulation in management education. *Simulation & Games: An International Journal, 20*(4), 409-438.
Mintzberg, H. (1973). *The nature of managerial work.* New York: Harper & Row.
Parente, D. H. (1994). *Strategic management instructor's guide.* Unpublished manuscript.
Priesmeyer, H. R. (1992). *STRATEGY!* Cincinnati, OH: South-Western Publishing.
Purkey, W. (1992, February). Quotation in issue on active learning. *The Teaching Professor, 6*(2), 6.
Wheatley, W. J., Roberts, R. M., & Einbecker, R. C. (1990). A complex simulation and community involvement yield an award-winning capstone experience. *Simulation & Gaming: An International Journal, 21*(2), 181-189.
Wolfe, P. J. (1993). A history of business teaching games in English-speaking and postsocialist countries: The origination and diffusion of a management education and development technology. *Simulation & Gaming: An International Journal, 24*(4), 446-463.

12

A Pan-American University
Network Simulation/Game

LEOPOLDO SCHAPIRA

Comments on and the results of the ICONS and IDEALS simulations have been presented at previous ISAGA conferences. In 1986, David Crookall, Robert Noel, Jonathan Wilkenfeld, and I showed how ICONS functioned (see Noel et al., 1987). In that demonstration, two groups in the United States, three in France, and another in Argentina, working simultaneously, simulated an international crisis around a missing nuclear missile. At the 25th anniversary ISAGA conference, some reflections on a new experience were shared.

The Project

In 1991 and 1993, ten university teams[1] from North, Central, and South America participated in the inter-American simulation PRODUCTION, TRAFFICKING, AND CONSUMPTION OF COCAINE ON THE CONTINENT. These simulation exercises were run by Jonathan Wilkenfeld, Department of Government and Politics at the University of Maryland, and myself, under a grant from the Inter-American Commission Against Drug Abuse, Organization of American States (CICAD-OAS). Student teams were linked by a University of Maryland host computer using the procedures and the software of ICONS, the international affairs simulation.

The issues of the simulation were reduction of consumer demand for cocaine and control of the production and commercialization of cocaine on the continent. The exercise comprised a sequence of three academic activities. In the first, each national team assumed the role of the Ministry of Foreign Affairs of its own country, starting out from a set of shared hypotheses (a scenario on the sociological, political, economic, and military situation of the problem). The teams carried out the necessary studies to formulate a picture of the situation and in a position paper shaped the objectives and strategies that would determine its behavior during the exercise.

The second stage was the simulation exercise. In this period, e-mail communications and on-line real-time conferences were set up. Teams exchanged diploatic correspondence with the aim of arriving at preliminary bi- or multilateral agreements on the main topics under discussion. During the on-line conference, attempts were made to arrive at final resolutions of the simulated international meetings. The third academic activity was another on-line conference, this time dealing with debriefing.

Besides the academic activity, the realization of the project required an institutional organizational effort: construction of the participant universities network and preparation, at a distance, of the schedule, simulation scenarios, and debriefing. In the first exercise, the search for appropriate participants (in social and political science institutes or in institutions concerned with the cocaine problem) was difficult. Personal contacts, academic directories, and article references were used as sources to build a preliminary list. Possible local group coordinators were invited to participate by telephone, fax, and e-mail.

Once the final local coordinators were committed, they were invited to the University of Córdoba with a double purpose: to train them in the use of ICONS communication facilities and simulation procedures and to build the simulation scenario and schedule. The meeting was very productive and generated a network of personal relationships. It was, however, an expensive undertaking. With that in mind, when it was time for the 1993 orientation for two new teams—Brazil and Bolivia—it was decided that the simulation director would visit the new local coordinator offices to teach them on-site about communication procedures and the nature of the simulation. This decision was based on the confidence that links built between the original participants during the first exercise would be sufficient to prepare, at a distance, the simulation scenario and procedures.

Although this assumption was correct, e-mail exchange provided less interaction than did the previous face-to-face work, and more time had to be devoted to exercises and team preparation activities. We found it difficult to find a balance between inexpensive e-mail work and the more beneficial and costly personal contacts.

Another matter that had to be taken into account during the organizational stage was the diversity of communication facilities available in each participant country. Some of the problems were solved by fitting on-line conference schedules to particular hours of the day when disruption (i.e., service interruption, congestion) in the telecommunication services of the intervening countries were less likely to occur.

There were more serious problems that had to be overcome so that all countries could participate. For example, in Bolivia, neither the interactive

Internet nor the Telnet was available. To overcome that problem, a double link was established. For the on-line work, they used direct international dialing instead of a data carrier. This expensive solution was partially supported by funds from the United Nations Development Program. In the e-mail correspondence period, they used a noninteractive address on Internet to receive and send messages. Their messages were sent to Maryland and from there distributed to participants in the ICONS community and vice versa.

In practice, this procedure produced a delay in their communications, which had an impact on their behavior during the simulation. In spite of this inconvenience, the high quality and vivid responses from the Bolivian team made them one of the important characters in the role-playing.

Context and Results

In the central and southern parts of America, a process of communication infrastructure improvement is taking place. In this process, computer networks, formerly used almost exclusively by the hard disciplines, are gradually being incorporated into the academic life of the social sciences. Both this technological development and a change of attitude on the part of the social scientists are taking place in territory that is still institutionally unconnected, despite the acknowledgment of a common past and of the possibilities for future integration projects.

Under these conditions, OAS is making great efforts to increase the electronic interconnection between Latin American countries and to facilitate exchange between people. The development of opportunities for direct contact is thought to ease the process of both identification of common objectives and the management of available resources. An important part of this policy should be to raise the level of communication among work teams and researchers in specific fields.

The development of an ICONS-like simulation exercise fits into the CICAD-OAS action strategies because it is implemented in a context of communication infrastructure growth, of gradual incorporation of the social sciences in the use of academic networks, and of the need to build continentwide cooperation. In this sense, the project is an example of horizontal cooperation in which a group of universities located in different countries of this continent develop scenarios and work techniques, coordinate a simulation, and draw conclusions in a debriefing. This is in essence a collective knowledge-building process.

The following are some considerations emerging from the 1991 and 1993 experiences that explain why CICAD-OAS exercises (including simulation, telecommunications, and an issue of vital interest to participants) can become the basis for a wider scope of undertakings:

- The activity encourages the development of a culture of negotiation. Such a culture is sometimes viewed with suspicion in Latin America.

- Each national university group follows certain fixed lines of thought that are taken for granted. The simulation by telecommunications processes helps to dissolve these rigid ideas and to bring into question the simplified, stereotyped, and uniform perspectives built by the international media.

- The exercise allows for an exchange of beliefs, myths, knowledge, attitudes, and aspirations among groups possessing different cultural contexts. Such communication enables participants to approach the issues with greater-than-usual creativity.

- Firsthand information (data, ideas, feelings) from the countries in which the cocaine trade takes place enables the participants to make use of real-world elements. This helps highlight the real situation and how it might develop.

- The participants felt that they were sharing an original and pioneering experience on a continental level. This led to the consolidation in 1993 of the network established in 1991.

- Starting with a proposal from the Costa Rican team (mostly composed of medical and psychology students) to establish horizontal communication systems among prevention-oriented institutions, it was decided by participants to go beyond the simulation to continue using the network to exchange concrete experiences.

- The simulation of events so close to the participants motivated them to continue exchanging their own opinions outside the exercise and also to coordinate non-simulated concrete actions.

- After becoming aware of the capabilities of communication, there was a feeling among participants that the simulation structure was not sufficient to contain what emerges from it.

Expansion and Action

The direct contact with the drug problem, the incentive of communications, and the simulation experience gave rise to initiatives to participate outside the boundaries of the simulation. The drug issue was a very involving one, considering the participants' ages and the context of the world in which they live. Through the exercise, which is oriented toward problem solving, participants felt a desire to continue resolving problems, but on a real-world basis.

This behavior shows the potential of this type of exercise to generate expanded actions that might prove useful for the participating organizations and promoters. A new institutional and telecommunication structure for upcoming exercises is being designed that considers the simulation as a source of this spillover effect. It is characterized as follows:

- Local coordinators and students can act as diffusion agents. They may contact members of OAS regional offices, government agencies, and institutions related to the drug problem and invite them to join the working team in a wider network. Such a network is the exercise's logical result. They may also bring in their colleagues who are interested in the problem.

- Once the enlarged network has been established, a new schedule of simulation-related activities can be planned. These may include distance education, discussions on the feasibility of student proposals, diffusion of CICAD-OAS aims, strategies for action, and dissemination of information. The wider network could be the place for a permanent interest group, acting as a parallel channel during the simulation or where discussions can be generated that surpass the simulation topic and time.

- Encouraging local teams in setting up a wider network would be advantageous not only regarding the diffusion and enrichment of the event, but also regarding the enlargement of possible local, interdisciplinary participation in future exercises.

- A natural complement to this policy would be a common database (e.g., on the international drug control treaties), to which all the participants from any part of the continent would have access. This base can be increased with material from the CICAD-OAS Documentation Center or any of the other invited organizations or by bibliographic and journalistic research carried out by the work teams in different countries.

- Surveys of on-line evaluations to check students' comprehension can be carried out using the simulation network.

- The network could be enhanced through use of new developments on the Internet, such as transmission of audio and images.

From the material entered into the database during the exercise, a face-to-face simulation could be designed, printed, and distributed to be run in high schools and other institutions.

Conclusion

The simulation on control of the supply and demand of cocaine provided many students and institutions with their first experience of the more sophisticated capabilities of the information superhighway. It opened the doors to further creative use of the medium. An additional benefit was dealing with an issue that hit close to home for many of the participants. That aspect drew the students more intensely into the experience and impelled them to think of what they could do, beyond the simulation, to solve the problems caused by the cocaine trade. Future simulation experiences are planned that will make greater use of telecommunications capabilities both within a simulation and in a wider network. The most exciting part of this experience lies in the extension of international networking to local networking. Opportunities are thus created to think globally and act locally.

Note

1. The following facilitators and institutions participated in the two runs of the simulation:

José Benes, Universidad de San José, Costa Rica

Anna Chisman, Inter-American Commission Against Drug Abuse, Organization of American States

Roberta Duran, Pontificia Universidad Católica de Santiago, Chile

Isabelia Leguizamón, Universidad de Los Andes, Bogotá, Colombia

Ana Maria Mesquita, GRA, Faculty of Medicine of the University of São Paulo, Brazil

Natalio Ortiz, Universidad Nacional de Salta—Gendarmería Nacional, Buenos Aires, Argentina

Daisy Pacheco, Universidad Nacional Abierta, Venezuela

Leopoldo Schapira, Universidad de Córdoba, Argentina

Carlos Wendorf, Pontificia Universidad Católica de Lima, Perú

Jonathan Wilkenfeld, Patty Landis, and Arturo Cordero, University of Maryland, United States

Reference

Noel, R. C., Crookall, D., Wilkenfeld, J., & Schapiro, L. (1987). Network gaming: A vehicle for intercultural communication. In D. Crookall, C. S. Greenblat, A. Coote, J. H. G. Klabbers, & D. R. Watson (Eds.), *Simulation-gaming in the late 1980's*. Oxford, UK: Pergamon.

13

Cross-Cultural Communication, the Internet, and Simulation/Gaming

Reports From the Field

JANET SUTHERLAND

DAVID CROOKALL

KIYOSHI ARAI

VALDIS BISTERS

AMPARO GARCIA CARBONELL

JUDY HO

LINDA MAK

PAULA W. SUNDERMAN

FRANCES WATTS

Project IDEALS[1] is the name given to a series of large-scale simulations involving student teams from educational institutions around the world. Two basic types of computer-facilitated simulations have been carried out: large-scale negotiations (SEASIM) and large-scale resource management decision making (COMMONS). The first type, the centerpiece of Project IDEALS, consisted of a six- to seven-week simulation/game, which involved from eight to nearly 30 teams of students in regional and global negotiations, somewhat similar in scope and intent to a Model United Nations (UN). There are two important differences, however, from the Model UN (see Muldoon, in press). Instead of coming together at a single location, as is typical of Model UNs, teams are located in many countries around the world. In the case of Project IDEALS in 1993, these were Australia, Austria, Canada, England, Estonia, Finland, Germany, Hong Kong, Japan, Latvia, The Netherlands, Russia, Spain, and the United States. The teams ranged in age from junior high school through university students to professionals. What once would have been insurmount-

EDITORS' NOTE: This chapter is a revised version of a paper that appeared in the proceedings of ISAGA '93, *Reform and Progress Helped by Simulation and Gaming,* edited by Eduard Rădăceanu and published by IROMA (Bucharest, Romania). We are grateful to the editor for granting permission to adapt this text.

89

able geographic and social distances were made far less problematic through the methodology of Internet simulation/gaming. This chapter provides a brief glimpse of this type of methodology, where content and people are the important elements, brought to life through the media of computer technologies and the Internet, and the methodology of simulation/gaming.

Roles, Organization, and Teamwork

Teams take on one of four basic roles: high-level national delegations, journalists, technical consulting firms, and non-governmental organizations (NGOs), such as environmental advocacy groups (similar to Greenpeace). With guidance from the facilitators, each team then works out an internal organizational structure consistent with its role and with the underlying pedagogical goals of the course. Frances Watts and Amparo Garcia Carbonell worked together, using the following approach, to facilitate an English-for-specific-purposes (ESP) team of telecommunications students from Valencia (Spain):

> We had 26 students whom we divided up initially into six groups. Since we had been having class already for two months, we were able to choose at least eight students whose written English was correct. We chose six as group editors and the remaining two were "roving" editors.
>
>   . . . the extroverted students [were] paired with introverts and strong students with weaker students.
>
>   . . . we tried to put a good speaker in each group, who was not necessarily the editor or best writer. This made for a good representation of the different skills. We also mixed the older students with younger.
>
>   And, last but not least in importance, the female students were mixed with the male students. This had the double effect of more fun and increased participation.

Although in most cases participating teams were formed within already existing courses, there were exceptions that required novel approaches to planning. Janet Sutherland, facilitator of the Regensburg (Germany) team, described one such approach:

> The *Ocean Report* team consisted of students from several different disciplines whose class schedules made it impossible to find a time during the normal teaching day to meet as a traditional class. Our solution combined informal, personal networking, electronic communications (e-mail, local electronic distribution lists and remote log-ins to the school's computers via modem) and informal dinner meetings for group debriefings and strategy sessions.

Despite, or perhaps because of, this non-traditional class configuration, both team members and facilitator reported a much stronger sense of commitment to and identification with the team than is usually the case with elective courses in the German polytechnic system. After the conclusion of the simulation, one student recalled (errors in the original):

> For me the most exciting thing in the simulation was the group dynamics. . . . I remember the time when the first issue had to be published. We sat in the digital lab, Thursday evening, not knowing what to write, how to write, . . . but we managed publishing the issue. Though we were not tightly organised . . . we always published the Ocean Report in due time and managed to take part at the teleconferences. Actually it was a less or more anarchic kind of organisation, where everyone did (wrote) what and when he wants (in most cases one minute before deadline).
>
> Despite of this we were a wonderful group. The result was good, too. Some more technical talented members, continuously improved the electronic environment. If I think of how terrible using POLNET was, at the beginning of the simulation and how comfortable it was at the end, I must say this was good work. Perhaps such kind of success, lead to this group. Or was it a kind of identification with the Ocean Report? Another reason for this group dynamics could be that the simulation has created a base for communication amongst the members. Discussions about events in the IDEALS world took place. There were common made experiences, funny chats at teleconferences, . . . all stuff, about that you can talk.

At least one team consisted entirely of non-students. Valdis Bisters facilitated a group of environmentalists in Riga (Latvia) whose team assignment was to represent an NGO concerned with marine environmental issues. For them, "the simulation was an excellent occasion to get out of [their] own shells and have one common topic to work on":

> We were a group of nine people quite diverse in educational backgrounds and interests age of 25 to 30. You could find physicist, chemist, hydrobiologist, computer designer, biologist, mathematician, economist and two philologists. Our role was very close to one we are trying to do in our centre but we never had such a good chance to work in the process of international negotiations.

Although Project IDEALS scenarios (unlike those of its progenitor, ICONS; see Wilkenfeld & Kaufman, 1993, for a description and Crookall & Landis, 1992, for a comparison) involve hypothetical rather than real countries and organizations, as the preceding comments indicate, role-type assignments tended nevertheless to be very similar to a team's actual interests or national situation. However, this was not always the case. Linda Mak's team at the Chinese University of Hong Kong (CUHK) took on a role in many respects quite unlike its actual situation:

> The CUHK team became Outlanders, people of a small and poor landlocked country, whose main concerns were gaining access to the sea and having a share

in the ocean's resources. . . . They learnt to be independent "delegates" representing Outland, as well as Hong Kong.

Entering into the hypothetical reality, these students found their perceptions of
their real-world classroom roles shifting:

> I find that teacher is not the only source of knowledge. Instead, each classmate has
> an influence on others . . . we can make a progress through mutual sharing and
> support. At first, I wonder why our teacher doesn't . . . try to dominate our dis-
> cussion. . . . We should learn to deal with crisis and make rational decisions in a
> very short time independently.

Another student wrote of a similar shift in perception concerning audience:

> The audience of this project is neither the teacher nor the class-mates. The audience
> is the students overseas. We are doing something important and representing, not
> only Outland, but also the Chinese University of Hong Kong.

Realistic Challenges in a Safe Environment

In the course of the negotiations, teams often have opportunities to think
about problems that have great relevance to their own local, regional, or national
situations. These problems can be safely explored, and strategies and solutions
tried out in a low-risk context, yet the learning that results yields insights that
can be applied to real-world situations. Bisters, for example, reports parallels
between the complexity of the simulation and the range of problems Latvia has
been confronting:

> If we look at the simulation topic and real life here in our region you may find a
> lot of similarities. It is very difficult for small countries just starting to build up
> their economies to deal at the same time with so broad spectrum of economic,
> environmental, and social problems.

Even teams whose simulation roles were far removed from their anticipated
real-world careers reported the simulation's challenges to be realistic and
relevant—and very different from those to which they were accustomed in
traditional classes. A German student noted,

> To be confronted with some kind of "real life" journalistic task was a absolutely
> new experience for me and we tried to take it as a team. I guess we did it not so
> bad, sometimes even surprisingly well. Everybody realised it is much more

difficult to make things better than just to criticise. In every case this was an absolutely new way of learning with others; we have learned a lot about the problem of the seas, international affairs in their difficulty and variety, and last not least about people in other countries and how difficult it is sometimes to communicate above cultural boarders.

Flexibility

The main objectives of Project IDEALS were broad and flexible enough to allow for a wide range of participant and team types, yet precise enough to provide sufficient focus for individual teams. By the third year of the Project, an impressive array of ages, nationalities, and academic disciplines were represented. An idea of the range can be gleaned from a brief list of a few of the participating teams: an Ontario (Canada) high-school class, New York City junior high school classes, a Moscow (Russia) class from the Institute of Electronic Machine Building (third- and fourth-year undergraduate and graduate students), an honors class in international relations in the Department of Political Science at the University of Louisville in Kentucky, a group of professional environmentalists affiliated with the University of Riga (Latvia), EFL (English as a Foreign Language) students from Asia, Europe, and South America, and a master's-degree class in environmental sciences at Brown University in Providence, Rhode Island.

On the face of it, so much diversity might appear overwhelming, but in practice, the (democratizing) nature of computer-mediated communication, which eliminates all visual cues as to age, background and status, meant that teams were perceived exclusively through their written words. In this electronically-mediated world, college-age students who otherwise might never deign to speak to (let alone listen to!) junior high students are able to be impressed by the quality of their performance—so much so that even when confronted with the facts, they at first refused to believe that the writers were 13-year-olds. Clearly, such feedback has positive effects on both sides, boosting the younger students' self-esteem and challenging the older students' preconceived notions of what constitutes competence and credibility.

Interdisciplinary Learning

The ultimate goal of each simulation/gaming was for teams to formulate and agree on policy related to some regional or global concern. They might, for example, have negotiated the text of a treaty governing the emission of CFCs, the use of the ocean's resources, or the future of Antarctica. The discussion and debate are carried on both locally and internationally, with students examining the technological, economic, social, cultural, and ethical dimensions of their and other teams' positions. Watts and Garcia (Spain) reports that the interdisciplinary nature of the simulation/gaming

> was very stimulating for the students. Not that they jumped for joy about the topic at first, though. Most knew nothing whatsoever about International Law or the Law of the Sea. But they come from a country that has kilometers and kilometers of coastline and they were vaguely familiar with the fishing quota problems that Spain has had with its neighboring countries of France and Morocco. They learned the definitions of the new concepts quite easily: Territorial sea, exclusive economic zone, deep sea mining, seabed exploitation, the right of innocent passage and so on.

Combining Content- and Skills-Based Learning

Students gained practice in working together as a team, in speaking and writing skills, in decision making and problem solving, in taking individual and team initiative and responsibility, and in interdisciplinary thinking. They gained an understanding of global issues, of other cultural perspectives, and of their own individual and culturally-influenced learning styles. The broad range of content- and skills-based learning that is possible within the framework of a large-scale Internet-based simulation/game such as Project IDEALS allowed individual learners and facilitators to focus on very different aspects without compromising the collective goals.

Students were encouraged and motivated to become fully involved, to work hard, and to take responsibility for their own learning. Project IDEALS avoids rote memorization and student dependence, concentrating instead on the professional, social, and ethical dimensions underlying the subject matter and the learning process. It thus constitutes an effective medium for the acquisition of the process-oriented kinds of international and work-related skills and orientations that are increasingly being demanded of our students. The overall effect is that students gain a measure of power over their own learning destinies and take advantage of a unique opportunity for learning from each other. This is true whether the main disciplinary focus of the host course is language, economics, history, or international relations.

Language Skills

Traditional language learning materials are based on a native/non-native paradigm; in other words, students are non-native speakers exposed to and expected to learn standard, native speaker rules, vocabulary, and usage patterns (primarily British or American English). This approach ignores the fact that, for the vast majority of English speakers worldwide, English is not their first language. Project IDEALS exposes both native and non-native speakers of the language to a much more realistic language panorama.

For some, particularly those in Asian and East European countries, participating in Project IDEALS provided the first opportunity to communicate directly with native speakers of English. Kiyoshi Arai (Japan) reported that most of his students in Japan had never had a chance to talk to foreigners. Moreover, students do not have incentives to learn English in ordinary life.

Both the language of diplomacy affected by some native-speaker teams and the student slang used in some informal communications bore little resemblance to the varieties of English found in most language textbooks. Non-native speakers are thus challenged and motivated to reach beyond their current skill levels to understand what is being said. On the other hand, native speakers who take for granted their ability to communicate in the language are challenged to formulate their messages in a way that takes into account a non-native-speaker audience. Students see the value of being able to communicate effectively because their audience is no longer limited to the teacher who reads their assignments.

Learner Responsibility

Another team in Hong Kong, facilitated by Judy Ho, went a long way toward learning how to learn and toward taking responsibility for their own learning. In a culture deeply rooted in the Chinese tradition of seeing oneself as a part of a relational hierarchy, classroom roles are marked by respect for authority and for the teacher as the authority figure. The Chinese preoccupation with *mien-tzu,* or face (the concern for protecting the other's self-image and feelings and for avoiding direct confrontation when communicating with another person), also affects classroom behavior. Chinese students have a great respect for and wish to maintain their teacher's mien-tzu, and the teacher is reluctant to admit any inadequacies on his/her part. However, taking responsibility for one's learning often requires that students work independently of the teacher; it may also entail shared decision making, even presenting opinions that differ from those of the teacher. Chinese students find situations that require these kinds of behaviors both emotionally and intellectually distressing.

Project IDEALS presented teams and facilitators with many opportunities to learn to take responsibility for learning. The first step was the students' own decision to take part, which meant thinking about their learning needs, interests, and abilities. During the simulation, students took responsibility for organizing their country and for representing its interests to the rest of the participants.

They decided on a form of government and on what ministries would be the most important and relevant for the type of country they represented, and they set goals and made policy. Moreover, the students took responsibility for learning and using the skills needed to complete the simulation task, including language, contingency planning, and conflict resolution skills.

Two characteristics of simulations encouraged the students to take responsibility for their learning. First, simulations are by nature unpredictable. There was no way in which the project director, let alone the local facilitators, could predict the course of the negotiations or their outcome. This eroded the sense of security to which Chinese students traditionally cling. Moreover, keeping pace with the number of messages from the telecommunications network and the rate at which they arrived required students to exercise their own discretion and to negotiate with other participants as fully responsible state officials.

Second, simulations require problem sharing among learners and between learners and teachers. The technical breakdowns that occurred in the course of the simulation were a prime example of this. In a sense, they tore apart the mien-tzu of the teacher, who was unable to prevent them. This, in turn, allowed the teacher to initiate a change in the teacher-student relationship by admitting that he/she could do nothing and in fact was in the same boat as the participants. However, because this occurred within the relatively less threatening context of the simulation, it was easier (than in more threatening traditional classrooms) for both the teacher and the learners to redefine the role of the teacher, a redefinition that was then carried over into non-simulation situations.

Although some traditional Chinese values discourage autonomy and individual responsibility, the simulation experience showed that certain others tend to enhance them, especially achievement orientation and emphasis on the cohesiveness of the in-group. Such factors impel participants to take responsibility for their sovereign country, to make autonomous decisions, and to act upon them with a force and conviction that would not be conceivable in an ordinary classroom. As Ho and Crookall (in press) reported,

> Through Project IDEALS, our students took part in an important and memorable experience. They were keenly aware of dealing with people from other cultures; they became critical thinkers; they learned to argue intelligently and to write effectively; they worked collaboratively with others; they made informed decisions. Not least of all, underlying these more practical pursuits, they rose to the challenge and opportunity of taking greater responsibility for their own learning. In addition, they shared in each other's learning; thus while they became autonomous from the teacher, they maintained the important social and collaborative aspect of the learning enterprise. Despite cultural constraints, the simulation project enabled them to develop certain knowledge, skills, and attitudes which are characteristic of learner autonomy.

Multi-Cultural Learning

One of the primary aims of Project IDEALS was to bring together students from different backgrounds within a nonthreatening, experiential learning environment where they could work in close-knit teams and share their diverse cultural perspectives on international issues and situations. Thus, teams composed primarily of American students ideally included international students. A German-based team included a student from Ghana, two from Great Britain, and, initially, two from Romania. Such multicultural teams gave students an opportunity to observe and reflect on their own as well as their teammates' interaction styles and ways of responding in a variety of situations. The following comment is taken from the journal of a Japanese student on a team at a U.S. university, who wrote this third-person narration of his own experiences (errors in the original):

> Furthermore, American way of listening the class surprised and discouraged him. He found that American students had no hesitation to interrupt the speaker and talk instead. In his culture, people try to listen to what the spokesperson is saying. Then he or she provides a rebuttal if the person has. Therefore, he was really afraid of being stopped in his rare, miserable speech in the middle; as a result, he had kept silence. However, he also found that this cultural difference was caused by the grammatical difference, that is, his language had a verb, which is the most important parts of the sentence, at the end, whereas, English has a verb next to the subject, which always comes beginning part of the sentence. Therefore, American students can guess and cut other's speech in the middle. On the other hand, people in his culture have to wait to see whether the speaker will do or won't do. These are his own interpretation toward American behaviors. In addition, he sometimes become disgusted with American students' strong opinions. The native students can show very strong opinions that will probably take more than hundreds years for him to say the same things. Since his culture doesn't allow people to give harsh ideas, he was not used to doing so and had kept silence in the class. . . . His listening ability has been getting better than before.

Arai (Japan), reported similar observations among his students:

> Japanese students thought that foreign students seemed not to have difficulty expressing their opinions. On the other hand, the Japanese have a tendency to listen first and respond to the other's opinions. Some Japanese students said that the Western way of expressing themselves sometimes looked egocentric.

In general, students tended to respond to the multi-cultural dimensions of the simulation/game in ways consistent with their nation's real-world geopolitical position and their own cultural paradigms. Thus Asian- and European-based teams speculated on whether the arrogance displayed by a U.S.-based team representing a newly wealthy, petroleum-producing country was real or put on (i.e., acted out because it was prescribed in the profile of the country the team represented). Such speculation suggests a high degree of congruence between the behavior of the team in question and the stereotypes of Americans held by many outside the United States. That students could move from certainty to speculation and questioning represents a significant move toward under-standing and acceptance of cultural differences.

Within individual teams as well, international students tended to comment on cultural differences more frequently than those operating within their own cultural context. Yet many students were reluctant to initiate conversations that might be interpreted as intrusive with students from other cultures and even other disciplines. However, facilitators who showed respect, acceptance, and an interest in learning about others' views were able to encourage similar positive attitudes and behaviors on the part of their students. Thus, a Ghanaian business student on a Germany-based team composed mainly of mathematics and com-puter science students was able to enrich his team's experience by providing information about Ghanaian culture and about his experiences living and studying in Germany as well as by sharing his interpretations of the IDEALS interactions. The value of such exchanges in a country with social tensions such as those Germany is currently experiencing can scarcely be overestimated, but they are also beneficial in cross-disciplinary courses in settings where students do not normally share classrooms with students from other majors—a common occurrence outside the United States (where the liberal arts tradition means undergraduate students regularly encounter students from outside their own disciplines). As one German student observed,

> At the beginning of the simulation program I was rather sceptical. . . . I couldn't imagine that this accumulation of people, none having ever worked on editorial things, should be a unit delivering a newspaper. Regarding the simulation project I was positively surprised there were participants from Estonia representing "Balancia" and even kids at the age of 12 or 14 (Waterwatch), playing a quite good role. Looking on the progress of the simulation I never thought that all participants could reach in such a treaty, as there resulted in the end, because till the last two/three weeks there had been such huge differences among the participating countries, so that I hadn't believed they could come together.

Another student on the same team reported,

> First of all the ideals project has trained my English capabilities. But this was just a side effect. Moreover it was a excellent exercise for teamwork and cooperation.

I found it really interesting how we organised ourselves at the beginning and how it worked afterwards.

Conclusion: A Brand New World

We conclude with the words of a Chinese student in Paula Sunderman's class at Mississippi State University. Her entries in her journal illustrate the richness of this kind of learning:

March 1992: They used slang, which I was not clear about, but I could sense the meaning. Sometimes I had to ask my American classmates for help. I am learning.

March 27, 1992: At last, I got the opportunity to experience the teleconference. I was excited and nervous, as if I would have to type all the response to the computer. Though I did not speak much, my mind worked very fast with those proposals. Economic zone, sea straits . . . those strange concepts were becoming familiar to me. I still had disagreement with others of my classmates: I preferred to sacrifice, that is, we give something. But they said we had nothing to give. Well . . .

April 3, 1992: After watching the film about Hong Kong, I sent a relatively long message to the class through e-mail. I like to share my culture with my classmates. I am glad to see that most of my classmates are interested in other cultures. I talked to my husband that I was getting more and more interested in different cultures, that I was thinking about finding a job related to cross cultures. From this Language and Culture class, I have learned to judge the world from all sides.

April 24, 1992: While I was filling in the questionnaire, I was thinking what I had learned from this simulation. . . . I felt that I had benefitted more than others, because it was easy for me, a foreign student, to experience different culture in a foreign culture. I have observed how the American students deal with negotiations, how they work with people, and what their attitudes are toward benefits.

April 29, 1992: The most precious fruit I have got from this Language and Culture class is that I have been led into a brand new world, the world of different cultures, which, hopefully, will affect my future career.

Note

1. The full name of Project IDEALS is Project for an International Dimension in Education via Active Learning and Simulation. The project received major funding from the U.S. Department of Education's FIPSE (Fund for the Improvement of Postsecondary Education). The project's director and principal investigator was David Crookall.

References

Crookall, D., & Landis, P. (1992). Global network simulation: An environment for global awareness. In D. Crookall & K. Arai (Eds.), *Global interdependence: Simulation and gaming perspectives* (pp. 106-111). Tokyo: Springer-Verlag.

Ho, J., & Crookall, D. (in press). Breaking with Chinese cultural traditions: Learner autonomy in English language teaching. *System: An International Journal of Educational Technology and Applied Linguistics.*

Muldoon, J. (in press). The Model United Nations revisited. *Simulation & Gaming: An International Journal, 26*(1).

Wilkenfeld, J., & Kaufman, J. (1993). Network simulation in international politics. *Social Science Computer Review, 11*(4), 464-467.

PART II

Policy Exercises

14

Policy Simulation and Crisis Management

The Harsh Winter Scenario

DANIEL G. ANDRIESSEN

In a joint effort, the Dutch Ministry of Home Affairs and KPMG Management Consultants used policy simulations to help develop and apply crisis scenarios. To clarify this use of policy simulations I would like to explain something about crisis management in The Netherlands. Then I will describe the purpose of crisis scenarios and the use of policy simulations in developing and applying them. To illustrate this I will give a brief description of the first scenario that was developed and of its results. This description is based on an evaluation of the simulation performed by Jaap van Lakerveld of the University of Leiden.

Crisis Management and Policy Simulations

Crises

A crisis can be described as a serious disruption of the basic structures, or an impairment of the fundamental values and standards of a social system (KPMG, p. 9). In this definition the word crisis exceeds incidents, accidents, major accidents and disasters. A disaster often involves a large-scale physical accident as a result of which people have to be rescued, fires extinguished and goods protected. Crises are worse; they are a disruption of basic social structures. Some crises start with physical accidents; for example the explosion at the nuclear plant in Chernobyl. Others do not result from disasters; for instance a growing stream of refugees can cause a major political, financial or social crisis.

The following are all crises that struck Dutch society during the past 2 years. Some of them were a result of disasters; others were minor disturbances that grew into major problems within several months. All of them called for effective and coordinated crisis management by the Dutch government at a local and national level:

- On September 17, 1992, a 14-year-old boy in Streefkerk, The Netherlands, developed the symptoms of polio. This was the beginning of an epidemic that lasted several months during which 68 people contracted the disease, two of whom died.
- On October 4, 1992, a Boeing 747-200 cargo aircraft crashed into a block of flats in a suburb of Amsterdam, killing 43 people and destroying hundreds of homes. Two weeks after this disaster the crisis started when thousands of illegal aliens tried to be officially recognized as victims of the disaster.
- In 1993, an average of 3,000 refugees entered the The Netherlands each month, and this number is still growing.

Crisis Management at a National Level

Crisis management can be described as "the entire set of measures taken and provisions made by the public authorities jointly with other organisations with a view to (acute) emergency situations in order to guarantee public safety in a broad sense" (KPMG, 1992, p. 11).[1] Crisis management can take place at all levels of government—from the commander of the local fire brigade on up to a crisis cabinet under authority of the prime minister. Because the situation in a crisis is more severe, crisis management is not the same as disaster relief, although disaster relief can be part of crisis management. One cannot prepare oneself for every aspect of a crisis. It is typical for a crisis that things happen that could not be predicted. Of course, one can make sure that all sorts of operational tasks that have to do with disaster relief (e.g., evacuation, firefighting, etc.) are well drilled, but one cannot prepare or drill oneself for the administrative and political aspects of a crisis.

Since the mid-1980s, the focus of crisis management in the Netherlands has shifted. Due to rapid international political developments the focus is no longer on civil defense in case of a military crisis. Instead, it is the government's view that special wartime provisions should also be used when dealing with the consequences of emergency situations and disasters in peacetime. The shift was made from a threat-oriented crisis policy (namely, war) to a policy based on the protection of vital interests and functions.

The civil defense structure within the central government was abolished. Instead, the assumption was established that each ministry has its own responsibility for including crisis management in its overall policy. This means that each ministry has one or more core activities in its portfolio and is responsible for the crisis management activities related to the core activities it represents. This has resulted in three complications:

- Crises tend to break through the barriers of ministerial autonomies. A crisis is rarely limited to one core activity only and hence will demand the involvement of various ministries, services, and organizations. This calls for coordination.
- The subject of crisis management is not very popular. It tends to be pushed aside constantly by day-to-day worries. With government budget under pressure, crisis management is a popular field for budget cuts.
- With the civil defense structure removed, there was no formal structure left to stimulate crisis awareness and enforce precautionary measures.

The Ministry of Home Affairs is responsible for the coordination of crisis management policy between the ministries. With the official civil defense structure removed, this type of horizontal coordination calls for "soft" coordinating tools, like creating the right conditions and stimulating enthusiasm. The Ministry wanted to increase the crisis awareness of its own civil servants and of those of the other ministries.

We decided to use scenarios and policy simulations as one of the tools to do so. Crisis scenarios and emergency exercises are very well known in the field of emergency management. The use of a policy simulation to create crisis management policy and to stimulate crisis awareness is new.

Crisis Management, Scenarios, and Policy Simulations

A scenario is the description of a hypothetical future situation. It shows in a plausible manner how, departing from the current situation, a future situation may develop. The objective of a scenario is not to predict the future; the prophetic value of a scenario is irrelevant. Many people tend to think in terms of probabilities when dealing with scenarios. This is dangerous, especially in the case of crisis management, because many of the biggest crises in the world were also the least imaginable.

Scenarios are an instrument for so-called learning organizations to gain insight into the possible effects of a changing environment on the organization. They are most commonly used as a tool for strategic management (see de Gues,

1988; Wack, 1985a, 1985b) or as a screenplay in an emergency management exercise. In crisis management, scenarios can be of use in several ways:

- They are an incentive for policymakers to give some thought to crises and increase crisis awareness.
- Scenarios encourage us to be fully aware of surprises; they are creative triggers to break through existing ways of thinking and to have assumptions re-discussed.
- By using scenarios, one can obtain a feeling for conditions that have to be met to make something happen.
- Scenarios are a tool to evoke a dialogue between actors.
- By developing several scenarios, one can develop mental flexibility.

Policy simulations are a powerful way to work with scenarios. Most policy simulations use some sort of scenario as a screenplay. It is less commonly known that policy simulations are also a helpful tool for the development of scenarios. This dual purpose of policy simulations makes them perfect instruments for crisis management policy.

Policy Simulations to Develop Scenarios

Crisis scenarios used for crisis management at a national level must have special characteristics:

- They must focus on the administrative and political aspects of a crisis, as opposed to the operational aspects.
- Because coordination is essential in crisis management, the crisis scenarios should cover problems that are the responsibility of more than one ministry.
- There is no one best way to cope with a major national crisis. The reactions of key actors such as ministries, the National Crisis Centre, and the local authorities are unpredictable, as are especially the political aspects of a crisis. This makes it impossible to develop a screenplay that covers all possible events. The scenario therefore must be very flexible.

To develop scenarios like these, we used a policy simulation to test a first draft of the scenario. The use of a policy simulation in this process is summarized in Figure 14.1.

Policy Simulations to Apply Scenarios

Once a scenario is developed, the next step is to apply it in such a way that the objectives are achieved. As stated before, several objectives are possible.

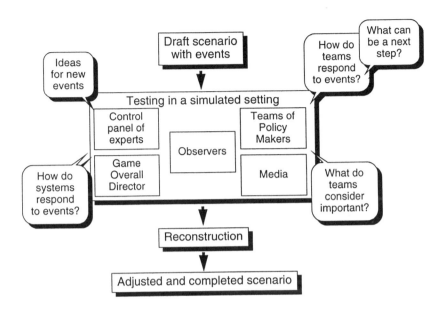

Figure 14.1   A policy simulation.

The use of a scenario in the form of a policy simulation is especially suited to accomplish the following objectives:

- Increase crisis awareness. A policy simulation that is set up as a realistic version of an actual crisis situation is a very powerful tool for increasing crisis awareness.
- Evoke a dialogue between actors. When the subject of the scenario is about a crisis concerning two or more ministries, the dialogue and the need for coordination can be central themes in the policy simulation; the consequences of a lack of coordination can be made visible.
- Provide insight into what may happen, which issues need attention when a crisis develops, and which information is important. When a team of experts is used to comment on the actions of the players and to give incentives, policy simulation can provide insight into what may happen when a real crisis occurs. This means the simulation is used as a research tool.
- Stimulate the ability to improvise. When the clock is ticking, the participants have to improvise to get the job done within the time limit.

This way of using a policy simulation is summarized in Figure 14.2.

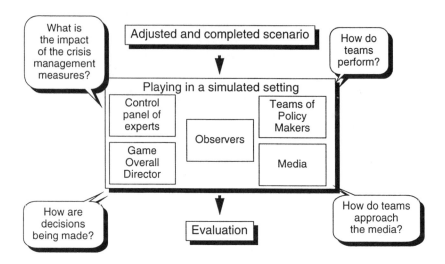

Figure 14.2 Structure of the scenario.

The Harsh Winter Scenario

The first scenario we developed featured a period of extremely cold weather. The development of this "harsh winter scenario" included a large-scale policy simulation.

Scenario

The basis for the scenario was written by the Royal Dutch Meteorological Institute and consisted of 11 weather forecasts (Figure 14.3). There were four phases in the scenario. During the first week (Phase 0), the temperature fell below 0° Celsius, but no problems arose yet. Phase 1 named Snow was characterized by heavy snowfall and blizzards. The main problem was transportation. In Phase 2, named Ice, there was a period of extremely low temperatures. The main problem was a possible shortage of natural gas. Phase 3, named Glazed Frost, was a period with rainfall, storms, and a temperature of around 0°, causing glazed frost. As a result, the electricity in large parts of the country failed.

Setting

There were four teams from four different ministries: Home Affairs, Transport and Public Works, Economic Affairs, and Welfare, Health and Culture. They consisted of heads of divisions with two or three subordinates. Each team had an official ministry communication manager and its own office.

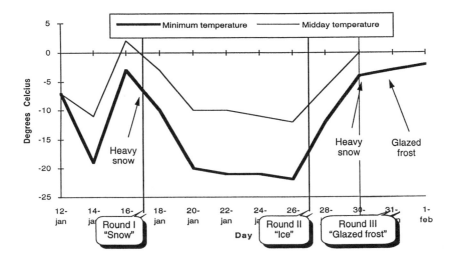

Figure 14.3 Phases in the scenario.

A control panel consisted of 12 experts in the field of energy, health, welfare, crisis management, transportation, and industry. The control room had three tasks:

- Simulate the outside world
- Answer questions from the teams regarding the situation in the world
- Give their opinion on actions taken by the teams

Two journalists played the role of the media. They did interviews on television and aired news items on the radio. Every team office had one observer. Finally, there was a game overall director, or facilitator, and his staff. About 50 participants were involved, and each had a separate meeting room.

Communication

Several means of communication were available to the simulation participants. There was a closed video circuit with monitors in every room. This was used in Rounds 1 and 2 to play videotapes showing the situation in the world and to broadcast interviews by journalists with spokesmen and experts. In Round 3 it was used for radio broadcasting because everyone was too busy to watch the television. Every half hour there was a special news bulletin regarding the situation in the world.

At the beginning of each round, a newspaper was distributed that contained a collection of news items about the situation. These simulated newspapers were inspired by news articles from cold winters in the past.

In each room, several telephones and fax machines were available. Team players were able to telephone other teams, "the outside world" (played by the control panel), the game facilitator, and the real world (for instance, their own department). Finally, there was a mail delivery system between all meeting rooms.

Session

The simulation took one full day and was divided into three rounds. In the first two rounds, the level of interaction between the teams and the control panel was limited and the game time was halted. These two rounds served as warm-ups for Round 3, where there was full interaction for 2.5 hours during which three days of the scenario were simulated.

An important task for the facilitator was to get the people in the right mood at the beginning of the simulation. Therefore, he played a video about Phase 0, which gave a journalist's impression of the harsh situation in Europe. Then the teams went into their own meeting rooms, where a second video was played describing the situation in Phase 1 on the simulated date of January 17, 1995.

In Round 1, the players had to answer questions asked by their minister and faxes containing cries of distress sent by interest groups. Some of the problems they had to deal with were the following:

- A train carrying chlorine was stranded in a suburb; the mayor demanded that it be removed.
- Public transport stopped completely.
- Three people were killed when a snowplow ran into a car; operators then refused to work because they feared being held responsible.
- The Dutch Islands were short of food and fuel.
- Hospitals were hard to reach; patients had to be transported by air.

During this round, game time was held up. The teams had one hour to answer faxes and questions. At the end of Round 1, each communication manager was interviewed about the situation on a closed video circuit, and three experts from the control room commented via video on the performance of the teams.

Between Rounds 1 and 2 there was a ten-day time leap in the scenario. Round 2 started with the situation on January 27, 1995, and had the same structure as Round 1. Some of the problems the teams had to deal with were the following:

- There was a very strong rumor that there was not enough natural gas; as this is the main heating fuel in the Netherlands for 95% of the households, this would be a very serious problem.
- Walls of ice forming in the sea threatened to crush the Dutch dikes.

- The national airport had a shortage of kerosene.
- Several homeless people froze to death.

At the beginning of Round 3 the game time was set to the morning of January 30, 1995. Every half hour in real time was equal to half a day in the scenario. Round 3 began with more questions from ministries and interest groups. From this point, the control panel started to intervene by sending messages to the teams. Some of these messages were prepared up front and were part of the draft scenario. The control panel had the freedom to invent new messages but only if they thought they were realistic. All the messages sent were registered, and the situation in the world at that moment was recorded on eight large flipcharts. The responses to these inputs came back to the control room by mail, telephone, or fax and this would then result in new messages by the control room. Some of the problems forming part of the scenario were the following:

- Electricity failed in the south of the Netherlands as a result of glazed frost.
- The Dutch Islands were short of food and fuel.
- In northern Netherlands, skating fanatics were planning the traditional *Elfstedentocht* (11-city skating tour).
- Several locks in waterways were threatened by ice.

Some of the problems created by the control panel were the following:

- A multiresistant bacteria spread throughout several hospitals.
- Because of thawing in Belgium and Germany, the water level of the Dutch rivers was rising rapidly.
- Transportation of containers from the harbor into the mainland was immobilized.
- There was a shortage of oil at the generating stations.

Results

As this simulation was the first of its kind, the Ministry of Home Affairs developed a broad evaluation scheme that asked three questions:

- A reconstruction of the day: What happened exactly?
- An inquiry into the opinions of the players: What did they think about the simulation?
- An evaluation of the way the scenario and the simulation were designed: Is this a good method to develop and use in crisis scenarios?

We will use the reconstruction of the day to adjust and complete the scenario. The simulation generated new ideas for events that could happen and gave information about things that go wrong and about important aspects of this sort of crisis.

The players were very enthusiastic about the simulation. They were positive about the insight the simulation had given them into the possible threats of a harsh winter. They also gained insight into the tasks and responsibilities of the different actors in a crisis. The simulation was a realistic portrayal of a possible future situation with individual and collective learning results. The players thought it would be useful for them and for others to carry out this sort of simulation again in the future. It clearly increased the crisis awareness of these policymakers.

The structure of the simulation was not perfect. In Round 3, the pace was too fast and the interactions were too complex. There was not enough time for the players to reflect on their actions. Therefore, the educational value of the simulation was not as high as it could have been. The construction and evaluation of the simulation could have been more focused and more efficient if we had pursued fewer goals. A complete reconstruction of events would have been less necessary.

Conclusion

Policy simulations are a powerful new tool in crisis management. They are useful in developing crisis scenarios and a good way to confront policymakers with crisis scenarios. They help increase crisis awareness, make the need for coordination visible, and generate information about what may happen, which issues need attention when a crisis develops, and which information is important.

Note

1. This definition was based on the definition used by Rosenthal (1989).

References

de Geus, A. P. (1988, March-April). Planning as learning. *Harvard Business Review*.
KPMG Management Consultants. (1992). *Crisis management: Handling the unexpected, the unknown and the undesired*. The Hague: Author.
Rosenthal, U. (1989). *Coping with crises: The management of disasters, riots and terrorism*. Leiden: University of Leiden Press.
Wack, P. (1985a, Sept.-Oct.). Scenarios: Uncharted waters ahead. *Harvard Business Review*.
Wack, P. (1985b, Nov.-Dec.). Scenarios: Shooting the rapids. *Harvard Business Review*.

15

A Policy Exercise for the Dutch
Health Care System for the Elderly

CISCA JOLDERSMA

JAC L. GEURTS

JULIETTE VERMAAS

GERTON HEYNE

In the Dutch health care system, a number of profound changes are taking place. Relations between parties in the field of health care are becoming less regulated by government intervention and more dependent on market forces. To survive in this new structure of health care, actors must alter their strategies. A policy exercise (PE) is a useful tool for learning to deal with such a situation (see Geurts, 1993). Toth (1988) defines a PE as a

> deliberate procedure in which goals and objectives are systematically clarified and strategic alternatives are invented and evaluated in terms of the values at stake. The exercise is a preparatory activity for effective participation in official decisions. (p. 237)

A PE offers a set of players in a policy network the possibility of exploring structural changes and finding ways to react to these changes.

In this chapter, a PE is described involving a gaming/simulation of chronic health care of the elderly in a Dutch region from 1990 to 2000. The game, called DIAGNOST, elaborates on a previously developed health care gaming/simulation (see Wenzler, Duke, Geurts, & Lugt, 1994). In contrast to the closed character of this earlier game, the underlying idea of DIAGNOST was that a gaming/simulation with an open, free-form structure should be developed. The driving force for developing an open game was a health-care PE previously developed in Great Britain (Office for Public Management, 1993).

The chapter first traces the effects of the gaming/simulation DIAGNOST and then discusses the open structure of the game. Prior to this discussion, background information is given about forthcoming developments in care of the elderly. These developments are then related to the objectives of DIAGNOST and to the game design. After a description of a game run, the results of the game are evaluated. Finally, some critical observations concerning the structure of DIAGNOST are formulated.

Background of the Problem

By establishing the Dekker Commission in 1986 the Dutch government began to develop a new structure for health care. In a new structure, direct negotiations between health-care providers and insurers will take place, and these negotiations will be accompanied by fewer government rules. The new structure of the health care system will introduce more elements of a market economy and is intended to stimulate the market parties to grow toward more entrepreneurship.

An important trend in chronic care of the elderly is an increasing growth of demand for care. The type of demand is also changing; elderly people want to live as long as possible in their own homes. The Dutch government has stated that it wishes chronic care of the elderly, more than previously, to be regarded as an integral regional chain of care in which several organizations provide related forms of care to the target group. Proper care provision along the complete chain is the collective responsibility of all parties.

Objectives of DIAGNOST

The aim of DIAGNOST is to provide administrators and other professionals in health care with a motivating learning and discussion environment. The objective is to bring about the following changes in their perspectives and behavior:

- Gain insight into the consequences of a changing health-care system and changing demand for elderly care
- Learn to behave more like entrepreneurs
- Learn to cooperate more with the chain of care
- Evaluate strategic options both from the perspective of the individual organization and from the perspective of the complete chain

These cognitive and behavioral objectives can be translated into two policy problems that managers in health care have to solve: an allocation problem and a co-operation problem (see Figure 15.1).

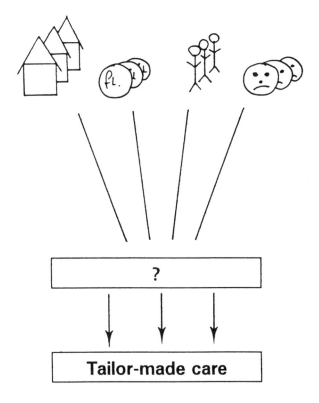

A: Allocation Problem

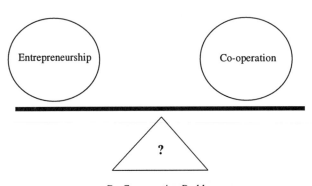

B: Co-operation Problem

Figure 15.1 Allocation and co-operation problems.

Managers in a deregulated health care chain face the problem of arriving at tailor-made care (see Figure 15.1a). Because of deregulation, an optimal allocation of funds, personnel, and infrastructure has to result from direct communication and negotiation between the regional providers and the financing institutions themselves. The parties in the chain are forced to develop new practices and policies that the old regulated system did not allow or did not implement.

In relation to the first problem, managers have to find a balance between individual entrepreneurship, on the one hand, and co-operation in the chain, on the other (see Figure 15.1b). The answers found to this second question will dictate the future styles of policy making in the field of elderly care.

The Relation Between
Design Criterion and Game Structure

Simulations are usually closed in the sense that the game designers' assumptions about how the world works structure the elements of the game. A game is often about playing against the rules; players test their understanding of the game designers' assumptions (Office for Public Management, 1993).

For strategic policy exercises, a rigid game structure has certain disadvantages. In a previously developed health care gaming/simulation, the game was structured toward one scenario of the future. The actions that participants could carry out were limited by the content and structure of the game (Wenzler et al., 1994). In our view, in a strategic policy exercise the participants must play with the rules. It should be possible for players to both generate and renegotiate the rules that govern organizational relationships in order to identify a range of possible futures (Office for Public Management, 1993).

In DIAGNOST, players have to generate futures themselves by negotiating and bargaining. Deregulation typically means that the dynamics of the new interactions are unpredictible. More than one scenario of the future is possible, and at present no one seems to know which scenario is most likely to be adopted in each of the very different care regions in the Netherlands. Therefore, a gaming/simulation with an open structure seemed the most appropriate for DIAGNOST.

The Game Design of DIAGNOST

Design Process

In broad terms, the design process of a game involves two activities: system analysis and game construction. The outcomes of the system analysis are the building blocks for the construction of the game.

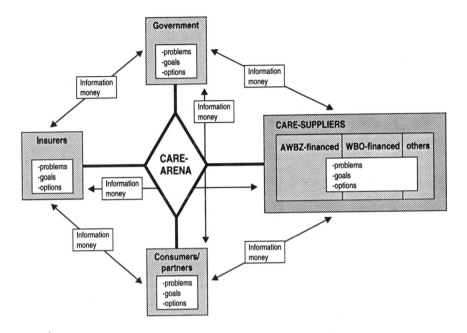

Figure 15.2   Schematic of DIAGNOST.

The design process of DIAGNOST basically followed the design steps described by Duke (1974). The DIAGNOST project was started in January 1993, and the system analysis was completed in October 1993. Members of the board of the client for DIAGNOST, the SWOOG[1], functioned as the steering committee of the project. The system analysis took place in intensive dialogue with this committee, in order to ensure validity and legitimacy of the end result (see Geurts & Vennix, 1989). The literature and documents were also reviewed. Figure 15.2 shows a simplified version of a result of the system analysis: the final schematic (Heyne, Vermaas, Wüstefeld, Joldersma, & Geurts, 1994a). The schematic portrays the most important stakeholders, including their positions and responsibilities. The relationships between the various actors are also shown.

Next, the analysis of the system was translated into a game on paper (Heyne et al., 1994b). After approval of the concept game by the steering committee, the project team went further with the development of the actual game and the construction of a prototype. In February 1994, this prototype was tested, and in March the second test run took place. The first official run took place on March 31, 1994.

TABLE 15.1 Suppliers, Their Products, and Their Financiers

Organization	Product	Financed by	Financer
Rest home (3)	Care, intramural	WBO[a]	Provincial government
Home care organization (1)	Care, extramural	AWBZ[b]	Insurer
Nursing home (3)	Nursing, intramural	AWBZ	Insurer
Home nursing organization (1)	Nursing, extramural	AWBZ	Insurer

NOTES: ( ) = organizations in the game; active participants in the game: 26.
a. WBO = Law on Rest Homes.
b. AWBZ = General Law on Special Medical Expenses.

Scenario and Roles

In the simulation, a fictitious country and a fictitious region are brought to life. The data are derived from a real region in the Netherlands. Players are responsible for provision and execution of chronic care for the elderly. The roles played by the participants are those of providers and financiers of care, such as the AWBZ[2] (see Table 15.1).

Table 15.1 shows that each provider delivers one product only. The most important political event is the announced abolition of the WBO.[3] This means that the local government will no longer be given a budget to finance WBO institutions (i.e., rest homes).

The consumers of care are included in the game because of their demand for elderly care. During the game, demand for intramural care decreases, and new products—semimural care and semimural nursing—rise in demand. The role of consumers is also simulated by the Assessment Committee, which consists of a group of experts in the field who give their opinion on the decisions taken by the participants. Other roles, such as the national government and general hospitals, can be played by the game operator.

Problem Structuring and Steps of Play

In the game, decisions regarding allocation and co-operation problems are made in primary and secondary processes. These processes and the steps of play are shown in Figure 15.3.

In the primary process of care delivery, suppliers of care negotiate budgets with financiers. The subjects under discussion are the kind of services that providers want to deliver, the volume of these services, and the number of staff required. Furthermore, providers of care have the option to cooperate and/or merge with each other. The outcomes of the negotiations are quantitatively assessed by two criteria: the ratio of staff hours per unit of service and the length of the waiting list for elderly care.

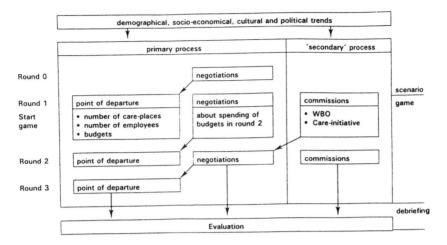

Figure 15.3   The steps of play in DIAGNOST.

In the secondary process, the participants take part in several policy work-shops set up by the government. In these groups, the players debate current policy issues such as the integration of entrepreneurship and co-operation in the chain.

As Figure 15.3 shows, the primary and secondary processes take place at the same time. In Round 1, the game structure defines the steps of play. After making an internal analysis of their own organization, participants have to take part in the financial negotiations and the policy committees. The negotiations and their implications as well as the findings of the committees are discussed and assessed.

In view of the changing relationships, the existing co-operative structures of Round 1 might be ineffective. This is why a new co-operative structure (and thus a new sequence of game steps) is allowed to emerge in Round 2. The participants may change the steps of the second game cycle.

The option of changing the steps of play makes the game more open to the actions and ideas of the participants. It gives the game a strategic character. The open strategic character is also guaranteed by the introduction of policy work-shops. The committee work connects the negotiations with the actual situation in the regions that the participants are from. In the committee meetings, participants can discuss new policy options for the problems of allocation and co-operation. These new options can be explored in the interaction between providers and financiers. The committees in the game contribute to a "reflection in action" (Schön, 1983). Furthermore, actors can discuss, within the safe environment of the game, the real situation in their home regions. The growing importance of the committees in the game contributes to a gradual move from budget negotiations in a simulated region to discussions of the actual situation.

DIAGNOST: Results and Evaluation

In this section, the results of the first run of DIAGNOST are analyzed. First, the findings are summarized, and then the evaluation by participants is reviewed. Finally, the resultant policy options are discussed.

The Premiere

A group of 30 people took part in the first official run of DIAGNOST, which lasted about 12 hours. The roles of care providers, care insurers, and local government were performed by directors and officials of real institutions in the Dutch province of North Brabant. Board members of SWOOG took seats on the Assessment Committee.

The game started with an introduction to the background and procedures of the game. Following the steps of play, the participants prepared their strategies. Each provider not only wanted to continue the present product but also intended to broaden the line of supply. All of the suppliers did, indeed, begin to cooperate with former competitors. Financial negotiations resulted in a greater supply of care but at the expense of quality of care. In the policy workshops, attention was given to cost control. One policy option that emerged from these committees was a redefinition of care in such a way that it included only chronic care and excluded living and house keeping components.

For the second round, the participants were allowed to adapt the steps of play. In contrast to the first round, the suppliers decided to prepare joint strategies for each health care cluster (rest homes, nursing homes, home organizations). Instead of negotiations with government and insurer separately, final negotiations were combined into one formal meeting. For the region as a whole, financial negotiations in the second cycle of the game resulted in less quantity but better quality of care. The rest homes were transformed into nursing homes and institutions for semi-mural care. In the plenary discussion, it was concluded that negotiations were dominated by the insurer, who used a more or less dictatorial style of decision making. The evaluation ended with a discussion on the real health care situation in the Netherlands.

Evaluation of the Game by Participants

Participants were asked to give their general impression of DIAGNOST. Descriptors included the following: very well put together, informative, enlightening, eye-opener, refreshing, good tool for getting the regional co-operation

TABLE 15.2 Partial Evaluation Results

	Yes	*To Some Degree*	Hardly	No
The simulation				
• makes clear that players are in thought and deed dependent on each other	22	3		
• has increased my insight into issues, strategies, and ideas	16	6	3	
• makes clear that development of a common vision is important	24	1		
• has increased my insight into anticipated developments	9	10	6	
• has demonstrated that an entreprenurial attitude is essential	18	7		
• is an adequate representation of reality	13	9		3
• has provided options that are valuable in actual policy making	12	10	1	1

process going, and exceptional model for prior testing of proposed policy consequences. The most important criticism of the simulation was directed toward the intense time pressure under which the participants had to work.

Participants were also questioned about the central problem of entrepreneurship versus co-operative behavior in the chain. Table 15.2 summarizes some of the answers. From these items, it can be concluded that the participants became aware that, in the future, both individual entrepreneurship and co-operation in the chain of care will be essential. Most participants recognized that they lack a common view. Participants changed their perspectives in an expected fashion. Furthermore, the majority of the participants saw the simulation as a valid representation of reality. For some, the simulation also provided a few options for real policy.

Styles of Policy Making

An optimal allocation of elderly care in a deregulated health-care system will require new styles of policy making. These new styles involve the manner in which a balance is found between individual entrepreneurship versus co-operation in the chain of care. To get an impression of these new styles, the interactions between participants were analyzed.

In the policy committee sessions, the participants together explored the concepts of entrepreneurship and co-operation and showed a clear understanding of each other's views and positions. Yet there is a discrepancy between the co-operative attitude in the joint workshops and the hard reality of the negotiations. The negotiations revealed a fierce competition between competitors, and participants did not behave as partners who are each other's complement. Mergers took place to guarantee organizational continuity.

The parties encountered great difficulty in implementing the desired balance between entrepreneurship and co-operation. When negotiations started, individual parties initially appeared to be driven by a desire to co-operate. However, under the pressure of circumstances, the actual compromises were, to a significant degree, dictated by political self-interest and self-defense. Becoming aware of changing trends and relationships in elderly care did not necessarily mean that actors changed their behavior in accordance with these changing circumstances.

With regard to the negotiation results, it can be assumed that a more market-driven health-care system does not automatically solve the allocation problem. No invisible hand can be found that regulates behavior of the participants so as to reach an optimal allocation. In fact, less regulation by the government resulted in more intervention by the insurance organization.

Conclusions

For strategic games such as DIAGNOST, an open structure is necessary. The open nature of DIAGNOST is operationalized through the possibility of changing the steps of play (in the secound round) and the increasing importance of policy committees. Changing the steps of play implies that some rules of the game are open to discussion (Duke, 1980). By introducing policy committees, participants are stimulated to generate new ideas, to reflect on their actions, and to make the connection with reality.

These open characteristics of the game contributed to participants' awareness of changing relationships in the health-care system of the future. The rigid steps of play in the first round stimulated participants to contribute their own framework of reference and experience. However, the second round made them aware that circumstances were changing and that new behavioral attitudes were necessary. The hard reality of the negotiations reminded them of the difficulties of implementing new ideas and new policy options that had been developed by the policy committees.

From the point of view of developing new styles of policy making, the game may not be open enough. The steps of play in the first round stimulated participants to stick to their own framework without taking a regional perspective on care for the elderly. Because the policy committees functioned more or less in isolation from the restricted negotiations between care providers and financiers, only certain real policy options came into view while other relevant ones were excluded.

One reason why only a few policy options came up might be that the game does not offer the participants enough time for experimenting with changing relationships. Had the game been extended to three of four rounds perhaps more relevant policy options would have come into view. Another explanation could be that the negotiation partners do not feel safe enough to change or adapt their behavior. The more realistic (hard, fierce) the negotiations in the game, the more participants will fear that negative consequences from the game will be transferred to the real world. All participants meet each other at regular intervals. It is possible that the game has not been able to create a completely safe environment for experimenting with new policy options.

The game DIAGNOST had two sets of objectives: cognitive and policy oriented. Rigid-rule games are often very appropriate for cognitive purposes. However, if both objectives are combined in one game, one must carefully search for the right mix of closing and opening characteristics. In a PE that stresses the importance of policy formulations and the exploration of shared future visions, discussion must dominate simulation.

Notes

1. The DIAGNOST project is an initiative of the Foundation for the Advancement of University Education and Research in Health Care (SWOOG) and the Tilburg Institute for Academic Studies (TIAS) and was undertaken by Tilburg University and IVA, the Institute for Applied Social Research.

2. The AWBZ (General Law on Special Medical Expenses) has as its goal insuring the population against the risk of special medical expenses. It deals with those medical risks not covered by the National Health Service or regular medical insurance. One can only stay in an AWBZ institution if the institution is acknowledged and if the insured individual has a so-called indication for this particular institution.

3. The WBO (Law on Rest Homes) implies a system of top-down allocation of financial resources, on the basis of which the provinces receive a budget to finance the rest homes, to the degree that the contributions of the inhabitants are not sufficient.

References

Duke, R. D. (1974). *Gaming: The future's language*. New York: Sage/Halsted.

Duke, R. D. (1980). A paradigm for game design. *Simulation & Games: An International Journal, 10,* 364-377.

Geurts, J. (1993). *Omkijken naar de toekomst: Lange termijn verkenningen in beleidsexercities* (Inaugurale rede). Alphen aan de Rijn: Samson H.D. Tjeenk Willink.

Geurts, J., & Vennix, J. (1989). *Verkenningen in beleidsanalyse: Theorie en praktijk van modelbouw en simulatie*. Zeist: Kerckebosch BV.

Heyne, G., Vermaas, J., Wüstefeld, C., Joldersma, F., & Geurts J. (1994a). *Chronische ouderenzorg in Brabant*. Tilburg: Foundation for the Advancement of University Education and Research in Health Care.

Heyne, G., Vermaas, J., Wüstefeld, C., Joldersma, F., & Geurts, J. (1994b). *DIAGNOST: The simulation in concept*. Tilburg: Institute for Applied Social Research.

Office for Public Management. (1993). *Learning from the future*. London: Author.

Schön, D. A. (1983). *The reflective practitioner: How professionals think in action*. New York: Basic Books.

Toth, F. L. (1988). Policy exercises: Objectives and design elements. *Simulation & Games: An International Journal, 19,* 235-255.

Wenzler, I., Duke, R. D., Geurts, J. L., & Lugt, P. (1994). Health care negotiations policy exercise. In F. Percival, S. Lodge, & D. Saunders (Eds.), *The simulation and gaming yearbook 1993* (pp. 275-284). London: Kogan Page.

16

Climate Policy

Management of Organized Complexity Through Gaming

JAN H. G. KLABBERS

ROB J. SWART

AAD P. VAN ULDEN

PIER VELLINGA

Government and industry policy makers and individual consumers base their response to the climate change issue on the balance between three types of considerations: perceived risks of climate change, socio-economic and technological feasibility of response options, and ethical aspects of an equitable distribution of responsibilities among different social actors. Especially in industrialized countries, they are overwhelmed by a profusion of complex and sometimes contradictory information from the scientific community.

Internationally, the Inter-governmental Panel on Climate Change (IPCC) prepares assessments that synthesize, integrate, and evaluate scientific knowledge in support of the policy-making process. Notwithstanding the consensus-building objectives of the Panel, the value-laden debate about the IPCC assessment reports and their policy maker summaries indicates that this is a tricky task (Bolin, 1994).

In the Netherlands, the National Research Programme on Global Air Pollution and Climate Change (NRP) was started in 1990, its main objective being to support scientific research that contributes to the policy debate. In the Netherlands, climate change is an established environmental policy theme, and in the 1990 National Environmental Policy Plan, greenhouse gas emissions targets were formulated. Gradually, it became evident that reaching these targets did not mesh easily with socio-economic objectives. Policy makers addressed the scientific community to gather usable information about the risks and response options related to climate change.

In this context, the NRP sponsored the project Policy Options Addressing Climate Change, aimed at enhancing dialogue between Dutch scientists and policy makers. The objectives of the project were to enhance communication among policy makers, third parties, and scientists; identify and explore the options for furthering Dutch climate policy; and generate a series of research and policy questions for programming purposes.

Managing Organized Complexity

Multiple Reality

Although the greenhouse metaphor originated in the natural sciences, the subsequent linkage of the results of scientific research with policy making implied a broader interpretation of the problems, causes, and options involved. As a consequence, the rationalist approach of the natural sciences is no longer predominant in the debate. Because of the complexity of the problem and the current scientific uncertainties, a variety of competing reality definitions exist that are based on different perceptions and positions of the major policy makers in government, industry, non-governmental organizations, and science. Policy-makers' appreciation of what science can do in such an arena is thus difficult to determine. The perceived controversy about climate change among scientists appears to be the main stumbling block for the general public and for policy makers in deciding on the urgency of measures. Communication between the science and policy communities also needs considerable improvement. Scientists should become more actively involved in the public debate. To balance options, social and technological scientists need to go beyond the stage of writing reports based on analytical studies and become more involved in action research.

Climate Policy and Organized Complexity

Developing an international climate policy while building on national policy perspectives is a tricky endeavor. In the social realm, one of the main characteristics of complexity is the existence of competing frameworks or reality definitions. Plurality of conceptions cannot be resolved by analytical problem solving per se. As a consequence, policy actors, in trying to cope with the problem of climate change and the social problems related to climate change, are dealing with situations where they have a fuzzy idea about what to accomplish and no clear idea about how to accomplish it.

The policy actors involved represent governmental and industrial organizations and institutions that are loosely coupled into networks. Problem solving in such a context involves a set of interactions as a means of finding an outcome that can be considered as moving toward a solution. These interactions constitute forms of organized complexity in which politics, economics, technology, and social choice are entangled. Schwarz and Thompson (1990) argue that these approaches are entangled because they all rely on cognition. In the policy realm, facts and the appreciation of facts cannot be clearly separated. Although societies have to look far into the future to cope with climate change, they must first understand today's problems, which, for several reasons, resist conventional analysis and problem-solving techniques (Kalff, 1989). Strategic problems can be characterized as follows:

- They lack a definite expression. The process of formulation and reformulation will never come to a conclusion.
- The formulation of the issue and the options to solve it are inseparable. Reformulation leads to different options, leading to reformulation of the issue.
- They have no closure. Restructuring the socio-economic system sows the seeds for the next round of restructuring.
- They are interconnected with risks and opportunities in other areas. There are many interrelationships between emissions of greenhouse gases, climate change, and the national economy that mutually influence each other.
- They are dynamic in nature. Each strategic commitment triggers action by stakeholders such as governments and industry, which rapidly renders the original problem formulation obsolete.
- Strategic problems are unique; history provides little guidance. There is no precedent of a long-term problem such as climate change, whereas the dynamics of social change are fluid and impredictable as ever.
- Strategic problems are molded by personal and social factors, loyalties, and interests. This is one of the reasons why the position of the various policy and institutional actors should be made clear.

Epistemology of Organized Complexity: Four Models for Problem Solving

Science so far has offered various forms of support in addressing climate change and climate policy. Paraphrasing Weiss (1977, pp. 11-15), three models for solving the problem of climate change have been widely used:

- The knowledge-driven model, in which "research has thrown up an opportunity that can be capitalized on."
- The decision-driven model, in which scientists respond to a problem largely posed by decision makers.
- The survey model, in which scientists engage in a complex search for opinions and behavior from a variety of sources.

All three models are, according to Lindblom and Cohen (1979), examples of analytical problem solving because they refer to alternative ways of bringing knowledge to bear. They reflect a notion of knowledge that has its origins in the intellectual traditions in science and in the philosophy of science. The more information a person acquires the more knowledgeable the person becomes. In this tradition, knowledge is viewed as a collection of abstract, context-independent concepts, and discrete instances of truths or information. The underlying notion of knowledge puts science in the position of observer (outsider), providing information or truths. This position is built on the belief that science should serve nonpartisan purposes. In organizational networks, however, policy is actually made by interaction among a plurality of partisans (Lindblom & Cohen, 1979). Each participating actor needs information, specialized to his partisan role in it. Knowledge in such a context is produced by meaning processing and by the sharing of interpretive schemata of the people involved; knowledge is a social construction. This type of knowledge is context dependent and not accumulative per se because historical and political conditions change. This implies that the facts and their context change.

Knowledge, according to the post-structuralist perspective, is produced by individuals within the possibilities of their discourse. Knowledge is what they express in discourses. It is action oriented and, in the spirit of Lewis Carroll (1865), based on the following recipe: How can we know what we think until we hear what we say? (see also Weick, 1979). Discourse, according to Foucault (1969/1972), is a system consisting of rules of formation and volitions that control what can be said within a particular field. Within the field of climate science the following discourses, among others, play a role: metereology; physics, chemistry, and biology; and economic, technology, demography, social sciences, and philosophy/ethics. All discourses are operationally closed in the sense that they produce statements that belong to that particular system of rules. The related knowledge is domain specific. As a consequence, each scientific discipline, following its discourse, speaks with a different voice.

Climate policy made by interaction among a plurality of partisans puts climate science in a double role. The first role is that of provider of information and truths within a specific discourse. The second, through (institutional) interactions with policy actors, is the role of fellow partisans jointly constituting the policy development process. Here the sciences play the role of insider/participant. The first role covers the three models for problem solving mentioned above. The second role requires another model, one based on notions of the learning organization (Senge, 1990). Policy, as a way of problem solving viewed in this way, is continuously aiming at enhancing the capacities of the learning organization. The building blocks are circular interactions among the participating actors.

This introduces the fourth model of climate change problem solving: the interaction/participative model, in which scientists develop the right conditions for interactions among actors/partisans by constituting adequate learning environments to enhance joint capacities. This interaction model and the related self-organizing learning environment have been used for framing the workshops described below.

Managing Organized Complexity
Through Free-Form Games

Several workshops were set up as free-form games; these are appropriate self-organizing learning environments (Klabbers, in press). During the subsequent workshops, participants received the rough material from previous activities in the form of questions, position papers, statements, or drafts of policy options. Participants were put in open-ended situations and were asked "What will you do? How will you handle this information?" Playing free-form games allows one to understand better the preoccupations of the policy actors while they emerge during the processing of meaning. Shubik (1983) suggests that the value of a free-form game may be closely related to the expertise and sophistication of both the players and the referees.

The workshops questioned the assumptions on which the situated knowledge of decision makers and researchers was based (Klabbers, in press). They helped in further articulating climate policy and climate science in a continuous process of reframing the issue of climate change. Free-form gaming provided a means for managing the complex process of developing five policy options.

The Project

Design

During the project, four consecutive workshops were set up in line with the ideas of the fourth model of problem solving. The three other models of problem solving were taken into account when appropriate. The coupling of the workshops was based on the macrocycle of policy-oriented research. In this macrocycle, five basic functions of scientific knowledge construction and knowledge utilization can be identified (see Figure 16.1):

- Formulation of goals; problem identification; formulation of the issue.
- Development of methods: development of explicit procedures for constructing knowledge for surveying the field.
- Science production: providing inputs to planning and decision-making processes.
- Science linking: coupling of research to intended users, leading to changing perceptions.
- Science utilization: information feedback to adjust goals and interventions.

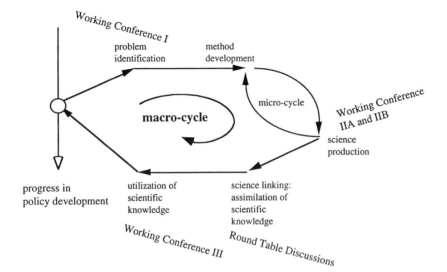

Figure 16.1 Macrocycle of policy-oriented research.

Figure 16.2 sketches the flow of activities in the project during the period April-November 1993.

Results, Their Context, and Interpretation

Results

The following five policy options were produced:

- No-regrets—a valuable policy even without climate change.
- Least-regrets—no-regrets plus anticipatory policy to cope with risks.
- Acceleration—accelerating (enhancing) forces within society to address and solve existing problems toward sustainable development via the right timing of policy measures.
- Technological innovation—technology as the single opportunity to balance societal needs with the carrying capacity of the natural environment.
- Institutional-cultural change—social, cultural, and institutional changes ultimately needed for sustainable development..

The detailed descriptions of each policy option, including plans of action and communication plans, are presented in Klabbers, Vellinga, Janssen, Swart, and Van Ulden (1994a, 1994b).

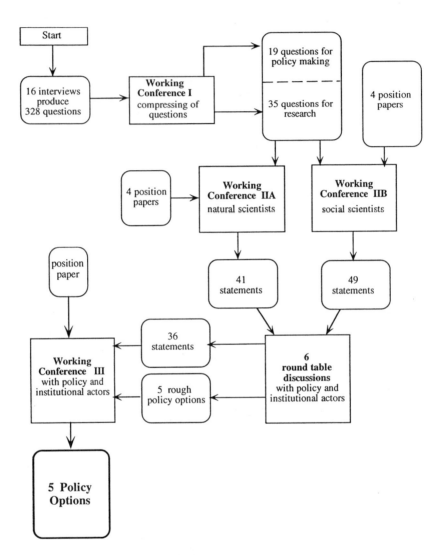

Figure 16.2   Flow chart of project.

Context

Step 1: Identification of the Problem of Climate Change

Instead of letting scientists define their own questions, key policy makers were interviewed at the start of the project and asked to identify the most important questions that they expected to be addressed by the scientific community. These policy makers included representatives from government, industry, environmental non-governmental organizations (NGOs), labor unions, and political parties. In a two-day working conference, a long list of questions abstracted from the interviews was revised and compressed into a more concise list. A two-step procedure was followed during the working conference, applying a gaming technique with "snowcards" (small cards colored to subject, each containing one question). Notwithstanding the consensus among Dutch climate policy makers negotiated during the National Environmental Policy Planning process, it appeared that participants' different perspectives on climate change were very closely related to their direct interests in the outcome of the policy debate.

The following four phases were distinguished (Klabbers, 1982, 1985; Mitchell, 1980):

- *Articulation:* Small leading groups in society encourage awareness in society. As a response, group building within major interest groups takes place. Science supports the conceptualization of the problem. The natural sciences have contrib-.uted considerably to the articulation phase by drawing attention to the greenhouse effect and its relationships with climate change and sustainable development. They have played a key role in conceptualizing the issue and in stimulating group-building processes within major (Dutch) interest groups.
- *Aggregation:* Coalitions are built among interest groups and policies are developed. The role of science shifts toward problem solving.
- *Allocation:* Public administration facilities are set up; budgets are defined and allocated; policies are implemented. Scientific assessments support actors to comply with the policy measures.
- *Review:* Policies are evaluated and fine-tuned. Science can help with performance evaluation.

Each phase of the policy cycle, coupled to the macro-cycle of policy-oriented research, requires different types of scientific support (Klabbers, 1985).

It became evident from the interviews that different types of policy makers could be associated with different phases in the above cycle. For example, some had not yet accepted climate change as a problem, and some were reluctant to take appropriate action, even if climate change was a problem. Many others were receptive, that is, promoting actions as a precautionary measure, while still others already had preconceived notions about the necessity of certain measures.

Some leading-edge companies and industry sectors showed a reactive response, defensively conforming to governmental environmental policy measures. This observation is in agreement with the findings of Winsemius and Guntram (1991). Other actors showed a receptive response, using their existing production configurations to meet criteria set by the government. Some showed a constructive response, accepting responsibility for their product or service. A few, such as environmental government institutions and non-governmental organizations, presented themselves as proactive, internalizing the environmental challenge as an element of quality management. Policy makers, who were still in the articulation phase, easily formed coalitions with third parties that showed a reactive response.

Step 2: Analyzing Research Questions

In the next phase of the project, all questions resulting from Workshop 1 were submitted to two selected groups of experts from the natural and social sciences, respectively. The basic question presented to the natural scientists was "Does the greenhouse effect exist, and if so, what are the risks?" The main concern put to the social scientists was "If climate change is a real danger, how can we cope with it from socio-economic, technological, and behavioral perspectives?" In addition to the questions from the first workshop, concise position papers, consisting of pertinent statements concerning the key questions of Step 1, were prepared by researchers before the meeting.

The different scientific discourses (mentioned above) had to be made explicit in the natural sciences workshop before the conversation became productive. A major issue during the discussion was popularity of traditional, mechanistic, and deterministic problem-solving techniques. It was concluded that, because of the poor predictability of (regional) climatic changes, the problem would be better approached using risk management. Consequently, the discussion focused on the shared certainties and uncertainties concerning climate change.

The clearly divergent interpretive schemata, based on different discourses, was one of the main reasons for initial problems in the dialogue in the social sciences workshop. Initially, the social scientists were unable to handle their own diversity in scientific cultures. They then agreed to discuss the assumptions underlying the statements expressed in their position papers and those communicated by the natural scientists. The debate followed from this.

In the end, a strong consensus for each disciplinary field emerged. From each distinct disciplinary perspective the problem of climate change appeared to be solvable on condition that the other disciplines would be successful in delivering their part of the solution. The real problem lay in the interactions between the disciplinary approaches.

Step 3: Enhancing the Dialogue

In the third step of the project, the results of the scientific assessment were fed back to the policy makers and third parties, grouped in roundtables. The participants were representatives of ministries, industry, transport and agricultural organizations, political parties, labor unions, environmental groups, and consumer organizations. Their response included a cautious exploration of policy options to take into account the scientific understanding of the problem of climate change and sustainable development. Some actors expressed their disagreement with the scientific statements. Lively debates helped divergent positions to converge.

Step 4: Exploring Policy Options

During the third working conference, policy makers and third parties jointly explored five options for pursuing a national climate policy. During the first day of the conference, the dialogue about scientific issues was stimulated and structured through POGE (Policy Options Addressing the Greenhouse Effect), a game developed by the project specifically for this purpose. The frame was adapted from Greenblat and Duke (1979). During the second part of this conference, a free-form gaming approach was used for each of the five options. As this working conference was problem driven and action oriented, emphasis was placed on mutual understanding and a shared will to bring forward viable options. The participants combined knowledge and experience in efforts to bring forward viable policy options.

Interpretation: Ordering Policy Options

The policy context of each of the five options is different. Therefore, each option should be understood as being supported by a particular coalition of policy makers and third parties. The time dependency and pervasiveness of each option is different. To combine them into an overall and comprehensive policy, the project team suggested combining them into time-dependent frameworks as shown in Figures 16.3 and 16.4.

Conclusions and Recommendations

The project has produced two types of results. The first included the policy options produced together with the related actions; the second, and probably more important, type of result is the process itself. There was an improvement in the communication and discussion among all the actors involved, which, over the longer term, could lead to a more solid foundation for action. Gaming has been shown to be an adequate approach to supporting both types of results.

The project does make clear that intensive communication among scientists of different disciplines and between scientists and decision makers can enhance mutual understanding and can support the appreciation of risks posed by climate change without falling into the trap of polarized debate. Also, it was found that the contribution of the scientific community and government policy makers to the development of a climate change policy is very important, but limited if other social interests and knowledge are not brought into the debate, notably through industrial and non-governmental organizations. Only then will the risks of climate change be managed adequately. The interaction/participative model of problem solving has demonstrated that this is a productive way to proceed in the climate change debate.

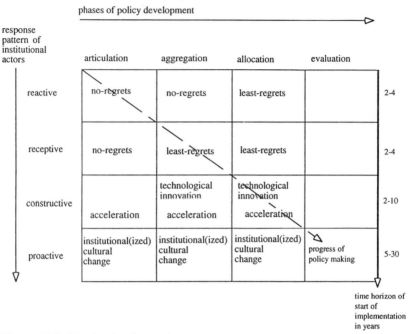

Figure 16.3 Matrix of policy options.

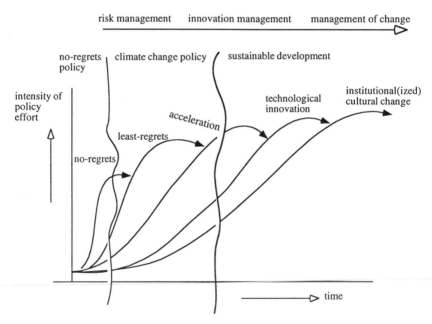

Figure 16.4 Overall strategy in relation to policy options.

References

Bolin, B. (1994). Next step for climate-change analysis. *Nature, 368,* 94.

Carroll, L. (1865). *Alice in wonderland.* London: Macmillan.

Foucault, M. (1972). *The archeology of knowledge and the discourse on language* (A. M. Sheridan Smith, Trans.). New York: Pantheon. (Original work published 1969)

Greenblat, C. S., & Duke, R. D. (1979). *Game-generating games.* London: Sage.

Kalff, D. J. A. (1989). Strategic decision making and simulation in Shell. In J. H. G. Klabbers, W. J. Scheper, C. A. T. Takkenberg, & D. Crookall (Eds.), *Simulation-gaming: On the improvement of competence in dealing with complexity, uncertainty and value conflicts.* Oxford, UK: Pergamon.

Klabbers, J. H. G. (1982). Futures research and public policy making: A context of use for systems theory and gaming. In D. B. P. Kallen, G. B. Kosse, H. C. Wagenaar, J. J. J. Kloprogge, & M. Vorbeck (Eds.), *Social science research and public policy making.* Windsor: NFER-Nelson.

Klabbers, J. H. G. (1985). Instruments for planning and policy formation: Some methodological considerations. *Simulation & Games: An International Journal, 16,* 135-160.

Klabbers, J. H. G. (in press). Problem framing through gaming: Learning to manage complexity, uncertainty and value adjustments. *Simulation & Gaming: An International Journal.*

Klabbers, J. H. G., Vellinga, P., Janssen, R., Swart, R. J., & Van Ulden, A. P. (1994a). *NRP project "Policy Options Addressing Climate Change": Reports of Working Conferences I, IIA and IIB, and III* (in Dutch). Bilthoven: NRP-RIVM.

Klabbers, J. H. G., Vellinga, P., Janssen, R., Swart, R. J., & Van Ulden, A. P. (1994b). *NRP project "Policy Options Addressing Climate Change": Executive summary.* Bilthoven: NRP-RIVM.

Lindblom, C. E., & Cohen, D. K. (1979). *Usable knowledge.* New Haven, CT: Yale University Press.

Mitchell, D. E. (1980). Social science impact on legislative decision making: Process and substance. *Educational Researcher, 9*(10).

Schwarz, M., & Thompson, M. (1990). *Divided we stand.* New York: Harvester Wheatsheaf.

Senge, P. M. (1990). *The fifth discipline.* London: Doubleday Currency.

Shubik, M. (1983). Gaming: A state-of-the-art survey. In I. Ståhl (Ed.), *Operational gaming.* Oxford, UK: Pergamon.

Weick, K. E. (1979). *The social psychology of organizing.* London: Addison-Wesley.

Weiss, C. H. (1977). *Using social research in public policy making.* Lexington, MA: D. C. Heath.

Winsemius, P., & Guntram, U. (1991). *Responding to the environmental challenge.* Amsterdam: McKinsey.

17

Simulation/Gaming for Long-Term Policy Problems

FERENC L. TOTH

Few issues raise as many big questions and as many big research budgets as the issue of global climate change. Thanks to an increasing fear of global warming and its possibly catastrophic impacts, atmospheric scientists are finally able to raise funds to clarify important issues of global bio-geochemical cycles of basic elements, and oceanographers receive support to explore fundamental problems of thermal circulation. We see a proliferation in projections of long-term global energy use. Despite the relative shortage of funds for impact assessments, the scientific community appears to be optimistic about our ability to improve our understanding of the multitude of social and environmental components involved in global environmental change.

In contrast, the policy community is much less optimistic about its own ability to find the right answer to the questions raised by the risks involved in global change. From the management perspective, there seem to be many more questions than answers: How is the climate likely to change, and how will it affect people's lives? How much would it cost us to slow or prevent these changes? Is it worth it to try? In recent years, representatives of the simulation/gaming community have joined those trying to sort out these vital questions.

This chapter was inspired by several games and simulations that address long-term problems like global climate change. As these problems climb ever higher on the social agenda, the number of games intended to shed light on them from an educational or management perspective is increasing.

Long-Term Management Problems

Looking at the games addressing long-term problems, we find two main types. Type 1 concerns slowly evolving systems with reasonably well-known characteristics, like a resource management game. Here the system itself is

$$\text{I} \longrightarrow \text{D}_1 \longrightarrow \text{U}_1 \longrightarrow \text{D}_2 \longrightarrow \text{U}_2 \longrightarrow \cdots$$

Figure 17.1 Sequential decision model.

evolving slowly, yet players get back a fairly immediate response. Thus, the response of the system to players' actions and decisions will be visible in one or two decision cycles. Some uncertainties arise, as, for example, in the case of a fishery management game, but they do not dominate the management problem and thus the gaming problem. For these systems, the gaming procedure depicted in Figure 17.1 seems to be appropriate. Here we have an initial state of the system (I) followed by a decision cycle (D_1), then an update of the system (U_1) by a simple calculus rule or a more complex computer model. Then a new decision cycle (D_2) is started based on this new, updated state of the world. Examples of games using this type of procedure are STRATEGEM (Meadows, Biesiot, & Geerts, 1986) and FISH BANKS, LTD. (Meadows, Fiddaman, & Shannon, 1989).

The situation is completely different with a slowly evolving system with a high degree of uncertainty or outright ignorance that can be expected to be resolved in the future. The system is evolving slowly, and this is combined with significant inertia due to irreversibilities both in the natural system and on the part of management. The issue of global climate change provides examples for both. By emitting carbon dioxide (CO_2) in the atmosphere, we face an irreversible problem, at least in the short to medium term, as it will stay there for 100 to 150 years. Similarly, if we invest and install technologies to reduce CO_2 emissions at substantial costs, these technologies are expected to operate over 20 to 50 years, and it would be difficult or impossible to recover the invested capital once it has been committed, even if it turns out that the risk of climate change has been exaggerated. The catch of the inertia problem in a gaming situation is that players can do whatever they want and yet the system will evolve along its long-term path as determined by its initially inherited starting point and the nonrecoverable historical emissions. An example is the GLOBAL WARMING GAME by de Vries, Fiddaman, and Janssen (1993).

The key issue for these games is ignorance and the resolution of at least some uncertainties in the future. Following the procedure in Figure 17.1, when we take the present as the initial state, players make decisions today, then the world is updated based on these decisions, although, as we have seen, their action will make little difference in the outcome of the system's update. It is simply unrealistic to assume that when players have to make decisions in the subsequent rounds that are assumed to take place 10, 20, or 30 years in the future, they still have to rely on the same knowledge base that was built into the initial conditions reflecting state-of-the-art knowledge of the time when the game was

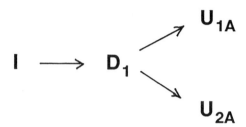

Figure 17.2   Decision model with learning.

constructed. We can safely assume that at least some uncertainties will be resolved over the next decade; therefore, the same policy makers whose decision dilemmas are modeled in these games will be in a different situation because of their increased knowledge. Therefore, for the second type of long-term problems characterized by significant uncertainties that might be realistically expected to reduce over time, the sequential decision model is not appropriate for gaming.

At this point, it is worth taking a step back and asking what the real question is in managing these Type 2 problems. There is a common misunderstanding, even among those who are involved in climate policy or any aspect of the global warming issue. The root of the problem is that when an expert report or a computer model suggests some kind of action today (regardless whether it is ambitious or modest) it is often taken as the policy recommendation for the next 100 years. In contrast, the real question for today is what should the policy be so as to enable us to position ourselves to revise our policy 5, 10, 20 years from now when at least part of the uncertainties will be resolved. This makes a huge difference in real-life policy making. Consequently, it must be represented in the games as well.

Improved Design

The previous section concluded that the learning element must be represented in the game design. Inclusion of the learning process in the game is illustrated in Figure 17.2. Here we start from an initial state representing current knowledge and the best available information (I), and run through the decision process. In the update, one would develop a new current state, the projected long-term future based on the players' decisions and based on the new knowledge that is expected to become available about the fate of greenhouse gases (GHGs) in the atmosphere, about regional and global climate change, and about its impacts. This new knowledge is, of course, hypothetical knowledge. It reflects what we assume today we could or might know 10 years from now.

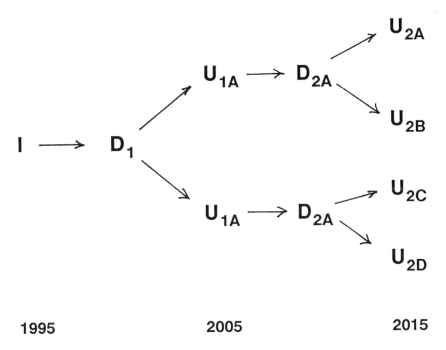

Figure 17.3 Possible game design including the learning process.

One possible way to implement this learning process in a game is presented in Figure 17.3. Here we assume that the game starts in 1995 and play the first decision round in that year. In the first update for 2005, in addition to user-provided strategies and their consequences, the game designers can inject their own or their clients' assumptions about the future. In U_{1A}, the assumption is that climate change turns out to be a big problem by 2005: big changes, fast changes, serious impacts. At the other extreme, in U_{1B} climate change turns out to be a small problem: The system will change slowly, changes will be moderate, and there will be only minor impacts.

At this update, this information would go back to the players for their next decision round. The new update might produce variations around four major cases: U_{2A}, U_{2B}, U_{2C}, and U_{2D}. It is probably not worth pushing the game any further along the time horizon. However, it is certainly useful to make several iterations and explore the various paths along the major branches of this decision tree.

Under this design, the game would involve several iterations to explore medium-term implications of our short-term actions instead of playing one full cycle from 1990 through 2100 in 10-year steps. Besides being unrealistic, by ignoring the learning component this type of design runs the risk of players realizing that, irrespective of their action, nothing happens in the first 4-5 cycles, with the result that they get bored and lose interest. This would undermine the teaching value of the whole exercise.

In contrast, repeated iterations over the first few decades would generate a large amount of self-created material on various branches of the decision/event tree that could be usefully analyzed, compared, and evaluated in the debriefing. This design represents real policy dilemmas of today's decision makers more realistically than does pushing the game through a 100-year time horizon. The teaching value about allocating resources into various activities, like GHG emission reductions, adaptation measures, technological development to support either, or more intensive research "to buy future information" on any aspect of the global warming issue is likely to be much higher. Analyzing the costs and benefits of various near-term strategies would help players explore and select the best strategies for today to be in the best position ten years from now when we expect to have more information available about the greenhouse problem.

The key issue here is policy making under uncertainty and with the potential for learning. The design outlined above seems to be more appropriate than the myopic sequential decision-making design. It could also help participants explore relative merits and shortcomings of the precautionary position versus the risk-management and insurance-based approaches to climate policy. Those advocating a precautionary strategy basically argue that nothing should be done unless no harm is proven. Whereas, the risk analytical approach says that we should consider global warming as an insurance problem: We buy insurance by making some initial investments so as to be in a good position for future decision points.

The proposed game design might also help participants understand the conservative versus possibilist positions. The conservative position maintains that climate change will be fast and within a few decades we can expect climates unprecedented in the history of human civilization, and this must be prevented at any price. At the other extreme, advocates of the possibilist position say that society will be able to adapt to climate change easily and that therefore the huge investments to drastically reduce emissions and significantly slow climate change are simply not justified.

The result of such a gaming design is expected to improve the educational value of the game; it will be a more interesting game and will also provide a much better understanding of the decision problem itself.

Possible Models to Draw on in Game Design

An increasing number of integrated climate-economy models is becoming available. Therefore, one would not even need to start from scratch to build a global warming game along the above design principles. Some of these integrated models explicitly include the learning process that might help game development.

The pioneering work in the field of climate economics is DICE (Dynamic Integrated Model of Climate and the Economy; Nordhaus, 1994). Given the extremely long time lags between GHG emissions and their economic impacts, the concept and models of optimal growth offer a convenient framework for analysis. Nordhaus took the model version formulated by Frank Ramsey in 1928 and extended it to include both impacts of anthropogenic climate change and the allocation of resources to reduce those emissions.

The optimization criterion in DICE is to maximize the discounted sum of the utility of per capita consumption, that is, the value of a traditional social welfare function. Paths of optimal growth affected by climate change are diverted from the unconstrained optimal path as a result of losses in output due to global warming and diverting resources to reduce emissions. Output is computed from a standard, constant-return-to-scale Cobb-Douglas production function. Together with the output of goods and services, GHG emissions are also generated according to a slowly declining emissions/output ratio.

A small set of equations traces the fate of GHG emissions in the atmosphere. First, their accumulation and transportation is determined. Then, their total radiative forcing and the climate dynamics are calculated by using a simple, three-layer reduced-form, coupled atmosphere-ocean model. The resulting globally and seasonally averaged temperature change drives a quadratic damage function to feed back climate impacts to the production function. Similar single-region, sectorally aggregated global models were formulated by Fankhauser (in press) and Maddison (1994).

A cost-benefit framework, developed by Peck and Teisberg (in press), was used to explore the relationship between the value of information about impacts and damages, and the optimal time path for emission control. Peck and Teisberg investigate the sensitivity of optimal carbon control strategies to parameters of their Carbon Emission Trajectory Assessment (CETA) Model (see Peck & Teisberg, 1992). The model has five modules. Emission projections and cost calculations are based on the Global 2100 model. Impact and damage assessments are treated similarly to DICE (see above).

Peck and Teisberg (1992) found that even modest learning rates tend to reduce the expected value of perfect information, which is defined as the difference between the net present value of expected consumption less damage if emission control can be completely based on the state of nature and the same figure under uncertainty and non-state-dependent controls. Moreover, rapid learning biases move CO_2 control levels downward but do not eliminate the desirability of some control.

Recent concerns about the possibility of abrupt climate change raises the question of possible thresholds in the climate system beyond which anthropogenic forcing might trigger unforeseeable changes. We do not know where those thresholds are, but some consider this an additional argument for undertaking immediate and drastic action to reduce GHG emissions. Therefore, it seems to be important to include this problem in operational games addressing global warming in order to compare the costs of early versus delayed actions with what they would buy in terms of long-term concentrations and temperature changes with a view to the possibility of abrupt climatic change.

Hammit, Lempert, and Schlesinger (1992) developed a two-stage decision model to explore the effects of uncertainty about the damages of climate change on how ambitious near-term GHG abatement strategy should be. They analyze two near-term (ten years) abatement policies: a moderate one with low emissions reduction involving energy conservation alone, and an aggressive strategy involving both energy conservation and switching to nonfossil fuels. Their model also includes the learning element; they assume resolution of uncertainty by the second decision point.

Recently, they extended their analysis (Lempert, Schlesinger, & Hammit, in press) to include the case of the potential impact of abrupt climate changes on the relative merits of the moderate and aggressive abatement policies. This required changes in the treatment of individual GHGs in their model. The conclusion from the modified model is that, although abrupt changes tend to increase the long-term costs of responding to climate change, they do not significantly affect the validity of earlier conclusions drawn from the smooth climate change case. That is, the cost difference is insensitive to the selection between moderate and aggressive abatement policies in the near term.

Another critical problem in the climate risk issue and its management is the irreversibility characterizing both anthropogenic emissions of most GHGs and investments to abate those emissions. The irreversibility problem is compounded by the facts that we have learned a lot over the past two decades and that we expect to learn a lot more over the next two about both the biogeophysical and the socio-economic aspects of climate change. Therefore, it may be worth waiting a little longer for better information before committing substantial irreversible investments in capital assets and infrastructure with long-life horizons. Incidentally, one important piece of information learned relatively recently is related to the irreversibility problem per se. If the CO_2 lifetime in the atmosphere is between 50 and 100 years, then its emission irreversibility is getting very close to that of committing fixed assets that are important in emissions or abatement.

Lempert et al. (in press) model the learning process using exogenously specified dates of when uncertainties are resolved. Kolstad's (1994) model includes a dynamic learning process. His study is based on an extended version of the DICE model and covers two basic processes considered irreversible over a reasonable time horizon. These processes have been mentioned earlier as particularly important to include in a global warming game: emissions (because CO_2 remains in the atmosphere for a long period) and mitigation investments (which are practically lost if they turn out to be unnecessary after they have been committed). Kolstad's results provide interesting insights into how relative time paths of the learning process and major emission reduction commitments might influence the magnitude of economic losses from overaction versus inaction. These results could usefully serve as a basis for calibrating a greenhouse game developed along the Type 2 design.

Another major issue in the management of global environmental risks like climate change is how to engage all nations, or at least a critical group contributing the bulk of GHG emissions, in a worldwide emission control scheme. This issue should also be considered when we design a teaching- or policy-oriented global warming game. Nations are likely to investigate their own cost-benefit ratios carefully before engaging in expensive commitments, although the ultimate decision will probably be motivated by other factors as well. Some politicians seem to have a ready answer to the who-bears-the-costs question by counseling that the rich (countries) must pay. In a new two-region version of CETA, Peck and Teisberg (in press) analyze the rich world (OECD) versus the poor world (rest of the world, or ROW) dilemma under three GHG control strategies that the OECD could adopt: emission controls to offset their own warming damages, emission controls to balance global damages, and side payments from OECD to ROW to participate in a globally optimal, emissions control policy. In contrast to Nordhaus's original version and to Kolstad's, Peck and Teisberg adopt a cubic damage function in their analysis. Whereas damages associated with a 3 C global warming amount to 2% of the global/regional output, they increase to 16% for a 6 C warming. Not surprising, there are dramatic differences in carbon tax and carbon emission paths, as well as in the welfare implications of various strategies. This stresses the importance of devising global control strategies that can achieve the greatest reductions at the minimum costs.

Summary and Conclusions

The discussion that followed my presentation at ISAGA '94 showed that many game designers face the problems of system inertia and learning when developing games to address policy problems involving long time horizons, system inertia, uncertainties, and the possibility of learning. Commentators mentioned technological development as another important example of slowly evolving systems that are difficult to model and game in an attractive fashion.

These problems can also be characterized as the myopia versus clairvoyance dilemma. Games based on systems dynamics models are typically myopic. Players make their decisions and the model is activated to compute the new state of the world. Players receive results of the update and make the next decision cycle, but they are not provided a long-term outlook of how the system would evolve as a result of what they are doing. Perhaps their decisions would be the same even if they knew the long-term consequences. However, this then would be a different story.

At the other extreme are economic models that involve perfect foresight and try to define the optimal path for 50 to 100 years based on this perfect foresight. An optimal path for a carbon tax would only be possible if one has good assumptions about the availability and price of carbon-free backstop technologies and other exogenous factors. Clairvoyance is not a realistic assumption either, but it helps players explore alternative futures based on their own strategies and different assumptions about the behavior of the system they learn to manage.

What game designers have not yet sufficiently explored is a broader issue. Behind all these modeling/simulations approaches, there are paradigms with sometimes completely different philosophical worldviews. In the case of systems dynamics, for example, one looks at the world as a mechanism that evolves along the path determined by its own internal rules. Introducing management and especially learning in these models is difficult, but necessary to make these games more realistic and more instructive for players.

References

de Vries, H. J. M., Fiddaman, T., & Janssen, R. (1993). *Outline for a global environmental strategic planning exercise* (GESPE project). Bilthoven: RIVM.

Fankhauser, S. (in press). Evaluating the social costs of greenhouse gas emissions. *Energy Policy.*

Hammit, J. K., Lempert, R. J., & Schlesinger, M. E. (1992). A sequential decision strategy for abating climate change. *Nature, 357,* 315-318.

Kolstad, C. D. (1994). Mitigating climate change impacts: The conflicting effects of irreversibilities in CO_2 accumulation and emission control investments. In N. Nakicenovic, W. D. Nordhaus, R. Richels, & F. L. Toth (Eds.), *Integrative assessment of mitigation, impacts, and adaptation to climate change* (CP-94-9). Laxenburg, Austria: International Institute for Applied Systems Analysis.

Lempert, R. J., Schlesinger, M. E., & Hammit, J. K. (in press). The impact of potential abrupt climate changes on near-term policy choices. *Climatic Change.*

Maddison, D. (1994). The shadow price of greenhouse gases and aerosols. In N. Nakicenovic, W. D. Nordhaus, R. Richels, & F. L. Toth (Eds.), *Integrative assessment of mitigation, impacts, and adaptation to climate change* (CP-94-9). Laxenburg, Austria: International Institute for Applied Systems Analysis.

Meadows, D., Biesiot, W., & Geerts, M. (1986). *STRATEGEM* (Research Rep. No. 13). Gröningen: IVEM RU.

Meadows, D., Fiddaman, T., & Shannon, D. (1989). *FISH BANKS, LTD.* Durham: University of New Hampshire, Institute for Policy and Social Science Research.

Nordhaus, W. D. (1994). *Managing the global commons: The economics of climate change.* Cambridge: MIT Press.

Peck, S. C., & Teisberg, T. J. (1992). CETA: A model for carbon emissions trajectory assessment. *The Energy Journal, 13*(1), 55-77.

Peck, S. C., & Teisberg, T. J. (in press). Global warming uncertainties and the value of information: An analysis using CETA. *Resources and Energy.*

18

A Policy Exercise for the Dutch Power Industry

IVO WENZLER

ROB WILLEMS

A. M. van 'T NOORDENDE

In recent years, the Dutch electricity production and distribution industry has come under increasing pressure to move toward a more market-oriented system. The process of European integration is accompanied by phrases like single market, competition, and internationalization. Whereas the European Commission strives for more competition, free access to European markets, and higher transparency of pricing, the Dutch electric power industry has exclusive rights over energy distribution and pooling of production costs.

Whether or not the European single market will eventually happen is as yet unknown. Nevertheless, our clients considered it wise to explore what effects such a market would have on the electricity industry in the Netherlands. For that reason, we were asked to develop a policy exercise that would simulate an electric power industry in which the changes proposed by the European Commission were already implemented.

During the course of developing and implementing the policy exercise, we as designers gained a number of insights into the design process that are worth mentioning. First, having the client's undisturbed attention and expertise available by staying in a hotel for a number of days proved to be extremely beneficial not only for the speed, but, more important, for the quality of the process. Second, we experienced that the design process in itself becomes an added value to the final product because most of the learning takes place in the design proces.

The objectives of the ELECTRICITY CONTRACT MARKET 2000 (ECM2K) policy exercise were twofold:

- Test whether a market-oriented electric power industry would be stable, in other words, whether continuous delivery of electricity would be guaranteed and whether electricity prices in such a market would be reasonable.
- Give the managers of Dutch electricity production and distribution companies the opportunity to experience what it would be like to act in a market-oriented electricity-power supply industry (EPSI).

System Analysis and Building the Exercise

The first step toward achieving the above objectives was a detailed system analysis with the aim of developing a comprehensive conceptual model of the future market-oriented EPSI. The core of the system analysis process was based on a few, highly interactive workshops with an interdisciplinary team. Each workshop was attended by a number of experts from our client's organization and by top managers from several electricity production and distribution companies. The knowledge gained in one workshop was incorporated into the growing conceptual model and was fed back to the experts participating in the next workshop. The final approval on the growing body of knowledge represented in the model was given by the project's steering committee, which consisted of several directors of a number of major electricity production and distribution companies.

The starting point in the system-analysis process was the identification of all relevant actors and development of detailed descriptions of their objectives, basic activities, and success factors. Once a consensus had been reached on these elements, the process continued by identifying basic links between the actors. With the definition of these basic links, a conceptual model began to emerge, with more than 20 different actors and about 100 links. Each link was then defined in terms of relations, processes, and flows. In the end, the conceptual model contained 12 different types of relations (contract, ownership, regulatory, etc.), four types of processes (monitoring, negotiation, etc.), and 14 types of flows (fuel, money, electricity, advice, etc.). Each of these types had different characteristics depending on the link of which it was a part. The end product of the system analysis phase was a large visual representation (schematic) of the conceptual model, accompanied by a written report describing in detail all elements of the model. This report served as a basis for the development of a policy exercise.

In building the ECM2K, we followed a design process we often use for building complex policy exercises, games, or simulations (Duke, 1980; Wenzler, 1993). The main purpose of this process is an effective translation of the mostly qualitative conceptual model into a qualitative and quantitative simulation model.

The process started with the development of a system components/exercise elements matrix that helped define which components of the conceptual model had to be represented in the exercise, and which elements (such as roles, steps of play, or the accounting system) of the policy exercise would represent those components. After the matrix was filled, its content was translated into a concept report, which was then presented to the steering committee for their comments and approval. Through a series of iterative steps and tests, the ideas presented in the concept report were translated into the final structure of the exercise. As with the system analysis, the core of the process of building the exercise was based on several interactive workshops between the design team and experts from the field of electricity production and distribution.

Structure of the Exercise

The best way to describe the structure of the ECM2K is through a description of some of its basic elements, such as roles, sequence of activities, decision support system, and accounting system.

Roles

There are two kinds of roles in this exercise: gamed roles (actually played by the participants) and simulated roles (played by facilitators or performed by the accounting system). The gamed roles are the following:

- *Producers:* These are divided into five different companies with three participants each, and their primary role is to produce and sell electricity to distributors, or directly to large clients.
- *Distributors:* These are divided into six different companies with three participants each. Their primary role is to ensure the steady supply of electricity to their clients, whether by buying electricity or generating it themselves.
- *Large clients:* These are divided into six different companies with two participants each. Their primary role is to ensure a steady supply of electricity in order to satisfy the demand coming from their core business.
- *Trader:* This player's objective is basically to buy at low prices and sell at high prices.
- *Regulator:* This player regulates the market and ensures its stability, primarily by modifying regulations and determining price limits.

The simulated roles, which are played by one facilitator per role, are the following:

- *Foreign electricity market:* This is the role through which participants can import or export electricity.
- *Spot market:* This is the market for short-term demand and supply of electricity.
- *Capital market:* At the capital market participants can borrow money for their capital investments.
- *Production unit market:* This is the place for buying electricity generating units.
- *Market information:* This is a place where the participants can get relevant information on market trends, such as electricity demand, electricity supply, and fuel prices.
- *Government:* This role helps and guides the activities of the regulator.
- *Dispatch and clearing:* The economic dispatch of electricity production and clearing of the buying contracts is performed by a computerized accounting system.

Sequence of Activities

The ECM2K is designed to last a day and a half. During that time, the participants play four to five cycles, each representing four years, with specially structured sector meetings taking place after the second cycle. The first cycle starts in the year 2000. Each cycle consists of four steps of play: strategy formation, negotiation, evaluation, and plenary meeting.

During strategy formation, the participants make their strategy for the negotiation phase by deciding on such questions as how many buying or selling contracts have to be negotiated and with whom, whether production capacity should be expanded or not and for how much, and whether it is necessary to make a loan.

In the negotiation phase, participants implement their strategy. They negotiate and conclude buying and selling contracts in both long-term and short-term markets, they buy new production units or decommission old ones, they get loans, and so on.

During the evaluation phase, the participants evaluate their own performance and position on the market. They base this evaluation on their annual reports and their experiences from the negotiation phase.

The last step of play is the plenary meeting, which is chaired by the regulator. Here all players meet to talk about the performance of the market as a whole, and, based on the recommendations given them by other participants, they decide what regulations have to change in the next cycle.

After the fourth (or fifth) cycle, the exercise ends with an extensive debriefing for each role. Producers, distributors, and free clients sit together and evaluate the electricity contract market as compared to the present situation in the Netherlands. These meetings are facilitated by one of the people who plays the

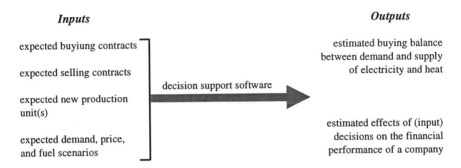

Inputs		*Outputs*

expected buyiung contracts

expected selling contracts

decision support software

expected new production
unit(s)

expected demand, price,
and fuel scenarios

estimated buying balance
between demand and supply
of electricity and heat

estimated effects of (input)
decisions on the financial
performance of a company

Figure 18.1   Inputs and outputs of the DSS.

regulator role. In a plenary meeting, a representative of each role presents the remarks that were made during the debriefing.

Decision Support System

During the first two steps of play, participants make many decisions involving changes in their unit or contract portfolios. To support this process and to help them explore the potential effects of decisions they make, they use a specially designed and fully computerized decision support system (DSS). Through this system, participants are able to explore what effects the buying and selling of electricity and/or buying of a production unit have on their financial perform- ance and energy balance. To obtain these estimated effects the players have to enter into the DSS the expected amount of electricity bought, the expected amount of electricity sold, the characteristics of new units, and their estimate of the future demand, price, and fuel scenarios. Figure 18.1 outlines the inputs and outputs of the DSS.

Accounting System

Once decisions have been made regarding the purchase of new units, or contracts have been negotiated and signed, all these decisions are recorded on specially designed forms. To cover the complexity of the environment in an appropriate way, we developed more than 20 different types of forms. Each form records a different type of decision that impacts the financial and energy performance of a particular company in the exercise. Forms include electricity contracts, heat contracts, unit purchase, unit life extension, loans, and payments. By the end of the second step, all decisions (forms) have to be handed to the facilitator responsible for the accounting system.

Because of the large amount of information to be processed and the need to integrate the decisions made by participants with the system of electricity dispatch and clearing of contracts, the accounting system was fully computerized. Once all decisions are entered into the computer, the accounting software creates a series of outputs for each company. The following is the list of reports that each company receives at the end of each cycle:

- Annual report consisting of balance sheet, cash flow report, and profit and loss account, with several ratios such as interest coverage and market share
- Energy balance report, an account of actual demand versus actual supply of electricity and heat
- Portfolio of loans and payments
- Production portfolio, a list of all production units that a company has and their characteristics, with the amount of time on-line for the current cycle
- Contract portfolio, a list of all buying and selling contracts (both for electricity and heat) with all their characteristics, including the contract clearing information for the current cycle

Results

To date, the exercise has been played seven times with participants from the top managers of the Dutch distribution and production companies, members of SEP (Dutch Electricity Generating Board), and our client EnergieNed (association of Dutch energy distribution companies). Between 40 and 50 participants took part in each of the runs. On each occasion the exercise was formally evaluated using a specially designed questionnaire. The results of this evaluation were promising: Between 87% and 93% of the participants were of the opinion that taking part in this exercise was useful.

Examples of comments are "the exercise gives you insight into the relationships and an overview of these relationships," "the exercise makes the consequences of decisions clear," and "the exercise gives you insight into the variety of possibilities open to several parties in the future."

Conference Session

At the ISAGA '94 session many questions were asked. The questions not only concerned more detailed aspects of the game, but also the possible application of the game in other parts of the world. After some discussion it was agreed that this game would be very suitable for countries considering liberalization of the electricity market, including the United States and European countries other than the Netherlands.

Conclusion

During the course of developing and implementing the ECM2K, we as designers have gained a number of insights into the design process that are worth mentioning. The first insight has to do with the speed with which the project took place. We had to develop, test, and implement the exercise in two months! The only way that would allow us first to develop a viable model of such a complex reality as the future electricity market and then to translate that model into a policy exercise was to involve the client in a different way from our usual method. The whole of the system analysis and exercise design process was centered around a series of highly structured and interactive workshops with the client. The workshops lasted for several days at a time and took place in a hotel conference room. The whole team stayed in a hotel and worked more or less nonstop. Having the client's undisturbed attention and expertise available in such a way proved to be extremely beneficial not only for speed, but, more important, for the quality of the process.

The second insight is related to the question of the nature of the product of a game/simulation or policy exercise design process. When the project started, our client expected us to design and deliver a policy exercise that would achieve the objectives already mentioned at the beginning of this chapter. In other words, the product we were asked to deliver was a policy exercise.

Nevertheless, almost from the very start of the system analysis the expectations started to change. The further we went into the system analysis and exercise development process, the greater was the client's interest in the process. The insights about the future electricity market gained during the development process increasingly influenced the mental models of our client. This in turn increased the value they attached to the conceptual modeling process and to the process of translating that model into a simulation model. At some point, this value almost became more important than the perceived value of the policy exercise itself.

For the past few years, in most of our gaming/simulation or policy exercise projects we have experienced that the design process in itself added value to the final product. What was different here was the extent of that added value. According to one member of the client's expert team involved in the process, once it was developed the policy exercise was almost not needed any more. The learning had already taken place.

References

Duke, R. D. (1980). A paradigm for game design. *Simulation & Games: An International Journal,*
    11(3), 364-377.
Wenzler, I. (1993). *Policy exercises: A new approach to policy development.* Nijmegen: Institute for
    Applied Social Science.

PART III

Research

19

A Guide to the Literature on Simulation/Gaming

DAVID CROOKALL

Simulation/gaming conferences are wonderful events—you participate in exciting exercises, you debate passionate issues, you meet lovely and loving people, you discover a world rich with action, ideas, and ideals, and you leave replenished spiritually and socially. However, conference sessions and written accounts of work accomplished could be improved considerably by drawing more fully on previous work as accounted for in the literature. Greater inclusion and fuller discussion of already published literature would improve much current work. The benefits for the simulation/gaming profession itself would be noticeable both in regard to cost-effectiveness in theory, practice, and research and in respect of the image that the profession projects and promotes among

AUTHOR'S NOTE: I should like to thank the following people for their helpful comments on drafts of this guide. Kiyoshi Arai (Kinki University in Kyushu, Japan), Michael Berney (Federal Judicial Center, Washington, DC, USA), General Carvalho (Ohio University, Athens, USA), Dan Druckman (National Research Council, Washington, DC, USA), Sandra Fowler (Consultant, Washington, DC, USA), Cathy Stein Greenblat (Rutgers University, NJ, USA), Jerry Katz (Saint Louis University, USA), Jan H. G. Klabbers (KMPC, Bemmel, The Netherlands), Barbara Steinwachs (Consultant, Penn Yan, NY, USA), Precha Thavikulwat (Towson State University, USA), Morry van Ments (Loughborough University of Technology, UK), and Joseph Wolfe (University of Tulsa, USA).

kindred disciplines. It is ultimately the publicly perceived legitimacy of our endeavors that is at stake.

With those aims in mind, I have compiled a selection of some of the essential references, which include general works (mainly books) and a few, more specialized ones (mainly articles or chapters). This guide does not include many thousands of other articles and chapters to be found in the simulation/gaming literature and in other journals and books. Any proper literature review must, of course, be extended to a much wider search, starting, of course, with the other chapters in this volume.

At the 25th annual conference of ISAGA, a significant effort was made to include and encourage the next generation. Sessions allowed both newcomers and aficionados to mix, and the younger people even organized their own plenary sessions, a feature not found in many conferences. However, an uncomfortable feeling arose in me and became more pronounced as the conference continued. It can be summed up in what one might term simulation/gaming amnesia. With notable exceptions, it seemed to me that some presentations (more particularly those by the younger than by the older delegates) implied that little previous work had been done in the field, while other presenters claimed that simulation/gaming is already a discipline.

As editor of a major journal in the field of simulation/gaming and also active in the development of professional standards for simulation/gaming, I became particularly concerned during the conference about what I felt to be a lack of familiarity with accomplishments and experience already laid down in books and journals. This was all the more poignant as the conference was ISAGA's silver anniversary and its theme embraced the idea of handing over to the next generation and encouraged us to look to the future of the profession.

As Micheal Berney has suggested, a healthy tension between simulation/gaming groups is to be encouraged; it can allow divergent perspectives on the same area to emerge, encouraging creative insights and fresh outlooks. For example, tension exists between academia and practitioners and between running a skills-oriented training workshop and producing an academic paper (conference presentation or publication). Those who work mostly in academic communities gain much of their credibility from research and publication. The growing numbers who are essentially practitioners (e.g., human resource trainers) must focus on their customers' needs and understand their world. Although some people work astride these two and experience the tension first-hand, many remain encamped in one or the other side.

The two camps have a great deal they can learn from each other. The practitioners have much to learn about the background of simulation/gaming, and demonstrating such knowledge would enhance their image in the eyes of their academic colleagues, especially when it comes to publications. Some people find it frustrating to listen to a beginning practitioner holding forth about, say, the difference between simulation and game as though nothing had ever been published about this. On the other hand, the academics have perhaps even more to learn from the practitioners, especially when it comes to using these tools in the classroom. Even more annoying are the dyed-in-the-wool academics who consider that simulation/gaming is just for company training or not worthy of their time. The word "Design" in the subtitle of the journal I edit was changed to "Practice" to reflect this need for complementarity between practice and theory, with research being the third element.

Most simulation/gamers usually like to think of themselves as a combination of practitioner, theorist, and researcher, possibly with leanings toward one favored direction. Whatever the emphasis of individuals, however, any group of people, particularly in attempting to establish a field of endeavor as a discipline, should take advantage of the tensions that exist and build upon previous work. We must not ignore the accomplishments recorded in the literature. It is notorious that American simulation/game authors almost never refer to the British literature and vice versa. My hope in providing the list of references below is that it will help simulation/gamers draw on past experience and well-established knowledge in the course of their practice and writing and that this will gradually help simulation/gaming attract the wider attention and respect we think it deserves. Trainers and academics, newcomers and experienced, practitioners and theorists, researchers and funders, Easterners and Westerners—all can enrich the creative process by drawing on the efforts already accomplished and made publicly available in publications of various kinds. In this way, too, future simulation/gaming conferences will be even richer places for the exploration of new ideas and the exchange of experience.

The Guide

The reference lists provided below, by necessity, constitute a very small selection from the available literature. The largest number of published items falls under the category of simulation/games themselves. This includes both single, stand-alone simulation/games and collections of simulation/games— books or spiral-bound volumes containing several. None of these are listed here for several reasons. They do not usually constitute a study or discussion on simulation/gaming, they are too numerous (including them here would at least triple the size of this guide), and they tend to be difficult to get (they are seldom held in academic libraries and tend to become obsolete or unobtainable relatively quickly). This chapter is a guide to the literature, not a guide to simulation/games. The references given here also tend to be of a more general nature, but these will often provide leads to more specialized items. This guide contains three main sections:

- *Metaconcerns:* Texts about simulation/gaming and topics in simulation/gaming, such as design, debriefing, and evaluation.

- *Applications:* Texts about the application of simulation/gaming to other fields, such as communication, business, and international relations.
- *Other sources:* A list of journals, associations, and electronic discussion lists in the field of simulation/gaming.

Metaconcerns

This section focuses on books, book chapters, and journal articles about the field of simulation/gaming itself—for example, what it is, how effective it is, and how we should do it—both how we should conduct exercises and how should we build the profession of simulation/gaming?

Main Works

A relatively large number of books have been written on simulation/gaming. The selection that follows contains essential references, many of which one would expect to see on a student reading list. Many of these also provide the basic blocks upon which our future work will be built.

Abt, C. C. (1970). *Serious games.* New York: Viking.

Ancelin Schutzenberger, A. (1990). *Le jeu de rôle.* Paris: ESF.

Armstrong, R. H. R., & Taylor, J. L. (Eds.). (1970). *Instructional simulation systems in higher education.* Cambridge, UK: Cambridge Institute of Education.

Armstrong, R. H. R., & Taylor, J. L. (Eds.). (1971). *Feedback on instructional simulation systems.* Cambridge, UK: Cambridge Institute of Education.

Avedon, E. M., & Sutton-Smith, B. (1971). *The study of games.* Huntington, NY: Krieger.

Boocock, S. E., & Schild, E. O. (Eds.). (1968). *Simulation games in learning.* Beverly Hills, CA: Sage.

Cecchini, A., & Indovina, F. (Eds.). (1989). *Simulazione: Per capire e intervenire nella complessita del mondo contemporaneo.* Milano: Franco-Angeli.

Duke, R. D. (1974). *Gaming: The future's language.* New York: Halstead.

Greenblat, C. S., & Duke, R. D. (Eds.). (1981). *Gaming-simulation: Rationale, applications: A text with parallel readings for social scientists, educators, and social workers* (updated and abridged ed.). Beverly Hills, CA: Sage. (Original full-length work published 1975)

Jones, K. (1987). *Simulations: A handbook for teachers and trainers* (2nd ed.). London: Kogan Page.

Kolb, D. A. (1984). *Experiential learning: Experience as the source of learning and development.* Englewood Cliffs, NJ: Prentice Hall.

Leif, J., & Brunelle, L. (1976). *Le jeu pour le jeu.* Paris: Armond Colin.

Mauriras-Bousquet, M. (1984). *Théorie et pratique ludiques.* Paris: Economica.

Megarry, J. (Ed.). (1977). *Aspects of simulation and gaming: An anthology of* SAGSET *Journal, Volumes 1-4.* London: Kogan Page.

Milroy, E. (1982). *Role-play: A practical guide.* Aberdeen, UK: Aberdeen University Press.

Shubik, M. (1975). *The uses and methods of gaming.* New York: Elsevier.

Simulation & Gaming: An International Journal of Theory, Practice, and Research. Thousand Oaks, CA: Sage. (Note that the official name of this journal has an ampersand (&) in the main title and an "and" in the subtitle. When referring to the journal, please use the form shown.)

The former name of the journal was *Simulation & Games: An International Journal of Theory, Design, and Research.*)
Simulation/Games for Learning (previously *SAGSET Journal*). London: Kogan Page.
Stolovitch, H. D., & Thiagarajan, S. (1980). *Frame games.* Englewood Cliffs, NJ: Educational Technology Publications.
Tamsey, P. J. (1971). *Educational aspects of simulation.* London: McGraw-Hill.
Taylor, J. L., & Walford, R. (1978). *Learning and the simulation game.* Milton Keynes, UK: Open University Press.
Thiagarajan, S., & Stolovich, H. D. (1978). *Instructional simulation games.* Englewood Cliffs, NJ: Educational Technology Publications.
van Ments, M. (1994). *The effective use of role-play: A handbook for teachers and trainers* (rev. ed.). London: Kogan Page.
Wohlking, W., & Gill, P. J. (1980). *Role playing.* Englewood Cliffs, NJ: Educational Technology Publications.

If I had to choose three references from the above, they would be the book by Greenblat and Duke and the one by van Ments and the journal *Simulation & Gaming.* Most of the books above deal with a wide range of specific topics, such as design, debriefing, the nature of simulation/gaming, and evaluation—all topics that also have their own specialized literature (see headings below).

Besides general texts, several conference proceedings and other books have been published. Proceedings tend to deal with a very wide range of topics. They have been listed here because, although they do contain much material that falls under the rubric of application (see next main section), they are also often equally concerned with simulation/gaming as a profession or as a field.

Arai, K., & Game Research Group. (Eds.). (1992). *Simulation/game evolution* (in Japanese). Tokyo: Koei.
Armstrong, R., Percival, F., & Saunders, D. (Eds.). (1993). *Simulation and gaming yearbook, 1993: Interactive learning.* London: Kogan Page.
Bruin, K., de Haan, J., Teijken, C., & Veeman, W. (Eds.). (1979). *How to build a simulation/game* (Vols. 1-2). Gröningen: Centrale Reproductiedienst der Rijksuniversiteit.
Craig, D., & Martin, A. (Eds.). (1986). *Gaming and simulation for capability* (Perspectives No. 11). Loughborough, UK: SAGSET.
Crookall, D., & Arai, K. (Eds.). (1992). *Global interdependence: Simulation and gaming perspectives.* Tokyo: Springer-Verlag.
Crookall, D., Greenblat, C. S., Coote, A., Klabbers, J. H. G., & Watson, D. (Eds.). (1987). *Simulation-gaming in the late 1980s.* Oxford, UK: Pergamon.
Crookall, D., Klabbers, J. H. G., Coote, A., Saunders, D., Cecchini, A., & Frisenna, A. (Eds.). (1988). *Simulation-gaming in education and training.* Oxford, UK: Pergamon.
Fitzsimons, A., & Thatcher, D. (Eds.). (1987). *Games and simulations at work* (Perspectives No. 12). Loughborough, UK: SAGSET.
Goldberg, D., & Graber, M. (1980). *Simulation/games in education, research and decision making.* Geneva: University of Geneva Press.
Gray, I., & Waitt, L. (Eds.). (1982). *Simulation in management and business education* (Perspectives No. 7). London: Kogan Page.
Hollinshead, B., & Yorke, M. (Eds.). (1981). *Simulations and games: The real and the ideal* (Perspectives No. 6). London: Kogan Page.
Jacques, D., & Tipper, E. (Eds.). (1984). *Learning for the future with games and simulations* (Perspectives No. 9). London: Kogan Page.

Klabbers, J. H. G., Scheper, W. J., Takkenberg, C. A. T., & Crookall, D. (Eds.). (1989). *Simulation-gaming: On the improvement of competence in dealing with complexity, uncertainty, and value conflicts.* Oxford, UK: Pergamon.

McAleese, R. (Ed.). (1978). *Training and professional education* (Perspectives No. 3). London: Kogan Page.

Megarry, J. (Ed.). (1979). *Human factors in games and simulations* (Perspectives No. 4). London: Kogan Page.

Miller, A., & Crookall, D. (Eds.). (1989). *Simulation and gaming: Pathways to progress* (Perspectives No. 14). Loughborough, UK: SAGSET.

Percival, F., Lodge, S., & Saunders, D. (Eds.). (1993). *Simulation and gaming yearbook: Volume 1. Developing transferable skills in education and training.* London: Kogan Page.

Race, P., & Brook, D. (Eds.). (1980). *Simulation and gaming for the 1980s* (Perspectives No. 5). London: Kogan Page.

Rădăceanu, E. (Ed.). (1994). *Reform and progress helped by simulation and gaming.* Bucharest: IROMA.

Saunders, D., Coote, A., & Crookall, D. (Eds.). (1988). *Learning from experience through simulations and games* (Perspectives No. 13). Loughborough, UK: SAGSET.

Stahl, I. (Ed.). (1983). *Operational gaming: An international approach.* Laxenburg, IIASA; Oxford, UK: Pergamon.

Thatcher, D., & Robinson, J. (Eds.). (1983). *Simulations in business, health and nursing education* (Perspectives No. 8). Loughborough, UK: SAGSET.

van Ments, M., & Hearden, K. (Eds.). (1985). *Effective use of games and simulations* (Perspectives No. 10). Loughborough, UK: SAGSET.

Evaluation (and Objectives)

The topic of evaluation is essential. In a nutshell, the basic question is how effective is simulation/gaming in achieving its objectives? Some simulation/ gaming scholars, such as Gerard Carvalho, believe that the objectives and the measurement system are decided on before efforts to achieve the objectives have been made. Only then is a judgment made of the achievement's value. Others, perhaps working in other-than-achievement-oriented cultures and educational settings would argue for a more open approach, in which objectives emerge during the design of the simulator or during the simulation as it is run. Both perspectives are valid within their own logic and may be seen as mutually exclusive. Whether that is the case or not, it is certainly important for the learning we wish to promote to have some form of evaluation, even if this is accomplished only during the debriefing. More important still for the profession is that some form of valid and sustained evaluation be accomplished, ranging anywhere from elaborate, objectives-based, achievement-oriented, quantitative, longitudinal study to more informal, subjective, and participatory assessment. Such evaluation will help practitioners and theorists to build a stronger case for simulation/gaming as well as to head off opponents who seem all too eager to spot false pitfalls in our endeavors. It is perhaps in this area that some of the greatest transatlantic simulation/gaming differences exist, but people have been known to cross the water. Several important articles and one book deal with the topic. Evaluation is also discussed in some of the main texts, such as Greenblat and Duke (listed earlier).

Bredemeier, M. E., & Greenblat, C. S. (1981). The educational effectiveness of simulations and games: A synthesis of findings. *Simulation & Games: An International Journal, 12*(3), 307-332.

Butler, R. J., Markulis, P. M., & Strang, D. R. (1988). Where are we? An analysis of the methods and focus of the research on simulation gaming. *Simulation & Games: An International Journal, 19*(1), 3-26.

Druckman, D., & Bjork, R. A. (1994). *Learning, remembering, believing: Enhancing human performance* (esp. chaps. 3 and 6). Washington, DC: National Academy Press.

Fletcher, J. (1971). The effectiveness of simulation games as learning environments. *Simulation & Games: An International Journal, 2*(4), 425-454.

Gredler, M. (1992). *Designing and evaluating games and simulations: A process approach.* London: Kogan Page.

Greenblat, C. S. (1973). Teaching with simulation games. *Teaching Sociology, 1*(3), 62-83.

Greenblat, C. S. (1975). Teaching with simulation games: A review of claims and evidence. In C. S. Greenblat & R. D. Duke (Eds.), *Gaming-simulation: Rationale, design, and applications.* New York: Sage/Halsted.

Horn, R. E., & Cleaves, A. (Eds.). (1980). *The guide to simulation games for education and training* (4th ed.). Beverly Hills, CA: Sage.

Laveault, D., St.-Germain, M., & Corbeil, P. (1992). A global model of simulations and game evaluation. In D. Crookall & K. Arai (Eds.), *Global interdependence: Simulation and gaming perspectives.* Tokyo: Springer-Verlag.

Pierfy, D. (1977). Comparative simulation game research: Stumbling blocks and stepping stones. *Simulations & Games: An International Journal, 8,* 255-268.

Randel, J. M., Morris, B. A., Wetzel, C. D., & Whitehill, B. V. (1992). The effectiveness of games for educational purposes: A review of recent research. *Simulation & Gaming: An International Journal, 23*(3), 261-276.

Rolfe, J. (1991). SAGSET 1990—The proof of the pudding: The effectiveness of games and simulations. *Simulation/Games for Learning, 21*(2), 99-117.

Seidner, C. J. (1976). Teaching with simulations and games. In N. L. Games (Ed.), *The psychology of teaching methods.* Chicago: National Society for the Study of Education.

Sudaby, A. (1976). A critical analysis of simulation games. *SAGSET Journal, 6*(3), 87-101.

Van Sickle, R. L. (1986). A quantitative review of research on instructional simulation gaming: A twenty-year perspective. *Theory and Research in Social Education, 14,* 245-264.

Wolfe, J. (1985). The teaching effectiveness of games in collegiate business courses: A 1973-1983 update. *Simulation & Games: An International Journal, 16*(3) 251-288.

Wolfe, J. (1990). The evaluation of computer-based business games: Methodology, findings and future needs. In J. Gentry (Ed.), *The guide to business gaming and experiential learning.* London: Kogan Page.

Facilitation and Debriefing

Many books contain chapters on how to run a simulation/game, often with a few (helpful but unfulfilling) words on debriefing. Although facilitation of simulation/games is often a tricky business, it is usually the debriefing that is the most delicate and problematic.

Debriefing is also the most important part of the simulation/gaming experience, whether the main purpose of the simulation/game is training or research. Debriefing is the analysis of and reflection on the simulation/game experience that participants and facilitator do, with the objective of transforming the experience into positive and lasting learning. One might say that debriefing is the reason for which a simulation/game is conducted. At the very least, a simulation/game in its design and in its implementation points toward and achieves its dénouement in the debriefing.

Debriefing actually is a very common activity engaged in by many people in their everyday lives. Although such activity is not labeled debriefing, it functions like it. Consider a group of teachers in the teachers' lounge busily discussing their last classes, venting their exasperation with particularly difficult students, holding forth about the inappropriate conduct of a colleague, or even deploring the latest budget cut. Such expression is in fact debriefing; through the discussion and interchange, such teachers are analyzing a particular experience they have recently lived through (or are still living through—we know the importance of in-session debriefing for particularly long simulation/games). Many people naturally tend toward discussion of personal experience with others whom they consider able to lend an ear and/or who have had a similar experience. One difference with formal debriefing is that such expression is not formalized or pre-structured and does not usually have an official facilitator. Other differences exist, of course, and these would make an interesting study, but underlying both types of debriefing is a human need to process experience with others.

Some experienced gamers (e.g., Precha Thavikulwat) are of the opinion that some games do not require formal debriefing, for example, when a simulation/game is used as a test or as a selection or qualification procedure (e.g., when pilots are qualified to fly a particular aircraft by their performance score in a flight simulator). Some simulation/games are designed to give practice, to automate procedures, such as solving factory production problems, and have feedback mechanisms built into the simulation/game. Another example might be computer simulations (i.e., no human participant) of various phenomena: social (e.g., crowd behavior), ecological (e.g., heat exchange in the oceans and the archetypal weather simulator) or physical (e.g., automobile engine).

However, participants in and witnesses to such simulation/games will inevitably talk about it afterward. People who have taken a test or been through a selection exam will get together and compare notes. People who have seen a run of a computer simulation will talk about their impressions. Researchers who are refining the prototype of a computer simulation will discuss at length about its accuracy, possible refinements, portability, and so forth. Thus, although no formal critical appraisal has been conducted, people will inevitably conduct their own informal debriefing.

Taking this a step further, any formal process of assessment of a situation is a form of debriefing. Examples are an inquiry into an airplane disaster, with results being fed back into airplane design and safety, and a performance appraisal with feedback (e.g., a teacher being inspected, an apprentice doctor, a learner driver). Debriefing is central to other activities and experiences than simulation/games. We have much to learn from them and they from us. Indeed, simulation/gaming is not such a strange thing after all.

Readers should be careful of articles and books that omit discussion on debriefing. Compared to the amount that has been written about other aspects of simulation/games, very little has been written about debriefing. For example, evaluation studies tend not to make debriefing an explicit and central element in the evaluation. Design issues need to include debriefing in a more prominent and decisive way than they currently do.

The following references provide a good start for those interested in facilitation and debriefing (also known by other terms, such as post-simulation analysis, feedback on participation, or discussion of the experience).

Barnett, T. (1984). Evaluations of simulations and games: A clarification. *Simulation/Games for Learning, 14*(4), 164-175.

Druckman, D. (1971). Understanding the operation of complex social systems: Some uses of simulation design. *Simulation & Games: An International Journal, 1*(2), 173-195.

Hammel, H. (1986). How to design a debriefing session. *Journal of Experiential Learning, 9*(3), 20-25.

Hart, L. B. (1992). *Faultless facilitation.* London: Kogan Page.

Heron, J. (1989). *The facilitators' handbook.* London: Kogan Page.

Lederman, L. C. (1984). Debriefing: A critical reexamination of the postexperience analytic process with implications for its effective use. *Simulation & Games: An International Journal, 15,* 415-431.

Lederman, L. C. (Ed.). (1992). Debriefing [Special issue]. *Simulation & Gaming: An International Journal, 23*(2).

Mahoney, R., & Druckman, D. (1975). Simulation, experimentation, and context: Dimensions of design and inference. *Simulation & Games: An International Journal, 6*(2), 235-270.

McMahon, L., & Coote, A. (1988). Debriefing simulation games: Personal reflections. In D. Crookall, J. H. G. Klabbers, A. Coote, D. Saunders, A. Cecchini, & A. Frisenna (Eds.), *Simulation-gaming in education and training.* Oxford, UK: Pergamon.

Pearson, M., & Smith, D. (1986). Debriefing in experience-based learning. *Simulation/Games for Learning, 16*(4) 155-172.

Rolfe, J. (Ed.) (1992). Simulations and gaming: Reliability, validity and effectiveness [Special issue]. *Simulation/Games for Learning, 22*(4).

Russell, T. (1994). *Effective feedback skills.* London: Kogan Page.

Thiagarajan, S. (1986). Debriefing. *Performance & Instruction, 25*(5), 49.

Thiagarajan, S. (1993). How to maximize transfer from simulation games through systematic debriefing. In F. Percival, S. Lodge, & D. Saunders (Eds.), *The simulation and gaming yearbook 1993: Developing transferable skills in education and training.* London: Kogan Page.

Thiagarajan, S. (1995). Guidelines for conducting a defriefing session and for developing a debriefing guide. In D. Saunders (Ed.), *The simulation and gaming yearbook, Vol. 3: Games and simulations for business.* London: Kogan Page.

van Ments, M. (Ed.). (1986). Debriefing simulation/games [Special issue]. *Simulation/Games for Learning, 16*(4).

van Ments, M. (1990). *Active talk: The effective use of discussion in learning.* London: Kogan Page.

Williams, T. (1992). Debriefing learning activities. *Simulation/Games for Learning, 22*(2), 91-94.

Other important discussions on this are found in the main texts mentioned earlier, especially those by van Ments, Greenblat and Duke, and Jones.

If simulation/games are conducted well and debriefed appropriately, they can be a powerful source of enrichment that goes well beyond that normally expected from other types of formal learning situations. Cathy Greenblat has commented that bringing members of different groups together in a simulation presents an opportunity for misunderstandings to arise, which can then be collectively considered, what she calls "understanding the misunderstanding."

Computer-Mediated and Network Simulation/Gaming

Growing numbers of simulation/game articles mention the use of computer technology in one form or another. Even greater numbers of computer-related publications contain articles on various types of simulations and games. Several trends noted over the past decade in the interface between computers and simulation games are these:

- The large number of excellent computer-mediated simulation/games that have been developed for education and training have undoubtedly improved the image of simulation/gaming in the mind of educators. Such activities or packages are seen by such people as computer-based instruction or multimedia or whatever the current buzzword is and thus as legitimate educational classroom material.

- The use of simulation/gaming methods by computer people has greatly improved the overall quality of educational software.

- However, a counter-trend is at work. The commercially produced zap-'em-up-type games have probably detracted from the image of simulation/gaming in the eyes of educators and the public at large. Simulation/gamers have been careful to avoid being associated with these types of games, despite their immense popularity.

- A more recent trend, spearheaded by a few commercial companies, such as Thinking Tools (formerly Maxis) and Koei, is an attempt to bring together the popular and the serious in what has been dubbed "edutainment," in which engaging and fun simulation/game software also has perceivable and sometimes acknowledged educational value.

- Virtual reality (VR) is a technology that has been developing in parallel with (and, seemingly, separate from) computerized simulation, despite the fact that at the heart of most VR systems is some form of computerized simulation/game. The parallel lines of development should be made to cross from time to time; much benefit could come from interaction between the two.

- Finally, network gaming has been developing steadily since Bob Noel's pioneering work. The expansion of the Internet has made this form of simulation/game more accessible (examples are ICS, ICONS, and IDEALS). A related and less academic form of game played via the Internet is what are known as MUDs. Here again, the dichotomy between academic and hobby can be seen, with few people being involved in both.

The issues involved in computer mediation of simulation/games are wide-ranging and discussed in both the simulation/gaming literature and other arenas.

Crookall, D. (Ed.). (1988). Computerized simulation in the social sciences [Special issue]. *Social Science Computer Review, 6*(1).

Crookall, D., & Landis, P. (1992). Global network simulation: An environment for global awareness. In D. Crookall & K. Arai (Eds.), *Global interdependence: Simulation and gaming perspectives.* Tokyo: Springer-Verlag.

Crookall, D., Martin, A., Saunders, D., & Coote, A. (1987). Human and computer involvement in simulation. *Simulation & Games: An International Journal, 17*(3) 345-375.

Garson, G. D. (1994). Computerized simulations in social science: A personal retrospective. *Simulation & Gaming: An International Journal, 25*(4), 477-487.

Garson, G. D. (1994). Social science computer simulation: Its history, design, and future. *Social Science Computer Review, 12*(1), 55-82.

Gredler, M. B. (1989). A further analysis of computer-based simulations. *Simulation/Games for Learning, 19*(2), 76-81.

Kalawasky, R. (1993). *The science of virtual reality and virtual environments.* Reading, MA: Addison-Wesley.

Pimentel, K., & Teixeira, K. (1995). *Virtual reality: Through the new looking glass* (2nd ed.). Blue Ridge Summit: Windcrest/McGraw-Hill.

Robinson, S. (1994). *Successful simulation: A practical approach to simulation projects.* London: McGraw-Hill.

Savetz, K. M. (1994). Internet games. *Internet World, 5*(3), 29-33.

Social Science Computer Review. Durham, NC: Duke University Press.

Whicker, M. L., & Sigelman, L. (1991). *Computer simulation applications: An introduction.* Thousand Oaks, CA and London: Sage.

Wilkenfeld, J., & Kaufman, J. (1993). Political science: Network simulation in international politics. *Social Science Computer Review, 11*(4), 464-467.

Willis, J., Hovey, L., & Hovey, K. L. (1987). *Computer simulations: A source book to learning in an electronic environment.* New York and London: Garland.

Wolf, C. J. (1987). ICS: Interactive communication simulations. In D. Crookall, C. S. Greenblat, A. Coote, J. H. G. Klabbers, & D. Watson (Eds.), *Simulation-gaming in the late 1980s.* Oxford, UK: Pergamon.

Design

Design has received much attention in the literature and continues to be an enthralling topic at simulation/gaming conferences for at least three reasons: (a) Design is concrete—you can touch the results, (b) it is creative—you develop an object, and (c) it is involving—you develop understanding in a passionate and intimate way.

It has been pointed out, most notably by Cathy Greenblat, that one cannot design a simulation/game of a system until one understands the system and that the design process also helps one to understand the system. Several people (most notably Fred Goodman, Richard Powers, and Richard Duke) have realized that one may learn more by designing a simulation/game than by participating in it. In other words, getting a group of people to go through the process of designing a simulation/game about a system may be more instructive (both for understanding the system and for development of research skills) than getting them to participate in an already-designed simulation/game about that system.

Designing a major simulation/game can be a lengthy and involved task, even for aficionados. Newcomers seem to want quick recipes, of which there are (fortunately!) few. Of course, participation in and experience with running a wide range of simulation/games can provide much insight into and feel for what constitutes a good simulation/game, and this will be invaluable in the design process. However, this cannot replace the above-mentioned need for research into the referent system, product objectives, intended audience, and so on. It is easy to theorize at length even if one has never designed and run a simulation/game oneself. It becomes more difficult with concrete design experience.

Designing a simulation/game is like learning from a simulation/game—you have to do it. You cannot read the highway code or a car manual and expect to be able to drive a car. Of course, such codes and manuals are extremely useful prior to and along with practice and for passing exams. However, any serious discussion about design, in-depth debate about the design process, whether in conference sessions or in writing, must look at and draw on the literature.

Crookall, D., Saunders, D., & Coote, A. (1987). THE SIMULATION DESIGN GAME: Examining the simulation design process by means of a game. In S. McClure & D. Thatcher (Eds.), *Games and simulations at work*. Loughborough, UK: SAGSET.

Duke, R. D. (1974). Gaming: The future's language. New York: Sage/Halsted.

Ellington, H., Addinall, E., & Percival, F. (1984). *Case studies in game design*. London: Kogan Page.

Ellington, H., Addinall, E., & Percival, F. (1992). *A handbook of game design*. London: Kogan Page.

Greenblat, C. S. (1988). *Designing games and simulations: An illustrated handbook*. Newbury Park, CA: Sage.

Greenblat, C. S., & Duke, R. D. (1979). *Game-generating games. A trilogy of games for community and classroom*. Beverly Hills, CA: Sage.

Jones, K. (1985). *Designing your own simulations*. London: Methuen.

Megarry, J. (1976). Ten further "mistakes" made by simulation and game designers. *SAGSET Journal, 6*(3), 87-92.

Shannon, D. E. (1992). Applying principles of graphic design to game design. In D. Crookall & K. Arai (Eds.), *Global interdependence: Simulation and gaming perspectives*. Tokyo: Springer-Verlag.

Stolovitch, H. D., & Thiagarajan, S. (1980). *Frame games*. Englewood Cliffs, NJ: Educational Technology Publications.

Thatcher, D., & Robinson, J. (1990). A game workshop for the design of games and simulations. *Simulation/Games for Learning, 20*(3), 250-263.

The volume by Greenblat is *the* reference on game design—no simulation/gamer can seriously do a study of simulation/game design without referring to this book, which now has an edition in Japanese.

The Nature of Simulation/Gaming

A number of authors have expressed their thoughts on what constitutes the essential nature of a simulation/game. This is also a topic that is raised time and again at conferences, particularly by newcomers as they try to grapple in their own mind with what a simulation/game actually is (or argue, just as vehemently, what it is not). Such discussions are often conducted as though parties to them were raising the issue for the first time, in other words, as though nothing had been said, let alone written, about the nature or concept of simulation/gaming.

My own proposal on this topic (published nearly 10 years ago) was as much an attempt to straighten out things in my own mind as it was to offer some coherent account that might be of use for others. With the passing of time, it has become clear to me that each newcomer and succeeding generation in simulation/gaming battles with these issues. It seems to me that this is both a necessary part of coming to terms with the complexity of the methodology and an intriguing intellectual journey because it involves establishing in one's mind a series of interlocking relationships among a series of elements from a wide variety of domains, such as play, game, simulation, learning, cognition, experience, involvement, motivation, research, theory, practice, systems, feedback, society, interaction, and computing.

However, such personal explorations should not, indeed cannot, state once and for all the nature of simulation/gaming. Pinning down a watertight definition is impossible given the nature of simulation/gaming and given its socially constructed character. It is far better that the definitions we offer remain tentative so that such openness will contribute to a continuing debate.

However, it is one thing for newcomers to attempt to work out things in their own minds and quite another to write or talk about things as part of an ongoing debate about the nature of simulation/gaming in general. In both cases, however, sessions at simulation/gaming conferences tend to tackle the topic without the rigor and reference that would be required in many other areas. Just as reference to past work in many research endeavors is usually a good starting point, so it is in the case of definitions of simulation/gaming and discussions on its nature.

The literature is replete with proposals for definitions; there is an immense variety of perspectives and conceptualizations. Such definitions may have implications for such topics as design and debriefing. The references below are starting points only, but many of them are essential ones. I have included a broader range of references than one might otherwise at first expect so as to encompass such areas as play and reality, as these have more to contribute to the debate than has traditionally been recognized.

Anderson, R. J. (1987). The reality problem in games and simulations. In D. Crookall, C. S. Greenblat, A. Coote, J. H. G. Klabbers, & D. Watson (Eds.), *Simulation-gaming in the late 1980s.* Oxford, UK: Pergamon.

Bateson, G. (1977). *Vers une écologie de l'esprit.* Paris: Le Seuil.

Bruner, J. S., Jolly, A., & Sylva, K. (1976). *Play: Its role in development and evolution.* Harmondsworth, UK: Penguin.

Caillois, R. (1958). *Les jeux et les hommes.* Paris: Gallimard.

Carse, J. P. (1986). *Finite and infinite games: A vision of life as play and possibility.* New York: Free Press.

Cecchini, A., & Frisenna, A. (1987). Gaming simulation: A general classification. *Simulation/Games for Learning, 17*(2), 60-73.

Crookall, D., Oxford, R. L., & Saunders, D. (1987). Towards a reonceptualization of simulations: From representation to reality. *Simulation/Games for Learning, 17*(3), 147-171.

Culin, S. (1975). *Games of the North American Indians.* New York: Dover. (Original work published 1907)

Goffman, E. (1961). *Encounters: Studies in the sociology of interaction.* Indianapolis: Bobbs-Merrill.

Greenblat, C. S. (1988). Extending the range of experience. In D. Crookall & D. Saunders (Eds.), *Communication and simulation: From two fields to one theme.* Clevedon, UK and Philadelphia: Multilingual Matters.

Huizinga, J. (1955). *Homo ludens: A study of the play-element in culture* (3rd ed.). London: Roy Publishers/Routledge & Kegan Paul.

Jones, K. (1988). *Interactive learning events: A guide for facilitators.* London: Kogan Page.

Klabbers, J. H. G. (1987). A user oriented taxonomy of games and simulations. In D. Crookall, C. S. Greenblat, A. Coote, J. H. G. Klabbers, & D. Watson (Eds.), *Simulation-gaming in the late 1980s.* Oxford, UK: Pergamon.

Klabbers, J. H. G., & van der Waals, B. (1989). From rigid-rule to free-form games: Observations on the role of rules. In J. H. G. Klabbers, W. J. Scheper, C. A. T. Takkenberg, & D. Crookall (Eds.), *Simulation/gaming: On the improvement of competence in dealing with complexity, uncertainty, and value conflicts.* Oxford, UK: Pergamon.

Kolb, D. A. (1984). *Experiential learning: Experience as the source of learning and development.* Englewood Cliffs, NJ: Prentice Hall.

Sharrock, W. W., & Watson, D. R. (1987). "Power" and "realism" in simulation and gaming: Some pedagogic and analytic observations. In D. Crookall, C. S. Greenblat, A. Coote, J. H. G. Klabbers, & D. Watson (Eds.), *Simulation-gaming in the late 1980s.* Oxford, UK: Pergamon.

Sisk, D. (1995). Simulation games as training tools. In S. M. Fowler & M. Fowler (Eds.), *The intercultural sourcebook: Cross-cultural training methods.* Yarmouth, ME: Intercultural Press.

Suits, B. H. (1978). *The grasshopper: Games, life and utopia.* Toronto: University of Toronto Press.

Winnicott, D. W. (1971). *Playing and reality.* London: Tavistock.

The topic is also the subject of important discussion in many of the books cited as main texts, particularly the one by Greenblat and Duke.

Game Theory

Some of those involved in simulation/gaming consider game theory to be outside our interests, and further that simulation/gaming has little, if anything, to learn from game theory. Those involved more closely with both areas would argue otherwise. One of these is Martin Shubik, who has worked to bring the two areas together and to show the contribution that each makes to the other. His books and others on game theory are listed below.

Aumann, R. J., & Hart, S. (1992). *Handbook of game theory with economic applications.* Amsterdam: Elsevier Science.

Brams, S. J. (1990). *Negotiation games: Applying game theory to be bargaining and arbitration.* London and New York: Routledge.

Brams, S. J. (1994). *Theory of moves.* Cambridge, UK: Cambridge University Press.

Brewer, G., & Shubik, M. (1979). *The war game.* Cambridge, MA: Harvard University Press.

Colman, A. M. (1982). *Game theory and experimental games: The study of strategic interaction.* Oxford, UK: Pergamon.

Hamburger, H. (1979). *Games as models of social phenomena.* San Francisco: Freeman.

Rapoport, A. (1960). *Fights, games, and debates.* Ann Arbor: University of Michigan Press.

Shubik, M. (1975). *Games for society, business, and war.* Amsterdam: Elsevier.

Shubik, M. (1975). *The uses and methods of gaming.* New York: Elsevier.

Shubik, M. (1984). *Game theory in the social sciences: Concepts and solutions.* Cambridge: MIT Press.

von Neumann, J., & Morgenstern, O. (1944). *Theory of games and economic behavior.* New York: John Wiley.

History

Traditionally, the history of simulation/gaming has attracted little attention. This may be due, in part, to its relative youth and to its rather amorphous character, compared to a more traditionally configured discipline, such as sociology. It may also be due to the wide dispersal of gamers across professions and in many countries worldwide. The following collections provide some insight into the development of the discipline.

Crookall, D. (Ed.). (1994-1995). 25th anniversary special issues of *Simulation & Gaming: An International Journal, 25*(2, June 1994; 4, December 1994), *26*(2, June 1995; 4, December 1995).

Greenblat, C. S. (Ed.). (1989). 20th anniversary special issue of *Simmulation & Gaming: An International Journal, 20*(2, June).

Megarry, J. (Ed.). (1977). *Aspects of simulation and gaming.* London: Kogan Page.

Some of the main texts also provide important insights into the origins of simulation/gaming, particularly those by Shubik, Guetzkow, Greenblat, and Duke, and Avedon and Sutton-Smith.

Bibliographies and Guides

A number of useful bibliographies and specialist surveys have been published over the years. Some of these are annotated and thus provide some idea of the contents of each item. A number of guides have also been published, focusing on simulation/games themselves, and should not, strictly speaking, appear here because I have excluded simulation/game packages from this guide. However, several of these guides contain extensive essays about simulation/gaming. This is particularly the case for the Horn and Cleaves guide and the Taylor and Walford book.

Coombs, D. H. (1980). Simulation/gaming journals: A review of the field. *Simulation/Games for Learning, 10*(2), 60-66.

Crookall, D. (1990). Learning more about simulation/games. In D. Crookall & R. Oxford (Eds.), *Simulation, gaming, and language learning.* Boston: Heinle & Heinle.

Dukes, R. L., & Matthews, S. (1993). *Simulation and gaming and the teaching of sociology* (5th ed.). Washington, DC: American Sociological Association.

Horn, R. E., & Cleves, A. (Eds.). (1980). *The guide to simulation games for education and training* (4th ed.). Beverly Hills, CA: Sage.

Steinwachs, B. (1992). *Some resources on simulation gaming and other experiential learning methods.* Penn Yan, NY: Organizational Planning & Participative Learning.

Taylor, J. L., & Walford, R. (1978). *Learning and the simulation game.* Milton Keynes, UK: Open University Press.

Many articles and books on simulation/gaming include extensive references to other works, and such leads should not be overlooked. A comprehensive bibliography of items published in the 1970s and before is contained in the book by Greenblat and Duke described earlier.

Professional Standards

Very little has been done in the vital area of professional standards in simulation/gaming, at least in terms of a document containing a code of ethical standards by which the profession operates. Other professions have fully developed codes by which their members are bound, which has helped establish their group as a bona fide and legitimate endeavor. Their identities and values embody codes of conduct created to guarantee the smallest possible risk to others and the greatest advantage to clients. Little has been published on this vital area in simulation/gaming, and when it has, it tends to be associated with debriefing.

The professional and caring simulation/gamer will ask a number of questions. Here are a few in relation to debriefing, and it is easy to extrapolate from there to other parts of the simulation/gaming enterprise. What is the status and importance of debriefing? How should it be conducted? What specific methods? When? By whom? What do you do if someone gets terribly upset? What if the simulation/game took longer than you bargained for and less time than necessary is left for debriefing? What does the profession do about people who fail to debrief (and thus give the profession a bad name)? Should we (who is we?) set up a board that certifies people as qualified to debrief? What body would administer such a program? What cultural differences have to be taken into account? Should standards be flexible enough to account for a large range of cultural differences, or should we have a series of standards, each suitable for a cultural group? What do we do about transgressions? Is any of the above feasible? Is it indeed desirable?

My personal answer to the last two questions is an unqualified "yes." A start has been made to answer these and other questions and to establish a set of professional guidelines. A working conference took place a couple of years ago at the University of Fukuoka in Japan (organized by Kiyoshi Arai and myself).

Some dozen people from around the world worked for five long days and began to formulate draft statements regarding professional standards specific to simulation/gaming. The operative word was specific; in other words, standards that are common across professions and not special for simulation/gaming were considered peripheral to our work. Since then, several workshops have been conducted at simulation/gaming conferences, most notably at a preconference workshop at ISAGA '94. Alongside this effort, the Simulation/Gaming Committee of SIETAR International, spearheaded by Daniel Yalowitz of Lesley College, Cambridge, Massachusetts, has also produced a set of guidelines, relating in particular to the interculturalists' use of simulation/games. We are planning to merge these two efforts, and we hope to make available the work of all these meetings in the not-too-distant future.

Applications

This section contains references that are essentially concerned with the use of simulation/gaming in other fields, such as social studies, counseling, and negotiation. At least two categorization systems could be used here—one that groups references into objectives, such as educational purposes, professional procedures and skills training, and research, and the other that uses the well-worn disciplinary areas—sociology, political science, ecology, and chemistry, to name just a few.

A matrix of objectives by disciplines would produce an unmanageable number of cells. Some references below would have to be cited in several cells, taking up space unnecessarily. Also, this sort of categorization tends to go counter to the integrative, cross-disciplinary spirit of much simulation/gaming. Thus, the items are grouped together, with the topic(s) covered in each work usually evident from the title.

Barthélémy-Ruiz, C. (1993). *Le jeu et les supports ludiques en formation d'adultes.* Paris: Editions d'Organisation.

Bell, R. C. (1990). *Board and table games from many civilizations.* Mineola, NY: Dover.

Béville, G. (1986). *Jeux de formation.* Paris: Editions d'Organisation.

Bideau, A. (1989). *Les jeux à l'école et hors de l'école.* Lyon: Editions E. Robert.

Brougère, G. (Ed.). (1992). *Valeurs et paradoxes d'un petit objet secret.* Paris: Autrement.

Cavanagh, T. K. (1970). *Simulation gaming in Canadian history.* Sherbrooke, PC: Progressive Publications.

Chadwick, R. W. (1972). Theory development through simulations: A comparison and analysis of associations among variables in an international system and an international simulation. *International Studies Quarterly, 16,* 83-127.

Chiarotto, A. (1991). *Les ludothèques.* Paris: Cercle de la Librairie.

Christopher, E. M., & Smith, L. E. (1987). *Leadership training through gaming: Power, people and problem solving.* London: Kogan Page.

Christopher, E. M., & Smith, L. E. (1991). *Negotiation training through gaming: Strategies, tactics and manoeuvres.* London: Kogan Page.

Clarke, M. (1978). *Simulations in the study of international relations.* Ormskirk: Helspeth.

Coleman, D. W. (Ed.). (1990-1992). Computerized simulations and games for language learning, Parts 1-3 [Special issues]. *Simulation & Gaming: An International Journal, 21*(4, pt. 1, 1990), *22*(2, pt. 2, 1991), *23*(1, pt. 3, 1992).

Coplin, W. D. (Ed.). (1968). *Simulation in the study of politics.* Chicago: Markham.

Coppard, L. C., & Goodman, F. L. (Eds.). (1979). *Urban gaming simulation: A handbook for educators and trainers.* Ann Arbor: University of Michigan Press.

Corbeil, P., Laveault, D., & Saint-Germain, M. (1989). *Jeux et activités de simulation: Des outils pour une éducation au développement international.* Hull, PQ: Agence Canadienne de Développement International.

Crookall, D. (Ed.). (1985). Simulation applications in L2 education and research [Special issue]. *System, 13*(3).

Crookall, D., & Oxford, R. L. (Eds.). (1990). *Simulation, gaming, and language learning.* Boston, MA: Heinle & Heinle.

Crookall, D., & Saunders, D. (Eds.). (1989). *Communication and simulation: From two fields to one theme.* Clevedon, Avon, UK: Multilingual Matters.

Druckman, D. (1993). The situational levers of negotiating flexibility. *Journal of Conflict Resolution, 37* 236-276.

Dukes, R. L. (1990). *Worlds apart: Collective action in simulated agrarian and industrial societies.* Dordrecht: Kluwer.

Dukes, R. L., & Seidner, C. J. (Eds.). (1978). *Learning with simulations and games.* Beverly Hills, CA: Sage.

Ellington, H., Addinall, E., & Percival, F. (1981). *Games and simulations in science education.* London: Kogan Page.

Fowler, S. M., & Fowler, M. (Eds.). (1995). *The intercultural sourcebook: Cross-cultural training methods.* Yarmouth, ME: Intercultural Press.

Fripp, J. (1993). *Learning through simulations: A guide to the design and use of simulations in business and education.* London: McGraw-Hill.

Gentry, J. (Ed.). (1990). *Guide to business gaming and experiential learning.* London: Kogan Page.

Guetzkow, H. (Ed.). (1962). *Simulation in social science: Readings.* Englewood Cliffs, NJ: Prentice Hall.

Guetzkow, H., Alger, C. F., Brody, R. A., Noel, R. C., & Snyder, R. C. (1963). *Simulation in international relations: Developments for research and teaching.* Englewood Cliffs, NJ: Prentice Hall.

Guetzkow, H., Kotler, P., & Schultz, R. L. (1972). *Simulation in social and administrative science: Overviews and case examples for the use of simulations in decision making.* Englewood Cliffs, NJ: Prentice Hall.

Guetzkow, H., & Valdez, J. J. (1981). *Simulated international processes: Theories and research in global modeling.* Beverly Hills, CA: Sage.

Inbar, M., & Stoll, C. S. (Eds.). (1972). *Simulation and gaming in social science.* New York: Free Press.

Jamieson, I., Miller, A., & Watts, A. G. (1988). *Mirrors of work: Work simulations in schools.* Lewes, East Sussex, UK: Falmer.

Jaulin, R. (Ed.). (1979). *Jeux et jouets: Essai d'ethnotechnologie.* Paris: Aubier.

Jones, K. (1982). *Simulations in language teaching.* Cambridge, UK: Cambridge University Press.

Katz, J. (Ed.). (1994). Simulation/gaming in entrepreneurship education [Special issue]. *Simulation & Gaming: An International Journal, 25*(3).

Keys, B., & Wolfe, J. (1990). The role of management games and simulations in education and research. *Journal of Management, 16*(2), 307-336.

Lewis, L. H. (Ed.). (1986). *Experiential and simulation techniques for teaching adults*. San Francisco: Jossey-Bass.

Livingston, S. A., & Stoll, C. S. (1973). *Simulation games: An introduction for the social studies teacher*. London: Collier Macmillan.

Mauriras-Bousquet, M. (Ed.). (1991, May). People at play [Special issue]. *UNESCO Courier*. (Also published in 34 other languages)

Moscardini, A. O., & Fletcher, E. J. (1991). *Applied simulation and system dynamics*. Northallerton, UK: Emjoc.

Moyles, J. R. (1989). *Just playing? The role and status of play in early childhood education*. Milton Keynes, UK: Open University Press.

Noel, R. C. (1963). *Theory and procedures for a simulation of international relations*. Englewood Cliffs, NJ: Prentice Hall.

Oswalt, I. (Ed.). (1993). Military simulation/gaming, Parts 1-2 [Special issues]. *Simulation & Gaming: An International Journal, 24*(3, pt. 1; 4, pt. 2).

Paul-Cavallier, F. (1993). *Jouons*. Geneva: Jouvence.

Pedersen, P. (Ed.). (1994). Counseling and counselor education [Special issue]. *Simulation & Gaming: An International Journal, 25*(1).

Provenzo, A. B., & Provenzo, E. F., Jr. (1990). *Favorite board games you can make and play*. Mineola, NY: Dover. (Original work published 1981)

Saunders, D. (Ed.). (1995). *The simulation and gaming yearbook, Vol. 3: Games and simulations for business*. London: Kogan Page.

Simulation & Gaming: An International Journal. Thousand Oaks, CA: Sage.

Simulation/Games for Learning (SAGSET's journal, now *Simulation and Gaming Yearbook*). London: Kogan Page.

Stadsklev, R. (1979). *Handbook of simulation gaming in social education*. University: University of Alabama Press.

Thatcher, D., & Robinson, J. (Eds.). (1984). *Business, health and nursing education*. Loughborough, UK: SAGSET.

Thorson, E. (Ed.). (1979). *Simulation in higher education*. Hicksville, NY: Exposition Press.

Toth, F. (1988). Policy exercises I: Objectives and design elements II: Procedures and implementation. *Simulation & Games: An International Journal, 19*(3).

Vajda, S. (1992). *Mathematical games and how to play them*. Chichester, UK: Ellis Horwood.

Ward, M. D. (Ed.). (1985). *Theories, models, and simulations in international relations: Essays in honor of Harold Guetzkow*. Boulder, CO: Westview.

Wenzler, I. (1993). *Policy exercises: A new approach to policy development*. Nijmegen: Stichting Katholieke Universiteit.

Wolfe, J. (Ed.). (1987). A practical guide of business gaming [Special issue]. *Simulation & Games: An International Journal, 18*(2).

Zoll, A. A. (1969). *Dynamic management education*. London: Addison-Wesley.

Other Sources

One of the most useful other sources of work on simulation/gaming is, of course, the periodical literature, such as *Simulation & Gaming: An International Journal*. The frequently asked questions that I encounter at conferences (and indeed at other times) can be answered by consulting the periodical publications, which give information about imminent events and new developments. Besides the literature on simulation/gaming, a great many other titles are relevant to the field. A couple of these have been cited above, for example on facilitation, but space here precludes others, such as research design books (which sometimes include a chapter on simulation/gaming as a research method) or books on political science, environmental concerns, policy, mathematical games, and counseling.

Periodicals

Many articles on simulation/gaming are published in journals such as *Teaching Sociology, Geography Teacher, History Microcomputer Review,* and *Social Science Computer Review.* Until recently, two major journals were devoted to the discipline of simulation/gaming; unfortunately, the excellent *Simulation/ Games for Learning* (SAGSET's journal) ceased publication a couple of years ago. This has been a great loss to the simulation/gaming community and to the field. We have been lucky, however, because the journal has been superseded by a yearbook devoted to simulation/gaming, which is listed with periodicals in Table 19.1.

Listservs

The Internet has become a rich resource for simulation/gaming in at least three ways. The first, of course, is its use as a means of communication for large-scale, multi-institutional simulation/games, such as POLIS, ICONS, and IDEALS, and multiuser dungeons (MUDs). The second is a means of communication among scholars—for example, for writing joint papers or making arrangements for working together. The third is its facilities for housing and distributing information and discussion, such as on Listservs. To join a discussion list, send the message *sub list_name your_first_name your_surname [any_comments]* to *listserv@node.* The list_names and the nodes of the main simulation/gaming lists are provided in Table 19.2. Usenet is another carrier of several groups related to simulation/gaming, such as abstract games, BRIDGE, DIPLOMACY, and video games.

Associations

Many associations exist in the area of simulation and gaming, although only ISAGA is truly international. ISAGA also often has the most well-attended annual conference, a conference that sparkles with attendees from an unusually wide range of disciplines and from an exceptionally large number of countries and cultures. Information on forthcoming ABSEL, ISAGA, JASAG, and NASAGA conferences is made available in the *Association News & Notes* section of *Simulation & Gaming: An International Journal* (see Table 19.1). Information on the main simulation/game associations is given in Table 19.3.

TABLE 19.1 Periodicals on or Related to Simulation/Gaming

Title and Type	Editorial and/or Comments	Publisher (subscription address)
Gaming & Education (occasional four-page newsletter)	David Millians 991-A Adair Avenue Atlanta, GA 30306, USA	Same
Handbook for Group Facilitators (annual game compendiums)	J. William Pfeiffer 8517 Production Avenue San Diego, CA 92121, USA	Pfeiffer & Co. Same address
Interactive Fantasy: The Journal of Role-Playing and Storytelling Systems (quarterly journal)	Andrew Rilstone Hogshead Publishing 29a Abbeville Road London SW4 9LA, England james@hogshead.demon.co.uk	James Wallis Same address
Journal of Experiential Learning and Simulation (JELS) (quarterly journal)	Ceased publication	Elsevier North Holland
Journal of Management Education (quarterly refereed journal)	Joan Gallos School of Education University of Missouri, Kansas City 5100 Rockwell Road Kansas City, MO 64110, USA	Sage Periodicals Press 2455 Teller Road Thousand Oaks, CA 91320, USA
Pédagogies Ludiques (quarterly journal on games in education and professional training)	Chantal Barthélémy-Ruiz Argine Consultants 88 boulevard de Courcelles 75017 Paris, France	Same
SAGSET Journal (quarterly journal)	Ceased publication; superseded by Simulation/Games for Learning and this in turn by Simulation and Gaming Yearbook	SAGSET & Kogan Page
Sigsim Simuletter (quarterly newsletter on computer simulation)	Harold J. Highland Association for Computing Machinery SIG on Simulation 11 West 42nd Street New York, NY 10036, USA	Same
Simages (occasional one-page newsletter)	Sivasailam Thiagarajan 4423 East Trailridge Road Bloomington, IN 47408, USA	Same
Simgames: The Canadian Journal of Simulation and Gaming (quarterly journal)	Ceased publication	

(continued)

TABLE 19.1 Continued

Title and Type	Editorial and/or Comments	Publisher (subscription address)
Simulation & Gaming: An *International Journal of Theory, Practice, and Research* (quarterly refereed journal on all aspects of simulation/gaming; its Silver Anniversary took place in 1994)	David Crookall TSH-UTC, BP 649 60209 Compiègne cédex, *France* Telephone: 44.23.46.23 Fax: 44.23.43.00 E-mail: crookall@omega.univ-lille1.fr or crookall@mx.univ-compiegne.fr Before submitting a manuscript, send a check for US$3 or a cheque for £2 or three IRCs, for a copy of the *Guide for Authors*	Sage Periodicals Press 2455 Teller Road Thousand Oaks, CA 91320, USA Telephone: 805-499-0721 Fax: 805-499-0871 or 6 Bonhill Street London EC2A 4PU, England
Simulation and Gaming Yearbook (yearly edited volume on all aspects of simulation/gaming)	Danny Saunders Enterprise Unit University of Glamorgan Llantwit Road Pontypridd Mid-Glamorgan CF37 1DL, Wales	Kogan Page 120 Pentonville Road London N1 9JN, England
Simulation Journal (monthly magazine on industrial applications)	Barbara Novak Simulation Council Box 17900 San Diego, CA 92117, USA	
Simulation Practice and Theory: *International Journal of the Federation of European Simulation Societies* (quarterly journal)	L. Dekker c/o Elsevier Sara Burgerhartstraat 25 1055 KV Amsterdam, The Netherlands	Elsevier Same address
Simulation/Games for Learning (quarterly journal)	Ceased publication; formerly *SAGSET Journal*; replaced by *Simulation and Gaming Yearbook* (see above)	SAGSET & Kogan Page Back issues available from SAGSET (see Associations)
Social Science Computer Review (quarterly, refereed journal)	G. David Garson Editor, *SSCORE* Department of Political Science North Carolina State University Box 8101 Raleigh, NC 27695, USA	Duke University Press 6697 College Station Durham, NC 27708, USA

Teaching Sociology (quarterly refereed academic journal)	Dean Dorn
	c/o American Sociological
	  Association
	1722 N Street NW
	Washington, DC 20036, USA
		American Sociological
		  Association
		Same address

TABLE 19.1 Continued

Title and Type	Editorial and/or Comments	Publisher (subscription address)
Wetenscappelijk Tijdschrift voor Informatica en Modelbouw in Interdiscplinaire Context (Occasional journal)	Cor van Dijkum & Dorien J. DeTombe Department of JGL Faculty of Social Science University of Utrecht Heidelberglaan 2 3584 CS Utrecht, The Netherlands	Box 3286 1001 AB Amsterdam The Netherlands

TABLE 19.2 Listservs Related to Simulation/Gaming

Listname@node	Focus
absel@toe.towson.edu	Forum for ABSEL
aeelist@pucc.bitnet	Association for Experiential Education
bes-list@unbvm1.bitnet	Discussion on the Business Enterprise Simulator
consim-l@ualtavm.bitnet	Conflict simulation/games
mcleod@sdsc.bitnet or scsi@biomath.rug.ac.be	Contacts for E-S3: Electronic version of *Simulation in the Service of Society*
games-l@brownvm.bitnet	Computer games (Peered)
games-l@krsnucc1.bitnet	Computer games (Peered)
games-l@utarlvm1.bitnet	Computer games (Peered)
glosas-l@uottawa.bitnet	Global Systems Analysis and Simulation
gspe-nl@hearn.bitnet	Discussions on policy exercises
ifsug-l@uhccvm.bitnet	INTERNATIONAL FUTURES Simulation Users' Group
isaga-l@uhccvm.bitnet	Forum for ISAGA
isss@jhuvm.bitnet	International Student Space Simulations
nyslux-l@ubvm.bitnet	New York Consortium for Model European Community Simulation
simurb-l@icineca.bitnet	Simulation/gaming in town planning and architecture
vrsurger@gwuvm.bitnet	Virtual Reality Surgical Simulator Group

Next Steps

Each individual must decide if any of the materials presented here is useful, and if so, to look at the work already accomplished and base new work on the previous or at least do new work that moves on from where we are now. We do not have the resources of some disciplines and cannot therefore afford to reinvent wheels. That is why we have conferences and proceedings, and that is

TABLE 19.3 Main Simulation/Game Associations

Abbreviation	Full Name	Contact
ABSEL	Association for Business Simulation and Experiential Learning	J. Bernard Keys School of Business Georgia Southern University Statesboro, GA 30460, USA or John Butler Sirrine Hall Clemson University Clemson, SC 29634, USA
AUSSAGA	Australian Simulation and Gaming Association	Elizabeth Christopher School of Business and Public Administration Charles Sturt University Bathurst, NSW 2795, Australia
AMPK	Austrian Management Planspiel Kongreß	Niki Harramach Harramach Management Beratung Stubenring 24 1010 Wien, Austria
EESAGA	Eastern European Simulation and Gaming Association	Current address unknown
EUNETSIM	European Network for System Simulation and Management Gaming	Walter E. Rohn Deutsche Planspiel Zentrale Vonkeln 51 5600 Wuppertal 12, Germany
GERSAFE	Groupe d'Etudes et de Recherche sur les Simulations Appliquées à la Formation et à l'Enseignement	Claude Bourlès GERSAFE IPSA-UCO 3 place André-Leroy 49008 Angers cédex 08, France
ISAGA	International Simulation and Gaming Association	Jan H. G. Klabbers ISAGA Secretary General Oostervelden 59 6681 WR Bemmel, The Netherlands or David Crookall Dépt. TSH, UTC, BP 649 60209 Compiègne cédex, France
JASAG	Japan Association of Simulation and Gaming	c/o JPCSA 2-D Kioi Royal-Heights, 3-29 Kioi-Cho Chiyoda-ku, Tokyo 1 02, Japan

TABLE 19.3 Continued

Abbreviation	Full Name	Contact
NASAGA	North American Simulation and Gaming Association	Sivasailam Thiagarajan Workshops by Thiagi 4423 East Trailridge Road Bloomington, IN 47408, USA or Barabara Steinwachs risingmoon at Keuka Lake 1128 East Bluff Drive Penn Yan, NY 14527, USA
Permis de Jouer		Chantal Barthélémy-Ruiz Argine Consultants, 37 rue Jouffroy dAbbans 75017 Paris, France
PHILSAGA	Philippines Simulation and Gaming Association	Current address unknown
SAGSET	Society for Active Learning (Formerly Society for the Advancement of Games and Simulation in Education and Training)	c/o Jill Brookes SEDA Administrator Gala House, 3 Raglan Road Edgbaston, Birmingham B5 7RA, England
SCS	Society for Computer Simulation	Suzette McLeod or Sandra LaFlair P.O. Box 17900 San Diego, CA 92177, USA or Philippe Geril SCS - European Simulation Office University of Ghent, Coupure Links 653 B-9000 Ghent, Belgium
S/G Committee, SIETAR	Simulation/Games Committee of the Society for Intercultural Education, Training and Research	Daniel Yalowitz Lesley College 29 Everett Street Cambridge, MA 02138, USA
SIGIS	Societa Italiana dei Giochi di Simulazione	SIGIS Via Taro 35 00199 Roma, Italy

why books are written and journals published. The avenues for research into simulation/gaming are many and wide, but we have to point the signposts carefully. A few are suggested here.

Ethnomethodology

The nature of simulation/gaming is clearly an area that attacts much interest. Without some close analysis of actual participation in simulation/games, it would seem to me fruitless and even misleading to attempt any definition of what simulation/gaming is, particularly from the participant's perspective. When considering the nature of simulation/gaming, the tools of ethnomethodology have been used on occasion to look at participants' meaning-making procedures, but such studies are largely ignored by the more positivist researchers.

Future research should employ ethnomethodology to analyze segments of simulation/games in operation. From that analysis could be drawn clear inferences about the nature of the activity from the perspective of the participant. Such analyses might also yield valuable indicators about how best to conduct and debrief these events and also about how to shape more sensitive and appropriate evaluation instruments. The work of social interactionists, such as Goffman (cited earlier), would bring much weight to our analyses and theorizing.

Debriefing

In the areas of debriefing and evaluation, the opportunities for conducting valuable research are wide open. Most evaluation studies ignore or simply gloss over the debriefing. Future studies should incorporate the debriefing as one of the major variables, and evaluation designs should be built around it. Table 19.4 gives an example of a comprehensive design that would take debriefing explicitly into account.

TABLE 19.4 Example of Design for Research on Debriefing

Group A: Game + Debriefing	Group B: No Game + Debriefing	Group C: No Game + No Debriefing
Data collection 1	(Data collection 1)	(Data collection 1)
Normal teaching	Normal teaching	Normal teaching
Data collection 2	**Data collection 2**	**Data collection 2**
Participation in simulation/game	**Normal teaching**	**Normal teaching**
Data collection 3, before debriefing	(Data collection 3)	(Data collection 3)
Debriefing 1, immediate (e.g., after simulation/game or next day)	(Debriefing 1)	nothing
Data collection 4	(Data collection 4)	(Data collection 4)
Normal teaching	Normal teaching	Normal teaching
Debriefing 2, later (e.g., 1 week)	**Debriefing** of normal teaching sessions	nothing
Data collection 5	**Data collection 5**	**Data collection 5**
Data collection 6, much later (e.g., 1 year)	**Data collection 6,** much later	**Data collection 6,** much later

NOTE: Parentheses indicate optional steps. Bold type highlights the most important steps.

Reader's Comments and Contributions

This is the first version of this literature guide. At some point, an updated version will be needed. You will be able to contribute to the field by sending me comments about the present version, particularly regarding any references that are missing and that you think should be in the next version. Please send me a copy of the item, or, failing this, complete bibliographic information, including postal address of the publisher. Your contribution will be acknowledged.

Certificate Programs and Collaboration

At least two certificate programs exist on the topic of simulation/gaming, one offered by the Université de Paris Nord (Villetaneuse, France) and the other by the University of Michigan (Ann Arbor, United States). Discussions are under way to create other programs, probably with an international dimension. Currently being envisaged are new programs in France, Italy, Japan, and the Netherlands. Current and future programs have a major role to play in furthering simulation/gaming in general and setting agendas for and conducting research in the area. Such programs should also work with other simulation centers, such as the Center for Business Simulation, Georgia Southern University (Statesboro, United States). Much can come from working together and even from pooling resources.

In Closing . . .

Lewis Carroll's *Through the Looking-Glass* embodies much of the paradoxical nature and playful character of simulation/gaming. Some might liken a simulation/game to the smile of the Cheshire cat. However, as a wry comment on the need to move forward in the field of simulation/gaming, I rather like the Walrus and his musing that "the time has come . . . to talk of many things."

20

The Educational Effectiveness
of Interactive Games

DANIEL DRUCKMAN

For almost a decade the National Research Council's Committee on Techniques for the Enhancement of Human Performance has examined a wide variety of approaches that make strong claims for improving performance. The results of our work are reported in a series of books published by National Academy Press (Druckman & Bjork, 1991, 1994; Druckman & Swets, 1988). Among the approaches examined in our most recent phase of work were role-playing exercises and interactive games. These techniques were considered in conjunction with team-building interventions, both of which are often accompanied by enthusiastic testimonials about their effectiveness for enhancing learning and performance. The results of a review of the research literature suggested that team-building exercises have stronger effects on morale and cohesion than they do on actual performance and thus raised questions about the impact of games on conceptual learning. The review in this chapter focuses on games used primarily for educational purposes, and draws implications for effectiveness from the results of evaluation studies (for the review of studies on team building and team development, see Druckman & Bjork, 1994, chap. 6). In the concluding section, I also raise issues concerning fidelity or realism, an important design consideration for games that attempt to simulate real-world environments.

Interactive Games

The terms simulation and games are often used interchangeably. In this chapter, I focus primarily on games that are role-playing exercises involving groups. This is often considered to be a type of simulation (see, e.g., Crookall, Oxford, & Saunders, 1987), although it differs from the mechanical simulators or training simulations used for developing specific skills. Most of the games discussed in this chapter are concerned less with the training of well-defined, mission-oriented operational skills and the transfer of those skills than with learning general and social skills in educational settings. Because of its popularity as a training and research device, the technology of game design and evaluation has been the subject of considerable research and conceptual work.[1] In what follows, I discuss issues related to the use of games and provide a summary of the evidence obtained to date on their effectiveness. Games are frequently used as exercises in team development packages designed by organizational consultants. One of the more popular games for facilitating team building is PUMPING THE COLORS, created by Gary Shirts. Rarely, however, are the exercises evaluated in terms of whether they accomplish their objectives. Even when used as tasks in studies comparing different team-building interventions, the game exercises are not evaluated (e.g., Hsu, 1984; Miesing & Preble, 1985; Norris & Niebuhr, 1980; Wolfe, Bowen, & Roberts, 1989). Thus, implications for the effectiveness of games used for team development must be derived from more general research on educational games. That research has addressed both cognitive and motivational effects of games; by so doing, it has implications for their effect on team-learning and team-building processes. However, measures of individual learning and motivation, used in most of these studies, may not translate into team outcomes. At issue are the effects of team members' development for a team's performance, and few studies to date have addressed this relationship (see Druckman & Bjork, 1991, chap. 12).[2]

The kinds of exercises used most often for training take the form of games played by students or trainees to discover new concepts or develop new skills. At issue is whether the intended learning—acquiring concepts or skills—occurs. This issue has been addressed by research designed to evaluate outcomes of the learning experience. Another issue is whether the new knowledge or skills can be used effectively in other environments. Beginning in the early 1960s, an active network of gaming researchers devoted their careers to finding answers to these questions. Many of these studies have been reported in the journal *Simulation & Gaming* and in a number of edited books that cover a variety of types of uses and applications. My review draws on this literature, emphasizing, in particular, work reported during the past 15 years. I concentrate on gaming technology in general rather than specific simulations intended to develop particular operational skills (for a discussion of simulators, see Druckman & Bjork, 1994, chap. 3). Games have a number of features that should facilitate learning. Among the features highlighted in the literature are involving students in an active learning situation (Glenn, Gregg, & Tipple, 1982), enhancing their control over the learning environment (Boocock & Schild, 1968), focusing on learning principles and referents for concepts (Greenblat, 1975), rapid feedback and the learning of strategies (Schild, 1968), enhancing motivation to learn (Bredemeier & Greenblat, 1981), and providing an opportunity to encounter problems in ways analogous to the way they are encountered in real-world contexts (Van Sickle, 1978). The key question is whether these features contribute to better learning.

Educational Effectiveness

Cherryholmes (1966) is often credited with the earliest evaluation of learning through game playing. On the basis of only a few studies completed prior to 1966, he concluded that only interest in the material being learned improved significantly; negligible changes occurred on cognitive and attitudinal variables. Somewhat more optimistic conclusions were reached 11 years later. Pierfy (1977) reviewed studies reported during the 1960s and 1970s that compared learning through games with other educational experiences. With regard to learning, 15 of 21 studies showed no significant difference between experimental and control groups, indicating that the games were not more effective than conventional instructional techniques. Of the other six studies, three showed games to be better, and three showed conventional methods to be better. With regard to retention, eight of 11 studies reported significant differences in favor of games, indicating that students retained information longer than those trained with more conventional approaches. With regard to attitude change, eight of 11 studies showed that games had a greater effect on attitudes (in terms of increased realism and approval of real-life persons) than conventional methods. For interest, seven of eight studies reported significantly more interest in the simulation activities than in the more conventional classroom activities, a finding that supports Cherryholmes' (1966) conclusion.

Pierfy (1977) goes on to indicate that deficiencies in research design render these conclusions tentative. He lists a number of sources of possible confounding factors in many of the studies, including unintended biases from game designers who also conduct the studies; unintended effects of instructor variables, when matched classes are taught by different instructors; Hawthorne effects, due to the difference between one group receiving a new method (game) while the other group is exposed to a familiar, conventional method; for some studies, administration of the post-test after a debriefing, allowing for the possibility that the post-test responses were influenced by the debriefing discussion; the techniques used in control classes may be regarded by students as vague, dull, and incomplete, so that any gains shown for the simulation classes are not strongly biased; and use of only a pre-test/post-test design—not adding groups without the pre-test—allowing for the possibility that the pre-test interacted in different ways with one or another method of instruction. These flaws are not limited to game evaluations; they also characterize much of the evaluation literature in general—and many of them can be remedied.

Stronger studies have appeared in more recent years, due in part to attempts by designers and users to incorporate evaluations in their packages as a matter of course. Comparability from one study to another can also be increased if the same categories of learning are used in constructing dependent variables, including knowledge of facts, analogies, game structure, skills needed for playing the game, knowledge of outcomes of various strategies used in the game, perceptions of the game, and attitudes toward the game (see also Fletcher,

1971). A variety of methods can be used to measure any particular learning objective, as Anderson and Lawton (1992) illustrate with respect to the objectives of basic knowledge, comprehension, application, analysis, synthesis, and evaluation. Furthermore, replication of studies in a variety of settings would help distinguish between findings that hold across situations from those that are specific to particular situations. Such replication can reduce the impact of confounding variables (see Campbell & Stanley's, 1963, discussion on heterogeneity of irrelevancies).

Another methodological concern is that even the best evaluations may not uncover causal mechanisms. Most of the studies reviewed by Pierfy (1977) were demonstration experiments that simply show effects of the instructional packages: Does it work? Few attempts are made to unpack the parts in order to determine what may account for the observed effects on learning or motivation: How does it work? This distinction was recognized in early appraisals of learning in simulation and games. In their wide-ranging survey of the issues, Boocock and Schild (1968) distinguish between the engineering and the science approaches to understanding. The former consists of demonstrating that a social technology produces gains; the latter is the identification of the mechanisms responsible for the gains. Few of the studies they examined searched for mechanisms; nor has there been any trend toward explanatory studies in more recent years. Investigators seem to have largely ignored the Boocock and Schild distinction.

Also missing in the research on simulations and games are issues raised by Bredemeier and Greenblat (1981) in their update of Pierfy's review. Bredemeier and Greenblat divide learning into three parts: subject matter, attitudes, and learning about oneself. With regard to subject matter, the available evidence suggests that games are at least as effective as other methods and are more effective aids to retention. With regard to attitudes, the evidence suggests that games can be more effective than traditional methods of instruction in facilitating positive attitude change toward the subject and its purposes. With regard to learning about oneself, they cite the results obtained by Johnson and Nelson (1978) showing that subjects who played games (versus those who did not) showed greater positive change on willingness to communicate. The positive effects on self-awareness may, however, depend on the extent to which the game was experienced in a positive way. Many of these conclusions support those reached by Pierfy (1977). They do not illuminate reasons for why the effects do or do not occur and therefore make only small contributions to the development of theory in this area.

More recently, Randel, Morris, Wetzel, and Whitehall (1992) updated the earlier reviews in an examination of 69 studies reported in a 28-year period. Overall, they found that 56% of the comparisons between simulation games and conventional instruction showed no difference, 32% found differences favoring games, 7% favored games but their controls were questionable, and 5% found differences favoring conventional instruction. Dividing the studies into six subject-matter areas, the authors found that the greatest percentage of results favoring games were in mathematics (seven of eight studies) and language arts (five of six studies). Although the largest number of gaming evaluations have been in the area of social science, the majority of these studies (33 of 46) showed no differences in performance between games and conventional instruction. A meta-analysis of social science simulations (Van Sickle, 1986) reported a small effect size. On the basis of these findings, Randel et al. (1992) concluded that games are likely to be more beneficial for topics "where very specific content can be targeted and objectives precisely defined" (p. 269). They also reaffirmed conclusions, reached in earlier reviews, that games show greater retention for students over time and elicit more student interest than conventional instruction. As did the earlier reviews, Randel et al. (1992) call attention to many of the design and measurement problems typical of the studies. They add to the earlier lists the possible confusion between effects produced by the game and those produced by the debriefing sessions. They also emphasize the importance of distinguishing between preferences expressed by players and what it is that they learn from the games.

The reviews make evident that there is much yet to be understood about the effects on learners of participation in games or simulations. Progress toward richer theory and application may depend on providing answers to the following questions: What accounts for the discrepancy between learners' impressions and subjective reports and the weak evidence on performance? What is the relationship between motivational and learning variables? How does involvement in the game affect learning? Why are motivation and interest stimulated by games? To what extent are effects due to instructor variables? For example, those instructors who are amenable to using games may be people who stimulate relaxed classrooms and facilitate later changes in classroom atmosphere. What aspects of games are expected to have what sorts of distinct effects on what sorts of participants? Does what one learns in a particular game transfer to other situations? To what range of situations do the lessons learned in a particular game apply? The promise of interactive games as vehicles for learning skills and concepts has been largely unrealized to date. That promise is based on the assumption that role-playing activities may do more than stimulate interest; they "may also involve students in an active learning situation that may teach them specific skills" (Glenn et al., 1982, p. 209). Although the evidence to date is inconclusive, the problems may rest not with the technology but with the way it is implemented and evaluated. A clearer definition of what is to be accomplished by the experience, how to accomplish it, and then how to evaluate effects would help, as would a theoretically based taxonomy of games that distinguishes among games used for different purposes (see Bredemeier & Greenblat, 1981). Game designers need to be guided by conceptual frameworks. Game evaluators need to increase their sensitivity to relevant methodological issues. Advances along both these lines will almost certainly strengthen the state of the art. They will also clarify the distinction between cognitive and motivational effects on participants in gaming exercises used for team development.

Game Fidelity: How Important?

Many games are attempts to reproduce features of particular real-world settings. An assumed advantage of simulating is that what is learned will transfer to the settings where the acquired concepts or skills will be used. Similarly, for researchers, it is assumed that knowledge acquired about behavior in simulated gaming settings will apply to behavior in the setting that is reproduced.[3] These assumptions turn on the relationship between game fidelity (referred to also as verisimilitude)—the extent of correspondence between the simulation/game and the setting being simulated—and transfer of the skills or understandings acquired in the simulation. This issue has received limited attention in the empirical literature. We simply do not know the extent to which transfer depends on fidelity.[4] However, it may be useful to consider some possible advantages and disadvantages of increasing the fidelity of learning environments.

The importance of fidelity may be a function of the purpose of the game or simulation. Transfer of learned skills to specific missions may benefit from a close correspondence between the learning and operating environments. Use of knowledge learned in simulated exercises across a range of situations may be enhanced to the extent that the learning environment is not narrowly constructed to reflect particular situations. Most generally, it would seem that when people are being trained for specific missions, some degree of fidelity between the learning and operating environments is important. Examples are pilot training, air traffic control training, and rehearsals for theatrical performances or concerts, and athletic contests (where, for example, the opposing team's moves are simulated or orchestrated). These are carefully defined skills often executed in rote fashion. They are also attempts to develop strategies to be deployed in specific situations likely to occur in the future. Along with the strategies comes teamwork. Building cohesion among team members in simulations may be more likely to carry over to the mission when the training task resembles the mission. Similarly, it is important to construct realistic what-if exercises when these exercises are used for contingency planning, that is, if the events occur, be prepared. Also, attempts to understand why particular events unfolded in the past is likely to benefit from high-fidelity simulation (see, e.g., Hermann & Hermann's, 1967, simulation of the outbreak of World War I).

One issue is just how much fidelity is enough to produce transfer of learned skills. Some have suggested that very high levels of fidelity are not cost-effective and may even be detrimental (Andrews, 1988; Patrick, 1992). Too much fidelity to an actual complex system can sometimes be worse than a simpler representation of the environment. This is particularly the case when novices are being trained to operate complex equipment: they are not ready to comprehend the subtle, fast, and transitory aspects of the equipment. Simpler tasks are more suited to the initial stages of learning. Furthermore, beyond certain levels, increasing the fidelity of a simulation may yield only small improvements in performance over a simpler device. A number of studies have shown no advantage for using realistic equipment over inexpensive cardboard mockups (e.g., Caro, Corley, Spears, & Blaiwes, 1984). The challenge is to determine which elements of the operating environment need to be preserved and which can be dispensed with in a simulation. Some are more important than others, and the distinction depends on the results of careful task analyses.

Fidelity is likely to be less important when simulations are used for general education, as in the gaming studies reviewed above, than for training to perform in more specific missions or contests. In fact, it can be argued that it would be advantageous to reduce fidelity when the aim is to convey general concepts or to enhance the learner's flexibility or long-term retention (see Greenblat's, 1975, discussion of the advantages of using simulations for concept learning; also see Druckman & Bjork, 1991, chap. 6, for training approaches that increase flexibility and adaptation to new environments). Fidelity is also less important when simulations are used as forecasting devices or as settings to conduct experiments that contribute to the development of theory in a field. Futuristic simulations cannot, by definition, benefit from information about those environments (e.g., Brody, 1963). Experimental simulations are often used to test hypotheses derived from theories relevant to a wide range of situations (Mahoney & Druckman, 1975).

Conclusions

Interactive games are widely used as exercises in educational and training programs. In educational settings, they are often used to facilitate concept learning. In training programs, they are used to contribute to the development of task-related skills. Their popularity in both settings is based mostly on judgments made by participants and developers rather than on carefully designed evaluation studies. Although the literature on games is large, many of the evaluation studies consist of demonstration experiments that do not attempt to uncover mechanisms for effects or of studies designed without proper controls for alternative explanations. However, the few well-designed studies to date, done mostly with educational games, suggest that although games are effective in instilling positive attitudes toward and interest in the subject matter they are not more effective than other methods as aids to learning. By producing stronger effects on motivational variables, games may be more useful for encouraging participation in a social learning process that exposes students to new concepts and ideas. They also expose students to teamwork activities but are probably more effective as vehicles for team-building than team-learning exercises. However, further research is needed to establish the value of games in team training. In fact, both team building or training and gaming interventions need to be unpacked to determine which parts of the packages are primarily responsible for impacts. In evaluating the effectiveness of games as learning environments, it is important to consider issues of fidelity—the extent to which a game resembles the environments where new skills and understandings will be used. In discussing this issue, I suggest that high levels of fidelity may be more important for the learning of specific job-related skills than for the learning of more general concepts. When the purpose of a game is to educate, it may be advantageous to reduce fidelity so as to increase the learner's flexibility in applying the new concepts. However, even when the purpose of a game is to train, very high levels of fidelity may not be cost-effective. Beyond a certain level of fidelity, any further performance gains may be offset by the added costs incurred in materials. Also, in the early stages of skill acquisition, the learner may simply not be ready to confront the complexity of the real-world setting or features of the task, including any equipment or material needed to execute or implement operations.

Notes

1. Games are used frequently for training in the military. A detailed survey of uses of simulations and games in the military is reported by Shubik and Brewer (1972). They identified approximately 135 active military simulations in use at the Department of Defense. To our knowledge, this survey has not been updated, nor have we been able to locate a similar survey of games developed for other uses. However, it is possible to get a rough estimate of popularity from various published sources. New games are mentioned in each issue of the journal *Simulation & Gaming* (formerly *Simulation & Games*), and a wide variety of packaged games are made available. Games are usually distributed directly by the designers, by the institutes or councils that sponsored the gaming activity, by small companies formed to market particular games, or by book publishers. Sales for most games number in the thousands, but a few, such as the well-known cross-cultural game BAFA BAFA, have sold well over 100,000 worldwide. However, sales may not be a good indicator of use for at least three reasons. First, the same packaged materials are used by many people: Gary Shirts, the designer of BAFA, estimates that players of his games number in the millions (personal communication). Second, many games are designed and used for relatively idiosyncratic purposes, such as classroom adjuncts to other teaching techniques, experimentation in specialized areas, or training of highly specialized skills. Third, many games are distributed for free or are available in texts that contain role-playing exercises.

2. Nor have there been many evaluations of the highly technical team exercises used for military training. Combat exercises have been simulated in the form of board games, computerized virtual realities, and field exercises that provide soldiers with broad experiences of many facets of combat over relatively long periods of time; see Oswalt (1993) for a review of current military applications. Unfortunately, few of these exercises have been evaluated systematically in terms of their effect on training goals. Most evaluations reported in the published literature have concentrated on games designed to improve skill in such areas as business management, language learning, negotiation, medical education and hospital administration, environmental management, and social science concepts. Thus, implications for the effectiveness of military simulations must be derived from a literature on non-military applications.

3. This is referred to as external validity. Some of the best treatments of this issue are found in the literature on international relations. A general treatment of the issue is given by Hermann (1967).

4. A meta-analysis of the team performance literature by Freeberg and Rock (1987) showed a relationship between task fidelity and performance. The more realistic the task, the better the performance because both teams coordinated their activities more effectively. This finding suggests that realism heightens team motivation and, perhaps, learning. It does not suggest that transfer improved with increased fidelity.

References

Anderson, P. H., & Lawton, L. (1992). A survey of methods used for evaluating student performance on business simulations. *Simulation & Gaming: An International Journal, 23,* 490-498.

Andrews, D. H. (1988, January). Relationships among simulators, training devices, and learning: A behavioral view. *Educational Technology,* pp. 48-54.

Boocock, S. S., & Schild, E. O. (Eds.). (1968). *Simulation games in learning.* Beverly Hills, CA: Sage.

Bredemeier, M. E., & Greenblat, C. S. (1981). The educational effectiveness of simulation games: A synthesis of findings. *Simulation & Games: An International Journal, 12,* 307-332.

Brody, R. A. (1963). Some systematic effects of the spread of nuclear weapons technology: A study through simulation of a multi-nuclear future. *Journal of Conflict Resolution, 7,* 665-753.

Campbell, D. T., & Stanley, J. C. (1963). *Experimental and quasi-experimental designs for research.* Chicago: Rand McNally.

Caro, P. W., Corley, W. E., Spears, W. D., & Blaiwes, A. S. (1984). *Training effectiveness evaluation and utilization demonstration of a low cost cockpit procedures trainer* (Rep. No. NAVTRAEQUIPCEN 78-C-001301). Pensacola, FL: Seville Training Systems.

Cherryholmes, C. (1966). Some current research on effectiveness of educational simulations: Implications for alternative strategies. *American Behavioral Scientist, 10,* 4-7.

Crookall, D., Oxford, R. L., & Saunders, D. (1987). Towards a reconceptualization of simulation: From representation to reality. *Simulation/Games for Learning, 17*(3), 147-171.

Druckman, D., & Bjork, R. A. (Eds.). (1991). *In the mind's eye: Enhancing human performance.* Committee on Techniques for the Enhancement of Human Performance, National Research Council. Washington, DC: National Academy Press.

Druckman, D., & Bjork, R. A. (Eds.). (1994). *Learning, remembering, believing: Enhancing human performance.* Committee on Techniques for the Enhancement of Human Performance, National Research Council. Washington, DC: National Academy Press.

Druckman, D., & Swets, J. A. (Eds.). (1988). *Enhancing human performance: Issues, theories, and techniques.* Committee on Techniques for the Enhancement of Human Performance, National Research Council. Washington, DC: National Academy Press.

Fletcher, J. (1971). The effectiveness of simulation games as learning environments: A proposed program of research. *Simulation & Games: An International Journal, 2,* 473-488.

Freeberg, N. E., & Rock, D. A. (1987). *Development of a small-group team performance taxonomy based on meta-analysis* (Final report to Office of Naval Research). Princeton, NJ: Educational Testing Service.

Fletcher, J. (1987). *Development of a small-group team performance taxonomy based on meta-analysis* (Final report to Office of Naval Research). Princeton, NJ: Educational Testing Service.

Glenn, A. D., Gregg, D., & Tipple, B. (1982). Using role-play activities to teach problem solving: Three teaching strategies. *Simulation & Games: An International Journal, 13,* 199-209.

Greenblat, C. S. (1975). Teaching with simulation games: A review of claims and evidence. In C. S. Greenblat & R. D. Duke (Eds.), *Gaming-simulation: Rationale, design, and applications.* New York: Halsted.

Hermann, C. F. (1967). Validation problems in games and simulations with special reference to models of international politics. *Behavioral Science, 12,* 216-231.

Hermann, C. F., & Hermann, M. G. (1967). An attempt to simulate the outbreak of World War I. *American Political Science Review, 61,* 400-416.

Hsu, T. (1984). A further test of the group formation and its impacts in a simulated business environment. In D. M. Currie & J. W. Gentry (Eds.), *Developments in business simulation and experiential exercises.* Stillwater: Oklahoma State University Press.

Johnson, M., & Nelson, T. M. (1978). Game playing with juvenile delinquents. *Simulation & Games: An International Journal, 9,* 461-475.

Mahoney, R., & Druckman, D. (1975). Simulation, experimentation, and context: Dimensions of design and influence. *Simulation & Games: An International Journal, 6,* 235-270.

Miesing, P., & Preble, J. F. (1985). Group processes and performance in a complex business simulation. *Small Group Behavior, 16,* 325-338.

Norris, D. R., & Niebuhr, R. E. (1980). Group variables and gaming success. *Simulation & Games: An International Journal, 11,* 301-312.

Oswalt, I. (1993). Current applications, trends, and organizations in U.S. military simulation and gaming. *Simulation & Gaming: An International Journal, 24,* 153-189.

Patrick, J. (1992). *Training: Research and practice.* San Diego: Academic Press.

Pierfy, D. A. (1977). Comparative simulation game research, stumbling blocks, and steppingstones. *Simulation & Games: An International Journal, 8,* 255-268.

Randel, J. M., Morris, B. A., Wetzel, C. D., & Whitehall, B. V. (1992). The effectiveness of games for educational purposes: A review of recent research. *Simulation & Gaming: An International Journal, 23,* 261-276.

Schild, E. O. (1968). The shaping of strategies. In S. S. Boocock & E. O. Schild (Eds.), *Simulation games in learning* (pp. 143-154). Beverly Hills, CA: Sage.

Shubik, M., & Brewer, G. D. (1972). *Models, simulations, and games: A survey* (RAND Rep. No. R-1060). Santa Monica, CA: RAND.

Van Sickle, R. (1978). Designing simulation games to teach decision-making skills. *Simulation & Games: An International Journal, 9,* 413-425.

Van Sickle, R. (1986). A quantitative review of research on instructional simulation gaming: A twenty-year perspective. *Theory and Research in Social Education, 14,* 245-264.

Wolfe, J., Bowen, D. D., & Roberts, C. R. (1989). Team-building effects on company performance: A business game-based study. *Simulation & Games: An International Journal, 20,* 388-408.

21

Jog Your Right Brain (JOG)

An Organizational Research Tool

PETER A. RAYNOLDS

A key aspect of humankind's transition to the new millennia is a shift toward a more holistic orientation, one in which individuals become more concerned with discovering and improving their relationships with all facets of their existence: self, family, employment, community, culture, global society, and environment. The Jog Your Right Brain (JOG) exercise is in tune with this shift. JOG is a multi-purpose exercise that encourages deep inquiry into any denotable subject area through two working topics addressed in a session. It is based on participants making holistic and intuitive choices from pairings of abstract pictures with respect to the topics. The results from any JOG session can be compared quantitatively and qualitatively with results from previous sessions.

At ISAGA '94, a complete JOG exercise was conducted and was followed by presentation and discussion of preliminary results from the use of JOG in recent organizational research studies. This chapter begins with a brief description of JOG and gives references for readers wanting to find out more. The remainder discusses JOG quantitative results obtained in five organizational settings.

Overview of the JOG Exercise

JOG begins with a data-gathering portion lasting 25-30 minutes. The projective differential (PD) technique (Raynolds, 1970; Raynolds, Sakamoto, & Raynolds, 1988; Raynolds, Sakamoto, & Saxe, 1981) is administered on four

AUTHOR'S NOTE: Gennie Raynolds has been an inspirational and creative supporter. She and I co-developed the JOG exercise, including the abstract visual stimuli it employs. We jointly conducted the JOG session at ISAGA '94 and at the organizational sessions covered in this chapter. She also participated in the analysis of all results reported here. Thanks go to Rajesh Swaminathan for constructing the figures and doing so in record time.

topics. Participants concentrate on a topic while pairings of abstract pictures (Raynolds & Raynolds, 1982) are rapidly shown (about 0.5 seconds each). Participants are instructed to choose the picture from each pairing that seems to be more like the topic. The same ten pairings, consisting of all of the combinations of five different abstract pictures, are shown in the same order for each of four JOG topics.

A topic is a concept, person, place, organization, quality, and so on, described by a word or short phrase. JOG sessions employ two working topics (chosen for the particular session) and two anchor topics (the same for all JOG sessions and providing the basis for later scoring and interpretation of results). The working topics provide virtually unlimited possibilities for moving a given session in a desired direction. This is what makes JOG a multi-purpose instrument.

Then, in a well-considered (reasoned) manner, participants rate the two working topics and also themselves on a 10-point scale (0 = *unfavorable,* 10 = *favorable*). These ratings reflect L-mode (left-brained) attitudes toward the two working topics and also self-esteem. In the final data-gathering step, participants are shown each of the five JOG pictures for about a minute and asked to give each one a name and/or brief description.

The second portion of JOG consists of scoring, interpreting and discussing results. This takes another 20-30 minutes. Participants tally their own R-mode (nonverbal) attitude scores toward the two working topics and a non-verbal self-esteem score. These are compared with the L-mode ratings obtained earlier. Identification scores are also tallied with respect to the working topics. Finally, the pictures (from the five JOG abstracts) chosen most often by each participant for the topics are labeled "epitomizing pictures," and the names given to them are discussed. This is an exciting opportunity for many participants to bridge their non-verbal and verbal appreciations of the topics.

Optional concluding portions of the exercise are open-ended and tailor-made for the particular session. They sometimes include a structured step (described in Raynolds & Raynolds, 1989a, pp. 16-18) that guides participants into deeper understandings and closure around one of the working topics. Sometimes, especially in organizational settings, subgroups are formed on the basis of epitomizing pictures. The groups explore the implications of the meanings they attach to their picture in connection with the organization and report their conclusions to the total group. This is often cast in the form of creative problem solving, with a goal of arriving at concrete action steps. The kinds of qualitative information elicited in this manner are presented in Raynolds and Raynolds (1989b, 1992). More detailed descriptions of JOG and its uses are given in Raynolds and Raynolds (1989a, 1989b, 1993), and JOG is reviewed by Ifill (in press). Raynolds (in press) provides descriptions of two case studies, one quantitative and one qualitative, involving the PD and JOG. They are presented as holistic tools for assessing transformational training effects arising in some educational programs including simulations, games, and experiential exercises.

The Use of JOG in Organizational Research

JOG produces nine quantitative measures that are relevant to organizational research. Both R-mode and L-mode attitudes toward the organization and member self-esteem relate to member morale and satisfaction. L-mode measures are subject to intentional or unintentional response bias, so the nonverbal JOG measure acts as an independent cross-check (see Raynolds et al., 1988, p. 401; Raynolds et al., 1981, pp. 636-637). Incongruence (both attitude and self-esteem) is the inconsistency between verbal and nonverbal scores. It reflects upon the communications climate in an organization. Low incongruence implies that members mean what they say they mean. This results in less distortion and confusion than if incongruence is high. Positive identification with the organization implies that members are personally involved with it. Members care about the organization's welfare as if it were their own. Shared vision reflects the degree to which members have the same perception, understanding, and feelings about an organization. In the author's view, it indicates the distinctiveness and coherence of the organization's image, culture, mission and goals. Alignment refers to the degree to which there is cooperativeness and a sharing of objectives by members and their organization. With a positive alignment, likes and preferences are in harmony with what the organization stands for and asks of them, this concept is discussed in a theoretical manner by Coffey, Athos, and Raynolds (1975, pp. 278-279). JOG holds promise in operationalizing the concept into a useful organizational diagnostic measure.

A computer program summarizes a group's responses at a JOG session and provides statistical measures of the significance of results. JOG has been administered to over 4,000 people worldwide, and results are being added to a database that allows each new administration of the exercise to be compared with previous ones. JOG results from multiple sessions can be analyzed further through various methods, including correspondence analysis (Lebart, Morineau, & Warwick, 1984; Saxe, 1991).

Three zones are distinguished. "Ideal" reflects the direction of participants' preferences. The next zone, "Involvement," could just as well have been labeled "Identification" because the topics falling within it were perceived as being close to one's real self. In other words, participants positively identified with them. The final zone is labeled "Alienation" because topics falling within it are more distant from Self topics. Furthermore, they are very far away from and in the opposite direction from Likes, or the participant-preferred topics.

JOG Organizational Comparisons

JOG organizational indicators were used in comparing five organizations. The purpose in presenting these preliminary highlights at ISAGA '94 was more to suggest the kinds of JOG data analyses that are possible than to provide

TABLE 21.1 JOG Organizational Indicator Results

| | Example Organizations | | | | |
| | Modern | | Post-Modern/ New Paradigm | | Four SAGA Conferences |
	1 (n = 76)	*2* (n = 17)	*3* (n = 6)	*4* (n = 49)	(n = 64)
L-mode indicators					
Attitude	Positive 5.63	Positive 5.65	Positive 9.67	Positive 7.61	Positive 6.83
Self-esteem	Positive 7.79	Positive 7.12	Positive 8.83	Positive 6.98	Positive 7.25
R-mode indicators					
Attitude	Negative 4.29***	Neutral 5.29	Positive 8.00***	Positive 6.08***	Positive 5.67**
Self-esteem	Positive 7.57***	Positive 6.59***	Positive 8.33***	Positive 7.18***	Positive 7.19***
Incongruence (attitude)	High 1.34*** (opposite)	Low 0.35	Moderate 1.67**	Moderate 1.53***	Moderate 1.16**
Incongruence (self-esteem)	Low 0.22	Low 0.53	Low 0.50	Low −0.20	Low 0.06
Indentification	Negative 4.09***	Neutral 4.59	Positive 7.67***	Positive 5.92***	Positive 5.67***
Shared vision	High 45.2***	Moderate 12.9*	High 31.0***	Moderate 17.1**	Low 8.3
Alignment (see Figure 21.1a-c)	Negative (Fig. 21.1a)	Negative (Fig. 21.1a)	Positive (Fig. 21.1b)	Positive (Fig. 21.1b)	Somewhat positive (Fig. 21.1c)

$*p < .05; **p < .01; ***p < .001$

comprehensive study findings. In all of the organizations and conferences, JOG was used first as an exercise for the benefit of the participants themselves. It provided them with a deeper awareness of their feelings and orientations toward the working topics. At the conferences and in two of the organizations, the first working topic was "my personal project," an important, but unresolved, and private endeavor being undertaken by each of the participants. One of the working topics was always the organization as it is now; that is, it referred to the organization's current operations or participants' perceptions of the current conference (ISAGA 1988, 1990, 1991, or 1992).

Table 21.1 displays results along the nine JOG organizational indicators previously described. Before the data were analyzed, the four organizations were categorized by the author into two classes. Example organizations 1 and 2 were considered modern, that is, traditional, bureaucratic, mechanistic, and having single-purposed bottom-line orientations. Example organizations 3 and 4 were seen as post-modern/new paradigm (see Boje & Dennehy, 1993; Ray & Rinzler, 1993). The latter organizations are distinguished by their active multi-dimensional commitment to diverse objectives such as social responsibility, member empowerment, community engagement, and environmental sensitivity. The ISAGA conference data were presented as an experiential baseline for the session participants.

As shown in Table 21.1, there are considerable differences in some of the JOG indicators for the five organizational topics. Noteworthy is the fact that results from the two modern organizations were less favorable than for the postmodern/new-paradigm organizations on four indicators: attitudes (both L-mode and R-mode), identification, and alignment. ISAGA conference results fell between the two classes of organizations on these JOG indicators.

On the three maps comprising Figure 21.1, several distinguishing features of the organizations become apparent, among them the perceived location of the organization in one of the three zones (ideal, involvement, or alienation) and the alignment of members with their organizations. The latter is represented by the two lines on the map for each organization/conference topic and the angle between the lines. The first line connects member Self topics with Likes (with the arrow pointing toward Likes). There is a difference between the location of Self and Likes. This is viewed here as an indication of the direction that members are pursuing for their own fulfillment. The second line, which starts at the same point, connects Self and organization (with the arrow pointing toward the organization). The angle between the two lines is an indication of the alignment between members and their organizations.

Modern organizations (Figure 21.1a) fall in the alienation zone and have negative (oppositional) alignments; that is, the members are headed one way and the organization is seen to be located in essentially an opposite direction. In contrast, post-modern/new-paradigm organizations (Figure 21.1b) fall within the involvement zone and have positive (harmonious) alignments. The four ISAGA conferences (Figure 21.1c) are within the involvement zone but have negative (oppositional) alignment. This pattern is also frequently found in relatively successful classroom settings. In Table 21.1, it is labeled "somewhat positive" because of ISAGA's location within the involvement zone. Note that the strength of opposition (suggested by the length of the line pointing toward the organization) is considerably shorter for ISAGA than it is for the modern organizations.

During the session and its debriefing, participants expressed mostly delight and surprise over the depth and scope of the JOG experience and research data it generates. There was a trace of concern expressed by one participant about possible dangers in delving so deeply, and ways of dealing with this were discussed.

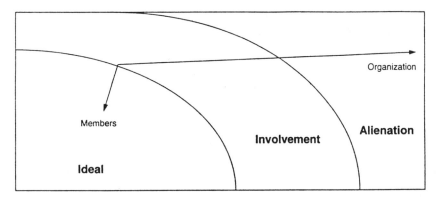

A. Organization 1 and 2 (modern)

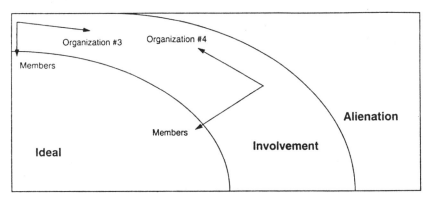

B. Organization 3 and 4 (post-modern/new paradigm)

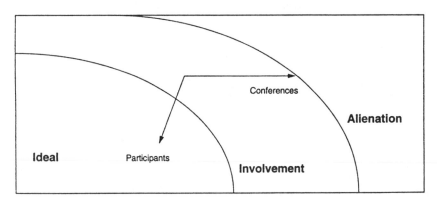

C. ISAGA (four conferences) summary

Figure 21.1 Organizational comparisons.

In conclusion, although JOG is a multi-purpose research instrument, it allows organizational assessments to be made in well-defined quantitative research dimensions. Based on holistic and intuitive nonverbal choice data, JOG is a research tool in tune with the emerging paradigms of the 21st century.

References

Boje, D. M., & Dennehy, R. F. (1993). *Managing in the postmodern world: America's revolution against exploitation.* Dubuque, IA: Kendall/Hunt.
Coffey, R. E., Athos, A. G., & Raynolds, P. A. (1975). *Behavior in organizations: A multidimensional view* (2nd ed.). Englewood Cliffs, NJ: Prentice Hall.
Ifill, D. (in press). [Review of} Jog Your Right Brain. *Simulation & Gaming: An International Journal.*
Lebart, L., Morineau, A., & Warwick, K. M. (1984). *Multivariate descriptive statistical analysis: Correspondence analysis and related techniques for large matrices.* New York: John Wiley.
Ray, M., & Rinzler, A. (1993). *The new paradigm in business: Emerging strategies for leadership and organizational change.* New York: Putnam.
Raynolds, P. A. (1970). The projective differential: A general purpose inkblot technique for studying denotable objects (Dissertation, University of California, Los Angeles, 1969). *Dissertation Abstracts International, 31,* 512A.
Raynolds, P. A. (in press). On taming the evaluation monster: Toward holistic assessment of transformational training effects. *Simulation & Gaming: An International Journal.*
Raynolds, P. A., & Raynolds, G. H. (1989a). Jog Your Right Brain: Fun in the classroom (and research too!). *Organizational Behavior Teaching Review, 13*(1), 7-22.
Raynolds, P. A., & Raynolds, G. H. (1989b). The "Jog Your Right Brain" exercise at ISAGA '88. In J. H. G. Klabbers, W. J. Scheper, C. A. T. Takkenberg, & D. Crookall (Eds.), *Simulation-gaming: On the improvement of competence in dealing with complexity, uncertainty and value conflicts: Proceedings of the International Simulation and Gaming Association's 19th International Conference, Utrecht University, The Netherlands, 16-19 August, 1988* (pp. 260-268). Oxford, UK: Pergamon.
Raynolds, P. A., & Raynolds, G. H. (1982). *Projective differential images.* Flagstaff, AZ: Projective Awareness Research Center (now Raynolds Research Center).
Raynolds, P. A., & Raynolds, G. H. (1992, July). *Jog Your Right Brain (JOG): A case study in knowledge elicitation and evaluation.* Paper presented at the International System Dynamics Conference, Utrecht University, The Netherlands.
Raynolds, P. A., & Raynolds, G. H. (1993). Jog Your Right Brain (JOG): A multipurpose exercise for simulation and gaming. In F. Percival, L. Lodge, & D. Saunders (Eds.), *The simulation and gaming yearbook, 1993: Developing transferable skills in education and training* (pp. 130-137). London: Kogan Page.
Raynolds, P. A., Sakamoto, S., & Raynolds, G. H. (1988). Consistent projective differential responses by American and Japanese college students. *Perceptual and Motor Skills, 66,* 395-402.
Raynolds, P. A., Sakamoto, S., & Saxe, R. (1981). Consistent responses by groups of subjects to projective differential items. *Perceptual and Motor Skills, 53,* 635-644.
Saxe, R. (1991). *CORANA: Correspondence analysis.* La Canada, CA: Saxe Research.

22

Discourse Analysis of Foreign Language Learners in Computerized Simulation

BEVERLY RISING

WALTER CEDAR

Cunningsworth and Horner (1985) spoke of simulations as providing "the most realistic context that can be established in a classroom . . . to bridge the gap between controlled language learning and the relative uncertainty of the outside world" (p. 217). They feared, however, that without proper preparation the simulation in itself could not actually "teach all the abilities necessary for participating in oral interaction" (p. 217). Our contention here is that the computer can add to manual simulation by providing necessary input, which permits the conversation to progress and allows for the practice of natural communication. This communication practice is recognized as being esssential for second-language (L2) learners. Using two types of computerized simulations and comparing the same subjects in both native-language and second-language discourse, the naturalness of the language elicited during the simulations was examined as were results from previous studies.

The study reported here is based on two complementary research frames. The first is discourse analysis, and more specifically the functions used by Abraham and Liou (1991), which can help in the study of the type of language used by students at the computer. The second is the framework proposed by Crookall, Martin, Saunders, and Coote (1986) and revised by Crookall, Coleman, and Oxford (1992) for the classification of simulation environments. These two frames can be combined to indicate the quality of language used during different types of simulations. As a result, L2 teachers may, by looking at the language that is really produced at the computer, be guided empirically in their choice of which computerized simulations are most appropriate for their students and how such simulations can be used most effectively.

As with most studies that deal with real discourse and its transcription and study, the number of subjects in ours is limited. An attempt was made, therefore, to replicate the situation and categories of study used by other authors to add to the existing information on discourse available. Although we could have added more categories to Abraham and Liou's (1991) system of functions, we decided to use theirs for comparison purposes. The only real change we would suggest is the use of syllables instead of words for counting purposes. In one language, word count may be an accurate enough indicator of time and length of utterance, but when used across languages as we did (Spanish and English), it distorts any comparative time/length measurement. In our study, the relationship between English syllables/words was 1.35, whereas the relationship between Spanish syllables/words was 2.05. In a multi-syllable language, such as German, the relationship would be even higher, and therefore the syllable count for comparison purposes would reveal length of utterance more exactly. Following Chapelle and Jamieson's (1991) outline for research validity, we discuss the target language context, the characteristics of the subjects, and the computer-assisted language learning (CALL) materials used.

Educational Background

The study, carried out at the Universidad Pontificia Comillas in Madrid, is a small part of a larger research project examining cognitive/affective factors and variables of learner behaviors of participants in computerized business simulations. Approximately 600 students are involved in either control or experimental groups with pre-tests and post-tests of both cognitive learning and affective variables. The final aim is to select the best pedagogical material for this particular university setting. The two students involved in this sub-study were enrolled in the European business administration program, which means that they spend two years of their university studies in Spain and the following two years in an English or American university. The students in this program are selected for their high academic averages and for their entrepreneurial personalities. They are dynamic, creative, and eager to learn. The students chosen for this substudy were not the best in the class nor the worst. As we wanted to extrapolate the results to the other study programs of the university (e.g., law, economics, and engineering), the students chosen were considered representative of the other students at the university. As mentioned above, the number of subjects was very limited, hence the necessity of trying to choose representative students.

The Subjects

The two subjects, Angela and Almudena, were selected from a class of 18 students and considered representative of the students at Comillas with regard to age, background, personality, intelligence, nationality, language ability, computer knowledge, and subject matter knowledge. The only difference is that approximately 50% of the student body is male, whereas both subjects were females. This was done intentionally to avoid any differences between subjects that could be attributed to gender. Both were 18, which is the age of most first- or second-year students in the Spanish university. Their language proficiency is about 550 on the Test of English as a Foreign Language (TOEFL). Although their abilities are very similar, one ranked herself as "fluent" on the pre-test, whereas the other judged her language ability as "good." When asked in a pre-test if they thought the computer would enhance their language learning, both responded that they neither agreed nor disagreed. They were both computer literate, having had classes in computer science as part of their curriculum and using them in several of their classes (marketing, etc.), and both rated themselves as "users" on the pre-test, a condition that again is representative of most of the students at the university.

The CALL Programs

The two programs used were not CALL programs as such. In line with other authors (e.g., Abraham & Liou, 1991), we have been piloting non-English as a Second Language (ESL) software for ESL use. The teachers have reported that for EPS (earnings per share) the added dimension of business created a dual motivation for the business administration students and at the same time freed the language teacher from having to also be an expert in business. With the appropriate software, the computer becomes the expert in the field and allows the language teacher to concentrate on language. The choice of the right type of program is therefore important, leading us to the raison d'être of our study.

The two programs used fell clearly into two different types of computer environments that we wanted to examine (see Crookall et al., 1992, for a more complete understanding of their categories of environments). The first was a computer-based simulation (CBS) entitled MILLIONAIRE II, and the second was a computer-assisted simulation (CAS) entitled INTERACTIVE CASES IN MANAGEMENT. The division of computer environments presented by Crookall et al. (1992) has four categories based on control, learner (L) or computer (C), and interaction, computer-learner (C-L) or learner-learner (L-L). The categories are as follows:

CDE: Computer-determined environment (low L and high C control/low L-L and high C-L interaction)

CCE: Computer-controlled environment (low L and high C control/high L-L and low C-L interaction)

CBE: Computer-based environment (high L and low C control/low L-L and high C-L interaction)

CAE: Computer-assisted environment (high L and low C control/high L-L and low
       C-L interaction)

In the CBS, the students, in pairs, act as investors in the stock market. They
have 15 companies' shares that they can buy and sell. They can call up company
descriptions, news of the week, trends in the market and in a specific sector, and
so on. The object is to become a millionaire. The language input from the
descriptions and the news is particularly useful for EPS.

Although this program could be classified as a CCE or as a CBE, depending
on the type of control and interaction that was being considered, and most
probably falls between the two, for the purposes of our study this is not really
problematic as the basic difference being analyzed is with a CAE. The important
aspect here is that the students cannot move away from the computer. They have
control in the sense that they can call up the information they need and can
choose to buy or sell as they wish, but they must make every move with the
computer; discussion is not possible without the information from the computer
available.

In the other simulation, or CAS, the students are presented with a company
and asked to make management decisions in areas such as marketing, production, and personnel. The information is given to the students in written form,
and they are presented with three to five options from which they must choose.
They select the option on the computer and in the end are told if the company
would hire them again, fire them, or give them a raise. Most of the discussion
can be done away from the computer if the students so desire. In our case, the
students chose to stay by the computer and simply ignored it when not using it.
As they are very accustomed to computers, it is no longer an extraneous element
in the classroom and causes them no inhibitions as far as speaking is concerned.

Quantity and Quality of Talk

Data Collection

In the CBS, dyads seated at each computer were audiotaped for 10 minutes
in English and then for 5 minutes in Spanish. They had 2 hours in which to play
the market, and most students asked to be given more time or to be allowed to
continue outside class. As a whole they were very outgoing and the recorder did
not interfere in any way with their normal behavior, as recording equipment is
commonly present in the classroom. The students merely thought the recorder
was being used to make sure they stayed in the target language, and they even
apologized to the machine if they slipped into a Spanish expression (about once
every 3 minutes). They were extremely surprised when they were asked to speak
in Spanish, and one group would not believe the teacher and continued in
English.

In the CAS, three dyads were both videotaped and audiotaped. The videotaping was intended to shed light on possible ambiguities of function that had been detected in the CBS recordings. Like the tape recorder, the video camera had little effect on normal classroom behavior. These dyads were allotted the same amount of time to play the game as in the CBS. For each simulation the teacher ensured that the students had sufficient background knowledge to make effective stock market and company management decisions.

Data Analysis

The recordings of the nine dyads who had played the CBS were then studied and the tape made by Angela and Almudena was selected as the most representative of the group. Consequently, their recording was selected as the one to be studied in the CAS. Transcriptions of Angela and Almudena's tape were made in the CBS in their L2 (English) and in their L1 (Spanish). In the CAS, only L2 was available. Transcriptions were prepared independently by the two researchers, compared, and then the final version of the transcription was prepared, following the system employed by Abraham and Liou (1991).

The three simulation transcripts were studied first for quantity of discourse. Measurements were taken of the words per minute (WPM) spoken by each of the subjects. This quantity of discourse was then examined for quality—the number of words per turn (W/T) and the number of turns per minute (T/M). The longer the turn, the more communicative practice taking place and therefore the richer the possibilities afforded the student for L2 improvement. Table 22.1 presents the data collected.

The WPM data in our study seem to fall into line with the speeds found by Piper (1986) and close to those found by Tong-Fredericks (1984) in her non-computer study. As mentioned by Abraham and Liou (1991), the pauses they registered for typing input could cause part of this discrepancy. Nevertheless, the students in this study seemed able to type and speak at the same time. Transcription of MI (machine interaction in silence) was four times higher in the CBS than in the CAS but relatively unimportant in both cases. The lower WPM in L1 (Spanish) is caused in part by the syllable/word difference between the two languages, although the syllables per minute was also lower in Spanish.

T/M showed a position between Abraham and Liou's and Piper's results, and W/T was very similar to Abraham and Liou's, doubling those found by Piper. The findings in the simulation used by Abraham and Liou (LEMONADE STAND) were similar to the CAS data. It was surprising to note that W/T was lower in the students' L1 using a CBS than in the CAS in L2.

Table 22.2 shows the individual differenes between speakers of basically the same language proficiency. Abraham and Liou (1991) also mention this phenomenon but point out the possibilities in their study of gender or cultural factors. As both of our subjects (Angela and Almudena) are of the same gender and the same cultural background, the differences must be sought in personality

TABLE 22.1	Average Number of Turns per Minute (T/M), Words per Turn (W/T), and Words per Minute (WPM)

Computer Study	T/M	W/T	WPM
This study			
CBS/L1	13.0	6.80	88.6
CBS/L2	19.7	4.65	92.3
CAS/L2	18.0	7.76	119.0
Abraham and Liou (1991)			
ARTICLES	8.85	5.50	48.7
ELIZA	6.70	6.00	39.0
LEMONADE STAND	7.50	7.00	2.4
Piper (1986)			
CLOZEMASTER	36.0	3.10	112.0
WORD ORDER	33.0	3.00	99.0
COPY WRITE	28.0	2.60	72.0
Non-computer studies (as reported in Abraham & Liou, 1991; Tong-Fredericks, 1984)			
Problem solving	13.0	8.50	111.0
Role-play	9.0	13.40	121.0
"Natural"	11.0	11.50	127.0

characteristics or learning behaviors. In the long run, research statistics must be based on numbers large enough to be significant, but our case could be indicative, pointing out possibilities that can be added to a suitable number of similar studies.

Two points should be made here. First, the CAS increased the W/T in the quieter student by nearly 100%, and the more talkative member in CAS surpassed the W/T found in the CBS in her native language. Second, the lower WPM in L1 could be attributed in part to the difference in syllable/word relationships between the two languages, to the strangeness of being allowed to speak their forbidden L1 in class, and/or to the lack of pressure to produce language in this situation.

Classification Into Functional Units and Categories

The categories developed by Abraham and Liou (1991, pp. 95-96) were used to make comparisons between this study and other studies of functional units easier. Their categories are as follows:

1. *Repeating:* Reading from screen or instruction sheet; repeating partner's or one's own utterance

TABLE 22.2 Comparison of the Two Speakers With Reference to Words per Turn (W/T) and Percentage Talking Time

Speaker	Game	W/T	Percentage of Talking Time
Angela	CBS/L1	8.42	53.0
Almudena	CBS/L1	5.90	47.0
Angela	CAS/L2	10.70	65.5
Almudena	CAS/L2	4.82	34.4
Angela	CBS/L2	6.66	66.0
Almudena	CBS/L2	2.65	34.0

2. *Managing mechanical aspects of tasks:* Management of the computer (also arithmetic calculations in their study)

3. *Managing discussion:* (a) managing mechanics of discussion (e.g., focusing discussion, extending previous contributions, rephrasing, requesting time to think) and (b) managing strategies for accomplishing tasks (e.g., suggesting strategies or answers, making decisions, telling partner to make decisions, evaluating previous courses of action, expressing purpose and cause/affect relationships, drawing conclusions, stating generalizations)

4. *Establishing facts needed to perform task:* (a) inquiring (e.g., asking for information, clarification, confirmation, or agreement, asking for partner's opinion, asking whether partner understands, expressing confusion or lack of understanding) and (b) responding (e.g., providing information, clarifying, confirming, agreeing, disagreeing, expressing understanding or awareness of situation, questioning truth of partner's assertion, making an observation about or showing lack of belief of computer responses)

5. *Showing concern for language form:* Asking or providing information about target language; spelling words for the typist; correcting spelling, punctuation, morphology, or grammar; analyzing grammatical structure

6. *Showing emotion and feeling for others:* Complaining, apologizing, reassuring, joking, showing excitement

Inevitably, discrepancies arose between each of our initial classifications of some utterances. Whereas one of us interpreted several units to be extensions of previous contributions, the other felt that the main purpose was to provide information for decision making. The audio and video recordings were consulted in cases of discrepancy. Intonation and paralinguistic features were major determiners in resolving differences.

A number of comments can be made about these observations. First, there is a much higher number of functional units for category 3a (managing mechanics

TABLE 22.3 Average Number of Functions per Minute

	Function Categories							
Program	1	2	3a	3b	4a	4b	5	6
This study								
CBS/L1	4.33	1.00	3.66	5.00	3.00	3.33	0.00	2.66
CBS/L2	3.00	0.66	1.66	3.66	3.00	5.66	0.00	0.66
CAS/L2	1.00	0.00	8.33	4.00	3.66	4.00	0.33	1.66
Abraham and Liou (1991)								
ARTICLES	3.98	0.48	0.53	2.76	1.63	2.81	0.58	0.09
ELIZA	3.14	0.18	0.95	2.08	1.50	1.44	1.03	0.04
LEMONADE STAND	1.39	0.74	0.89	3.28	1.76	3.05	0.07	0.09

TABLE 22.4 Average Number of Words in This Study and per Function per Program

	Function Categories								
Program	1	2	3a	3b	4a	4b	5	6	Average
This study									
CBS/L1	1.38	3.67	2.90	5.80	3.33	2.76	0.00	3.87	3.33
CBS/L2	2.89	4.00	2.60	6.60	4.22	5.88	0.00	5.00	4.87
CAS/L2	3.67	0.00	3.44	10.80	6.54	3.50	9.00	1.00	5.03
Abraham and Liou (1991)									
ARTICLES									3.80
ELIZA									3.80
LEMONADE STAND									4.50

of discussion) in the CAS than in any of the other programs. Second, an even higher number of words/function occurred in the CAS than in CBS/L1, which indicates the high quality of discourse in the CAS. Third, category 4a (inquiring) is of special interest to the ESL teacher because asking for information, clarification, confirmation, and so on creates "comprehensible input" (Krashen, 1985), which is thought to be especially useful for L2 learners. In the CAS/L2, this category had the highest frequency of functions per minute of all the programs for which we had data and was double the number reported by Abraham and Liou (1991). Fourth, high numbers in one function category may not indicate the overall use of that category but simply that a single unit was particularly long; for example, 9 in CAS/L2 category 5 refers to only one speech act (see Tables 22.3 and 22.4).

Conclusions

As in most studies of this type, the obvious conclusion is that more research is needed in this field. Moreover, we advocate the use of syllable count rather than word count for reasons of precision, especially in cross-language studies.

From the data presented here and in similar studies, it appears that a substantial difference in the language produced (both in quantity and quality) occurs during different kinds of computer simulations. The software program type, or computer environment, is therefore one of the principal variables to be taken into account when choosing pedagogical material for ESL and EPS classes.

References

Abraham, R. G., & Liou, H.-C. (1991). Interaction generated by three computer programs. In P. Dunkel (Ed.), *Computer-assisted language learning and testing: Research issues and practice* (pp. 85-109). New York: Newbury House.

Chapelle, C., & Jamieson, J. (1991). Internal and external validity issues in research on CALL effectiveness. In P. Dunkel (Ed.), *Computer-assisted language learning and testing: Research issues and practice* (pp. 37-59). New York: Newbury House.

Crookall, D., Coleman, D. W., & Oxford, R. L. (1992). Computer-mediated language learning environments: Prolegomenon to a research framework. *CALL, 5*(1-2), 93-120.

Crookall, D., Martin, A., Saunders, D., & Coote, A. (1986). Human and computer involvement in simulation. *Simulation & Games: An International Journal, 17*(3), 345-375.

Cunningsworth, A., & Horner, D. (1985). The role of simulations in the development of communication strategies. *System, 13*(3), 211-218.

Krashen, S. (1985). *The input hypotheses: Issues and implications.* New York: Longman.

MILLIONAIRE II. (1992). [Computer simulation]. (Available from Compton's New Media, 2320 Camino Vida Roble, Carlsbad, CA 92009)

Piper, A. (1986). Conversation and the computer: A study of the conversational spin-off generated among learners of English as a foreign language working in groups. *System, 14*(2), 187-198.

Tong-Fredericks, C. (1984). Types of oral communication activities and the language they generate: A comparison. *System, 12*(2), 133-146.

23

The Effect of Time Pressure, Team Formation, and Planning on Simulation/Game Performance

WILLIAM J. WELLINGTON

A. J. FARIA

Over the nearly 40 years that business simulation games have been in use in college courses, interest in the teaching and learning possibilities of business games has grown enormously. The body of empirical research examining all aspects of gaming is large and continues to grow. Comprehensive reviews of this research base can be found in Greenlaw and Wyman (1973), Keys (1976), Wolfe (1985), Miles, Biggs, and Schubert (1986), and Randel, Morris, Wetzel, and Whitehill (1992). Despite the widespread use of business games and the large research base, it is still not clear what the optimal learning conditions are for business games. This chapter examines three important factors that may have a bearing on student simulation/ game performance.

Background

Some of the factors that are thought to affect the simulation learning environment and participant performance and that have been investigated are listed in Table 23.1. This chapter examines the effect of decision time pressure, method of team formation, and formal planning on team performance in a computerized marketing simulation/game. This represents the first reported study of direct competitive performance under these conditions.

Past Research

Although the body of research on simulation gaming is extensive, very few studies have examined decision time pressure, method of team formation, and

TABLE 23.1 Studies of Factors Affecting Performance in Business Simulations

Factor	Studies
Personality characteristics of team members	Bruschke, Gartner, and Seiter (1993), Patz (1992), Rotter (1966)
Previous academic achievement	Gosenpud and Miesing (1992), McKenney and Dill (1966), Rowland and Gardner (1973), Vance and Gray (1967), Wellington and Faria (1991), Whiteley and Faria (1989), Wolfe (1978)
Ethnic origin of team members	Blanchette and Brown (1993), Faria (1986), Moorhead, Brenenstuhl, and Catalanello (1980)
Team size	Faria (1986), Gentry (1980), Remus and Jenner (1977)
Previous business experience	Halterman and Sampson (1993), Trinkaus (1981)
Team organizational structure	Edge and Remus (1984), Wellington and Faria (1992)
Degree of instructor explanation	Faria (1986), Platt (1993), Wolfe (1978)
Simulation grade weighting	Faria (1986), Gomolka and Mackin (1984)

formal planning. Only three studies, for example, have examined decision time pressure (Aplin & Cosier, 1979; Sampson & Sotiriou, 1979; Walker, 1979). Each of these studies compared team performance when decisions were spread over an entire semester versus concentrated within a shorter time period. The Aplin and Cosier (1979) study, for example, compared team performance of companies making 12 decisions spread over a 16-week period versus 12 decisions made within a two-week period. The conclusion from all three studies was that team performance was not hampered by having decisions concentrated within a shorter time frame.

A major problem with the three studies, however, is that all teams that had shorter decision time periods were competing against other teams under time pressure. None of the studies compared teams under time pressure against teams under no time pressure.

Three studies have reported on method of team formation (Hsu, 1986; Hsu & Eng, 1984; Wolfe & Box, 1986). In each of these studies, teams in which the students self-selected were compared to teams selected by the course instructor. Unfortunately, the dependent variable examined in each of the studies was team cohesiveness, not team performance. As such, no studies have reported on method of team selection and team performance.

Formal planning has been the focus of three studies (Curran & Hornaday, 1987, 1990; Hornaday & Curran, 1988). In these studies, team performance, as measured by earnings per share and several related variables, was compared between teams that had to develop a formal business plan and those that did not.

In the 1987 Curran and Hornaday study, no differences in performance were found. In the 1988 study, it was reported that the teams that were required to develop a formal business plan outperformed (achieved higher total earnings) those that did not develop a formal plan. Unfortunately, however, the planning and non-planning teams were in separate sections of a business policy course and did not compete against each other. In the 1990 study, formal planning teams did compete against non-planning teams and no significantly different earnings results were found. Comparisons in this study, unfortunately, were made across all industries and not simply between planning and non-planning teams in the same industry. As such, the contribution of planning to company performance is still not clear.

Methodology and Hypotheses

The study reported here was designed to overcome the drawbacks found in the previous research and to directly compare the earnings performance of teams in a computerized business simulation game competing under varying time pressure, planning and team formation circumstances. The study was undertaken in a second-year marketing course using COMPETE: A Dynamic Marketing Simulation (Faria, Nulsen, & Roussos, 1984) and involved 116 teams of three or four students each, competing in industries of four or five companies. The teams competed over 12 decision periods representing three years of business operation.

The treatment conditions used in this research were as follows:

- Time pressure (two levels): (a) no time pressure (teams had three to five days between receiving their output and submitting their next decision) and time pressure (teams had 80 minutes between receiving their output and submitting their next decision).
- Team formation (three levels): (a) systematic selection (teams formed by the course instructor to balance the skills and abilities of the companies based on factors such as previous courses taken, majors, work experience, interests, age, and class level), (b) self-selection (students formed their own teams), and (c) random selection (course instructor assigned students to teams at random).
- Formal planning (three levels): (a) strategic plan (teams required to develop and implement a strategic marketing plan covering the last eight periods of the competition), (b) objectives report (teams required to submit a company objectives report detailing performance goals for the three years of the simulation competition), and (c) no formal planning (teams not required to submit any formal written plans).

TABLE 23.2 Study Treatment Conditions

Group Formation Method	Time Pressure	Planning Method	Number of Teams
Random	Yes	None	10
Random	Yes	Objective setting	15
Random	Yes	Strategic plan	9
Systematic	No	None	13
Systematic	Yes	Objective setting	9
Systematic	No	Strategic plan	8
Self-selected	No	None	16
Self-selected	No	Objective setting	20
Self-selected	Yes	Strategic plan	16

A nested treatment design was developed with nine treatment conditions (the time pressure treatments were nested within the three methods of team formation by three modes of formal planning) to which the 116 student teams were assigned as shown in Table 23.2. The study design, unfortunately, could not be perfectly balanced due to the fact that the simulation/game used accommodated a maximum of five teams to an industry. Nine teams per industry would be needed for simultaneous interaction. However, across the many industries established, all treatments did interact.

The following hypotheses were formulated to be tested:

H1: Mean earnings per share will be significantly higher for the no-time-pressure teams than for the time-pressure teams.

H2: Mean earnings per share will be significantly higher for the strategic-marketing-plan teams than for the objectives-report teams, which, in turn, will be significantly higher than for the no-formal-planning teams.

H3: Mean earnings per share will be significantly higher for the systematically selected teams than for the self-selected teams, which, in turn, will be significantly higher than for the randomly selected teams.

H4: Earnings per share levels will be significantly different among the nine treatment groups.

The assumptions used in formulating these hypotheses were that the existence of time pressure should hamper team decision making, formal planning should enhance team performance, systematic team participant selection should improve performance, and interactions among these treatments should result in different earnings performance among the nine treatment groups.

Team performance, as measured by earnings per share (EPS), was examined at the end of each year of competition and for the three-year period of simulated competition. The resultant values were examined using analysis of variance.

TABLE 23.3 ANOVA Results

	Time Pressure		Team Formation Method		Formal Planning		Treatment Group	
Year	F Value	Significance	F Value	Significance	F Value	Significance	F Value	Significance
1	.05	.824	.64	.527	1.12	.330	1.72	.100
2	.14	.703	1.66	.195	.67	.513	.73	.662
3	.18	.667	3.68	.028**	.11	.892	.98	.452
1-3	.00	.962	2.72	.070*	.48	.618	.98	.457

*Significant at .10 level; **significant at .05 level.

Team performance was selected as the dependent variable for this study as it represents a goal-oriented outcome. A goal orientation is critical to simulation competitions as it acts as the motivating force for competing in the simulation exercise and provides a yardstick for measuring decision-making outcomes. A profit maximization motive was employed in the current competition to represent the typical real-world assumption of economists "that businessmen in competitive industries have to try to maximize their profits" (Caves, 1982, p. 2). To ensure that students would be motivated by profit, grades were assigned on the basis of earnings-per-share performance.

Results

Table 23.3 presents the ANOVA analysis findings, all of which resulted in the rejection of all four hypotheses. There is no significant difference in earnings per share between the time-pressure and no-time-pressure teams in any year of the simulation competition and overall; thus Hypothesis 1 was rejected. There were also no significant differences in earnings in any year of the competition and overall between the strategic-marketing-plan teams, objectives-report teams, or the no-formal-planning teams, so Hypothesis 2 was rejected.

There is a significant difference in earnings by method of team formation in Year 3 of the competition and overall (the three years combined). The self-selected teams achieved significantly higher earnings than the systematically selected teams overall (at the .10 level) and in Year 3 alone (at the .05 level). This was not in the direction hypothesized, however, and so Hypothesis 3 was also rejected.

Finally, there were no significant differences in earnings across the nine combination treatment conditions. Therefore, the combination of different levels of time pressure, method of team formation, and level of formal planning had no significant effect on earnings per share performance; thus Hypothesis 4 was rejected.

Discussion

The finding that performance was not affected by time pressure was surprising given the complexity of the simulation game used, the detail of the computer output returned (12 pages of financial data, sales and market share information, selected competitive data, and many charts and graphs), and the fact that the time-pressure teams had only 80 minutes to analyze their previous output and submit their next decision. Meanwhile, their competitors had several days over which to schedule meetings, analyze results, and make their decisions.

It is possible that time-pressure groups may have equalized their treatment using "compensatory rivalry" (Cook & Campbell, 1979, p. 54) because, despite the best efforts of the investigators, the time-pressure groups discovered they were competing against no-time-pressure groups. The time-pressure groups thus may have compensated by spending more time between decision periods analyzing past results and preparing for the upcoming period. Also, teams under time pressure may have been more efficient in arriving at decisions by spending less time socializing and debating fruitlessly.

The finding that there was no difference in earnings performance despite mode of planning was also unexpected, especially in light of the finding on time pressure. Given the number and complexity of decisions in the COMPETE simulation, planning was believed to be an important factor for improving performance. It was thought that strategic planning might compensate for time pressure, but the findings did not support any relationship between time pressure and planning. Apparently, requiring teams to develop formal plans does not ensure they will produce superior plans, and thus better results, than objective setting or non-planning teams.

The lack of difference in performance between formal planning and non-planning teams may have occurred because, outside of competitors' decision making, simulation environments tend to be fairly stable. It is also possible that simulation environments tend to stress short-run over long-run decision making. If this were not the case, teams that fall behind early would never be able to catch up and such simulation games would quickly lose the interest of students because the winners and losers would be decided too soon. Furthermore, all students have very limited experience with simulation environments and this lack of experience may make planning efforts less effective than they might otherwise be.

The significant findings on method of team formation suggests that simulation teams will perform much better when they are allowed to self-select. It is believed that group cohesion was higher in the self-selected groups than in the assigned groups, although cohesion was not measured directly. This could be due to the fact that self-selecting students formed teams with their friends and acquaintances on the basis of things in common. The method of systematic selection was designed to produce heterogeneous groups where students had more differences than similarities. It was felt that these varying strengths would be brought to bear in the competition. This did not seem to be the case.

The implications of these findings are that simulation teams perform better when they are allowed to self-select their members. In addition, instructors who use self-selection will benefit in that they do not bear any responsibility for teams that perform poorly due to lack of cohesion. After all, the students chose their group members.

Students faced with time pressure to make decisions performed as well as students under no time pressure. This indicates that the time-pressure students were able to adapt themselves well in the face of a time constraint. The implication is that instructors can require more decisions in simulation games, with shorter decision turnaround, without being concerned that team performance will suffer.

It would appear that performance rewards for planning are not evident. However, given the notion that strategic planning might have its greatest performance impact over more simulation decisions, the expected positive impact of planning might show itself over a longer simulation experience. Possibly four or five years of simulated competition are needed.

Conclusions

Team formation by self-selection was the method of grouping that produced the best level of performance in the study. The performance of the students under the decision time pressure of 80 minutes was as good as that of students having several days. Formal planning requirements did not produce superior performance results versus no planning requirements. Although the lack of a planning requirement does not preclude a team from developing a plan, the requirement of a formal written plan does not seem to matter with respect to earnings performance. Therefore, if instructors wish students to develop formal business plans, it is recommended that the planning exercise be presented as a process rather than an illustration that planning will produce superior performance.

References

Aplin, J. C., & Cosier, R. A. (1979). The use of intensive simulation in executive development and academic settings. In S. C. Certo & D. C. Brenenstuhl (Eds.), *Proceedings of the Sixth Annual Conference of the Association for Business Simulation and Experiential Learning*. ABSEL.

Blanchette, D., & Brown, N. (1993). Shared cultural perspectives: An experiential exercise using international students. In S. Gold & P. Thavikulwat (Eds.), *Proceedings of the Twentieth Annual Conference of the Association for Business Simulation and Experiential Learning*. ABSEL.

Bruschke, J. C., Gartner, C., & Seiter, J. S. (1993). Student ethnocentrism, dogmatism, and motivation. *Simulation & Gaming: An International Journal, 24,* 9-21.

Caves, R. (1982). *American industry: Structure, conduct, performance.* Englewood Cliffs, NJ: Prentice Hall.

Cook, T. D., & Campbell, D. T. (1979). *Quasi-experimentation: Design and analysis issues for field settings.* Boston: Houghton Mifflin.

Curran, K. E., & Hornaday, R. W. (1987). An investigation of the relationships between formal planning and simulation team performance and satisfaction. In L. Kelley & P. Sanders (Eds.), *Proceedings of the Fourteenth Annual Conference of the Association for Business Simulation and Experiential Learning.* ABSEL.

Curran, K. E., & Hornaday, R. W. (1990). Formal planning and simulation team performance. In J. Wingender & W. Wheatley (Eds.), *Proceedings of the Seventeenth Annual Conference of the Association for Business Simulation and Experiential Learning.* ABSEL.

Edge, A. G., & Remus, W. E. (1984). The impact of hierarchical and explitarian organization structure on group decision making and attitudes. In D. M. Currie & J. W. Gentry (Eds.), *Proceedings of the Eleventh Annual Conference of the Association for Business Simulation and Experiential Learning.* ABSEL.

Faria, A. J. (1986). A test of student performance and attitudes under varying game conditions. In A. C. Burns & L. Kelley (Eds.), *Proceedings of the Thirteenth Annual Conference of the Association for Business Simulation and Experiential Learning.* ABSEL.

Faria, A. J., Nulsen, R. O., & Roussos, D. S. (1984). *COMPETE: A dynamic marketing simulation.* Plano, TX: Business Publications, Inc.

Gentry, J. W. (1980). The effects of group size on attitudes toward the simulation. In D. C. Brenenstuhl & W. D. Biggs (Eds.), *Proceedings of the Seventh Annual Conference of the Association for Business Simulation and Experiential Learning.* ABSEL.

Gomolka, E. G., & Mackin, J. L. (1984). Individual versus group grade: An exercise in decision making. In D. M. Currie & J. W. Gentry (Eds.), *Proceedings of the Eleventh Annual Conference of the Association for Business Simulation and Experiential Learning.* ABSEL.

Gosenpud, J., & Miesing, P. (1992). The relative influence of several factors on simulation performance. *Simulation & Gaming: An International Journal, 23,* 311-325.

Greenlaw, P. S., & Wyman, F. P. (1973). The teaching effectiveness of games in collegiate business courses. *Simulation & Games: An International Journal, 4,* 259-294.

Halterman, C. C., & Sampson, N. S. (1993). Antecedent biases of experiential learners: Trainee occupation and subgroup activity. In S. Gold & P. Thavikulwat (Eds.), *Proceedings of the Twentieth Annual Conference of the Association for Business Simulation and Experiential Learning.* ABSEL.

Hornaday, R. W., & Curran, K. E. (1988). Formal planning, simulation team performance, and satisfaction: A replication. In P. Sanders & T. Pray (Eds.), *Proceedings of the Fifteenth Annual Conference of the Association for Business Simulation and Experiential Learning.* ABSEL.

Hsu, T. (1986). A further test of group formation and its impact in a simulated business environment. In D. M. Currie & J. W. Gentry (Eds.), *Proceedings of the Eleventh Annual Conference of the Association for Business Simulation and Experiential Learning.* ABSEL.

Hsu, T., & Eng, D. J. (1984). Effects of different organizational arrangements on interpersonal behavior. In W. G. Briggs (Ed.), *Proceedings of the Northeast Meetings of the American Institute for the Decision Sciences.* Atlanta, GA: American Institute for the Decision Sciences.

Keys, B. (1976). A review of learning research in business gaming. In B. H. Sord (Ed.), *Proceedings of the Third Annual Conference of the Association for Business Simulation and Experiential Learning.* ABSEL.

McKenney, J. L., & Dill, W. R. (1966). Influences on learning in a simulation game. *American Behavioral Scientist, 10,* 28-32.

Miles, W. G., Biggs, W. D., & Schubert, J. N. (1986). Student perceptions of skill acquisition through cases and a general management simulation. *Simulation & Games: An International Journal, 17,* 7-24.

Moorhead, G., Brenenstuhl, D. C., & Catalanello, R. (1980). Differential predictors of academic performance for white and non-white samples. In D. C. Brenenstuhl & W. D. Biggs (Eds.), *Proceedings of the Seventh Annual Conference of the Association for Business Simulation and Experiential Learning.* ABSEL.

Patz, A. L. (1992). Personality bias in total enterprise simulations. *Simulation & Gaming: An International Journal, 23,* 45-76.

Platt, R. G. (1993). Matching student-teacher cognitive style. In S. Gold & P. Thavikulwat (Eds.), *Proceedings of the Twentieth Annual Conference of the Association for Business Simulation and Experiential Learning.* ABSEL.

Randel, J., Morris, B. A., Wetzel, C. D., & Whitehill, B. V. (1992). The effectiveness of games for educational purposes: A review of recent research. *Simulation & Gaming: An International Journal, 23,* 261-276.

Remus, W., & Jenner, S. (1979). Playing business games: Attitudinal differences between students playing singly and as teams. *Simulation & Games: An International Journal, 10,* 75-86.

Rotter, J. B. (1966). Generalized expectations for internal versus external control for reinforcement. *Psychological Monographs, 80,* 69.

Rowland, K. M., & Gardner, D. M. (1973). The uses of business gaming in education and laboratory research. *Decision Sciences, 4,* 268-283.

Sampson, N. S., & Sotiriou, C. E. (1979). Business policy simulation and the intense course structure. In S. C. Certo & D. C. Brenenstuhl (Eds.), *Proceedings of the Sixth Annual Conference of the Association for Business Simulation and Experiential Learning.* ABSEL.

Trinkaus, J. W. (1981). Participant type differences in response to experiential methods. In D. C. Brenenstuhl & W. D. Biggs (Eds.), *Proceedings of the Seventh Annual Conference of the Association for Business Simulation and Experiential Learning.* ABSEL.

Vance, S. C., & Gray, C. F. (1967). Use of a performance evaluation model for research in business gaming. *Academy of Management Journal, 10,* 27-37.

Walker, C. H. (1979). Comparing performance during three managerial accounting simulation schedules. In S. C. Certo & D. C. Brenenstuhl (Eds.), *Proceedings of the Sixth Annual Conference of the Association for Business Simulation and Experiential Learning.* ABSEL.

Wellington, W. J., & Faria, A. J. (1992). An examination of the effect of team cohesion, player attitude, and performance expectations on simulation performance results. In J. Gosenpud & S. Gold (Eds.), *Proceedings of the Nineteenth Annual Conference of the Association for Business Simulation and Experiential Learning.* ABSEL.

Wellington, W. J., & Faria, A. J. (1991). An investigation of the relationship between simulation play, performance level and recency of play on exam scores. In W. Wheatley & J. Gosenpud (Eds.), *Proceedings of the Seventeenth Annual Conference of the Association for Business Simulation and Experiential Learning.* ABSEL.

Whiteley, T. R., & Faria, A. J. (1989). A study of the relationship between student final exam performance and simulation game participation. *Simulation & Games: An International Journal, 20,* 44-65.

Wolfe, J. (1978). The effects of game complexity on the acquisition of business policy knowledge. *Decision Sciences, 9,* 143-155.

Wolfe, J. (1985). The teaching effectiveness of games in collegiate business courses: A 1973-1983 update. *Simulation & Games: An International Journal, 16,* 251-288.

Wolfe, J., & Box, T. M. (1986). Relationships between team cohesion dimensions and business game performance. In A. C. Burns & L. Kelley (Eds.), *Proceedings of the Thirteenth Annual Conference of the Association for Business Simulation and Experiential Learning.* ABSEL.

PART IV

Professional Matters

24

Gaming-Simulation in Perspective

ROBERT H. R. ARMSTRONG

ISAGA's 25th anniversary is a time for celebration, marking a milestone in the development of international collaboration and communication in the field of gaming-simulation that augurs well for the future. It is also a time for reflection.

Beginnings

In retrospect, it is difficult to define precisely the expectations of those who gathered in Bad Godesberg 25 years ago. We were a diverse group brought together by a common interest in the use of gaming-simulation, although there was no clear agreement on a definition of what constituted gaming-simulation. Equally, there was variety in the types of approach and purposes for which they were being used. Despite the differences we believed there were benefits to be gained from sharing experiences.

Prior to Bad Godesberg, national and regional associations existed. Individuals were in contact, forming what have been described as secret colleges. Bad Godesberg represented a significant step in broadening the base for cooperation by recognizing that use of gaming-simulation had spread worldwide.

At the time of the Bad Godesberg meeting, the use of games for serious purposes was not new. War games were well established, with extensions into the field of international relations. Management games had proliferated since the mid-1950s. Academics in the field of urban planning had recognized the potential of gaming-simulation in the 1960s. Alongside these developments there was a growth in the use of games for classroom teaching.

If gaming-simulation was not new at the time of Bad Godesberg, then what was? I suggest that there were three concerns in the minds of participants, providing us with common ground for discussion of problems:

- A feeling of dissatisfaction with the restrictive nature of the analytical approach to problems in our subject areas
- A wish to explore the potential of a systems approach to societal problems as a framework for the consideration of multi-disciplinary problems
- A desire to refine and extend the use of gaming-simulation in our areas of interest

It was felt that gaming-simulation provided a framework for the development of a multidisciplinary methodology that could make a contribution to teaching and research. We hoped exchange of experience and ideas would assist with development of such a methodology. Fulfillment of the hope meant stepping outside the ordered disciplines of the subjects in which we had been trained.

Venturing into the field of gaming-simulation involved learning new skills and modes of operation. The multi-disciplinary nature of gaming-simulation meant giving serious attention to other subjects. Discussion of professional conduct in the use of gaming-simulation became necessary. These considerations created a situation where it was possible to think of gaming-simulation as containing the seeds of a new subject.

If the emergence of a new subject was a possibility, then ISAGA at its birth was confronted with a challenging agenda. After 25 years, how successful have we been in addressing that agenda? Can we echo Ackoff's (1974) comments when he wrote, "The subjects I teach did not exist when I was a student" (p. 77). Can we now discern the outlines of a new subject?

What Is Gaming-Simulation?

Gaming-simulation is a synthesis of some elements of a game, and a simulation, or analog, of some aspect of reality. The game elements consist of people playing roles and taking decisions appropriate to those roles. Definition of roles can lie anywhere along a continuum from abstract/symbolic to realistic. Constraints on decision-making behavior can be embodied in rules or emerge during an exercise as a result of roles interacting.

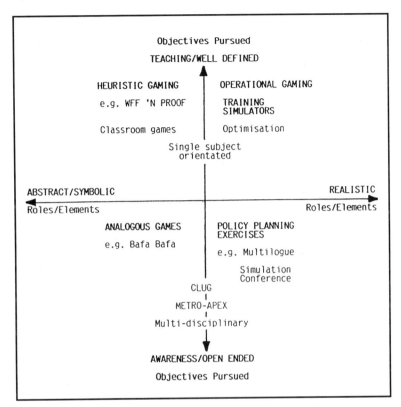

Figure 24.1 A schematic classification of gaming-simulation approaches.

The simulation, in the form of a scenario or model, contains aspects of the environment within which the decision-making roles have to act. In the exercises, participants assess the relevance of the aspects from the viewpoint of their assumed role. As in the case of role definition, elements of a simulation can be placed on a continuum from the abstract/symbolic to the realistic.

Ignoring this range of possibilities of the form that can be taken by components means we implicitly exclude certain types of gaming-simulations from our definition of the subject area. Margaret Hobson and myself were guilty of such implicit exclusion in our definition of the area appropriate for use of gaming-simulation, illustrated in Figure 24.1 (Armstrong & Hobson, 1972, p. 87). By placing gaming-simulation techniques in the lower right quadrant we defined the content of the planning exercise in which we were interested, ignoring the contribution made by other forms of gaming-simulations. Not only did this type of definition implicitly ignore the diverse nature of the elements and roles that can make up gaming-simulations, it also ignored equally diverse purposes for which they can be used. As with elements and roles, the range of

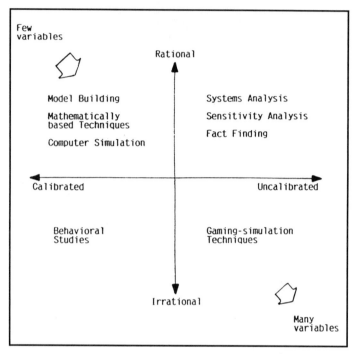

Figure 24.2   A schematic representation of some techniques available in situations
described by the two dimensions of rationality (consistency of behavior)
and calibration (measurability).

purposes can be defined by a continuum from teaching/well-defined to creation
of awareness/open-ended. When this continuum is juxtaposed with the abstract-
to-realistic continuum defining elements and roles, the schematic classification
illustrated in Figure 24.1 emerges.

The quadrant format makes too stark a contrast between the different types
of approach. Placing any given gaming-simulation exercise in a precise position
in Figure 24.1 is difficult. Nevertheless, it provides a useful framework for
examination of the contribution made by various approaches. Hopefully, it
emphasizes what we have in common.

Figure 24.2 was an attempt to distinguish gaming-simulation from other
approaches. It was deficient in that it placed too much emphasis on the relationship between calibration and a limited definition of a continuum describing
modes of behavior.[1] The objective was to contrast the apparent order, certainty,
and precision of the approaches in the upper left quadrant with the characteristics of the lower right quadrant where disorder and uncertainty might reign.
It was felt that abandoning, or moving away from the scientific and analytical
approach required justification. We assumed that any departure from the scientific and analytical approach could be viewed as the adoption of a methodology

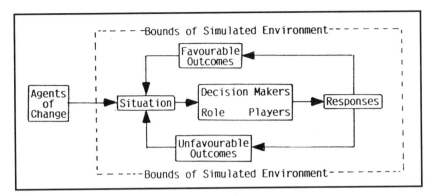

Figure 24.3   Gaming-simulation: An outline definition.

lacking the rigor required for serious academic research. By concentrating on an attempt to define the problem areas and failing to define the essential characteristics of the approach, we fell into the trap of not seeing the forest for the trees.

The essence of gaming-simulation is interaction of decision makers within a simulated environment. This is illustrated in Figure 24.3. Such an illustrative definition is capable of including any type of simulated situation involving human decision makers. It is not confined to complex situations where many variables and decision makers are operative, and the elements that comprise the situation can be of any type. The calibrated-to-non-calibrated continuum remains relevant but is not essential to the definition of the types of situation where the use of gaming-simulation is appropriate.

Central to the distinctive nature of gaming-simulation is the decision-making behavior of role-players. In the course of an exercise, learning involves changes in, or reinforcement of, the understanding and perceptions of the role-players. Gaming-simulation differs from most other learning situations in that it is non-linear in character. There is no defined sequence of steps leading to production of any given outcome. This is true even in those cases where the exercise has a well-defined objective stated in terms of knowledge or skills to be learned. The complex nature of interactions between the scenario and role-players means that predictions of the precise course of an exercise cannot be made. Intuition, use of value judgments, and lack of knowledge can be as important as expertise, or rational behavior. The interaction of these diverse bases for decision making is in marked contrast to the ordered approach, which is characteristic of formal educational settings, and the scientific and analytical approach. It is the admixture of diverse bases for decision making and the possibilities inherent in their interaction that give gaming-simulation its potential richness as a learning environment. In addition to the acquisition of accepted and habitual answers to problems, gaming-simulation provides opportunities for developing new insights, which can lead to original responses to problems.

Concentration on the rationality continuum in defining the position of gaming-simulation in the classification of techniques implicitly ignored the potential for interaction of the different bases of decision making. However, it did have the merit of drawing attention to the part played by non-rational elements in decision making.

It is a truism to say that all decision making is concerned with the future. Decisions are either a response to change or an attempt to initiate change. If there were no possibility of change, decision making would be redundant. Gaming-simulation gives participants the opportunity of developing an awareness of the impact that their decisions and those of others can have on the process of change. The development of such awareness takes place in an environment where responsibility for decisions and their consequences rests with the person making them. Rote learning is replaced by a process of exploration in which the learner assumes the responsibility for what is learned. In this sense, the participant in a game-simulation exercise becomes the authority rather than submitting to authority.

Although elements of trial and error are involved, they are not the whole story. Success or failure of strategies adopted has to be judged against movement toward the achievement of explicit or implicit objectives, within the context of a changing environment. An important element in the learning process is the opportunity to reassess objectives and evaluate contributions made by other decision makers. This process of reassessment and evaluation can result in the development of new preceptions of the nature of change, leading to innovative approaches to problems. It is this possibility that gives gaming-simulation the characteristics of a "futures language" (Duke, 1974) rather than the content or purpose.

How Effective Is Gaming-Simulation?

Evaluating the effectiveness of gaming-simulation is an area that requires more attention. Difficulties result from differences in purposes pursued and in defining the precise nature of the outcomes of gaming-simulation in terms that are comparable with those of other approaches.

Lack of well-documented outcomes is a factor contributing to difficulties in assessing effectiveness of exercises defined by the lower half of Figure 24.1. Without records, yardsticks against which subsequent developments can be assessed cannot be established. Ensuring that adequate documentation is available for later analysis must be part of the structure of exercises.

The structure of the ALEA exercises, illustrated in Figure 24.4, was a response to the problem of evaluating outcomes of exercises designed for use as part of the planning process. Recording information requested, answers provided, contracts between roles, and reasons for them ensured that reference points were established for subsequent review. Use of the NEXUS format

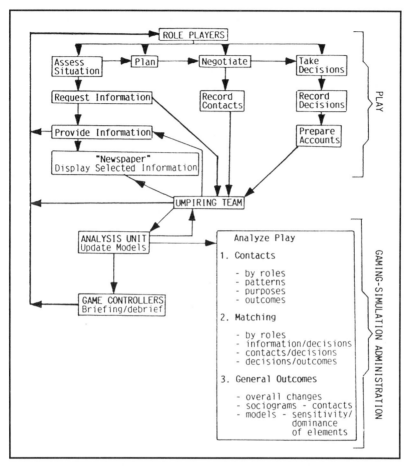

Figure 24.4 Outline of information flows and activities in an ALEA gaming-
simulation exercise.

(Armstrong & Hobson, 1970) as the accounting system enables assumed consequences of each decision and event to be stored and recalled for later
discussion. This means that the assumptions underlying the models can be
subject to critical review. The flexible nature of the NEXUS format means that
the consequences of unexpected decisions can be recorded, thus ensuring that
they are available for assessment at a later stage.

These characteristics of the record-keeping systems in an ALEA exercise
provide a framework capable of allowing for the introduction of new elements
during the course of the exercise. As the exercise progresses, participants can
redefine the nature of their roles and the types of decisions appropriate to their
perceptions of a changing situation. An ALEA exercise can encompass fundamental changes occurring in the nature of the problems to be explored. This

means that the initial definitions of roles and scenario can be stated in minimal terms providing a set of reference points for role-players rather than imposing constraints. Further, progress of an exercise is not determined by the operation of models containing the designer's perceptions of relationships and their nature. Outcomes are not solely the result of feeding new quantitative data into a set of equations. The flexibility built into the structure means that as important as changes in values of variables is the possibility of change in the nature of relationships between variables. The framework provided by an ALEA exercise gives participants the opportunity of adapting the components of an exercise as their perceptions, insights, and awareness develop.

An attempt to increase the effectiveness of both gaming-simulation and the committee process led to development of the simulation conference methodology (Armstrong & Hobson, 1973, pp. 211-228) illustrated in Figure 24.5. This involved placing the ALEA gaming-simulation exercise into the context of the use of other approaches designed to provide information for the planning process. Broadening the approach by including people likely to be affected by the planning process with those involved in it makes the approach a suitable vehicle for the promotion of public participation.

Use of DELPHI, CROSS IMPACT, and NEXUS provides a structured framework for large numbers of people to consider complex issues in an environment where committee noise is minimized. Use of these approaches makes it possible to obtain a record of perceptions and assumptions concerning the issues at the time when they are under consideration. The information obtained can then be used as the basis for the models in subsequent gaming-simulation exercises. The exercises become ones in which participants subject their own perceptions and assumptions to examination rather than those of the game designer. The exercise becomes the property of the participants.

The use of models embodying the perceptions of people involved in the planning process introduces participants to possible implications of decision making based on the use of their perceptions in an interactive situation, enabling implicit assumptions to be examined in a dynamic setting. When the exercises are used in an educational setting, they allow students to gain insights into the perceptions of those involved in decision making. The amount of time required can be a problem, although there is evidence suggesting that this diminishes over time.[2]

Lack of congruence of the perceptions with reality is not a major problem. There are three reasons for this:

- No decision-making process is based on accurate perceptions of reality. In most decision-making situations the perceptions brought to bear are implicit rather than explicit. Making them explicit produces improvement.
- As all decision making is concerned with the future, assumptions concerning the future will not be congruent with what eventually emerges. The future cannot be

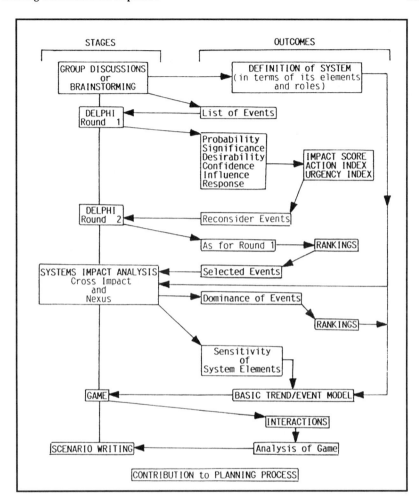

Figure 24.5 Outline of the simulation conference process.

forecast accurately. The evolution of the future in human affairs depends on a complex process of interaction of responses to change made by numerous decision makers. In human affairs, the concept of cause and effect as an explanation of change has limited usefulness. Models and the assumptions on which they are based cannot predict the future accurately.

• Keeping records of what perceptions were at the time when planning alternatives were being considered makes it possible, at a later stage, to check their accuracy.

In committee settings, the possibility of perceptions and assumptions being in error receives little attention when decisions are made. Further, the linear nature of committee agendas ignores the complex relationships that can exist between items. Committees can be dominated by single issues, and sometimes hidden agendas can dominate. Other problems could be cited. Insofar as the ALEA and Simulation Conference formats help to overcome some of these problems, they make a contribution to the planning process.

At first sight, the discussion of the ALEA and simulation conference formats may appear to be a digression from the subject of the effectiveness of gaming-simulation. Such an impression would be mistaken for two reasons:

- Both formats were developed to deal with aspects of policy formulation in areas where other approaches to such problems are deficient in some respect. In expressing concern over the effectiveness of gaming-simulation we are prone to forget that one reason leading us to use it is dissatisfaction with the effectiveness of alternative approaches. The justification for doing what we do is that gaming-simulation is an attempt to do things that other approaches cannot do or do not do very effectively. Once we formulate our objectives in terms of the gaps left by other approaches, then discussion of the effectiveness of gaming-simulation gains meaning.
- The components used in the ALEA and simulation conference formats have many features in common with those used in other exercises. Indeed, the ALEA format is an explicit statement of procedural elements present in most gaming-simulation exercises.

The concern with effectiveness is not a distraction. It provides a safeguard against complacency and the possibility of deteriorating professional standards.

Where to From Here?

There is nothing new in what has been said above. It represents a rehash of questions raised 25 years ago and some responses to them. The number of gaming-simulations and practitioners has increased. The level of professional expertise has improved. Both these things represent progress, but problems remain. I will discuss one in my own area of interest, that of planning and public participation.

In the design and use of gaming-simulations, the problem of scale arises. An example is the relationship between representation of time in an exercise and real time. Other examples can be found in the use of physical models and the size and influence of decision-making groups. Defining principles that can be used to determine a reasonable scale for each element in an exercise is one aspect of the problem.

In everyday situations, many of the perceptions and assumptions determining our recognition of issues are derived from experience of the scale of the temporal, physical, and human environment in which we live—our perceptual environment. Reducing the scale of elements of that environment results in the production of a new perceptual environment. Sometimes, this can create problems.

As a digression, it is worth remembering that a similar problem affects research and development in the physical sciences when successful bench experiments are scaled up to make them operational. It is not uncommon for problems to arise, making it difficult to produce an operational product.

On occasion, the reduced scales used in an exercise can serve to sharpen perceptions of the holistic nature of a situation. Equally, it is probably true that there are occasions when distortion of perceptions occurs. Some exercises have avoided the problem by use of standard units having no direct relationship to a real-life counterpart. The use of representational units having a defined scale relationship with each other in the context of the exercise means that parts of the scenario assume an analogous relationship to reality. CLUG (Feldt, 1972) is an example of the successful use of this device for teaching purposes.

Compression of time is a problem of scale that manifests itself in various ways. The interval between a decision being taken and consequences becoming apparent varies in reality from a relatively short time to a lengthy period. In most cases in a gaming-simulation exercise, the existence of such a difference is ignored, and the consequences of decisions taken during a period of play are presented together at the end of the period.

War gamers are able to avoid the problem. Field exercises can equate the scales of the real and the simulated in almost every respect in the examination of tactical situations. Sand-tray exercises overcome some of the problems by allowing the opposing sides to take turns in making decisions.

Inability to match the passage of time in an exercise to the scale of decisions creates difficulties in establishing congruence with the dynamic interaction and flow of decisions in reality. With public participation exercises this can eliminate an important aspect of the interaction of interest groups with governmental bodies. It is common for interest groups to react strongly to interim consequences before the intended outcomes are visible. Sometimes, this is the result of decision makers and those affected having different perceptions of the passage of time. This arises in urban development when immediate irritations with construction work outweigh possible long-term benefits. Reactions of interest groups can lead to modification of plans, producing different results from those intended originally.

Some may argue that it is overly ambitious to expect gaming-simulation to encompass all the steps characterizing change over time. There is merit in this argument, but accepting it diminishes the potential of gaming-simulation for exploring the dynamics of the flow of decision making in complex situations.

Conclusion

This brief review of gaming-simulation and its effectiveness has not answered the question of whether we can discern the outlines of a new subject. In my mind, it is still an open question. Maybe we have yet to complete the transition from order to complexity and are still enmeshed in reconciling the differences in approach and objectives represented by our diverse interests.

Notes

1. Some have questioned the use of irrational as a description of the contrast to rational. Replacing irrational by intuitive (Duke, 1974, p. xv) introduces a new emphasis and draws attention to an important distinction. Perhaps a compromise can be found in the use of arational.

2. Bob Blackburn, Deputy Fire Officer for West Sussex, adapted the approach for use with the county's Fire Brigade Committee. He found, following a period needed for members to become familiar with the format, that the time required for conducting meetings tended to decline (Blackburn, 1971).

References

Ackoff, R. L. (1974). *Redesigning the future.* New York: John Wiley.

Armstrong, R. H. R., & Hobson, M. (1970). *The use of gaming-simulation techniques in the decision-making process* (Rep. No. ESA-PA-MMTS-21). Washington, DC: United Nations.

Armstrong, R. H. R., & Hobson, M. (1972). *Introduction to gaming-simulation techniques.* Birmingham: Institute of Local Government Studies, University of Birmingham. (Reprinted in *Gaming-simulation: Rationale, design and applications,* by C. S. Greenblatt & R. D. Duke, Ed., 1974, New York: John Wiley)

Armstrong, R. H. R., & Hobson, M. (1973). Where all else fails. In J. E. Moriaty (Ed.), *Simulation and gaming* (National Bureau of Standards Special Publication No. 395). Washington, DC: U.S. Department of Commerce, National Bureau of Standards.

Blackburn, R. B. (1971). Planning games are more then just fun. *Fire: Journal of the British Fire Services, 63,* 788.

Duke, R. D. (1974). *Gaming: The future's language.* New York: Sage/Halsted.

Feldt, A. G. (1972). *CLUG, community land use game: Player's manual.* New York: Free Press.

25

The Future of Simulation/Gaming in Britain

HENRY I. ELLINGTON

A milestone such as the 25th anniversary of ISAGA presents an ideal opportunity to look back at what has been achieved and, just as important, to look forward at what has still to be achieved. In this chapter, I attempt to do both, drawing on my 21 years of experience in simulation/gaming to predict the likely future role of games and simulations in British education and training. I then deal with how I envisage such techniques contributing to primary education, secondary education, tertiary education, and training, showing that this contribution seems certain to be significant in all four sectors, but is likely to be greater in some than in others.

Primary Education

Here, the potential for the use of gaming and simulation techniques is virtually unlimited but as yet largely untapped. Since being freed from the shackles of the 11+ examination back in the 1960s, primary teachers have had considerable freedom regarding curricular variation and innovation. This has resulted in primary education becoming much more pupil centered than was the case when I was at school, when, sitting in rows, rote learning and mindless conformity were what was expected of children. Now, however, primary pupils are encouraged to be self-reliant, creative, and imaginative, with traditionally taught lessons being largely replaced by self-paced individualized learning and group learning based on cross-disciplinary projects. Primary education has also become much more process centered than was the case in the past, with pupils being helped to develop problem-solving, communication, interpersonal and other life skills rather than simply being crammed full of facts.

During the past eight years, I have been involved in a number of major curriculum development projects in the primary sector, including problem-based learning (Ellington, Addinall, & McNaughton, 1989), computer-based learning (Ellington & Addinall, 1990) and the use of gaming and simulation techniques (Ellington, 1992; Ellington & Fowlie, 1994). This latter work has convinced me that games and simulations are capable of making a tremendous contribution to primary education. First, it has shown that well-designed educational games and simulations are capable of achieving virtually all types of educational aims and objectives—lower cognitive, higher cognitive, affective, psychomotor, and interpersonal—with pupils of all ages. Second, it has shown that most primary school teachers have all the intrinsic skills needed to design perfectly workable classroom games and simulations for use with their own pupils, provided they are given a little basic guidance on how to do so. Third, it has shown that primary pupils are themselves capable of designing educationally useful games and simulations, provided they are given appropriate guidance and support from their teachers, and that they can get even more out of participating in this design and development process that they do from actually playing the games. Fourth, it has shown that games and simulations can be much more powerful educational tools when used in combination (e.g., using simple board games or card games to back up a complicated role-playing simulation) than when used in isolation. As was stated at the start of this section, the potential for the use of educational games and simulations in the primary sector is virtually unlimited, and I confidently expect much of this potential to be exploited during the next 25 years of ISAGA's existence.

Secondary Education

Although the potential for the use of educational games and simulations is just as great in the secondary sector as in the primary sector, the nature of British secondary education makes it unlikely that this great potential will be fulfilled to the same extent. To put it bluntly, much of the good that is done in our primary schools is undone once our children are subjected to the rat race of secondary education, which is rigidly subject based rather than holistic, content centered rather than process centered, and totally dominated by the need to prepare pupils for examinations. The curriculum is also grossly overcrowded, leaving teachers with little scope to introduce curricular innovation or to try to help their pupils develop wider skills. True, the situation is slightly better in Scotland than in England and Wales, as Scotland's different examination system currently leaves some room for creative teaching at the sixth-form level, but recent government proposals seem likely to remove this advantage.

Although I am not optimistic that things will get much better during the next 25 years, I draw some crumbs of comfort from two current trends. First, the general availability of micro-computers in secondary schools, together with the increasing availability of high-quality computerized simulations, is making the study of subjects such as science, technology, and economics much more meaningful and experiential than was the case in the past (Percival, Ellington,

& Race, 1993). The great potential of such computerized simulations has been pointed out by many authors during the past 15 years (see, e.g., Ellington, Addinall, & Percival, 1981; Megarry, 1978), and it is extremely satisfying to see at least some of these predictions actually coming to pass. Second, more and more secondary teachers are coming to appreciate the great potential of interactive games, simulations, and case studies in developing higher cognitive skills of all types, in developing communication and interpersonal skills, and in demonstrating how their own specialist subjects relate to the real world. Since 1973, I have been heavily involved in promoting the use of such exercises in secondary schools through projects such as THE POWER STATION GAME (Ellington & Langton, 1975) and work with the Association for Science Education (Ellington, Addinall, Percival, & Lewis, 1979) and the Scottish Education Department (Ellington & Addinall, 1984). In this time, such exercises have become increasingly accepted as mainline instructional techniques capable of achieving worthwhile educational objectives rather than simply as time fillers and optional extras (Ellington, 1994). I hope that the people responsible for the secondary curriculum will recognize the tremendous contribution that such exercises are capable of making and will, in the future, allow greater room for their use.

Tertiary Education

Paradoxically, there is now much more scope for the use of innovative teaching techniques such as games and simulations at the tertiary level than there is at the secondary level. Indeed, the use of such techniques is now being actively encouraged via initiatives such as the government's Enterprise in Higher Education program, which is currently pumping money into Britain's higher education institutions to promote an enterprise culture (my own university, for example, received a million pounds between 1988 and 1993). Because tertiary-level teachers also have much more say in what they teach and how they teach it than do secondary school teachers, they are in a much better position than the latter to make use of time-consuming methods such as games, simulations, and interactive case studies.

Games and simulations are likely to play two increasingly important roles in tertiary education during the next 25 years. First, computer simulations will become progressively more widely used in teaching all branches of science and engineering, all financial subjects, all subjects involving design, and many of the social sciences. Such simulations will enable students to gain access to otherwise inaccessible situations (e.g., control of a nuclear reactor), carry out simulated experiments, and design virtually any type of system. Indeed, such laboratory-mode computer-based learning will eventually replace much of the work that currently takes place in conventional laboratories and studios (but not all, as students will always require some genuine hands-on experience).

Second, manual games, simulations, and case studies will become more widely used in the teaching of virtually all academic subjects, mainly as vehicles for developing higher cognitive skills such as decision making and problem solving, for achieving affective objectives of all types, and for developing communication, interpersonal, and other life skills. I have seen these various uses of manual games and simulations spread throughout tertiary education during the past 20 years and seen such use accelerate during the past few years as a result of the stimulus of the government's Enterprise funding (Ellington & McIntosh, in press). I am confident that this trend will continue.

Training

Here the situation is very similar to that of tertiary education, with most training organizations and individual trainers becoming increasingly aware of the valuable role that games, simulations, and case studies of all types are capable of playing in their work. I have considerable firsthand experience of the use of games and simulations in training—particularly in management training (Ellington, Addinall, & Langton, 1982)—and I have seen just how effective they can be in this sector. I envisage them being used in much the same ways as in tertiary education and am confident that this use will again flourish during the next 25 years.

Conclusion

Twenty-five years ago, the use of educational games and simulations was largely confined to the teaching of a few subjects—notably, business studies, geography, and the social sciences—and even then were used by only a few enthusiastic teachers. The subsequent spread of the use of such techniques to all sectors of education and training and to the teaching of virtually all subjects has been one of the great success stories of educational technology during the past 25 years. I am certain that it will become an even greater success story during the next 25 years.

References

Ellington, H. I. (1992). A case study on the use of games and simulations in primary schools. *Simulation/Games for Learning, 22*(3), 195-209.

Ellington, H. I. (1994). Twenty years of simulation/gaming: Reminiscences and thoughts of a Scottish practitioner. *Simulation & Gaming: An International Journal, 25*(2), 197-206.

Ellington, H. I., & Addinall, E. (1984). Designing educational games for less able pupils. In C. W. Osborne (Ed.), *International yearbook of educational and instructional technology 1984/85* (pp. 31-44). London: Kogan Page.

Ellington, H. I., & Addinall, E. (1990). Teaching primary pupils about energy using an interactive database. In B. Farmer, D. Eastcott, & B. Lentz (Eds.), *Aspects of educational and training technology* (Vol. 23, pp. 99-102). London: Kogan Page.

Ellington, H. I., Addinall, E., & Langton, N. H. (1982). How technologically based simulation exercises can be used in management training. In L. Gray & I. Waitt (Eds.), *Perspectives on academic gaming and simulation* (Vol. 7, pp. 144-151). London: Kogan Page.

Ellington, H. I., Addinall, E., & McNaughton, B. (1989). Introducing problem-based learning into the primary schools: A major initiative in the Grampian Region. In C. Bell, J. Davies, & R. Winders (Eds.), *Aspects of educational technology* (Vol. 22, pp. 193-199). London: Kogan Page.

Ellington, H. I., Addinall, E., & Percival, F. (1981). *Games and simulations in science education.* London: Kogan Page.

Ellington, H. I., Addinall, E., Percival, F., & Lewis, J. L. (1979). Using simulations and case studies in the ASE's Science in Society project. In J. Megarry (Ed.), *Perspectives on academic gaming and simulation* (Vol. 4, pp. 55-66). London: Kogan Page.

Ellington, H. I., & Fowlie, J. (1994). Designing "toolkits" to help teachers develop new skills: Two case studies. In R. Hoey (Ed.), *Aspects of educational and training technology* (Vol. 28, pp. 98-101). London: Kogan Page.

Ellington, H. I., & Langton, N. H. (1975, September). THE POWER STATION GAME. *Physics Education,* pp. 445-447.

Ellington, H. I., & McIntosh, P. W. (in press). Innovative teaching at a Scottish University: Report on a survey carried out in 1993. In F. Percival et al. (Eds.), *Aspects of educational and training technology* (Vol. 29). London: Kogan Page.

Megarry, J. (1978). Retrospect and prospect. In R. McAleese (Ed.), *Perspectives on academic gaming and simulation* (Vol. 3, pp. 187-207). London: Kogan Page.

Percival, F., Ellington, H. I., & Race, P. (1993). *Handbook of educational technology* (3rd ed.). London: Kogan Page.

26

Opportunities and Challenges for Gaming/Simulation

A Dutch Perspective

JAC L. GEURTS

The Dutch are, at least quantitatively, a very conspicuous group in ISAGA. Although ours is a small country, over the years many Dutch representatives have come to the ISAGA meetings. One of the philosophical founding fathers of the gaming tradition is the Dutchman Johan Huizinga, author of the famous book *Homo Ludens*. Our country has produced two secretary generals for ISAGA: Henk Becker and Jan Klabbers.

Gaming/simulation is very popular in the Netherlands, even more than our quantitative presence at ISAGA meetings indicates. Why? At first sight this seems hard to explain. For example, Huizinga observes his fellow countrymen's scant receptiveness to rhetoric. Aldous Huxley called my country "a haven for rationalists," which is not necessarily a great help for gaming, a technique that relies so much on intuition and judgment. And Richard Hill, a British consultant who specializes in role-playing to improve management performance says, "It does not work with the Dutch; you cannot make them compete with one another publicly."[1]

But, as Hill correctly states, we are a bunch of very (perhaps overly) educated individuals: assertive, individualistic, and almost dogmatic in our democratic attitudes. We are pluralistic and we are anti-hierarchical. We are also a society in which decisions are made in a very complex network of organizations. William Shetter (1987) says,

> The Dutch occupy one of the world's most densely populated countries and they structure life by means of a seemingly irrevocable commitment to a meticulously detailed, but at the same time flexible, system of interlocking organizations. (quoted in Hill, 1992, p. 136)

In the Netherlands, organizational and public decision making follows complicated paths of coordination and communication; we avoid conflict, sit in meetings, stimulate stakeholder participation, and believe in win/win situations. If the United States is the country of lawyers and litigation, the Netherlands is the country of consultants and communication. We have the highest density of consultants per capita in the world!

I think that gaming does well in the Netherlands because of two reasons: We had strong individuals who believed in the technique and propagated it, and we have the perfect society for the technique, a technique that (a) helps to understand the complexities of institutional arrangements, (b) bridges and integrates multiple perspectives, (c) productively uses and integrates the experience of many individuals, and (d) allows decision makers to experiment with policy options in a safe environment that fits very well into our public and private decision-making culture.

I do agree, however, with the British consultant: We do not like certain aspects of gaming. For example, we hate to make fools of ourselves. We are not extrovert pragmatists like the typical U.S. manager. However, we have other reasons to take gaming very seriously and we obviously do so.

What can ISAGA members learn from the success of gaming in the Netherlands? I would like to point at two aspects: the organization of our profession and the need for more focus on the policy- and decision-making applications of gaming. I make some remarks on the first point but draw most attention to the second point because it is at the core of my personal interest in gaming.

Lesson 1: Professional Organization

It is beyond the scope of this chapter to describe the whole gaming landscape in the Netherlands. On the one hand, gaming is a respected field of research in several universities: Leiden, Rotterdam, Delft, Nijmegen, Tilburg, and Utrecht, all of which have simulation groups. At the same time, gaming is well grounded in professional management consulting. More than I have observed in other countries, gaming is a successful business in the Netherlands, but, like almost everything else that we do, gaming is pluralistic, individualistic, and weakly coordinated. This loose structure of gaming as a profession has its pros and cons. The pros are, of course, flexibility and innovativeness. On the negative side, the loose structure does not help the development of quality control procedures, standardization of pricing, and the definition of delivery standards. Nor is it good for mutual learning, joint promotion, or the emergence of a common gaming warehouse. Gaming needs professional integration with the commercial side of the discipline. An indicator of this is the fact that some of the professional game suppliers and design organizations in the Netherlands have created a network called Game Expertise Netherlands (GEN), aiming at several of the supporting functions I mentioned above.

I think this also has a bearing on ISAGA. Unfortunately, I have to conclude that ISAGA does not have strong ties with the consulting industry, nor does it attract enough attention from internal consultants in large companies and public agencies, nor from the professional training groups in those organizations. ISAGA is oriented toward academia, educators, and applied research institutions. That is a focus it should not lose. However, ISAGA has to broaden its scope. There is much more good gaming out there than we hear about in ISAGA. There is a great market for our tools and ideas, but academics are not trained to open up that market. From a scientific point of view it is a waste of research opportunities if gaming experts in the consulting field are not in close contact with gaming-oriented researchers and methodologists. I call upon the ISAGA Steering Committee to take it as a challenge to broaden the scope of ISAGA in this sense.

Lesson 2: Practicing With Policy

The need for professionalization on the consulting side of our discipline is also linked to a second noteworthy aspect of gaming in the Netherlands. I have a hunch—admittedly, it is no more than a personal impression—that gaming, more in my country than elsewhere, is becoming accepted as a policy aid and as a tool for organizational change. This difference with other countries is, of course, only a matter of degree. Everywhere in the world there is the ambition and the experience to apply gaming/simulations to policy problems. Although the technique may be most well-known and most frequently applied in training and educational situations, over the years several gaming colleagues have published accounts of successful contributions of this technique to policy problems and decision making, both in intra-organizational and inter-organizational settings.

Currently, we are witnessing a tendency in the gaming field to use the label "policy exercise" when referring to the application of gaming/simulation in policy development (see Geurts, 1993; Toth, 1988). The popularity of this concept is perhaps a good indicator of the gradual development of a separate and maturing body of knowledge on how to apply gaming/simulations specifically in policy and decision contexts. Perhaps it is true that, with regard to the policy-analytical role of gaming/simulation, ambitions are still greater than successes. However, I also believe that the visibility of successful gaming applications in the policy field to those not involved in the gaming world has been rather limited. In journals specializing in strategic management and policy analysis one finds little mention of the gaming technique. I hypothesize that a quantitative content analysis of recent volumes of these journals would reveal a much higher frequency of appearance of techniques such as scenario writing, Delphi, system dynamics, and strategic decision analysis than of applications of gaming/simulation. There are at least three possible explanations for this phenomenon:

- *Maturity:* Gaming/simulation is still not as widely used and accepted for policy and strategic decision making as the other methods.
- *Sectarism:* Gamers do not write enough about their methodology in media other than those intended for a gaming audience.
- *Conceptualization:* There is a gap between the conceptualizations of how gamers define their discipline and the conceptualizations understood and considered relevant in policy sciences and strategic management theory.

All three explanations are probably valid and do not seem to be independent of each other. The most serious problem is the lack of concepts and research linking gaming/simulation to current theory in policy science. I accept that policy-oriented gaming may not be as developed as it could be, but that does not justify the current lack of visibility. I also believe that gaming/simulation as a school of thought is too much involved with itself. I think, however, that the best way to get out of this disciplinary autism is by working on a theoretical frame that can integrate gaming/simulation and policy science via the linking concept of participatory policy analysis (PPA). For this, gamers should focus on three activities:

- Publishing illustrations of productive uses of gaming/simulation in policy settings in policy-oriented journals
- Conceptualization of gaming/simulation-based policy exercises as special forms of PPA, focusing on both the criteria for PPA and the functions for PPA that are suggested in the current policy analysis literature
- Creation of a conceptual frame of reference that can guide scientific research on policy exercises and that tries to link contexts of use, conditions of use, design parameters, and effect variables

The gaming discipline should work at a gradual closing of the conceptualization gap mentioned earlier. We need to stimulate gamers to communicate more with the relevant fields of policy sciences. I strongly believe that gaming/simulation has much to offer to current policy and management science. As stated before, certain paradigms have gained in popularity in the policy and management literature. These schools will be very receptive to ideas behind the discipline of gaming/simulation. Gurus in organization and management science claim that there are certain dominant trends in organizational dynamics all over the world. Internationalization of markets, politics, and technical infrastructure makes organizations so complex that the metaphor of the machine

bureaucracy is out of date. Networks are a better way to describe the organizations of the future. Organizations more and more become professional
ad hocracies—not like the Napoleonic army but like the typical law firm.
Professionals, says Moss Kanter (1983), need to be involved in decision making
for a professional organization to work. The new buzzwords are flat, network,
pluralistic, and participatory. In that sense, the Netherlands is almost like a
laboratory. The new dimensions of future organizations are already at work in
our society. So, gamers of the world, come and study us!

The above-mentioned trends have put back on the popular reading table of
many practitioners approaches to decision making that stress organizational
learning and communicative or participatory policy development. Books such
as *The Fifth Discipline* (Senge, 1990), *The Rise and Fall of Strategic Planning*
(Mintzberg, 1994), and, somewhat earlier, *The Change Masters* (Moss Kanter,
1983) have put the conceptualization of strategy making as learning (Senge),
communication (Mintzberg), and participation (Moss Kanter) on the agenda of
every strategy development discussion (see also de Geus, 1988; Hart, 1992).

Richard Duke's *Gaming: The Future's Language,* first published in 1974, has
created a theoretical basis for the technique of gaming/simulation. Duke explains the value of gaming/simulation for policy and management processes by
focusing on the three perspectives previously mentioned here. It is more than
remarkable that his and related publications emerged at a time when the
rationalistic planning traditions were still dominant in the practical policy
fields. Duke's book seems to me like the right message delivered at the wrong
time. But the times are changing. Precisely in this *fin de siècle,* there is ample
reason for gamers to stimulate policymakers and managers to rediscover our
discipline and the leading concepts behind it.

Note

1. The observations and quotations on the Dutch in this chapter are taken from Hill (1992).

References

Duke, R. D. (1974). *Gaming: The future's language.* New York: Sage/Halsted.
de Geus, A. (1988, March-April). Planning as learned. *Harvard Business Review,* pp. 70-74.
Geurts, J. L. A. (1993). *Omkijken naar de toekomst.* Alphen a/d Rijn: Samsom Tjeenk Willink.
Hart, S. L. (1992). An integrative framework for strategy-making processes. *Academy of Manage-
    ment Review, 17*(2), 327-351.
Hill, R. (1992). *We Europeans.* Brussels: Europublications.
Mintzberg, H. (1994). *The rise and fall of strategic planning.* Hemel Hemstead, UK: Prentice Hall.
Moss Kanter, R. (1983). *The change masters.* New York: Simon & Schuster.
Senge, P. M. (1990). *The fifth discipline.* New York: Doubleday/Currency.
Shetter, W. H. (1987). *The Netherlands in perspective.* Leiden: Martinus Nijhoff.
Toth, F. L. (1988). Policy exercises. *Simulation & Games: An International Journal, 19*(3), 235-276.

27

Debriefing the Debriefing Process

A New Look

LINDA C. LEDERMAN

FUMITOSHI KATO

In the world outside the academic classroom, few things about which people need to learn are systematically presented in pre-planned ways for which there are objective tests. Much of what people learn in day-to-day life results from a process of discovery. Thus, learning by means of the process of discovery is a familiar part of the human experience.

Experiential learning in the classroom incorporates those real-life processes of discovery into the educational setting. Experiential learning in the classroom takes place as a result of the experience in which learners engage and the analysis of that experience for the lessons to be plumbed from it. Central to the experience from which the lessons are to be drawn is the post-experience analytic process, generally referred to as the debriefing session (Greenblat & Duke, 1975). The process has begun to receive more attention in the literature than it had previously (Lederman, 1992). Still there is much that remains to be studied about debriefing. This chapter focuses on the debriefing process, with special attention to identifying and exploring theoretical issues as yet unexamined.

Experiential Learning and Debriefing

Experience-based learning is based on the assumption that experiences are the raw data out of which learning is created. Learning takes place as the instructor (facilitator) guides the learner (participant) through the experience, followed by the analysis of the learning that derives from that experience. The post-experience analysis is referred to as debriefing (Lederman, 1983). In summarizing the literature on debriefing, Lederman (1992) has pointed out that not all authors use the term "debriefing" to mean the same thing. Debriefing is variously defined as learning through reflection of a simulation experience (Lederman, 1983; Lederman & Stewart, 1986; Lee, 1984; Pearson & Smith, 1986; Raths, 1987; Thatcher & Robinson, 1990), emotional recovery from critical incidents (Bergmann & Queen, 1987; Donovan, 1983; Walker, 1990), work-related tasks, such as appraisal and synthesis of input from focus groups (De Nicola, 1990) or job performance analysis (Bobele, 1987), or team building and identifying managerial strengths (Bailey, 1990). Another use of debriefing reported by Lederman (1992) is in psychological studies. When subjects have participated in psychological experiments, to debrief them is to inform them (American Psychological Association, 1979), to reverse laboratory-induced experiences (Tennen & Gillen, 1979), to undo negative consequences, to inform and educate, and to check on the method used (Mills, 1976).

The historical roots of the debriefing process lie in military campaigns and war games (Pearson & Smith, 1986). Debriefing was the time after a mission or exercise when participants were brought together to describe what had occurred, to account for the actions that had taken place, and to develop new strategies as a result of the experience. In the educational setting, this process is referred to as the debriefing, the pull-out or the post-experience analysis (Lederman, 1983). During the experience, the emphasis is on the doing, on playing the game. In the debriefing, the emphasis is on making sense of what has happened. It is that part of the process in which participants are guided by the facilitators of the game or simulation in a reflective process about the use of the experiences that occurred during participation. Participants are taught how to analyze their experiences, to evaluate them, to interpret them, and to incorporate them into their own understanding of the issues modeled by the activity.

Much of what people learn, particularly experientially, is a subjective, personalized, individual, and thus idiosyncratic way of knowing, which Boulding (1956) refers to as subjective knowledge. Subjective knowledge is, he says, "more like an image of reality than an objective reality itself, an image as a way of seeing reality" (p. 3). The kind of knowledge that is the product of experience is highly subjective; it is the product of the interaction between the individual and the experience (Lederman, 1984). To the extent that no two individuals are ever completely alike, the knowledge that one individual gains can never be identical with that subjectively experienced by another. Experiences change learners' perceptions and knowledge of reality—their cognitive maps (Miller, Halanter, & Pribram, 1960). In the post-experience analysis, new cognitive maps or images that have been created during the experience are examined and analyzed (Lederman, 1984).

Thus, the debriefing session is a critical component of the experience-based learning situation. The purpose of the debriefing is for those who have experienced something (the learners) to be guided into insights about the meanings of those experiences and the lessons they are drawing from them. It is the process through which participants are guided in reflection on their experience of the simulation/game. Their experiences are examined, discussed, and turned into learning (Thatcher, 1986; Thatcher & Robinson, 1990). There are two underlying assumptions to the debriefing process: first, that the experience of participation has affected the participants, and second, that a discussion of the experience will enhance the participants' ability to learn from that experience.

Elements of the Debriefing Process

Debriefing is a purposeful and planned activity (Pearson & Smith, 1986). It can take place either immediately after an experience or sometime later. Although the atmosphere created by the person leading the debriefing is one of comfort and openness, debriefing has a structure that involves a number of elements, processes, and phases. Lederman (1992) defines these as the guide, the participants, the experience, the impact of that experience, the recollection of it, the mechanisms for the reporting out on the experience, and the time to process it. The debriefing session uses the present moment as a mechanism for reflection back onto the experiences that have transpired, the interpretation of those experiences, and the evaluation of the soundness of those interpretations. The conduct of the session depends on the educational purposes of the experience and the approach of the guide. Essentially, this involves reviewing and describing the experiences through which participants have come, their thoughts, feelings and reflections on those actions, and the assessment and application of these experiences and the meanings attributed to them to real-life situations. These can be classified into three phases: systematic reflection and analysis, intensification and personalization, and generalization and application (Lederman, 1992).

What We Can Learn
Through the Debriefing Process

The process of debriefing is an integral part of the simulation and gaming approach for learning. It is the means through which one's learning is facilitated. A systematic examination of the elements and steps of the debriefing process, as well as the basic skills of the facilitators (Lederman, 1992), may contribute to the effective design and implementation of simulations and games. It is also important to explore what we—as facilitators and/or researchers of experience-based learning—can learn from the debriefing process itself and from the examination of it.

An Expanded Look at the Debriefing Process

Through the debriefing process, participants are taught how to analyze their experiences, to evaluate them, to interpret them, and to incorporate them into

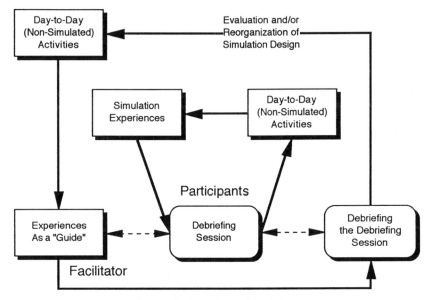

Figure 27.1 A model of the relationships between the steps of experience-based learning.

their own understanding of the issues modeled by the activity. What is not usually acknowledged is that, in debriefing processes, facilitators are also learning. How and what are they learning? Through the interactive process of debriefing, they are learning about the participants, the process of learning, and themselves as guides in the simulation. By shifting our focus from the experiences of the participants to that of the facilitator, we can begin to explore the alternative dimension of the debriefing process. From the standpoint of facilitators, we tend to understand the debriefing process as a simple recounting of the simulation, allowing them to learn from the experiences of the participants. However, we suggest that to focus on the facilitator means to portray the debriefing process beyond such simple recounting of simulation experiences, that is, to acknowledge the debriefing session as an opportunity for facilitators to discover and learn about the learners (participants) and about themselves.

Figure 27.1 illustrates a simplified model of the relationships between the steps of experience-based learning of both the participants and the facilitator. As shown, each of the steps creates a continuous process. The idea of experience-based learning favors the notion of continuity, and thus learning is, essentially, regarded as a never-ending process. For example, the final phase of the debriefing process is characterized in terms of the generalization and application of the experience (Lederman, 1992). Whereas the participants attempt to link their immediate simulation experiences with a broader context of their day-to-day (non-simulated) activities, the facilitator's emphasis is on the doing, on guiding the debriefing session, after which the facilitator is motivated to ask "What did I learn from this experience (as a guide)?" This self-directed questioning has a significant implication in regard to the training/education of the facilitator. By asking such questions—by debriefing the debriefing process—facilitators can evaluate and learn about their skills as guides playing important roles in simulations and games.

Experiencing this process enables facilitators to look back (forward) and establish a link with past (future) debriefing sessions. Viewed this way, the debriefing session is not simply the final part of the simulation, but also an initial part of subsequent simulations. Reflections on the debriefing session may lead to re-examination and re-organization of the structural properties—roles, interactions, rules, goals, and criteria (Ruben, 1977)—of the simulation itself. Thus, from the standpoint of the facilitator and/or researcher, the debriefing process may be used as an impetus to improve the design of the simulation.

This expanded look at the debriefing process has at least two important implications. First, as illustrated, it brings forward the fact that process orientation is inherent in the idea of the debriefing itself. Although the forms may vary depending on the characteristics and/or design of simulations, a debriefing session usually takes place in a form of discussion. Thus, a debriefing session is, by its nature, interactive. Viewed this way, it becomes clear that in the debriefing process both participants and facilitator(s) will engage in communication processes with an explicit focus on joint construction of the situation. Second, in relation to the process nature of the debriefing, this perspective allows us to acknowledge that a simulation, as an event, is embedded in a broader context of one's learning process. Mediated by debriefing processes, simulation experiences are linked together in that both participants and facilitator(s) become aware of their personal involvement in learning processes. This view emphasizes that the debriefing process offers a continuity of experiences, which makes the experience of education an educational one (Dewey, 1929).

Ethical Issues in the Debriefing Process

Simulations and games are powerful tools. The post-experience discussion requires careful use of that tool. People are learning by what they are doing. The facilitator is responsible for what he or she asks students to do and an analysis of his/her behavior with them. Students bring to the activity behaviors that are often self-disclosing. Often, the levels of disclosure go beyond their conscious awareness. This puts a burden on the teacher to determine the built-in protections of the potentially naive participants to assure that the learning is not inappropriately costly emotionally or intellectually. Furthermore, people are ultimately learning about self, and ethics are involved in providing that learning. The experience-based learning environment is a living laboratory of human behavior, an environment in which a database of behavior is created. It is the ethical responsibility of the facilitator to determine the parameters within which behavior is encouraged and/or analyzed.

Cultural Dimensions of the Debriefing Process

Besides the ethical issues, the facilitator's responsibilities regarding cultural issues are important as well. In the teacher/student dyad, partners are born, raised, and mentally programmed in different cultures or sub-cultures prior to their interaction in the learning institution (Hofstede, 1986). Cultural differences, stereotypes, biases, interpersonal perceptions and interpretations, and breaches of cultural norms or misbehaviors are potentially embarrassing. It is the facilitator's responsibility to consider the potential consequences for participants dealing with these issues, perhaps for the first time, and to create a climate in which it is safe and reasonable to explore what emerges. Considerations such as these lead to a review of the complexities added to the debriefing process when the teacher and learners have diverse cultural backgrounds.

There are many differences in the process of communication that can influence how meaning is interpreted and therefore how the debriefing process is guided. Differences in the styles of self-presentation, for example, are always open to misinterpretation because they are differentially valued in the cultures in which they have been learned. The definition of the situation and what is expected and appropriate to it are part of the element of the context of communication. These are culturally derived and therefore likely sources of differences among people from various cultural backgrounds. These differences, however, do not need to make the process of debriefing less effective. The facilitator guides rather than leads, asks rather than tells, and observes rather than predetermines. It is these skills and the paradigm out of which they grow—the perspective that experience-based learning is individual and interpretative— that provide an isomorphy between the processing of the experiences and differences that are culture bound. There are always differences between people as they experience something. It is the recognition of these differences that underlies the rationale for conducting the debriefing as a guided exploration. The debriefing session is not designed to tell the participants about themselves. It is designed to guide them through the process of reflection and self-reflection.

It is important to consider that values and assumptions are, to some extent, already embedded in the ways that simulations are designed. In a process of simulation, participants can only react to the situation in ways that the simulation's structural properties allow. In other words, once individuals have decided to experience the simulation, they enter the reality created and presented by its facilitator (and the designer of the simulation) and have to identify with a selected role the characteristics of which are predetermined by the structural properties of the simulation. Thus, a participant's ability to imagine the possible interactions and their outcomes in the simulation is largely dependent on the ways in which the simulation is guided. Moreover, when a certain property of the simulation becomes pervasive and begins to look natural and proper, its embedded cultural assumptions tend to disappear into the background of the simulation itself. That is, it becomes difficult for both participants and facilitator to recognize and/or question the ways in which they (can) act in the simulated reality.

As noted, the facilitator's task is to guide the participants to reflect on, to intensify, and to generalize their experiences. By doing so, the process itself leaves out other possible ways of debriefing. In other words, in the process of debriefing, the facilitator constantly faces a series of decisions on what questions and discussions to incorporate (or not incorporate) into the process itself. Further, the process is largely dependent on a set of values and assumptions based on the facilitator's cultural background, including past experiences (future visions). Therefore, through the debriefing process, the facilitator is, knowingly or not, communicating his or her cultural values and assumptions to the participants, and that process, in turn, functions to shape and reshape participants' cultural values and assumptions. Acknowledging that the act of debriefing can be an active attempt to produce influence—to create an impact— we need to become sensitive about the cultural issues regarding the debriefing process.

Conclusion

The potential for communication and understanding exists in the debriefing session. The debriefing process favors diversity and continuity. It is through the skillful guidance of the processing of the experience that participants and facilitator(s) can come to know themselves and others better. When those others are from diverse cultural backgrounds and experiences, the potential exists for understanding between people that is often missing in other learning contexts.

References

American Psychological Association. (1979). Ethical standards for psychologists. *American Psychologist, 2,* 56-60.

Bailey, B. A. (1990). Developing self-awareness through simulation gaming. *Journal of Management Development, 9*(2), 38-42.

Bergmann, L. H., & Queen, T. R. (1987). The aftermath: Treating traumatic stress is crucial. *Corrections Today, 49*(5), 100, 102, 104.

Bobele, K. (1987). Self-rating performance: How to reinforce the right job behavior. *Management Solutions, 32*(8), 41-45.

Boulding, K. E. (1956). *The image: Knowledge in life and society.* Ann Arbor: University of Michigan Press.

De Nicola, N. (1990). Debriefing sessions: The missing link in focus groups. *Marketing News, 24*(1), 20, 22.

Dewey, J. (1929). *Experience and education.* New York: Macmillan.

Donovan, E. J. (1983). Responding to the prison employee-hostage as a crime victim. In J. N. Tucker (Ed.), *Correctional officers power pressure and responsibility* (pp. 17-24). College Park, MD: American Correctional Association.

Greenblat, C., & Duke, R. (1975). *Simulation-gaming: Rationale design and application.* New York: John Wiley.

Hofstede, G. (1986). Cultural differences in teaching and learning. *International Journal of Intercultural Relations, 10,* 301-320.

Lederman, L. C. (1983). Differential learning outcomes in an instructional simulation: Exploring the relationship between designated role and perceived-learning outcome. *Communication Quarterly, 32*(3), 198-204.

Lederman, L. C. (1984). Debriefing: A critical reexamination of the postexperience analytic process with implications for its effective use. *Simulation & Games: An International Journal, 15*(4), 415-431.

Lederman, L. C. (1992). Debriefing: Toward a systematic assessment of theory and practice. *Simulation and Gaming: An International Journal, 23*(2), 145-160.

Lederman, L. C., & Stewart, L. P. (1986). *Instructional manual for THE MARBLE COMPANY: A simulation board game.* New Brunswick, NJ: Rutgers University, School of Communication, Information, and Library Studies.

Lee, H. C. (1984). Power sharing and the social studies: Project description. *EDRS Document,* No. 9.

Miller, G., Halanter, E., & Pribram, K. (1960). *Plans and the structure of behavior.* New York: Holt, Rinehart & Winston.

Mills, J. (1976). A procedure for explaining experiments involving deception. *Personality and Social Psychology Bulletin, 2,* 3-13.

Pearson, M., & Smith, D. (1986). Debriefing in experience-based learning. *Simulation/Games for Learning, 16*(4), 155-172.

Raths, J. (1987). Enhancing understanding through debriefing. *Educational Leadership, 45*(2), 24-27.

Ruben, B. D. (1977). Toward a theory of experience-based instruction. *Simulation & Games: An International Journal, 8*(2), 211-231.

Tennen, H., & Gillen, R. (1979). The effect of debriefing on laboratory induced helplessness: An attributional analysis. *Journal of Personality, 47*(4), 629-642.

Thatcher, D. (1986). Promoting learning through games and simulations. *Simulation/Games for Learning, 16*(4), 144-154.

Thatcher, D., & Robinson, M. J. (1990). ME-THE SLOW LEARNER: Reflections eight years on from its original design. *Simulation & Gaming: An International Journal, 21*(2), 291-302.

Walker, G. (1990). Crisis-care in critical incident debriefing. *Death Studies, 14,* 121-133.

28

Elbow's Methodological Belief

Some Uses and a Caution

RICHARD B. POWERS

Critical thinking, which Elbow (1983) calls methodological doubt, has a long tradition in many academic fields (e.g., science, philosophy, and law). It is a valuable and necessary method for examining ideas, but it does not go far enough. The main problem is that in arguing against new ideas we too quickly and easily dismiss them before we come to experience them fully. Hence, we lose out and end up with beliefs that might be called immature or underdeveloped. What Elbow discovered is a technique, which he labeled methodological belief, that complements methodological doubt and, when used in conjunction with it, results in what he believes is a superior method of arriving at a belief or of making a decision. Methodological belief is so called because it is systematic, requiring training and practice for proficiency just as methodological doubt does.

Development of Methodological Belief

Elbow invented methodological belief in his writing classes. Prior to its use, as is true in many classrooms, outgoing students monopolized discussions, argued, interrupted, and rarely listened to each other, whereas shy students remained silent. In attempting to improve class discussions, he introduced a rule that said listeners could not say anything when a speaker was offering an idea or interpretation of a writer. Interesting things sometimes happened with the use of this rule, so he introduced another rule that demanded even more of his students. Listeners now had to actively try to believe the idea being expressed, and questions were permitted only in an attempt to clarify. Because all speakers had a chance to speak without interruption and to experience others attempting to believe their ideas, the atmosphere in class became conducive to exchanging a variety of opinions. Tolerance of unusual or strange ideas became more acceptable than earlier. With the introduction of this exercise, he observed several changes in his students: improved "hearing" of the other, greater ease in reaching agreements, and more skill in taking the perspective of the other.

Differences Between the Doubting and the Believing

The essence of Elbow's approach is to practice systematically doing what is difficult by going against the cognitive grain. We try to believe that which is strange, difficult, or abhorrent and to doubt that which is familiar, easy, or loved. The two exercises differ also in the model of knowledge assumed:

> The central event in the doubting game is the act of trying to see what's WRONG with someone's thinking or to DENY their perception. It implies a scarcity model of knowledge, namely that one side must win and be right and the other wrong. The central event in the believing game, on the other hand, is the act of affirming or entering into someone's thinking or perceiving. It implies a pluralistic model of knowledge: the idea that the truth is often complex and that different people often catch different aspects of it, and that we get closer to seeing correctly by entering into each others' conflicting perceptions or formulations. (Elbow, 1983, p. 11)

Elbow (1983, 1986) says that because both methodological doubt and methodological belief are games they are simply devices to assign weights and make decisions according to criteria we construct. When we adapt a particular method (i.e., methodological belief) it does not follow that we commit ourselves to a given course of action. Fears that one might be unduly influenced by having to swallow an unpalatable idea, for instance, are unfounded, and Elbow attempts to allay such fears by stressing that the person can use the doubting exercise after using the believing exercise. Only then is that person in a position to use criteria to make a decision or accept a belief. The systematic use of both exercises should result in a much larger perspective or a much better decision in a choice situation than if either method was relied on exclusively.

Use of the Believing Exercise

I introduced Elbow's systematic approach to examining beliefs to an audience of about 40 attending ISAGA '94. After an overview of his ideas, the audience practiced methodological belief on a relatively novel proposal selected because it was not likely to elicit a strong negative emotional response. The proposal was that "our national representatives (both houses) should be selected by a lottery." After practice with this proposal, the audience read an article by W. J. Smith (1993) arguing against the use of assisted suicide for the terminally ill.

The audience was then divided into two groups: one (about 10 individuals) either supported the author or was not strongly against him, and the other (25-30 individuals) was strongly opposed to the author's beliefs. The larger group, practicing methodological belief, attempted to adopt the author's arguments uncritically for a brief time. The smaller group were instructed to question the larger group in a sympathetic manner as if it were a single person. In this way, all the nuances of the author's belief with respect to the moral incorrectness of assisted suicide might be fully aired.

After this exercise, a debriefing followed in which participants were asked if they had been able to practice methodological belief with both the non-controversial and the controversial belief. Most had no difficulty and in fact thoroughly enjoyed exploring all the implications of a lottery system for selecting our representatives. This exercise was akin to a brainstorming session, with the blackboard quickly filling with novel and interesting ideas—for example, the age limit for inclusion in the lottery pool was gradually lowered to 12 years as people successively advanced plausible reasons why age restrictions of 35, 21, or 18 were not defensible. I detected no resistance to the exercise.

The second exercise proved much more difficult, and although attempts were made to answer the questions asked by the small group, the answers became more extreme over time and delivered with more fervor. Some of the people in the large group admitted in the debriefing to playing a part, believing that this was what they were supposed to do, much as a seasoned debater might do in a debate by adopting the pro side of an issue one day and the con side the next day. The intensity of the positions advanced produced an increasing hostility and sense of incredulity on the part of the small group of questioners, and the intent of the exercise was soon lost to both sides.

Whereas those in the large group responded that they could indeed use methodological belief for the lottery issue, they reported extreme difficulty, even for a few minutes, uncritically accepting the author's argument that assisted suicide was morally wrong. Some confessed that they simply could not do it, even though they tried. One outspoken individual wondered aloud whether she might not "be wasting her time" doing an exercise like this with an issue she had come to believe firmly. As an illustration of her point, she stated that she was a radical environmentalist and argued forcefully that she had already examined the ideas of the other side(s) and found them wanting. Why should she entertain them all over again? She was an advocate, and her time, she believed, could best be used to convince others of the correctness of her position. The idea also came out in the discussion that an important or core belief, one tied to environmental ethics, for instance, helped define who a person was, and any procedure that attempted to change such a belief was threatening and bound to elicit a defensive action from the person. In effect, why should a person willingly participate in an exercise that might leave a core belief changed and bring into question an individual's identity?

In response to my question in the debriefing of whether any participants had changed their belief regarding assisted suicide, no one in the larger group admitted having done so. This was not surprising because of the atmosphere in the room that, as mentioned earlier, had taken on the character of play acting during the second exercise. Of course, a willingness to try methodological belief does not arise overnight. So I did not expect that any one who had given much thought to the assisted suicide issue and developed a position would change in one encounter with Elbow's method. With practice, though, he would argue that change in an important belief is likely:

> And yet, of course, I think that something real and weighty goes on when people play the believing game. The "belief" it calls for is real enough in the sense that it asks us genuinely, if temporarily, to change the way we see something and understand it. If we come to experience the full force of several competing views, our final position is likely to deepen and change. (Elbow, 1983, p. 12)

Some Difficulties

Elbow's support for the effectiveness of his believing exercise is based on his experiences in classrooms with his students. Could it be that the student audience is a bit more willing to try something that a teacher thinks worth doing than are other audiences (e.g., adults in a public forum listening to an "expert" who can exercise no fate control over them)? I think so, and I believe Elbow underestimates other difficulties as well, which I now discuss.

Defenses Against Trying the Believing Exercise

Elbow's position is that we need not fear "swallowing an unpleasant belief" because we can guide ourselves to our final belief by going through a series of steps: using the believing exercise, then the doubting exercise, then assigning criteria, and finally, making a decision or adopting a belief. But his attempt to allay our fears is not convincing. A psychological barrier to engaging in his exercise seems inevitable because many of our core, important beliefs help define who we are and he is asking that we engage in an activity that disturbs our sense of self. Because he has experience with this technique, he knows that it can be effective in changing beliefs. Otherwise, why suggest it? Knowing all this, I understandably resist the exercise or outright refuse to play. Why should I want my heartfelt beliefs, beliefs that I may have struggled to acquire and worked hard to defend, changed? For what reason(s)? The greater good? Truth? I resist for several reasons but mainly, it seems to me, because I do not want to undergo the pain and discomfort of redefining who and what I am.

Ethics, or "Why Should You Change Me?"

But suppose I do agree to engage in the exercise? Gabriel Marcel (1964, p. 214) suggests in his essay on tolerance that as soon as I allow credence to your beliefs by tolerating their existence, I admit the possibility that mine might be wrong or, at least, not as correct as I first believed. So, by agreeing to undergo the exercise (showing tolerance) I have undergone the first step in revising my belief, and this is, indeed, serious business. Voluntary compliance has been found to be one of the necessary steps in producing cognitive dissonance (Crano & Messé, 1982). I would expect some cognitive dissonance from those who were successful in believing even part of the other's position. How might it be reduced? One way would be to alter my beliefs. Another might be to discover something additionally wrong with the opposing side's argument. But, and this is the heart of the matter, it is not at all clear to me as an ethical person how to proceed if I were going to tackle a thorny issue in my community, say, a ballot measure allowing physician-assisted suicide under certain conditions. Should I promise to go through the methodological doubt procedure right after the methodological belief procedure to assure people that they would end up with their original position intact and with a minimum of emotional wear and tear? But why would I do this? The reason why I use methodological belief is *because* I want you to change your belief(s)! In summary, as an expert attempting to persuade, I might use methodological belief (and would suggest its being used systematically by my audience) in the hope that people on the other side of the issue experience cognitive dissonance and that they reduce it by coming around to the position I advocate, at least to the extent of voting for my position.

So, an ethical use of methodological belief may require that I obtain your informed consent to proceed. Is this enough? It seems that more may be required of me, but what, exactly, is not obvious. Consider the following questions for which I have no simple answers: By what right do I meddle in your belief system and rearrange it so that it is somehow better, or more in accord with mine, or more in accord with the majority, or more in accord with the "truth," however socially defined? Why is it desirable to have you experience the multiple truths or multiple perspectives that I or some other "worthy" person find valuable? Will the community be better off if we are all trained to see multiple perspectives? A large segment of our population (various fundamentalist groups) would disagree with this view, I think. The widespread adoption of methodological belief may be a common good, but I believe a much stronger case needs to be made for the conditions under which it may be ethical to use it.

The dilemma is one that surfaces with Elbow's method and is present any time we desire to intervene with an effective method in an educational program. Methodological doubt is acceptable, especially when core beliefs are at issue, precisely because it is not particularly effective in changing beliefs! In fact, it tends to harden them. Watch any public debate and note the effects on both the speakers and the audience. Both sides part company with their views more entrenched than when they arrived, and I believe academics and the educated public know this. So, because methodological doubt as a technique of persuasion is ineffective, it is acceptable and even promoted (the debate format) in our schools. For similar reasons, tobacco companies give money to school campaigns (speakers at assemblies, etc.) that rail against the evils of tobacco use, but they steadfastly refuse to curtail advertising. Why? They long ago learned that advertising is very important in maintaining sales, but that school campaigns are ineffective in reducing smoking rates among children and teens. So why not support the anti-smoking campaigns? It won't hurt and it's good public relations!

Relevance to the Field of Simulation/Gaming

In discussing the problems of trying out a contrary belief; one of the workshop participants said that in a good game one is not confronted so directly with a challenge to one's beliefs. Rather, what takes place is a slow, growing involvement in the game, the assumption of a role (either explicit or implicit), and then interaction with other players in that new role. Hence, one is more likely to be persuaded of the value of a contrary or new belief because the learning or persuasion process is subtle and appears to result from one's experiences in the game. Players in a good interactive game frequently report that they forget all about the game director—the game belongs to the players and so their discoveries appear independent of outside agents like a game facilitator or teacher.

This description of what transpires in a good game corresponds to my experience, and it may be the case that a good game "invites players to try on a new belief" with results similar to those of Elbow. After playing a cultural diversity game, for instance, players may see more value in having a diverse workforce or in putting their children in an educational program that explicitly teaches about other cultures or religions. But because a game or simulation may be belief changing and because it does not openly say that one's beliefs may be transformed, it may be on more slippery ethical ground than Elbow's exercise. It seems to me that it is all too easy for the game designer to slip into the posture of "knowing what's best" for gaming consumers.

Conclusion

I suggest that we need to take more pains in the introductory part of a game, especially one involving a controversial and widely contested issue, to warn our audience. Perhaps we should say something like the following:

These are some of my values and they are (or probably are) part of the underlying model in my game. My experience has shown me that many players get deeplyinvolved in this game and may have an important belief challenged and even altered. We will spend some time in the debriefing questioning my ideas and the model of the world I assume to be correct and valuable. I hope that this procedure will allow you to emerge with your own balanced and informed perspective. Now, do you want to play the game?

References

Crano, W. D., & Messé, L. A. (1982). *Social psychology.* Homewood, IL: Dorsey Press.

Elbow, P. (1983, April). *Critical thinking is not enough.* Reninger Lecture delivered at the University of Northern Iowa.

Elbow, P. (1986). *Embracing contraries: Explorations in learning and teaching.* New York: Oxford University Press.

Marcel, G. (1964). *Creative fidelity.* New York: Farrar, Strauss.

Smith, W. J. (1993, June 28). The whisper of strangers. *Newsweek,* p. 8.

29

History Lessons and Prospects of Gaming/Simulation in the CIS

VICTOR I. RYBALSKIY

In this chapter, I attempt to outline events, using illustrations from my own experience, that took place in the former USSR, now called the Confederation of Independent States (CIS). I explain how the gaming movement developed under these unfavorable conditions before and after the mid-1980s. I then describe problems of the gaming movement after the overthrow of the Communist regimes and the splitting of the Soviet empire into Russia, Ukraine, and other countries. Among those problems cited, it is most important to help the former Communist-bloc scientists create or adapt for their countries not only modern business games, but also games aimed at conserving the environment and developing human personality. I believe that the best games will be created jointly by Western and CIS scientists.

Gaming and Life Under Communism

The first business game was created in Leningrad more than 60 years ago by Birshtain and her colleagues. But such a "not serious" undertaking could not obtain official Soviet support for development. However, without such support, in a totalitarian country nothing had the right to exist. Therefore, research and the working out of the field of business games was effectively closed for 35-40 years and revived only in the 1960s and 1970s. But it goes without saying that these games had to base themselves only on a socialist ideology and Soviet management methods. Such games had the right of existence as long as they promoted the realization of decisions made by the Communist Party. It was clear that these games propagandized and reflected, in both nuance and detail, the

EDITORS' NOTE: This chapter is a modified version of an article that appeared in *Simulation & Gaming: An International Journal, 25*(2), 236-244.

principles of a planned economy. In accordance with these principles, all major economic questions were decided from above. Moscow gave out all the assignments and allocations, and the nation's factories had to obediently fulfill these assignments. Accordingly, these games dealt with the tactical problems of logistics and production scheduling rather than with creative entrepreneurship.

Another feature of those years was a lack of business games devoted to ecological problems. Only through empty words and phrases did socialism's leaders care for preservation of the environment. In reality, the preservation of nature and a caring for the people were considered an unnecessary luxury, a question of minor importance compared to industrial production activities. Not without reason, then, enterprise managers were judged by momentary output indexes. State firms operated according to the principle "After us—the deluge." This is the atmosphere that allowed the Chernobyl accident to take place near Kiev in 1986, and there are many other industrial regions in the CIS that are now unfit for living. Last year, the life expectancy of adult men in Russia was only 60 years. That means that men in Indonesia, the Philippines, and in many parts of Africa live longer than the average man in Russia (the life expectancy for an American man is 72 years). Last year, the death rate in Russia was 15 for every 1,000 people, in the United States only nine. On the other hand, the birth rate in Russia was only nine for every 1,000 people, in the United States 16. Of course, such an unprecedented decline in life expectancy and birth rate is a result not only of environmental pollution. Epidemics of alcohol abuse, bad food, and retarded medicine have also played their parts. In short, it is a result of the communist regime, which during its 70 years demanded that people sacrifice their health and lives for communism.

A third feature of Soviet gaming was the failure to create games for improving human personality, opening and developing such important and noble human qualities as charity, mercy, democracy, responsiveness, and individualism. These characteristics were for many years considered not only unnecessary, but also harmful to the Soviet people because they reflected bourgeois morals. The state promoted the slogan "Pity humiliates man." It is not by mere chance that a scornful and contemptuous attitude was adopted by waiters, salesmen, tailors, and other service people.

A Few Enthusiasts and Few Achievements

Despite these unfavorable conditions, some very good business games were created by a few enthusiasts: Siroejin, Gidrovich, and Porkhovnik in Leningrad; Komarov and Siskina in Novosibirsk; Arutunov, Burkov, Yefimov, Geronimus, Marshev, Ivanovskiy, and Krukova in Moscow; and scientists of my native Kiev Civil Engineering Institute and Cybernetics Institute (Ivanenko). Valuable ecological gaming models were suggested by Kavtaradze in Moscow, and the first personal improvement games (SUPER, PRESIDENT) in Kiev were created and played. All these efforts were resolutely supported after 1986 by Yagodin, Minister for National Education. For many years, an annual seminar entitled "Business Games" was held in Leningrad. A few conferences were held in Moscow, Novosibirsk, Kiev, and Chelyabinsk. The 15th anniversary conference of ISAGA was held in May 1985 in Alma-Ata, Kazakhstan. In 1981, a special education center was created by the Kiev Civil Engineering Institute to train professors and teachers in the use and creation of simulations and games. In a 12-year period, over 2,000 people from 300 universities, scientific institutes, and enterprises were trained at this center. A few years ago, the Social Simulation Game Modeling Designers Association was officially established.

However, despite all our efforts, we were unable to inspire the widespread adoption of business games in enterprises and universities. There were several reasons for this. First, despite gaming's obedience to the central planning dictates of the Soviet system, it rarely met with understanding and support from the managers of the socialist factories (there being no other kind of factories in the former USSR). Who needs games when the socialist system is based on commands rather than self-initiative? Second, educational games were not needed by the majority of leaders and professors of the country's universities and institutes. They were accustomed to giving lectures with old notes, which they renewed only with references to the regular congress of the Communist Party of the Soviet Union and to new decisions made by the Party. It was clear that these professors were in no hurry to learn and to use new teaching methods, including business games. It was quite possible to be sluggish under the conditions of a planned economy and still survive.

The fact is that the planned system decided how many engineers, physicians, agronomists, teachers, and so forth each university and institute had to graduate. The quality of the university and institute students was determined by the university itself and did not have to stand the test of the labor market because all graduates were automatically assigned positions in various state enterprises and government bureaus. Therefore, most of the universities merely attempted to fulfill their graduation requirements, graduating even the illiterate, if necessary. The number of students who failed or discontinued studies was trifling. Even the school's dropout rate was centrally planned! Unsatisfactory final marks died out as did the dinosaurs. Even grade "C" could be recorded in the country's official Red Book of endangered species. It was clear that business games could not be popular under such conditions.

In the 1980s, after many years of experiencing difficulties in applying gaming methods from "below," I found that these activities could be dangerous when in the hands of the "top" authorities. In this regard, I feel a sense of guilt because I finally convinced the leadership of the Ukrainian Department of Higher Education of the usefulness and productivity of gaming methods. Unfortunately, they used a purely Soviet way and began to generate them with "iron hand" directives. Orders, and soon decrees, were prepared by the appropriate ministries. To carry out these dictates and thoughtless plans, as well as to receive awards and advantages, people were consciously or unconsciously encouraged to engage in forgeries and humbug. I remember in the beginning of the 1980s that Ukraine's Minister of Higher Education suddenly made an initiative and ordered every university department to devise three business games within the year. Understand, not two or four, but exactly three as a convenient, easily calculated statistic. It's enough to make a cat laugh, but no one could raise an objection against such ridiculous order. It was a terrible program, but it was very difficult to struggle against what was the essence of the Soviet system. The result was such that, across the land, simple and naive exercises began to be called business games. Thus, business games were soon discredited, but the minister's order was realized. Only after a few years were we able to convince the minister to substitute for his absurd order another less formal one to stop the mass nonsense that had been created. By that time, large catalogs of mainly precocious business games were published in Leningrad and Kiev, legitimizing hundreds and thousands of simple exercises as real business games. The USSR very quickly left the rest of the world behind in the quantity of business games produced, although almost all were not true business games. In short, there were reports of achievements instead of true achievements.

Foreign Collaboration

Until 1985-1986, most Soviet scientists were allowed to collaborate only with their colleagues who lived in the socialist countries (East Germany, Poland, Czechoslovakia, Hungary, Rumania, etc.). Now, with great pleasure and gratitude, we remember our friendly and scientific relations with Gernert (East Berlin), Switalski, Naumenko, and Dlugoz (Warsaw), Borack (Prague), Radaceanu (Bucharest), and many others. However, only a few Soviet scientists were allowed to participate in international conferences in capitalist countries. Before the 1990s, for example, I received many invitations to participate in a certain forum, but higher authorities and the KGB never approved my appearances in the capitalist countries. Sometimes the authorities said that I had "suddenly fallen ill" or was "too busy to attend."

Eleven years ago I published in the Novosibirsk magazine *EKO* a proposal to create competitive conditions within the USSR's universities and institutes to arouse student interest in knowledge and learning. Needless to say, those in the higher ranks did not know about this experimental proposal. The experiment's results exceeded all expectations, but when one high official learned of the experiment he said to me, "You must understand that this is horse of another color, that competition is not our way. Competition and individualism are the diseases of capitalism. Our way is socialist emulation so we do not lose contact with the masses. On the contrary, we must help all students to reach an equally high level." Naturally, my gaming experiments could not be condoned and could not continue. True, I could not continue my experiments for other reasons: A representative of the KGB accused me of disloyalty after he heard me discuss in a seminar the advantages of American computers over Soviet-made ones. Although this accusation was ridiculous, but could have been the end of me, an about-face by the government in the mid-1980s changed many things. "Speak the truth, but leave immediately after" the Slovenian proverb teaches us.

Changes Wrought by Perestroika

In 1985 when perestroika was declared by Mikhail Gorbachev, serious changes began. I could publish a few important articles in Moscow newspapers which laid bare the truth and revealed the depth of the ineffectiveness of the Soviet system of vocational training and education. Before perestroika, such articles could not be published and were considered as anti-Soviet agitation. During this period the first textbooks on business games were published in Kiev. Not only was a special education center established in Kiev to train the Soviet professors and managers in the creation and use of simulation and gaming, but short-term courses were later offered also in Moscow, Leningrad, and Odessa.

The overthrow of the communist regimes in the USSR and other East European countries not only opened the way for creating games and using them effectively, it also brought new problems for scientists. At first, their contacts with Western scientists, and especially with ISAGA, were made easier and increased manifold. Russian, Ukrainian, and other specialists could easily participate in international conferences, obtaining foreign experience without the fear of official reprisals. For example, for the first time in my life I was allowed to visit some capitalist countries (the United States, Japan, and Israel). For the first time, some Soviet scientists became members of ISAGA; a few of them were later elected to its Steering Committee. In 1991, with the participation of Western scientists, we held in Kiev the 18th International Seminar on Gaming-Simulation in Education and Scientific Research. A similar seminar took place in St. Petersburg. The well-known American scientists Meadows, Greenblat, Wolfe, and others participated, putting their expertise to work to our problems. They also demonstrated their effective business games.

New Life: New Problems and New Prospects

After the Iron Curtain crashed down, many abnormal problems disappeared, but new problems arose. First, former Communist-bloc scientists have no funds for travel. Their salaries, if they are not businesspeople, are relatively low by international standards. For example, the salary of my friend in Kiev, who is both a professor and a doctor of medicine, is only $50 monthly. The developed world must help CIS scientists with foreign contacts and joint undertakings.

Second, the majority of the games we created before cannot help us under the new conditions in the CIS. I was pleased to learn that, to foster creation of new simulations and to better understand their application in the CIS, Joseph Wolfe has obtained five-year funding for an annual Marie Birshtain research competition. This should provide an international audience for the efforts of each republic's scientists and bring an international perspective to the judging of these efforts. The benefit to CIS scientists is twofold: It helps them create new games for use in the CIS today, and it facilitates their contacts with Western colleagues and helps them learn and understand democratic methods of governing.

Third, it is imperative to quickly create for or adapt to the conditions of the CIS business games that simulate the modern market economy. It is very important to implement these games as aids in replacing the socialist economic system with something that meets the demands of market conditions. Unfortunately, this transition has taken on a deformed and corrupted shape. Western scientists can help solve this problem, as described in Wolfe's 1991 report delivered in Kiev, "Prospects for the Transfer of American Market-Oriented Business Games to Post-Socialist Countries." At the same time, I believe that the best games will be created jointly by Western and CIS scientists because both can bring their insights into the game design process.

Fourth, business games are needed that examine and develop an understanding of the government's most important and complicated economic reforms such as currency reform, a flexible banking system, and equity market structures. Fifth, there is a need for the creation or adaptation of wide-net ecology games that provide for not only the conservation of nature but also its restoration or renewal.

Sixth, last but not least in significance or importance, sets of personality-improving games must be created. These games have to help develop individuals' feelings of charity, empathy, individualism, and democracy. Personality-improving games have to demonstrate that bitterness, insidiousness, selfishness, and aggressive actions are not only immoral, but often disadvantageous. By way of illustration, a trilogy of games, PRESIDENT I, II, and III, allows participants to run a country—its economy, its politics, and its social order, respectively. On completion of these games, the participants analyze theirs strategies and actions, taking into account both their personal winnings and the levels achieved by their countries. It is important to evaluate the state of a country as it pertains to the leadership of a president. This analysis may serve as the basis for discussing such aspects as competence, democracy, authoritativeness, resourcefulness, responsiveness, ability to cooperate with neighbors, and, in particular, the tendency to compete or confront. When I moved to the United States in 1993 I brought with me PRESIDENT II, which concentrates on political dimensions. It is currently under development and will run on a personal computer.

I hope that the end of the communist regime in Russia, Ukraine, and other East European countries will see an increased use of business games to help them overcome their current difficulties and accelerate their economic, personal, and spiritual development. Unfortunately, the past year has seen communists and ultra-nationalists in post-communist countries become stronger and more numerous. But the worst of it is that they are supported by many more people than before. If Vladimir Zhirinovsky, who heads the largest faction of ultra-nationalist deputies in the Russian state Duma, or another like him comes into power, all democratic reform would doubtless come to an end and no one would need our new games. However, I take the optimist view that a better future awaits us and that all our efforts will not be in vain.

30

Policy Exercises

The First 10 Years

FERENC L. TOTH

The year of the 25th anniversary conference of ISAGA also marked a small, but encouraging, jubilee for the expanding community involved in policy exercises (PEs). It was ten years earlier (1984) that I began work on developing a new approach to facilitate science-policy interactions by improving the tools available for scientific synthesis for policy purposes. In a few years, an increasing number of policy analysts and other practitioners adopted the methodology that has come to be known as PEs. The International Policy Exercise Group (IPEG) was established in 1989 to serve the interests of the PE community, but it remained largely inactive for a variety of reasons. However, the background for the method itself and for many practitioners is in simulation and gaming. Over the years, the annual ISAGA conferences have become important fora for presenting recent results and new ideas related to PEs. ISAGA '94 allocated a full-day session for reviewing and discussing the state of the art and provided an excellent opportunity for the PE community to re-organize itself. The enthusiasm about and the results from this session provide a powerful motivation to make meetings of IPEG an organic part of the annual ISAGA conferences in the future.

The Origins

The history of PEs began in 1984 when Bill Clark organized a conference titled "Sustainable Development of the Biosphere" at the International Institute for Applied Systems Analysis (IIASA) in Laxenburg, Austria, as a start-up to a major international project on global environmental issues. The project had many components. Although, over history, people have encountered many environmental problems, the nature and the character of these problems started to change in the 1960s and 1970s as societies moved from simple, short-term, and local problems to long-term ones (e.g., nuclear waste management or global climate change) and large-scale (continental to global-scale) problems (e.g., acid rain or stratospheric ozone depletion), and toward complex syndromes of environmental change, where several human activities affect a range of environmental components and the impacts would feed back to many human activities.

Clark (1986) felt that these new environmental problems and the new challenges we were facing in managing them would require new approaches to pull together all relevant scientific knowledge and to communicate them to key policy makers. His opinion was that the scope of techniques, models, and methodological approaches we were working with at that time had not been appropriate to address these new types of problems. At one extreme we had complex models, and at the other extreme were ad hoc expert committees (blue ribbon panels). Each approach had its own merits and shortcomings. There was clearly room for a new approach to address complex issues in a policy context.

In his contribution to the conference and subsequent book on sustainable development, Garry Brewer (1986) reviewed his experience of scenario-based, free-form games, that is, war-gaming experiments. He concluded that they might be a useful starting point for the new approach that he called the policy exercise. His proposal was that we should learn and adopt whatever is useful and relevant from the war-gaming technique and formulate PEs to help manage global environmental problems. Brewer defined a PE as

> a deliberate procedure in which goals and objectives are systematically clarified and strategic alternatives are invented and evaluated in term of the values at stake. The exercise is a preparatory activity for effective participation in official decision processes; its outcomes are not official decisions. (p. 468)

In his commentary on Brewer's book chapter, Nick Sonntag (1986) noted that another approach he was using in his environmental consulting activities might also provide useful elements to PEs. AEAM, the Adaptive Environmental Assessment and Management technique, is based on close interactions of interest groups, policy makers, and modelers/analysts.

I started out with these writings and guidance from Bill Clark as I began to design the various building blocks and procedural components of what later became known as the PE technique. My background at that time was policy analysis, operational gaming (STRATEGEM and related activities at IIASA), and several international AEAM projects and workshops. In the summer of 1985, we conducted a three-month-long brainstorming session with a group of graduate students who participated in IIASA's Young Scientists' Summer Program (YSSP) and whose background matched the various methodological approaches on which the PE technique drew (AEAM, policy analysis, war gaming, and negotiations analysis). By the end of the summer, we had an improved frame and many more building blocks for PEs. These preliminary results were critically reviewed at a workshop organized by Garry Brewer at Yale University. Results of this workshop and comments and suggestions from others were crucial for me in preparing the first procedural, implementation-oriented, technical document on PEs (Toth, 1986).

My own, more operational definition of the PE was also formulated during this initial development phase:

> A PE is a flexible structured process designed as an interface between academics and policymakers. Its function is to synthesize and assess knowledge accumulated in several relevant fields of science for policy purposes in light of complex practical management problems. It is carried out in one or more periods of joint work involving scientists, policy makers, and support staff. A period consists of three phases (preparations, workshop, evaluation) and can be repeated several times. At the heart of the process are scenario writing of "future histories" and scenario analysis via the interactive formulation and testing of alternative policies that respond to challenges in the scenarios. These scenario-based activities take place in an institutional setting reflecting the institutional features of the problem at hand. They are enhanced by a series of complementary activities. (Toth, 1986, p. 6)

There are two basic types of participants in a PE: policy makers as members of one or more policy team(s) and experts serving on the control team. Their activities at the policy exercise workshop are coordinated and moderated by a facilitator. If there are more policy teams their relationship can be co-operative or competitive, depending on the problem with which they are dealing.

The First Experiments

The obvious and most convenient places to test PEs were the various case studies organized in the framework of the IIASA biosphere project. Two such studies were being conducted in the mid-1980s, one of which addressed the problem of the forestry sector in Europe. The study analyzed the issues of how forests and the forestry industry in Europe would evolve under different management strategies, environmental stresses, and overall economic trends. Project leader Sten Nilsson, Peter Duinker, and I designed and implemented a series of test runs and several real PEs in the framework of this study. The first tests of the workshop components, facilitation techniques, and scenario processing procedures were conducted in summer 1986. These tests involved another group of graduate students who participated in the IIASA YSSP. Steve Underwood made an excellent contribution in implementing these experiments. The experience gained in these test runs were summarized in Part 2 of the Practicing the Future series (Toth, 1988).

The next phase in the forestry project consisted of a series of small-scale experimental exercises that involved representatives of the Swedish forestry industry, the Timber Committee of the United Nations Economic Commission of Europe (UN ECE), and graduate students in forestry at the University of Uppsala. The final exercise in this series involved senior company managers in forestry and the timber industry along with national-level policy makers from many European countries. Results from these experiments have been reported in Duinker, Nilsson, and Toth (1993).

The most important characteristics of these exercises were the following. The scenarios used in the exercises were largely based on conventional wisdom. This is understandable. Conducting the first experiments with something new, we were worried about how the whole procedure would be received by experts and policy makers involved in the forestry project. Therefore, we were very careful as we presented the non-traditional features of the exercise, like surprise-rich scenarios and competitive future history writing. Moreover, the exercises relied heavily on computer models. We ran the one and only global forest-product trade model and a series of national forest inventory models. The models were used in the preparations phase, in scenario development, as well as for scenario updates during the workshops. Finally, the PEs had a large original research component to support them. This was the first time we realized that if we were to engage and get full commitment for participation from serious policy makers there must be a significant research component behind the exercise because the chance to get new information from the original source is a major attraction for this community.

The most important result of these early PEs was that they confirmed the original design. I learned that this hybrid method drawn together from war games, AEAM, and operational games worked and was felt to be useful by most participants. The first experiments helped me to clarify some basic, conceptual issues related to the objectives for the methodological development. They also provided valuable experience of the operational and procedural aspects of the design elements. Many new ideas evolved and were tested, and substantial preparatory activities were identified as being crucial for a successful exercise. Of course, my team had many technical difficulties. These included problems of integrating computer models into the scenarios and the exercise procedure, integrating results from the background computer models in a consistent way, and finding fast and efficient ways for scenario updates.

Another series of PEs in the biosphere project were conducted for a case study on future environments for Europe. Project leaders Bill Stigliani and Laurent Mermet were the key people in designing and implementing these exercises. In contrast to the forestry PEs, there was a strong commitment to develop and work with surprise-rich scenarios, there was not much computer modeling involved, and, given the constraints of the study, there was little chance to establish a major original research component in-house. Instead, the project relied on a large network of researchers and focused on synthesis. The results of these exercises have also re-confirmed the basic procedures and elements of the original design and have provided useful insights for the European scene.

Selected Applications

The next set of applications of the PE technique originated from the Villach Conference on Global Climate Change that called for studies to look at regional impacts of climate change in more detail and to analyze possible policy responses based on regional impact assessments. One response by the United Nations Environment Program (UNEP) was the project titled "Socio-Economic Impacts and Policy Responses Resulting From Climate Change: A Study in Southeast Asia." The project involved an international core group of consultants and national study groups (NSGs) assembled under the leadership of designated government agencies in Indonesia, Malaysia, and Thailand. I was responsible for designing and implementing the socio-economic impact assessment and the policy response component of the study. Generating policy responses to large-scale biophysical changes that largely originate outside the study region was the central task for the project.

Given the scope and geographical boundaries of the project, the main emphasis was on developing and evaluating adaptive response strategies, although various aspects of greenhouse gas abatement had been repeatedly raised by various contributors to the study. The core team prepared a set of climate change scenarios for the region and provided computer models and other analytical tools for the NSGs to do their detailed impact assessments at the regional level. The three main impact areas investigated in this study were agriculture, water resources, and coastal changes due to sea level rise.

The PEs served as tools for synthesizing results of the various impact assessments and for generating and evaluating various response options by engaging an elite group of senior policy makers from the relevant government agencies. The two main exercises in the project were conducted in 1990 at Genting Highlands for Malaysia and in Jakarta for Indonesia.

The PEs in Southeast Asia presented a major challenge because they involved the first cross-cultural transfer of the methodology. ISAGA members are very aware of the possible traps and pitfalls of transferring various types of operational games from one culture to another. The PE approach is deeply rooted in the North American and to some extent in the West European culture where debates and challenging each other's ideas and opinions are the norm in exploring and presenting controversial issues. Taking this tool to the Asian culture, where open criticism is very rare, honoring superiors is a basic rule, and loss of face is the worst thing that can happen to someone, was anything but simple. It was necessary to change some of the procedural steps in order to allocate elements of the Asian culture that were relevant for a successful and stress-free participation in a PE. This mainly affected toning down the competitive and criticism-oriented interpersonal elements and gearing the exercise toward consensus seeking and cooperation.

Another important characteristic of the Southeast Asia exercises was a large original research input, including computer models, with the best available results from the general circulation models (GCMs), detailed local scenarios of climate change, and a number of models that were calibrated by the local teams based on their local data. The PE also involved a thorough and detailed preparations phase: 1.5 years between the first project meeting and the PE workshops. This manifested again what I earlier defined as the golden rule for PEs: namely, that 80% of the effort goes into the preparations and 80% of the output is generated at the workshop, but it is not possible to get the second one without making the first investment. I also conducted a series of detailed interviews with senior policy makers (deputy-minister level) in all three countries to get their perception of the problem, to raise their interest, to ensure their commitment to the project and the PE, and to structure the exercise from project focus to scenarios writing so that by the time they participated in the workshop their expected role and activities were clear to them. Finally, we had a very good mix of science and policy participants at the exercises (about one to three) that provided sufficient scientific expertise but kept the focus on policy issues.

Among the lessons we learned from these PEs, the importance of using multiple scenarios was probably the most significant. When only one climate-change scenario was fully developed and taken to the exercise, participants took the single scenario as a prediction of climate change and its impacts, and they criticized details in the scenario instead of working on the policy responses. Another important insight came out of the sub-group dynamics and the looking-outward component adopted from the AEAM approach. Following the first round of developing policy responses for individual sectors (agriculture, water, coastal regions), policy participants were recombined into new groups to analyze the interrelationships between the three areas. It soon turned out that indirect, cross-sectoral effects of climate change are more important in many impact areas than direct ones (e.g., agriculture, irrigation, and water resources; coastal agriculture, sea-level rise, and drainage). Finally, the Southeast Asia exercises have shown that, when addressing long-term problems like global climate change and its regional impacts, in order to get their attention and commitment the scenarios must be formulated to have direct relevance for policy makers today. This was achieved by formulating the climate impacts issue in the context of persistent current problems and strategies to solve them by linking them to long-term government objectives and to major long-range development programs. Toth (1992) presents a detailed account of the Southeast Asia PEs.

Another interesting application of the PE approach to the climate change problem was organized by Jill Jaeger (then with the Stockholm Environment Institute), Bill Clark, and Nick Sonntag. Their objective was to study the issues related to sustainable development in a world undergoing anthropogenically induced climate change. This exercise created broad-scale future histories of global development. These scenarios had an explicit surprise orientation as participants wanted to explore non-conventional paths of future development and society-environment interactions. Computer models were not used in this PE, which illustrates the qualitative and explorative nature of the exercise. Although it was called a PE, none of the participants was active in a senior policy-making position. So it is no wonder that one participant in the debriefing session asked why this was called a PE and not simply a futures exercise or some such term (see Jaeger, Sonntag, Bernard, & Kurz, 1991).

Despite the numerous uncommon features of this exercise, or precisely because of them, it has contributed to the increasing amount of practical lessons about PEs. First, the technique has proved to be useful as a research tool. The time constraints placed on preparations and workshop activities and on potential participant policy makers have been reconfirmed. This constituted an independent proof of the two and a half to three-day design that the IIASA team that I led has been pursuing. Another lesson was related to the preparations and preworkshop information made available to participants. These were confirmed as being vital in making participation in the workshop more productive, thus increasing the amount and quality of the output and reducing the time necessary to produce it.

A number of other PEs have been conducted by various teams in North America and Europe. Given my limited knowledge about them, I prefer to leave it to those involved to draw and publish lessons from them. Having said that, it is probably true that an incomplete overview of what is going on in the field appears to be a problem for most of us involved in PEs. Therefore, I next address the problem of communication and sharing experience across the growing PE community.

IPEG: Past, Present, and Future

By 1989, a sufficient amount of PE-related experience had accumulated to justify the need for an informal but organized exchange of views, ideas, and practical lessons and to the promotion of joint activities. The International Policy Exercise Group (IPEG) was established to serve these objectives. IPEG had its first meeting in December 1989 in Toronto. Although the meeting was an unqualified success, five years passed before IPEG's next meeting, held under the auspices of ISAGA '94. The central issue remains the same: how to learn from each other's experience and document both the successful design innovations and the pitfalls others should avoid.

Results of and experience from the increasing number of PEs are scattered in the literature. Many reports remain at the "grey level" of publication forever: Institute reports, working papers, project documents, and similar texts are not entered in the large computerized databases and do not show up even in thorough literature searches. When reports from PEs do get into the published literature, they tend to focus, understandably, on substantive results of the project and the exercise. Little time and energy is devoted to methodological lessons from the exercise because we are already preoccupied with the next project.

Given the above constraints, it is not surprising that hardly any systematic review and critical appraisal of the methodological development can be observed over the past few years. Communication between PE professionals has also been very limited, although it is clear that we could gain a lot from learning about each other's projects.

The IPEG session at ISAGA '94 made a major contribution to alleviating these problems. First of all, it provided an important forum for presenting recent PE projects. It was great to see the proliferation and diversity of projects adopting PEs as their methodology for synthesis and policy analysis. Second, the decision to create an up-to-date list of PE-related publications will facilitate communication and learning, and might also serve as a basis for a major methodological review. The intention to make IPEG a permanent part of the annual ISAGA conferences would clearly be the first step toward solving the information and communication problem. Editor David Crookall's offer to provide space in *Simulation & Gaming* for PE-related issues is also extremely valuable. It is now up to the PE community to grab these opportunities and turn PEs from an innovative, experimental technique into a mature, well-established methodology by the end of the second decade of its history.

References

Clark, W. C. (1986). Sustainable development of the biosphere: themes for a research program. In W. C. Clark & R. E. Munn (Eds.), *Sustainable development of the biosphere*. Cambridge, UK: Cambridge University Press.

Brewer, G. D. (1986). Methods for synthesis: Policy exercises. In W. C. Clark & R. E. Munn (Eds.), *Sustainable development of the biosphere*. Cambridge, UK: Cambridge University Press.

Duinker, P. N., Nilsson, S., & Toth, F. L. (1993). *Testing the "policy exercise" in studies of Europe's forest sector: Methodological reflection of a bittersweet experience* (WP-93-23). Laxenburg, Austria: International Institute for Applied Systems Analysis.

Jaeger, J., Sonntag, N., Bernard, D., & Kurz, W. (1991). *The challenge of sustainable development in a greenhouse world: Some visions of the future*. Stockholm: Stockholm Environmental Institute.

Sonntag, N. C. (1986). Commentary on methods for synthesis: Policy exercises. In W. C. Clark & R. E. Munn (Eds.), *Sustainable development of the biosphere*. Cambridge, UK: Cambridge University Press.

Toth, F. L. (1986). *Practicing the future: Implementing the "policy exercise" concept* (WP-86-23). Laxenburg, Austria: International Institute for Applied Systems Analysis.

Toth, F. L. (1988). *Practicing the future, Part 2: Lessons from the first experiments with policy exercises* (WP-88-12). Laxenburg, Austria: International Institute for Applied Systems Analysis.

Toth, F. L. (1992). Global change and the cross-cultural transfer of policy games. In D. Crookall & K. Arai (Eds.), *Global interdependence*. Tokyo: Springer.

31

The Use of Simulations/Games
to Fill Russia's Managerial Needs

JOSEPH WOLFE

Russia has embarked on a journey that will ultimately create a more democratic, open, and market-based economy. A number of faltering, tentative steps have been taken and the task is enormous. Given communist ideology's rejection of everything that was "capitalist" in nature, the economic elements and institutions supportive of the market mechanisms that facilitate a market-based economy were either lacking, in disrepair, or relegated to backstreet black market or otherwise illegal activities. Methods for equitably privatizing the state-owned enterprises have not been found, a competitive and independent commercial banking system is lacking, equity markets and venture capital acquisition methods are crude, and negotiations are often not "at arm's length." Russia's parliament is just now initiating reforms in its commercial law, and local and national infrastructures need to be significantly upgraded.

Although these problems are associated with institutions and the society's physical and legal structure, their resolution comes about through the activities and decisions of the nation's set of current and emergent managers and government officials. If economic reform and a market-based democratic nation is to emerge, changes must be made on a number of fronts, with a key element being alterations, additions, and deletions to the country's managerial focus, decision-making techniques, and business decision-making skills and abilities. This chapter discusses the role that simulations and games might play in bringing about a change in the managerial abilities possessed by Russia's new managers, government officials, and workers. Given Russia's educational traditions and the existing incentives and disincentives to learn and to engage in new workaday behaviors, the pragmatic and utilitarian nature of the experiential teaching tools of simulations and games presents numerous opportunities for their use, although accompanied by a number of factors that might frustrate their successful implementation.

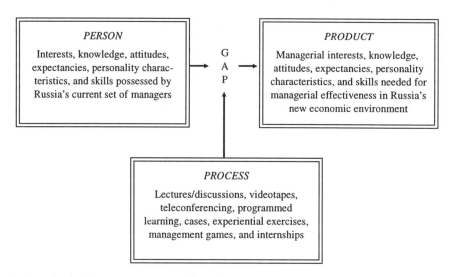

Figure 31.1   A person, process, and product model of MED efforts.
SOURCE: Adapted from Campbell, Dunnette, Lawler, and Weick (1970), p. 475.

The Management Development Process

Campbell, Dunnette, Lawler, and Weick (1970) have presented a model of the management development process that takes a person, product, and process approach. As shown in Figure 31.1, and applied to Russia's current set of managers, the model's "person" component is the set of personal attributes Russian managers bring to the training and development situation. These attributes entail their current skills, interests, attitudes and personality characteristics. They also bring to the situation certain expectancies based on their positive and negative experiences with socialism (Zinoviev, 1983) and with the education and development techniques used on them in the past. These expectancies will have a motivating or demotivating effect on the managers' attempts to (a) learn new management techniques and skills and (b) assess the degree to which they feel new personal attributes are required of them in Russia's current economic situation.

The model's "process" component is composed of the arsenal of tools and techniques by which educators can change individuals who are subjected to them. The tools commonly used in Western Europe and North America are lectures/discussions, videotapes and teleconferencing, programmed learning, cases, experiential exercises, management games, and internships. These may be more or less correct for Russian managers. The model's "product" component is the reformed or new set of skills, interests, attitudes, expectancies, and personality characteristics the trained managers now bring to their real-world situation given the effectiveness of the management education and development program. Based on this model, the success or failure of a management development technique is a function of the subject's nature, the reward structure existing in the society and workplace, and the propriety of the technique given the situation's constraints and opportunities.

Russian Management's Attributes and Background

Russia's current set of managers possess a set of personal attributes that have been pragmatically correct (Andrle, 1976; Granick, 1972; Lane, 1981), although many believe that certain attributes will have to be discarded, other attributes enhanced, and many new ones created (Lawrence & Vischoutsicos, 1990; Winiecki, 1988; Zinoviev, 1983). Based on many studies and observations about the backgrounds and skills of Russia's managers, certain predominant characteristics emerge (Abalkin, 1989; Granick, 1972; Lawrence & Vischoutsicos, 1990; Manevich, 1985; Richman, 1965; Zhuplev, 1992, 1994). Because of Russia's great size and communism's promise of a full-employment economy that would produce vast quantities of material goods, 80%-85% of its managers had college degrees in engineering or other technical fields. Only a small fraction had business degrees, which were in economics, although some management retraining occurred during their careers. Because of the predominance of the country's state-owned enterprises, this technocratic pattern still exists. In the communist era, management was a controversial combination of Marxist-Leninist ideological tenets and pragmatic Taylorism as both a body of knowledge and a practical field. Management practice in general and human resource management in particular was dominated by an ideology advanced and enforced by the Communist Party. Because of the restrictions against private enterprise, the only way to obtain professional self-realization and recognition was via advancement through the industrial sector's official hierarchy.

In the late 1980s, however, all this began to change. A series of reforms initiated under Gorbachev's perestroika followed by Yeltsin's "shock therapy" campaign in the early 1990s introduced dramatic changes. The basic ideology of unified central planning and procurement, and the social safeguards related to business management were destroyed or abandoned. Managerial careers and individual lifestyles were no longer strictly dependent on adhering to strict institutional or personal loyalty to the state and its official ideology. Formal education or the pursuit of systematic professional development no longer guarantees economic wealth. The system that once directed and coordinated management education and development efforts with personal careers across various republics, regions, industries, and companies ceased to exist. Accordingly, many Russian managers and budding entrepreneurs are seeking methods by which they can capitalize on the new situation. Insight into the skills they both possess and lack can be gained from recent research by Hisrich and Gratchev (in press) conducted on 32 Russian entrepreneurs. They found them

TABLE 31.1 Self-Rating of Management Skills

Management Skill	Ratings					
	Poor	Fair	Good	Very Good	Excellent	No Opinion
Finance	12	9	6	0	0	2
Dealing with people	3	11	11	4	0	0
Marketing/sales	6	8	12	1	1	1
Idea generation	3	12	7	6	1	0
Business operations	2	9	13	3	1	1
Organizing and planning	2	5	17	3	0	2

TABLE 31.2 Ranking of Most Important Training Needs (in percentages)

Accounting	81
Finance	77
Management	74
Leadership	72
Marketing	71
Business law	69
Entrepreneurship	66
Human resource management	63
Organizational culture	56

to be energetic, independent, competitive, and self-confident but weaker with respect to social activity, anxiety, flexibility, goal orientation, and a generalist perspective. The Russian entrepreneurs were also asked to rate their own management skills on a five-point scale. As shown in Table 31.1, they felt they were poorest in finance, followed by marketing/sales. They thought they were a little stronger in their "people dealing" skills and idea generation than in their skills in business operations and organizing and planning. When the Russians were compared to a comparable group of American entrepreneurs, both groups felt their skills in marketing and finance were the weakest; however, the American entrepreneurs felt they had much stronger skills in business operations and organizing and planning.

Further insight into the training and development needs of Russia's new managers, and perhaps the level of motivation to learn from management education and development efforts, can be gleaned from a pilot study of 266 entrepreneurs enrolled in the U.S. government-sponsored program "Business for Russia" (Gratchev, 1994). Although they were fairly elite, fluent in English, under 40 years of age, and came from such cities as Moscow, St. Petersburg, Khabarovsk, Samara, and Vladivostok, their business deficiencies were profound and organizationally broad based, as presented in Table 31.2.

The Ideal Product of a Management
Development Program for Russians

The previous section has given a strong indication of what the product of and management development effort should look like, although opinions in this regard are not unanimous (Hunter, 1978; Kiezun, 1991; Ryshkov, 1986). It is believed, however, that the new Russian manager will have to move from a purely operational, technical orientation to one that is more broad and eclectic. The new manager must also be conversant across all the firm's functional areas and must do this in a macro-economic environment possessing turbulence and high ambiguity. Accordingly, the manager must be able to embrace and capitalize on the opportunities offered by quickly changing events and circumstances. Although this judgment about the attributes of the new Russian manager appears to be strangely familiar to that rendered for American and West European managers, the depth of detail and the amount of unlearning and new learning needed by the Russian manager is far greater. More detail into the amount of learning and unlearning that will have to occur has been provided by Mikhail Gratchev (1994):

> Some management areas when being transferred from the West may be modified as Russians have had certain relevant experiences with those areas such as in organization and planning. Other management skills will have to be created "from zero," such as human resources management because the previous system was state-centered, administrative and ideological and missed important market features such as competitive labor markets, individual job descriptions or labor arbitration. (p. 6)

The effects of the turbulent nature of the Russian situation should also influence the time perspectives and the resources available to the new Russian manager. As observed by Anatoly Zhuplev (1994),

> In the years to come major economic progress will have to be achieved through internal, domestic efforts as Russia's exports will not be internationally competitive for a number of years. This harsh reality, with its accompanying high transitional turbulence and uncertainties, will force the country's management education and development (MED) efforts to adopt a short-term perspective and applications that inculcate short-term survival skills and recipe-type recommendations at the micro-economic level such as industries, regional economies, and company management as opposed to its usual long-term view at the macro level. This major shift from macro to micro is being enhanced by western management concepts and techniques brought to Russia more and more often as a result of booming international business activities. Along these lines, the need and demand for MED among existing managers, and those preparing themselves for business careers, are

expected to evolve within concrete, pragmatic topics and subject areas. Those subjects with the greatest demand under the current transition are strategic survival and strategic management, accounting and financial management, small business and entrepreneurship, international business, marketing, public relations, and computer applications for business. (pp. 2-3)

Process Tools and Techniques

The problems and opportunities afforded any technique for bringing about a change in a manager's skills, attitudes, and knowledge can be traced at least partially to the experience that Russia's managers have had with past programs and techniques.

Over a career, a typical Russian manager was exposed to many government and ministry-associated MED programs and their teaching tools and techniques at both home and abroad (Gvishiani, 1972; Kiezun, 1991; Popov, 1975; Puffer & Ozira, 1990; Rybalskiy, 1994; Stolyarenko, 1983; Vikhanskiiy, 1988; Wolfe, 1993b). A number of observations have been made on the differences and similarities between the content and the delivery of American versus Russian MED efforts (Puffer, 1981; Shekshnia, 1992; Vikhanskiiy, 1992). The reactions of Russian managers to American management programs and development techniques, as well as the transferability of those techniques, has also been noted (Fogel, 1990; McCarthy, 1992; Puffer, 1992; Wolfe, 1993a, 1993b).

In the recent past MED programs have ranged from seminars lasting a few hours to intensive programs lasting several months. In the early days of Russia's economic reform, many Russian management consultants and educators flooded the market with short programs, often of questionable quality (Veselov, 1992). Many Western consultants and educators soon followed suit, but they tended to concentrate on longer programs. The major teaching techniques used in Russia's MED programs have been lectures, cases, games and simulations, and role-plays, with the greatest emphasis being on lectures due to a shortage of trained Russian faculty members and a residual mindset from the communist period (Panevin, Rinefort, & Payne, 1992). Limited funding for the development of hands-on course materials has also reinforced the use of the lecture method. Although the most effective management development techniques are of the interactive variety that obtain attitude and behavior change by encouraging involvement, accountability, initiative, and risk taking and emphasize problem solving and an action orientation, these qualities were discouraged during the communist period (Puffer, 1994), thereby justifying the use of passive, centrally-controlled lecture techniques.

The opportunity for simulations and games in Russian MED programs is somewhat problematic. A number of these interactive techniques were used during the communist era and therefore are not seen as foreign or exotic. Operating at the dyad or individual level, some Russian managers have had experience with role-playing. This method's most frequent applications dealt with the human resource issues of leadership style, superior and subordinate relations, and decision making and delegation. Conforming to Russia's love of the theater and drama, further role-playing techniques have included "paratheater," a play in which the manager takes the roles of playwright, director, and manager. In another exercise called "Dueling," participants take turns being the boss and exercising power (Tarasov, 1992).

Operating at the large group or organizational level, open games similar to the noncomputerized learning environments created by the ORGANIZATION GAME (Miles & Randolph, 1979) and the LOOKING GLASS (Lombardo, McCall, & DeVries, 1983) in the United States have been employed, and Russian experts are continuing to refine these techniques (Walck, 1993). These games have been used for systemwide organizational and community change and can last many days or even weeks. Russia has also had a relatively long history in the use of computerized teaching games (Wolfe, 1991, 1993a), and Western simulations have recently shown utility in various postsocialist applications (Wolfe, 1993b). Senior executives from the Aviation Ministry competed in a computerized marketing strategy game, BRANDMAPS, during their training program at California State University at Hayward in 1989 (Wiley, Kamath, & MacNab, 1992) and Portland State University's Free Market Business Development Institute used a Russian translation of the BUSINESS MANAGEMENT LABORATORY (Jensen, 1990) at their sites in Archangl'sk, Novgorod, Rostov-on-Don, and Tambov in spring 1994.

Despite the favorable response afforded these games and simulations, serious impediments to their widespread application exist. Russia's educational system is struggling to survive, having been left without adequate financing and other support by the state, and its most capable faculty are leaving for private business or expend their greatest energies doing consulting work. Many others are simply trying to obtain teaching positions abroad. In my experience, modern personal computers are lacking or nonexistent, especially at the nation's provincial universities, institutes, and academies, simple supplies such as printer ribbons and paper are scarce, and classrooms and buildings are often unheated and in disrepair. Faculty members themselves, who have the responsibility of teaching the country's new managers and have worked for years under heavy teaching loads, have typically shown little interest in dedicating themselves to their students through the use of labor-intensive and mentally draining experiential learning techniques. Because their salaries are low and relatively fixed, Russia's hyper-inflation which amounted to 840% in 1993 and is expected to be about 150% in 1994, has forced them to seek outside employment. Any technique requiring extra time and effort on their part is looked upon with disfavor, despite the superior learning associated with those techniques.

Besides the class time and administrative effort needed to support simulations and games in ongoing classroom situations, much up-front time is required in either creating them or adapting Western-style games to the Russian situation.

So far, West European and North American publishers have been reluctant to translate their simulations into Russian due to copyright problems, the large amounts of reprogramming time required, and the prohibitive price that would have to be charged for the student manuals, given that a typical manual retails for $28 to $34 and an average Russian worker earns about $35 per month.

For the near term, it appears that simulations and games, regardless of whether they are computer based or hand scored, may be a curiosity at Russia's provincial schools and company training programs and an unusual experience for those attending the nation's elite schools in major cities or working in the largest firms. For the situation to improve markedly in the long term, the pursuit of creative teaching must be made financially rewarding, and release time must be provided so that faculty can learn how to teach experientially, adapt or create simulations that are relevant to the Russian situation, and gain confidence in the use of the simulation techniques chosen. This is a very large bill that is not likely to be filled given Russia's current economic situation and the priorities the country faces. To a major degree, then, enlightened aid that is primarily nonfinancial and collaborative must be provided by those experts from the West.

References

Abalkin, L. (1989, February 8). The moonlike paysage. *Komsomolskaya Pravda.*

Andrle, V. (1976). *Managerial power in the Soviet Union.* Lexington, MA: Lexington Books.

Campbell, J. P., Dunnette, M. D., Lawler, E. E., III, & Weick, K. E. (1970). *Managerial behavior, performance, and effectiveness.* New York: McGraw-Hill.

Fogel, D. S. (1990). Management education in Central and Eastern Europe and the Soviet Union. *Journal of Management Development, 9*(3), 14-19.

Granick, D. (1972). *Managerial comparisons of four developed countries: France, Britain, U.S., and Russia.* Cambridge: MIT Press.

Gratchev, M. V. (1994). *Management transfer to Russia: Strategic interests.* Symposium position paper prepared for presentation at the Academy of Management, Vancouver, Canada, August 1995.

Gvishiani, J. M. (1972). *Organization and management: A sociological analysis of Western theories.* Moscow: Progress Publishers.

Hisrich, R. D., & Gratchev, M. V. (in press). The Russian entrepreneur characteristics: A prescription for management. *Journal of Managerial Psychology. 9*(5).

Hunter, H. (1978). *The future of the Soviet economy.* Boulder, CO: Westview.

Jensen, R. L. (1990). *The BUSINESS MANAGEMENT LABORATORY.* Homewood, IL: Irwin.

Kiezun, W. (1991). *Management in socialist countries: USSR and Central Europe.* Berlin: Walter de Gruyter.

Lane, D. (1981). *The rites of rulers. Ritual in industrial society—The Soviet case.* Cambridge, UK: Cambridge University Press.

Lawrence, P. R., & Vischoutsicos, C. A. (1990). Managerial patterns: Differences and commonalities. In P. R. Lawrence & C. A. Vischoutsicos (Eds.), *Behind the factory walls: Decision making in Soviet and U.S. enterprises* (pp. 271-286). Boston: Harvard Business School Press.

Lombardo, M. A., McCall, M. W., & DeVries, D. L. (1983). *The LOOKING GLASS.* Glenview, IL: Scott, Foresman.

Manevich, E. (1985). *Labour in the USSR: Problems and solutions.* Moscow: Progress Publishers.

McCarthy, D. J. (1992). Developing a program for Soviet managers at Northeastern University. In S. M. Puffer (Ed.), *The Russian management revolution: Preparing managers for the market economy* (pp. 187-192). Armonk, NY: M. E. Sharpe.

Miles, R. H., & Randolph, W. A. (1979). *The ORGANIZATION GAME.* Santa Monica, CA: Goodyear.

Panevin, Y. L., Rinefort, F. C., & Payne, S. L. (1992). East-West cooperation on Russian management development: Russian views and a U.S. response. *Journal of Business Affairs, 18*(2), 5-9.

Popov, G. K. (1975). *Organization of management processes.* Moscow: Ekonomika.

Puffer, S. M. (1981). Inside a Soviet management institute. *California Management Review, 24,* 90-96.

Puffer, S. M. (1992). The Fuqua School of Business program for Soviet executives. In S. M. Puffer (Ed.), *The Russian management revolution: Preparing managers for the market economy* (pp. 227-233). Armonk, NY: M. E. Sharpe.

Puffer, S. M. (1994). *The process of management education in Russia: An assessment of program design and pedagogical techniques.* Symposium position paper prepared for presentation at the Academy of Management, Vancouver, Canada, August 1995.

Puffer, S. M., & Ozira, V. (1990). Hiring and firing managers. In P. R. Lawrence & C. A. Vischoutsicos (Eds.), *Behind the factory walls: Decision making in Soviet and US enterprises* (pp. 151-182). Boston: Harvard Business School Press.

Richman, B. (1965). *Soviet management: Within significant American comparisons.* Englewood Cliffs, NJ: Prentice Hall.

Rybalskiy, V. (1994). Recollections from a country where freedom was simulated. *Simulation & Gaming: An International Journal, 25*(2), 236-244.

Ryshkov, N. (1986, March 9). Guidelines for the economic and social development of the USSR for 1986-1990 and for the period ending in 2000. *Moscow News,* Supplement.

Shekshnia, S. V. (1992), The American MBA program: A Russian student's view. In S. M. Puffer (Ed.), *The Russian management revolution: Preparing managers for the market economy* (pp. 178-185). Armonk, NY: M. E. Sharpe.

Stolyarenko, A. (1983). *The psychology of management of labor collectives.* Moscow: Progress Publishers.

Tarasov, V. K. (1992). Personnel technology: The selection and training of managers. In S. M. Puffer (Ed.), *The Russian management revolution: Preparing managers for the market economy* (pp. 121-148). Armonk, NY: M. E. Sharpe.

Veselov, S. (1992). Miznes-obrazovanie v Rossii: Spros 50 raz bol'she predlozheniia. *Buznes MN (Moskovskie Novosti), 40*(28), 15.

Vikhanskiiy, O. S. (1988). *Historical experience of the USSR national economy management system development, Part 1: Forming the fundamentals of the management system.* Moscow: Moscow State University Press.

Vikhanskiiy, O. S. (1992). Let's train managers for the market economy. In S. M. Puffer, (Ed.), *The Russian management revolution: Preparing managers for the market economy* (pp. 33-48). Armonk, NY: M. E. Sharpe.

Walck, C. L. (1993). Organization development in the USSR: An overview and a case example. *Journal of Managerial Psychology, 8*(2), 10-17.

Wiley, D. L., Kamath, S. J., & MacNab, B. (1992). "Sedpro": Three Soviet executive development programs at California State University at Hayward. In S. M. Puffer (Ed.), *The Russian management revolution: Preparing managers for the market economy* (pp. 201-214). Armonk, NY: M. E. Sharpe.

Winiecki, J. (1988). *The distorted world of Soviet type economies.* Pittsburgh, PA: University of Pittsburgh Press.

Wolfe, J. (1991). On the transfer of market oriented business games to Eastern bloc cultures. *Social Science Computer Review, 9*(2), 202-214.

Wolfe, J. (1993a). A history of business teaching games in English-speaking and postsocialist countries: The origination and diffusion of a management education and development technology. *Simulation & Gaming: An International Journal, 24*(4), 446-463.

Wolfe, J. (1993b). Experiences with transferring American business school faculty, theory, and teaching methods to a postsocialist economy: A Delphi panel study. In E. Rădăceanu (Ed.), *Proceedings of the ISAGA '93 Conference* (pp. 1-10). Bucharest, Romania.

Zhuplev, A. (1992). Management education in a time of change. In S. M. Puffer (Ed.), *The Russian management revolution: Preparing managers for the market economy* (pp. 11-26). Armonk, NY: M. E. Sharpe.

Zhuplev, A. (1994). *Russia's transition: Management education and career progress.* Symposium position paper prepared for presentation at the Academy of Management, Vancouver, Canada, August 1995.

Zinoviev, A. (1983). *Homo Sovieticus.* London: Polonia.

About the Contributors

Daniel G. Andriessen is a management consultant for KPMG, The Netherlands, specializing in policy analysis and the use of policy simulations. His academic background is in administrative science and methodology. For the past two years he has been advising the Dutch Ministry of Home Affairs on crisis management policy. He can be contacted at KMPG Management Consultants, Churchillplein 6, 2517 JW, The Hague, The Netherlands; telephone 31+ 703-382110; fax 31+ 703-584508.

Kiyoshi Arai has been interested in computerized simulations for many years, particularly in citizen participation in regional planning. His background is in physics, economics, and engineering. He has been working in the field of social engineering for ten years. He is a member of the Editorial Board of *Simulation & Gaming: An International Journal*. He can be contacted at Industrial Engineering and Management, Kinki University in Kyushu, Iizuka-shi 820, Japan; telephone 81+ 948-24-1591-32.

Robert H. R. Armstrong is a founding member of ISAGA. Until 1978 he taught in the Institute of Local Government Studies at the University of Birmingham in Great Britain, after which he moved to Australia where he taught in the Australian Centre for Local Covernment Studies at Canberra College of Advanced Education. He now works as an independent consultant. He can be contacted at 76 Baracchi Crescent, Giraland, ACT 2617, Australia; telephone 61+ 06-241-2846.

Hamilton Beazley received his MBA from Southern Methodist University and is a doctoral candidate in organizational behavior and development at George Washington University and a doctoral teaching fellow. He co-created SECRET'S OUT, a television game show that aired on the BBC during the 1984-1987 seasons, and co-developed JACQUES-IN-THE-BOX, a board game that explores the small group dynamics theories of Wilfred Bion and the management theories of Elliott Jaques. He is currently studying the role of the psychological contract and its effect on management. He can be contacted at the School of Business and Public Management, George Washington University, Washington, DC 20052, USA; telephone 1+202-994-7375 (work), 1+202-686-6850 (home); e-mail beazley@gwis2.circ.gwu.edu; fax 1+ 202-994-4930.

Valdis Bisters has a B.Sc. in physics and M.Sc. in ecology and natural resource management. He currently works as Director of University of Latvia Ecological Centre. His main field of interest is environmental science, environmental management, environmental modeling, systems thinking, and development of learner-directed learning environments. He took part in Project IDEALS and has developed the project "Simulation and Gaming Set in Environmental Education," which is funded by the Regional Environmental Center for Central and Eastern Europe, and runs training workshops on team building, systems thinking, and the application of simulation and gaming methods for environmental NGO groups, schoolteachers, university training staff, and students. He is a member of ISAGA Steering Committee. He can be contacted at Ecological Centre, University of Latvia, Rainis blv.19, Riga LV-1586, Latvia; telephone 371+ 2-225304; e-mail root@cesams.edu.lv; fax 371+ 7-820384.

William C. Bradford is a doctoral candidate in political science at Northwestern University and a member of the International Studies Association and the American Political Science Association. He received a bachelor's in English Literature and a master's in Middle East Politics and International Relations from the University of Miami. His first game, KARAMEH, a historical simulation of the Karameh crisis of March 1968, was the first simulation to be conducted at the birthplace of political-military gaming, Northwestern University, in more than 20 years. He is currently running PROJECT PAX IS-LAMICUS at Northwestern University with the assistance of a grant from the Institute for the Study of World Politics. He can be contacted at the Department of Political Science, 301 Scott Hall, Northwestern University, 601 University Place, Evanston, IL 60208, USA; telephone 1+ 708-864-2479.

Amparo Garcia Carbonell began her teaching career in the field of electronic international communication and languages for artificial intelligence environments. In 1986, she acquired a double profile on joining the Department of Languages of the Universidad Politécnica de Valencia, where she forms a research team together with Frances Watts, bringing new experiences in the use of telematic networks in language learning to the university. The pilot experience began in the School of Telecommunication Engineering with Project IDEALS and continues with Project ICONS, which has opened up a new line of research on the possibilities for using new technologies and simulation/

gaming. She is co-organizer for the 26th Annual Conference of the International Simulation and Gaming Association (ISAGA '95) to be held at the Universidad Politécnica de Valencia, Spain, July 18-21, 1995. She can be contacted at ETSIT-UPV, Camino de Vera 14, 46022 Valencia, Spain; telephone 34+ 63.87.75.35 or 63.87.75.30; e-mail agarciac@upvnet.upv.es; fax 34+ 63.87.71.99.

Walter Cedar resides in Madrid, where he has been teaching English in the Schools of Economics and Law at the Universidad Pontificia Comillas (UPCO) for more than 20 years. He is currently pursuing doctoral studies. His research interests lie primarily in the fields of discourse analysis, code switching, and testing. He can be contacted at Idiomas, UPCO, Alberto Aguilera 23, 28015 Madrid, Spain; telephone 34+ 1-542-2800, ext. 2144; fax 34+ 1-559-6569.

Douglas W. Coleman is Director of English as a Second Language at the University of Toledo in Toledo, Ohio. An active member of ISAGA since 1986, he has recently focused much of his work on the development of simulation-based activities for college-level ESL composition. He is an associate editor of *Simulation & Gaming: An International Journal.* He can be contacted at the Department of English and Literature, University of Toledo, 2801 W. Bancroft Street, Toledo, OH 43606-3390, USA; telephone 1+ 419-537-2514.

David Crookall organized the 17th Annual ISAGA Conference on the Côte d'Azur (France), after which he worked for several years in the United States where he was Principal Investigator for Project IDEALS, a worldwide, multi-institutional, cross-cultural, Internet- and computer-mediated simulation/game, which received major funding from the U.S. Department of Education's Fund for the Improvement of Postsecondary Education (FIPSE). He recently returned to France to work in the Institut d'Etudes Politiques (Sciences Po) de Lille, and is currently in the Département Technologie et Sciences Humaines of the Université de Technologie de Compiègne. He is editor of *Simulation & Gaming: An International Journal* and serves on the editorial boards of several periodicals, among them *Social Science Computer Review, Journal of International Communication,* and *Simulation and Gaming Yearbook.* He has authored many articles, edited several books, and conducted numerous workshops and conference sessions in many countries around the world. He can be contacted at the TSM-UTC, BP 649, 60206 Compiègne cedex, France; telephone 33+ 44.23.46.23; e-mail crookall@omega.univ-lille1.fr or alternatively crookall@mx.univcompiegne.fr; fax 33+ 44.23.43.00.

Chris J. Cunningham is Senior Lecturer at the University of New England, Australia, and teaches courses in environmental design and urban planning. He grew up in the Blue Mountains of New South Wales and was an eyewitness to the region's devastating bushfires of 1951, 1957, 1968, and 1977, which explains his interest in community responses to such disasters. He is also interested in the use of simulations/games for motivating and teaching undergraduate students and has published a number of articles with Elizabeth Teather on their experiences in this area. He can be contacted at the Department of Geography and Planning, University of New England, Armidale, New South Wales 2351, Australia; telephone 61+ 67-73-2864 (work), 61+ 67-72-7665 (home); e-mail ccunning@metz.une.edu.au; fax 61+ 67-71-1787.

Daniel Druckman is Principal Study Director of the National Research Council in Washington, D.C. and Adjunct Professor of Conflict Resolution at George Mason University. He has been a research scholar at the International Institute for Applied Systems Analysis (IIASA) near Vienna, Austria. Besides gaming and simulations, his research interests are conflict resolution and negotiations, non-verbal communication, group processes, political stability, and modeling methodologies. He has written or edited several books and has published numerous articles and chapters on these topics. He currently serves on the editorial boards of the *Journal of Conflict Resolution, Negotiation Journal, Simulation & Gaming: An International Journal,* and *Journal of Applied Social Psychology.* He can be contacted at the National Research Council, 2101 Constitution Avenue, NW, Washington, DC 20418, USA; telephone 1+ 202-334-2355; e-mail ddruckma@nas.bitnet; fax 1+ 202-334-3829.

Richard D. Duke is Professor of Urban and Regional Planning at the University of Michigan. He initiated a course of study in gaming/simulation at this university in 1967; subsequently (1985) he founded a Certificate Program in Gaming/ Simulation Studies through the university's Rackham Graduate School, which he currently chairs.

Professor Duke called the first meeting of the International Simulation and Games Association (ISAGA) in Bad Godesberg in the summer of 1969 and was a founding member of the North American Simulation and Games Association (NASAGA). Currently, his primary interest is in gaming theory and the development of policy games, particularly for use by large organizations in envisioning alternate futures for strategic planning purposes. The central focus of these instruments is improved communication in complex environments.

He is the author of numerous books and articles. A book presently under development addresses the design of policy games; this will employ brief case studies of various complex systems to illustrate workable design concepts. He is President of Multilogue International; over the past decades his company has worked with many large organizations around the world to develop a variety of policy exercises; these have been used both for decision making as well as for training and related purposes. Past clients include many *Fortune* 500 companies, municipalities, and governments. He can be reaced at Multilogue International, 329 Lake Park Lane, Ann Arbor, MI 48103, USA; telephone: 1+ 313-769-0467; fax: 1+ 313-663-3690.

Henry I. Ellington has headed the Educational Development Unit at Robert Gordon University, Aberdeen (formerly Robert Gordon Institute of Technology) since 1973. He was awarded a professorial title in 1990. Highly active in the simulation/gaming field throughout this time, he has been involved in the development of over 70 games, simulations, and case studies, many of which have been published by organizations such as the Scottish Education Department, Association for Science Education, Institution of Electrical Engineers, United Kingdom Atomic Energy Authority, Shell UK, and Phillips Petroleum. He has also published over 100 papers in the field and is co-author (with Eric Addinall and Fred Percival) of three books on gaming and simulations. He served on the Governing Council of SAGSET for nine years and is currently Chairman of the Association for Educational and Training Technology. He can be contacted at Educational Development Unit, Robert Gordon University, Kepplestone Annexe, Queens Road, Aberdeen AB9 2PG, Scotland; telephone 44+ 224-263340; fax 44+ 224-263344.

A. J. Faria is Professor and Chair of the Department of Marketing at the University of Windsor. He has taught at Georgia Southern University and Wayne State University, worked for Chrysler Corporation and Nabisco, and served as a consultant to over 50 corporations. He is author of five books, five chapters in books, more than 30 journal articles, and 70 conference papers, five of which have won conference best-paper awards. He can be contacted at Faculty of Business Administration, University of Windsor, Ontario N9B 3P4, Canada; telephone 1+ 519-253-4232, ext. 3101; e-mail ad9@server.uwindsor.ca; fax 1+ 519-973-7073.

Jim Freeman specializes in computer simulation. Before joining UMIST in 1981 he was a statistician at the Distributive Industry Training Board where he was responsible for computer-based training. He has published widely in his field and been involved in developing numerous management simulation packages, particularly business games, for organizations such as Cyanamid, Makro Self-Service Wholesalers, and the Greater Manchester Police. In 1992-1993, he was a visiting professor in the Department of Finance and Management at the University of Alberta, Canada. He can be contacted at the Manchester School of Management, UMIST, P.O. Box 88, Manchester M60 IQD, England; telephone 44+ 61-200-3430 (work), 44+ 298-24275 (home); e-mail freeman@ac.uk.umist.sm.v2; fax 44+ 61-200-3505.

Jac L. Geurts is Professor of Policy Science and Chair of the Policy and Organization Program at Tilburg University in the Netherlands. Before joining the Tilburg faculty, he worked as a senior strategic consultant within Philips International and held several academic positions at the University of Nijmegen and Michigan. He serves on the editorial board of *Simulation & Gaming: An International Journal.* He can be contacted at Tilburg University, Policy and

Organization Program, Room S165, P.O. Box 90153, 5000 LE Tilburg, The Netherlands; telephone 31+ 13662069; e-mail jguerts@kub.nl; fax 31+ 13662370.

Gene B. Halleck began using simulations with her English-as-a-Second-Language students after attending David Crookall's in-service simulation/gaming workshop at Pennsylvania State University. More recently, as an Assistant Professor in the English Department at Oklahoma State University, she taught a graduate seminar on materials development for English as a Second/Foreign Language (ESL/EFL) using simulations as the basis for the course. During ISAGA '94, seven of her students from the ESL program presented the simulations and games they had created during the seminar. Energized by this experience, the group formed a company, ELITE Games, to create more simulation/ gaming materials for use in teaching English. She serves on the editorial board of *Simulation & Gaming: An International Journal.* She can be contacted at the Department of English, 205 Morrill Hall, Oklahoma State University, Stillwater, OK 74078-0135, USA; telephone 1+ 405-744-9474 (work), 1+ 405-377-5954 (home); e-mail halleck@osuvm1.bitnet; fax 1+ 405-744-6326.

Gerton Heyne is a senior consultant at the Institute for Applied Social Research of Tilburg University in The Netherlands. He was the leader of the DIAGNOST project. He can be contacted at Tilburg University, Policy and Organization Program, Room S167, P.O. Box 90153, 5000 LE Tilburg, The Netherlands; telephone 31+ 13-663153; e-mail f.jodersma@kub.nl (must say "Attn: Gerton Heyne"); fax 31+ 13-662370.

Judy Ho has had extensive ESL teaching experience in Hong Kong and Australia. Her learner groups included adult migrants, secondary school students, and tertiary students. The participation of her students of the City University of Hong Kong in Project IDEALS has proved to be a valuable experience for both the facilitator and the participants. She is currently writing instructional materials and is a university lecturer (designate) of the Department of English, Lingnan College, Hong Kong. Among her research interests are ESL teaching methodology, learner autonomy, intercultural communication, and literacy. Her contact address is P.O. Box 84367, Hunghom Bay Post Office, Hong Kong; telephone/fax 852+ 2364-6263.

Cisca Joldersma is Lecturer/Researcher in Policy Science at Tilburg University in the Netherlands. Before joining the Tilburg faculty, she worked as a researcher in public administration and public policy at Twente University. She can be contacted at Tilburg University, Policy and Organization Program, Room S167, P.O. Box 90153, 5000 LE Tilburg, The Netherlands; telephone 31+ 13-663153; e-mail f.jodersma@kub.nl; fax 31+ 13-662370.

Fumitoshi Kato currently works as a Teaching/Research Associate in the Department of Environmental Information at Keio University, Japan, and is a doctoral candidate in the School of Communication, Information, and Library Studies at Rutgers University. He has two master's degrees, one in economics from Keio University, Japan, and the other in communication theory from the University of Pennsylvania. One of his research topics is the use of computers for simulations and gaming, with a particular focus on the relationships between simulated (electronic) realities and day-to-day realities. He can be contacted at the Department of Environmental Information, Keio University, 5322 Endo, Fujisawa, Kanagawa 252, Japan; telephone 81+ 466-47-5111 (work), 81+ 427-66-3210 (home); e-mail fk@sfc.keio.ac.jp; fax 81+ 466-47-5041.

Jan H. G. Klabbers is a management and policy consultant and general secretary of ISAGA. He is an associate editor of *Simulation & Gaming: An International Journal*. Formerly, he was a professor at the universities of Leiden, Utrecht, and Erasmus. He can be contacted at Klabbers Management & Policy Consultancy Inc. (KMPC), Oostervelden 59, 6681 WR Bemmel, The Netherlands; e-mail jklabb@antenna.nl; telephone/fax 31+ 8811-62455.

Linda C. Lederman is Chair of the Department of Communication at Rutgers University and specializes in instructional and interpersonal communication with an emphasis on experiential learning. She has written five books, 20 book chapters and/or journal articles, presented more than 100 conference papers and professional seminars, and designed/published a variety of communication simulations and games including IMAGINE THAT! and L & L ASSOCIATES, and with Lea P. Stewart, SIMCORP, LINDLEE ENTERPRISES, THE MARBLE COMPANY, and PASS IT ON, and with Fumitoshi Kato, IMAGINE THAT! ONDISC. She is immediate past editor of *Communication Quarterly* and an associate editor of *Simulation & Gaming: An International Journal*. Her research focuses on the use of qualitative methods, especially simulations and games and focus-group interviews, to generate data on affective and behavioral dynamics associated with verbal communication. She can be contacted at the Department of Communication, Rutgers University, New Brunswick, NJ 08903, USA; telephone 1+ 908-932-8285 (work), 1+ 609-921-2911 (home); e-mail lederman@zodiac.rutgers.edu; fax 1+ 908-932-6916.

John Lobuts, Jr. is Professor of Management Science and has taught with the Behavioral Science Faculty at George Washington University in Washington, D.C. since 1970. He has served as Director of Off-Campus Programs, Assistant Dean for Undergraduate Programs, and Assistant Dean for Graduate Programs. In 1985, he returned to full-time teaching. Areas of academic interest are group dynamics, organizational communications and conflict resolution. He has published articles in the *Journal of Business Ethics, Journal of Creative Behavior, Journal of Secondary Education, Journal of Business Education,* and *The Realtor*; contributed chapters to several books published in America and in Europe; and delivered invited papers in China, Romania, The Netherlands, Germany, Scotland, France, and Korea. He also is an associate editor of *Simulation & Gaming: An International Journal.* He can be contacted at the School of Business and Public Management, George Washington University, Washington, DC 20052, USA; telephone 1+ 202-994-6918 (work), 1+ 301-929-1310 (home); e-mail lobuts@gwuvm.gwu.edu; fax 1+ 202-994-4930.

Drew Mackie trained as an architect and planner but has worked with games and simulations for the last 25 years. He initially used games as an aid to teaching, but lately his games have been used to analyze and predict policy outcomes for business and government. His greatest interest at the moment is the preparation of simple games for complex situations, and he was the originator of the SIMPLEX game format, which allows insights into complex policy situations using a very simple game format. He can be contacted at Tibbalds Monro, 20 Winton Grove, Edinburgh EH10 7AS, Scotland; telephone 44+ 31-445-3068; fax 44+ 31-445-5930.

Linda Mak is a language teacher at the English Language Teaching University, Chinese University of Hong Kong. Since 1992, she has been involved in the establishment of a new Independent Learning Centre (ILC). She specialized in CALL (Computer Assisted Language Learning) and, with the help of the Computer Centre, she not only set up the computer network of the ILC, but also developed the first multi-media computer simulation program, 1997 Dilemma, on campus. She has just finished a Mosaic Centre Information Guide to be put on the Internet. Her exploration in computer technology and English Language Teaching started in Spring 1993, when she joined Project IDEALS with a group of her undergraduate students. Since then, she has participated in several international e-mail projects, including the AT&T Global Learning Network, an e-mail project organized by Helsinki University (Finland) that involved 20 student discussion lists and a teacher list. She can be contacted at ELTU, Chinese University of Hong Kong, Shatin, NT, Hong Kong; telephone 852+ 2609-7461; e-mail linda-mak@cuhk.hk; fax 852+ 2603-5157.

Ivar Männamaa is a student in the Department of Psychology at the University of Tartu, Estonia. He participated in the design of two simulation projects for high schools in Estonia (based on Project IDEALS), in which his main task was to articulate the simulation's educational task with its procedural possibilities. Development of morality and social identity are his research themes in psychology; therefore, the working out of rules of conduct has been his main interest in the sphere of gaming. He can be contacted at the Department of Psychology,

University of Tartu, Tiigi str. 78, Tartu, Estonia; e-mail ivar@maf.ut.ee; telephone 372+ 7-422830 (home).

Mieko Nakamura is Assistant Professor at Ryutsu Keizai University, where she teaches general statistics and a seminar on behavioral science. She specializes in individual and group decision making and has a great interest in simulation and gaming in the classroom. She is editor of the JASAG News & Notes section in *Simulation & Gaming: An International Journal.* She can be contacted at Faculty of Economics, Ryutsu Keizai University, 120 Hirahata, Ryugasaki, Ibaraki 301, Japan; telephone 81+ 297-64-0001 (work), 81+ 298-73-2589 (home); e-mail sjk12106@mgw.shijokyo.or.jp; fax 81+ 297-64-0011.

Nina N. Nemitcheva has been doing training and research in psychology for six years as Professor at the Management Training Center. She is responsible for intensive training in communication, negotiation, English and Russian as foreign languages, and development of new programs. She also practiced sociology and did research for 15 years at the Scientific Research Institute of Complex Sociological Investigations at the State University of St. Petersburg where she is a Candidate in Philosophy (equivalent to a doctorate) and from which she obtained a Diploma in Psychology (equivalent to a master's degree). She can be contacted at the Management Training Center, St. Petersburg State Technical University, 29 Polytechnicheskaya Street, St. Petersburg 1195251, Russia; telephone 812+ 552-62-42 (work), 812+ 20-19-72 (home); fax 812+ 1-552-60-95; e-mail gugel@ipmo.spb.su (must begin message with "To: Nina Nemitcheva").

Diane H. Parente is a faculty member at the State University of New York, College at Fredonia and a doctoral student in the dissertation stage at the State University of New York at Buffalo School of Management. She has many years of business experience and is interested in an active learning approach to teaching. Her research interests are in manufacturing strategy, innovation, and strategic management. She can be contacted at the Department of Management Science and Systems, State University of New York at Buffalo, 310D Jacobs Management Center, Buffalo, NY 14260-4000, USA; telephone 1+ 716-645-3252 (work), 1+ 716-741-2401 (home); e-mail v160efad@ubvms.cc.buffalo.edu; fax 1+ 716-741-4120.

Richard B. Powers is Professor Emeritus of Psychology at Utah State University. He has designed several simulation/games and promotes them whenever he can as a way of introducing the feeling component in education. He currently works with the Oregon Peace Institute, conducting workshops on conflict management and related topics, and is also on the Portland board of the Alternatives to Violence Program. He can be contacted at P.O. Box 276, Oceanside, Oregon, 97134, USA; telephone 1+ 503-842-7347; fax 1+ 503-842-4654.

Peter A. Raynolds received his doctorate in behavioral sciences in management (organizational behavior) from UCLA in 1969. A stint in the Navy started him in simulation/gaming for training, and he has been involved ever since. His present professional focus is on developing holistic R-mode (so-called right-brain) techniques and applying them in combination with conventional methods to current problems in education, government, and industry. He is doing this within the context of post-modern, new paradigm, and holonomic thinking. He can be contacted at the College of Business Administration, Box 15066, Northern Arizona University, Flagstaff, AZ 86011, USA; telephone 1+ 602-523-7350 (work), 1+ 602-526-4111 (home); e-mail raynolds@nauvax.ucc.nau.edu; fax 1+ 602-523-7331.

Beverly Rising lives in Madrid, where she has taught English at the Universidad Pontificia Comillas (UPCO) for 23 years. She is currently Head of Studies for Language at the university and teaches in the international business administration program. Her current research involves computerized business simulations for foreign language learning. She can be contacted at Idiomas, UPCO, Alberto Aguilera 23, 28015 Madrid, Spain; telephone 34+ 1-542-2800, ext. 2144; fax 34+ 1-559-6569.

Victor I. Rybalskiy has been a full Professor at the Kiev Civil Engineering Institute since 1971. In 1979, he was awarded the State Prize of the USSR for creating efficient automated management systems. Most of his research and publishing activity, which consists of 30 books and almost 400 articles and reports, has been conducted in the area of automated management systems and business gaming. In 1981, he established and then led for 13 years a special education center to train the USSR's professors and managers in the creation and use of simulations and games. In 1989, he became a member of ISAGA's Steering Committee and was president of the Eastern European Simulation and Gaming Association for 1991-1992. He was the main organizer of the International Seminar on Gaming-Simulation in Education and Scientific Research held in Kiev in 1991. Since 1993 he has lived in the United States, where he continues his research work in the area of business and personality development games. He can be contacted at the Association of Engineers and Scientists, 45 East 33rd Street, Suite 3-24, New York, NY 10016, USA; telephone 1+ 718-259-7978 (home); fax 1+ 718-851-3591.

Leopoldo Schapira was one of ten facilitators in an inter-American simulation using ICONS. He can be contacted at the Centro de Investigaciones Jurídicas y Sociales, Universidad Nacional de Córdoba, Caseros 311, 5000 Córdoba, Argentina; telephone 54+ 51-241-921 (work), 54+ 51-241-921 (home); e-mail schapira@uncbjs.edu.ar; fax 54+ 51-241-921.

Paula W. Sunderman is Associate Professor of English and Director of TESOL at Mississippi State University. Project IDEALS introduced her to simulations, and she is currently involved in using the Internet and World Wide Web for teaching and research. She has introduced her students to Internet and World Wide Web, and she incorporates activities that require facility in these in her teaching. Her publications include articles and books in teaching English as a second or foreign language, pragmatics and 20th-century literature, particularly that of contemporary Arab women's writing. She can be contacted at Department of English, P.O. Box E, Mississippi State University, Mississippi State, MS 39762, USA; telephone 1+ 601-325-3644; e-mail pwsl@ra.msstate.edu; fax 1+ 601-325-7283.

Janet Sutherland has taught English and American Studies in Germany since 1977, both in academic institutions and in the private sector. In recent years, she has added cognitive and Internet training to her teaching and research activities. Project IDEALS allowed her for the first time to combine a long-standing interest in simulations in language learning with her interest in computer-mediated communication. She is currently involved in a three-year, TEMPUS-funded cooperative project, the goal of which is to re-structure post-secondary technical education in Romania. An Internet activist, she has been introducing secondary and post-secondary teachers to the Internet and its potential uses in education. She is the Forum Editor of TESL-EJ, an electronic journal for teachers of English as a foreign and second language, and she has written and edited a number of articles in the areas of computer-mediated communication, second-language learning, and simulations. She can be contacted at Fachbereich für Informatik und Mathematik, Fachhochschule Regensburg, Postfach 12 03 27, 93025 Regensburg, Germany; telephone 49+ 941-2427; e-mail janet.sutherland@rz.fh-regensburg.d400.de or alternatively sutherland@vax1.rz.uni-regensburg.d400.de; fax 49+ 941-3883.

Rob J. Swart is currently head of the Global Change Department of the Dutch National Institute of Public Health and Environmental Protection (RIVM) and advisor to the United Nations Environment Programme. He can be contacted at the National Institute for Public Health and Environmental Protection, P.O. Box 1, 3720 BA Bilthoven, The Netherlands; telephone 31+ 30-743-026; fax 31+ 30-250-740.

Ferenc L. Toth is an economist and policy analyst interested in problems of natural resource and environmental management. His activities in simulation/gaming started in 1983 when he was involved in the development of STRATE-GEM-1, a computer-based management training game. Later he designed, tested, and applied the policy exercise approach to provide a structured communication forum between scientists and policy makers who study and manage long-term, large-scale, and complex environmental problems like global climate change. He can be contacted at the Department of Social Systems, Potsdam Institute for Climate Impact Research, Postfach 601203, 14412 Potsdam, Germany; telephone 49+ 331-288-2554; fax 49+ 331-288-2600.

Terje Tuisk graduated from the University of Tartu as a biologist and is now a master's student in the Department of Education. He designed and ran a simulation/game called SIMUVERE (based on IDEALS) with a group of students, graduate students, and lecturers during the past two school years. He is involved in both the newly founded Active Learning Centre at the University of Tartu and an Estonian-Finnish cooperative project in the field of population security. Currently, he is creating a distance education network for continuing education throughout Estonia. He can be contacted at the Department of Education, University of Tartu, Ulikooli 18, Tartu, Estonia; e-mail ttuisk@math.ut.ee; telephone 372+ 2-434342.

A. M. van 't Noordende studied industrial engineering and management science at Eindhoven University of Technology, Faculty of Industrial Engineering. He graduated in 1987 in finance and marketing and then joined Andersen Consulting in its Hague office where he has been involved in both marketing strategy and information technology projects. Recently, he was project leader in the Horizon 2000 project, initiated by 11 of the biggest utilities in the Netherlands to develop a vision of the nation's future electricity market. This project eventually resulted in the ELECTRICITY CONTRACT MARKET 2000 policy exercise. He can be contacted at Andersen Consulting, Stadhoudersplantsoen 24, P.O. Box 29743, 2502 LS The Hague, The Netherlands; telephone 31+ 70-3425725; fax 31+ 70-3454867.

Aad P. Van Ulden received his doctorate in fluid mechanics from Delft University and has over 20 years' experience in atmospheric climate research. He can be contacted at the Royal Netherlands Meteorological Institute, P.O. Box 201, 3730 AE De Bilt, The Netherlands; telephone 31+ 30-206-447; fax 31+ 30-210-407.

Pier Vellinga is Professor of Environmental Sciences and Global Change and Director of the Institute for Environmental Studies at Free University, Amsterdam. He is a member of the Intergovernmental Panel on Climate Change (IPCC) and vice chair of IPCC's third working group adaptation. He can be contacted at the Institute for Environmental Studies, Free University, De Boelelaan 1115, The Netherlands; telephone 31+ 20-444-9515; fax 31+ 20-444-9553.

Juliette Vermaas holds a master's degree from the Policy and Organization Program at Tilburg University, The Netherlands. She was involved in the development of the DIAGNOST game. She can be contacted at Tilburg University, Policy and Organization Program, Room S167, P.O. Box 90153, 5000 LE Tilburg, The Netherlands; telephone 31+ 13-663153; e-mail f.jodersma@kub.nl (must say "Attn: Juliette Vermaas"); fax 31+ 13-662370.

Frances Watts, a native American, has lived in Spain for 25 years. She is currently in the Department of Languages of the Universidad Politécnica de Valencia, where her classes in the School of Telecommunications Engineering have participated in both the Project IDEALS and Project ICONS simulations. Her research interests include language testing and the evaluation of the integration of multimedia into the language learning curricula. Teamed with Amparo Garcia Carbonell, she is exploring ways to use new technologies in language learning. She and Carbonell are the organizers of the 26th Annual Conference of the International Simulation and Gaming Association (ISAGA '95), which will be held at the Universidad Politécnica in Valencia, Spain, July 18-21, 1995. She can be contacted at ETSIT-UPV, Camino de Vera 14, 46022 Valencia, Spain; telephone 34+ 63.87.75.35 or 34+ 63.87.75.30; e-mail fwatts@upvnet. upv.es; fax 34+ 63.87.71.99.

William J. Wellington is Assistant Professor of Marketing at the University of Windsor. He has authored a number of marketing and simulation papers and has won an ABSEL best paper award. He is currently completing a principles of marketing textbook for Prentice Hall. He can be contacted at Faculty of Business Administration, University of Windsor, Ontario N9B 3P4, Canada; telephone 1+ 519-253-4232, ext. 3151; e-mail r87@server.uwindsor.ca; fax 1+ 519-973-7073.

Ivo Wenzler applies the gaming/simulation methodology to complex policy issues. Until 1992 he worked as a research scientist at the University of Michigan and as a senior associate at Multilogue International. At both places his primary activity was designing policy exercises and large-scale gaming/ simulations for clients all over the world. In 1992, he accepted a position as head of the Policy Advice Group at the Institute for Applied Social Science (ITS) at the Catholic University of Nijmegen. The primary activity of the Policy Advice Group is to help integrate policy needs with policy-related research activities by applying the gaming/simulation methodology. He can be contacted at the Institute for Applied Social Sciences, Toernooiveld 5, P.O. Box 9048, 6500 KJ Nijmegen, The Netherlands; telephone 31+ 80-653598; e-mail u8000041@vm.uci.kun.nl; fax 31+ 80-653599.

Rob Willems studied general social science at the University of Utrecht, graduating in 1991 and then working there as a research scientist where he took part in research for the Dutch Ministry of Traffic and Transport. The aim of the research was to help managers of the ministry explore the future with the help of system dynamics. In 1994, he started working for the Policy Advice Group at the Institute for Applied Social Science at the Catholic University of Nijmegen where he took part in the construction of the ELECTRICITY CONTRACT MARKET 2000 policy exercise. He can be contacted at the Institute for Applied Social Sciences, Toernooiveld 5, P.O. Box 9048, 6500 KJ Nijmegen, The Netherlands; telephone 31+ 80-653598; e-mail u8000041@vm.uci.kun.nl; fax 31+ 80-653599.

Joseph Wolfe is Professor of Management in the College of Business Administration at the University of Tulsa, Oklahoma. For several years he has been active in promoting simulation/game use in the Confederation of Independent States, formerly the USSR. He recently obtained five-year funding for an annual Marie Birshtain research competition, the goal of which is to stimulate creation of new simulations by CIS scientists for application in business and education. He is an associate editor of *Simulation & Gaming: An International Journal*. He can be contacted at the Department of Management and Marketing, College of Business Administration, University of Tulsa, 600 S. College Avenue, Tulsa, Oklahoma 74104, USA; telephone 1+ 918-631-2428; Internet mgt_jaw@vax.1.utulsa.edu; fax 1+ 918-631-2142.

Simulation & Gaming: An International Journal

The official journal of ISAGA is *Simulation & Gaming: An International Journal of Theory, Design, and Research (S&G)*—the ampersand is official. *S&G* is the world's foremost journal devoted to academic and applied issues in the fast-expanding fields of simulation, computerized simulation, gaming, modeling, role-play, play, interactive learning, structured exercises and active, experiential learning, as well as in related research methodologies. The broad scope and interdisciplinary nature of *S&G* is demonstrated by the variety of its readers and contributors, such as sociologists, political scientists, economists, psychologists, and educators, as well as experts in such areas as international studies, management and business, environmental issues, policy and planning, leadership and decision making, conflict resolution, cognition, learning theory, communication, cross-cultural communication, language learning, media, educational technologies, and computing.

The journal contains academic papers, empirical studies, technical reports, simulation/game and book reviews, ready-to-use simulation/games, announcements, and association news. From time to time special theme issues are published. Recent themes have included debriefing, counselor education, and entrepreneurship.

You are invited to submit a manuscript for publication in *S&G*. Before sending a manuscript, however, you should consult the *Guide for Authors*. To obtain this, send a self-adhesive, self-addressed label and three international reply coupons (IRCs, obtainable from all post offices) or a check for US$5 or a cheque for £3 (people from economically poor countries need not send these) to: David Crookall, Editor *S&G*, TSH - UTC, BP 649, 60206 Compiègne cédex, France.

Subscription details can be obtained from the publisher: Sage Publications, 2455 Teller Road, Thousand Oaks, CA 91320, USA; telephone 805-499-0721; fax 805-499-0871; or 6 Bonhill Street, London EC2A 4PU, UK; telephone (0)71-374-0645; fax (0)71-374-8741; or P.O. Box 4215, New Delhi 110048, India.

SAGE PUBLICATIONS, INC.
P.O. BOX 5084
THOUSAND OAKS, CA 91359-9924